D0784543

Scott Fitzgerald

Dr Jeffrey Meyers, a Fellow of the Royal Society of Literature, taught for thirty years in universities in America, England and Japan. Most recently, he has been Jemison Professor at the University of Alabama in Birmingham, USA. He has published biographies of Katherine Mansfield, Wyndham Lewis, Ernest Hemingway, Robert Lowell and his circle, D. H. Lawrence, Joseph Conrad and Edgar Allan Poe, and has also written and edited three books about biography. He lives in Berkeley, California.

SCOTT FITZGERALD

A BIOGRAPHY

Jeffrey Meyers

PAPERMAC

First published 1994 by HarperCollins Publishers, Inc., New York

First published in Great Britain 1994 by Macmillan

This edition published 1995 by Papermac
an imprint of Macmillan General Books
25 Eccleston Place, London SW1W 9NF
and Basingstoke

Associated companies throughout the world

ISBN 0 333 59935 7

135798642

A CIP catalogue record for this book is available from
the British Library

Printed and bound in Great Britain by
Mackays of Chatham plc, Chatham, Kent

For Valerie Hemingway

CONTENTS

ILLUSTRATIONS

ILLUSTRATIONS

Acknowledgments

It is a pleasure to acknowledge the assistance I received while writing this book. My friend Jackson Bryer encouraged and helped from the very beginning; and the University of California at Berkeley appointed me a Visiting Scholar. For interviews I would like to thank Sally Abeles-Gran, Ellen Barry, Helen Blackshear, Fanny Myers Brennan, Tony Buttitta, Alexander Clark, Honoria Murphy Donnelly, Virginia Foster Durr, Marie Jemison, Frances Turnbull Kidder, Eleanor Lanahan, Ring Lardner, Jr., Joseph Mankiewicz, Margaret Finney McPherson, Julian and Leslie McPhillips, Edgar Allan Poe III, Landon Ray, Frances Kroll Ring, Budd Schulberg, Courtney Sprague Vaughan and Hugh Wynne.

During my quest for Bijou O'Conor I also interviewed Sir Brinsley Ford, the Earl of Minto, Michael O'Conor, Gillian Plazzota and Sir William Young; and received letters from Frances Bebis, Anthony Blond, Claire Eaglestone of Balliol College, Margaret Elliot of the Elliot Clan Society, William Furlong, Francis King, Joyce Markham of the Foreign and Commonwealth Office, the Honourable Mary Alington Marten and the National Portrait Gallery, London.

During my search for Beatrice Dance I received help from Bond Davis, Helen Handley, Joan Sanger and Dan Laurence as well as from the Bexar County Courthouse, the Historical Society of San Antonio, the San Antonio Bar Association, the San Antonio Conservation Society and the San Antonio Public Library.

For other letters about Fitzgerald I am grateful to Sally Taylor Abeles, David Astor, Dr. Benjamin Baker, John Biggs III, Jonathan Bishop, Sarah Booth Conroy, Anthony Curtis, the Marquess of Donegall, Maureen, Marchioness of Donegall, Susan Mok Einarson, Armand Forel, Ian Hamilton, Valerie Hemingway, John Howell, Samuel Lanahan, Whitney Landon, Richard Lehan, Allan Margolies, Samuel Marx, Linda Miller, Dr. Paul Mok, David Page, Henry Dan Piper (who sent me the notes of interviews he conducted in the 1940s), Anthony Powell, Ruth Prigozy, Cecilia Lanahan Ross, Marie Sauer, Meryle Secrest, Henry Senber, Dodgie Shaffer, Robert Squier, Joan Kennedy Taylor, Rosalind Wilson, Archer Winsten and Roger Wunderlich.

I received useful information from the following institutions and libraries: the Alabama Department of Archives and History; the Archdiocese of Baltimore (Reverend Paul Thomas); the Association of Theatrical Press Agents and Managers; Bryn Mawr School, Baltimore; BBC Television (Jill Evans); the Lord Chamberlain's Office, Buckingham Palace; Highland Hospital (Carol Anne Freeman); Montgomery Museum of Fine Arts; National Archives and Records Administration, St. Louis; the National Portrait Gallery, Washington, D.C.; National Sound Archive, London; Harold Ober Associates; Hôpital de Prangins; Public Broadcasting Service, Alexandria, Virginia; Scott and Zelda Fitzgerald Museum, Montgomery, Alabama; the Embassy of Switzerland; and Sheppard and Enoch Pratt Hospital (Eleanor Barnhart). Also: the Firestone Library, Princeton University (the main collection of Fitzgerald's papers); Catholic University of America; Cornell University; Harvard University; Southern Illinois University; the University of Alabama, Birmingham; the University of Alabama, Tuscaloosa; the University of Cincinnati; the University of Delaware; the University of Pennsylvania; Stanford University and Yale University.

As always, my wife, Valerie Meyers, scrutinized each chapter and compiled the index.

Preface

The novelist Jay McInerney, writing in the *New York Review of Books* in August 1991, summarized the limitations of the previous biographies of Fitzgerald and mentioned "Bruccoli's hagiographic *Some Sort of Epic Grandeur*, Mellow's peevish, sordid *Invented Lives*, as well as Scott Donaldson's folksy psychoanalysis in *A Fool for Love* . . . Arthur Mizener's excellent and grim *The Far Side of Paradise*, Andrew Turnbull's biographical memoir *Scott Fitzgerald* and Nancy Milford's feminist revisionist *Zelda*. What doesn't emerge from any of these books is the sense of a coherent personality." Fitzgerald himself pessimistically pointed out the difficulty of capturing the essence of a writer: "There never was a good biography of a good novelist. There couldn't be. He's too many people if he's any good."

Yet the romantic and tragic Fitzgerald, who seemed to embody the two decades between the wars, continues to fascinate and to inspire attempts to capture his elusive personality. Though I have profited in various ways from the earlier biographies, my book on Scott is more analytic and interpretive. It discusses the meaning as well as the events of his life and seeks to illuminate the recurrent patterns that reveal his inner self. This biography places much greater emphasis on Scott's drinking; on Zelda's hospitals and doctors, especially Oscar Forel and Robert Carroll; on his love affairs, before and after Zelda's breakdown, with Lois Moran, Bijou O'Conor, Nora Flynn, Beatrice Dance and Sheilah Graham. It also focuses on his personal relations with his mentors at the Newman School, Father Fay (who was in love with Scott) and Shane Leslie; his Princeton friends, Edmund Wilson and John Peale Bishop; the humorist and screenwriter Donald Ogden Stewart; the polo star Tommy Hitchcock; the Hollywood executive Irving Thalberg; the journalist Michel Mok; and his daughter, Scottie, who wrote a great deal about him. I also say much more than I did in my 1985 biography of Hemingway about the most important literary friendship of the twentieth century.

Fitzgerald is a subject no one has a right to mess up. Nothing but the best will do for him. I think he just missed being a great writer, and the reason is pretty obvious. If the poor guy was already an alcoholic in his college days, it's a marvel that he did as well as he did. He had one of the rarest qualities in all literature. . . . The word is charm—charm as Keats would have used it. . . . It's a kind of subdued magic, controlled and exquisite.

—Raymond Chandler

Chapter One

ST. PAUL AND THE NEWMAN SCHOOL, 1896–1913

I

At the turn of the century St. Paul, Minnesota, where Scott Fitzgerald grew up, was a small Midwestern city with a genteel atmosphere and a highly stratified society. Scott's parents, both Catholic and of Irish descent, came from very different social backgrounds. Even as a boy, he had a keenly developed sense of social nuance. He learned, from observing his odd, insecure parents, to worry about where his family belonged in "good" society. Fitzgerald's novels portray the restless American middle and upper classes in the early decades of the century, and his fictional themes evolve from his origins in St. Paul. His young heroes are, like himself, fascinated by money and power, impressed by glamour and beauty. Yet they know they can never fully belong to this secure and prosperous world, that the goal of joining this careless, dominant class is an illusion.

In his *Notebooks* and his *Ledger*—a month-by-month account of his own life, which he began in 1919 and kept until 1936—Fitzgerald recorded all the details that would help him define exactly who he was and where he stood. He wanted not only to describe how he was shaped by his social background, but also to differentiate himself from it. In his *Notebooks* he later analyzed the social structure of St. Paul. Situated on a prairie and next to a great river, far from cultural centers, the city took its tone from the East and Europe rather than from Mid-western agriculture or the Mississippi river trade. At the head of the social hierarchy were the older established families who practiced the learned professions and considered themselves superior to the self-made businessmen and the obscure, Gatsby-like upstarts: "At the top came those whose grandparents had brought something with them from the East, a vestige of money and culture; then came the families of the big self-made merchants, the 'old settlers' of the sixties and sev-enties, American-English-Scotch, or German or Irish, looking down upon each other somewhat in the order named—upon the Irish less from religious difference—French Catholics were considered rather distinguished—than from the taint of political corruption in the East. After this came certain well-to-do 'new people'—mysterious, out of a cloudy past, possibly unsound." The upper class of this self-consciously snobbish society, which was based on "background," good manners and the appearance of morality, lived on Summit Avenue. This elegant Vic-torian boulevard—filled with "turreted, spired, porticoed and cupolaed 'palatial' residences"—ran westward from the Catholic Cathedral of St. Paul to a bluff overlooking the commercial town and a bend of the Mis-sissippi River.

The most imposing mansion on Summit Avenue belonged to the abstemious and laconic multimillionaire James J. Hill. Born in humble circumstances in Ontario, Canada, in 1838, he had made St. Paul the headquarters of his Great Northern Railway and fulfilled his pioneer's dream by driving it across the Western wilderness to the Pacific coast. Hill, a financial ally of J. P. Morgan, was "a short, thick-set man, with a massive head, large features, long black hair, and a blind eye. . . . He had no small scruples [and was] rough-hewn throughout, intolerant of opposition, despotic, largely ruling by fear."[1] No man did more for St. Paul, as exemplar and benefactor, than this empire builder and railroad magnate.

Scott's Aunt Annabel McQuillan had been maid of honor at the wedding of Hill's daughter. In boyhood he was fascinated by the fabu-lous wealth and influence of this legendary figure, who inspired Fitzgerald's imagination and frequently appeared in his fiction. In his first novel, *This Side of Paradise* (1920), the hero, Amory Blaine, speaking of the futile attempt to make business interesting in fiction, remarks: "Nobody wants to read about it, unless it's crooked business. If it was an entertaining subject they'd buy the life of James J. Hill." Later on, when advocating government ownership of industry during an argument with the rich father of his Princeton friend, Amory states: "we'd have the best analytical minds in the government working for something besides themselves. We'd have . . . Hill running interstate commerce."

In "Absolution" Rudolph's dreary father, Carl Miller, works as a freight agent in one of Hill's transport camps and adores his omnipotent boss: "His two bonds with the colorful life were his faith in the Roman Catholic Church and his mystical worship of the Empire Builder, James J. Hill. Hill was the apotheosis of that quality in which Miller himself was deficient. . . . [He grew] old in Hill's gigantic shadow. For twenty years he had lived alone with Hill's name and God." Hill was also one of the models for Gatsby's wealthy patron, Dan Cody. After Gatsby's death, his old father, ignoring the criminal basis of Gatsby's fortune, tells Nick Carraway: "If he'd of lived, he'd of been a great man. A man like James J. Hill. He'd of helped build up the country."² If the Hollywood executive Irving Thalberg was Fitzgerald's last tycoon, Hill was certainly his first. Hill's astonishing success not only fulfilled the American dream and revealed the power of boundless wealth, but also showed Fitzgerald that a man from St. Paul could become a significant figure in the great world.

II

Fitzgerald's family had some claim to Eastern culture. His great-great-grandfather was the brother of Fitzgerald's namesake, Francis Scott Key, a Maryland lawyer who wrote "The Star-Spangled Banner" during the British naval bombardment of Baltimore in 1814. Despite its limp opening ("O say can you see"), its livid rockets and martial rhetoric soon made the song famous, and it was eventually adopted as the American national anthem. Fitzgerald was acutely aware of the embarrassing contrast between the genteel but impoverished and the crude but wealthy elements in his background, which always made him feel like a parvenu. As he told the socially ambitious writer John O'Hara: "I am half black Irish and half old American stock with the usual exaggerated ancestral pretensions. The black Irish half of the family had the money and looked down upon the Maryland side of the family who had, and really had, that certain series of reticences and obligations that go under the poor old shattered word 'breeding.' . . . [So] I developed a two-cylinder inferiority complex." Though his parents were listed in the St. Paul Social Register, they lived on the money that had been made by Grandfather McQuillan, an Irish immigrant and wholesale grocer, who had left a fortune of several hundred thousand dollars when he died at the age of forty-three in 1877.

Francis Scott Key Fitzgerald, the product of these warring strains, was born on September 24, 1896, in a rented apartment at 481 Laurel Avenue, near (but not on) Summit Avenue in St. Paul. Like many American writers, including Ernest Hemingway, he was the son of a weak father and strong mother. His father, Edward, born near Rockville, Maryland, in 1853, had attended Georgetown University but did not graduate. He married Mollie McQuillan in February 1890 and took her on a honeymoon to Europe, where she had traveled on four previous trips. On their first day in Paris, as he urged her to hurry so he could tour the fascinating city, she innocently replied: "But I've already seen Paris!"

Edward was a small, ineffectual man with well-cut clothes and fine Southern manners. He loved to tell stories of his boyhood adventures during the Civil War, and was fond of reading the Romantic poetry of Byron and Poe and drowsing over the miscellaneous knowledge in the *Encyclopædia Britannica*. The absolute antithesis of James J. Hill, Edward was quite obviously a gentleman—and a failure. When Scott was born, Edward was the middle-aged proprietor of a small but grandly named wicker furniture business, the American Rattan and Willow Works, which was doomed to be eclipsed by his more energetic competitors.

As a boy, Scott was not only troubled by his father's failure in trade, but also ashamed of his mother's eccentric dress and peculiar behavior. Born in St. Paul in 1860, Mollie McQuillan was educated at that city's Visitation Convent and at Manhattanville College in New York. A voracious but indiscriminate reader of sentimental poetry and popular fiction, she was often seen carrying piles of books from the local library. She toted an umbrella even in fine weather and wore mismatched shoes of different colors. Mollie was also accustomed to blurting out embarrassingly frank remarks without realizing their effect on her acquaintances. She once stared at a woman whose husband was dying and said: "I'm trying to decide how you'll look in mourning."

Edward tactfully remarked that she just missed being beautiful. But one relative, who thought she had missed by quite a lot, described the pathetic, wispy little wife as "the most awkward and the homeliest woman I ever saw." Andrew Turnbull, Fitzgerald's biographer, observed that "her sallow skin had grown surprisingly wrinkled, there were dark discolorations beneath her pale eyes, and her fringing, cascading hair was a byword. . . . Somewhat broad for her height, she walked with a slight lurch, and she spoke in a droll manner, dragging and drawling her words."[3] Fitzgerald inherited his elegance and propensity to failure from his father, his social insecurity and absurd behavior from his mother.

The most influential event of his childhood took place before he was born. His two older sisters, Mary and Louise, suddenly died during an epidemic, at the ages of one and three, while their mother was pregnant with Scott. Another infant, born four years later in 1900, lived only an hour. The Fitzgeralds—like the family of Franz Kafka, whose two young brothers died soon after he was born—were devastated by these losses. (Mollie kept Louise's dolls in tissue paper until the end of her life.) The death of his sisters may have made Scott feel guilty about surviving. It certainly led to an unnaturally close connection between the overprotective, middle-aged mother and the spoiled, delicate child.

The family tragedy also strengthened the bond between Scott and his father, who tried to protect the boy from his mother's grief-stricken hysteria. In an autobiographical passage from *Tender is the Night*, Fitzgerald wrote that his hero, Dick Diver, "was born several months after the death of two young sisters and his father, guessing what would be the effect on Dick's mother, had saved him from a spoiling by becoming his moral guide." Fitzgerald later connected his sisters' deaths to his vocation as an author: "Three months before I was born my mother lost her other two children and I think that came first of all though I don't know how it worked exactly. I think I started then to be a writer." Though Fitzgerald did not explain this cryptic statement, he probably meant that he had been born out of suffering, had been singled out for a survivor's special fate and had been made to feel that his life was particularly precious. His existence somehow had to compensate for their absence.

III

Though Scott was a robust infant, weighing ten pounds six ounces at birth, he became a sickly and much-coddled child. When he was two years old, his mother, fearing that his persistent cough might lead to consumption, took him to a health resort. The following year his parents sent him to an infants' school, but he wept and wailed so much that they took him out again after one morning. The family physician, M. R. Ramsey, recalled that the stubborn and spoiled young Scott "was a patient of mine when he was a small boy and until he went off to prep school. He was a very difficult and temperamental patient and refused to accept any regime which was not to his liking. This attitude he preserved throughout life."[4]

In April 1898, after Edward's furniture business had collapsed, he moved his family to Buffalo, New York, and became a soap salesman for Procter & Gamble. They remained in Buffalo for the next decade, except for two and a half years in Syracuse from January 1901 to September 1903. But upstate New York, unlike St. Paul, left a negative impression on Scott's character. At the end of *Tender is the Night,* Dick Diver starts an unsuccessful medical practice in Buffalo, where his father had died, and then drifts about to Batavia, Lockport, Geneva and Hornell. Fitzgerald always associated upstate New York with isolation and failure.

Scott's only surviving sister, Annabel, was born in Syracuse in July 1901, and his first childhood memory was the sight of her howling on a bed. The self-absorbed boy was not close to her as a child, though he offered the teenage girl substantial advice about how to attract men, and rarely saw his attractive but conventional sister in adult life. Annabel later married and had two daughters. Her husband, Clifton Sprague, became an admiral and won the Navy Cross at the battle of Leyte Gulf in 1944.

Two years after Annabel's birth, while the family was still in Syracuse, the six-year-old Scott had some frightening experiences and acquired his first badge of courage: "He begins to remember many things, a filthy vacant lot, the haunt of dead cats, a hair-raising buck-board, the little girl whose father was in prison for telling lies, a Rabelaisian incident with Jack Butler, a blow with a baseball bat from the same boy—son of an army officer—which left a scar that will shine always in the middle of his forehead." Despite his heroic scar, another boyhood friend recalled that the handsome Scott was considered a sissy because he was afraid of a dead cat in the alley. On September 24, 1903, just after he returned to Buffalo and was desperately trying to reestablish his childhood friendships, Scott sent out invitations to his seventh birthday party—to which no one came. Heavy rain kept the indifferent children at home, and the humiliated Scott, consoled and spoiled by his mother, was allowed to eat the entire birthday cake, including some candles, by himself. He was a great eater of tallow until well past the age of fourteen.

In the summer of 1907 Scott went to Camp Chatham in Orillia, Ontario, north of Toronto on Lake Simcoe, where he swam, rowed, fished, played baseball and was extremely unpopular. When he played catcher without a mask, a ball cut his forehead. He became a hero despite his lack of athletic ability, but was so insufferably pleased with himself that he lost his short-lived prestige. One of his earliest letters, posted from camp to his mother, set the pattern of his future corre-spondence with agents and editors: "I wish you would send me five dol-lars as all my money is used up." The ten-year-old also tactfully discour-aged his mother from visiting him at camp and embarrassing him in front of the other boys: "Though I would like very much to have you up here, I don't think you would like it as you know no one here except Mrs. Upton and she is busy most of the time. I don't think you would like the accommodations as it is only a small town and no good hotels."[5]

Scott later admitted that he disliked his mother. He blamed her for spoiling him (which his father could not prevent) and emphasized the great difference in their characters and beliefs: "Mother and I never had anything in common except a relentless stubborn quality," he told his sister, "but when I saw all this it turned me inside out realizing how unhappy her temperament made her." In "An Author's Mother," he described Mollie's absurd appearance and mentioned her disapproval of his career: "She was a halting old lady in a black silk dress and a rather preposterously high-crowned hat that some milliner had foisted upon her declining sight. . . . Her son was a successful author. She had by no means abetted him in the choice of that profession but had wanted him to be an army officer or else go into business. . . . An author was something distinctly peculiar—there had been only one in the middle western city where she was born and he had been regarded as a freak. . . . Her secret opinion was that such a profession was risky and eccentric."

Fitzgerald once recorded a disturbing dream about his mother in which he felt ashamed of her for not being young and elegant, and for offending his sense of propriety by her peculiar behavior. He called her "a neurotic, half insane with pathological nervous worry." And in *This Side of Paradise* he created the antithesis of Mollie Fitzgerald in his ideal mother, Beatrice Blaine: charming, stylish, well-educated, beautiful, wealthy and well-connected. Though Fitzgerald never dedicated a book to his father, he did, as a joke, offer *Tales of the Jazz Age* (1922) "Quite inappropriately, to my mother." To Fitzgerald, the real matriarch of the family was Mollie's younger sister, Annabel McQuillan, a dessicated spinster who had all the character and culture so noticeably lacking in his mother.

Edward adored his small, blond, blue-eyed boy, whose refined and delicate features resembled his own, and who was full of energy and imagination. In a poignant essay on his father, Fitzgerald described how Edward would dress his son in starched white trousers and walk into downtown Buffalo to buy the Sunday paper and smoke his cigar. Scott always used his well-bred father, who believed in the old-fashioned virtues of honor, courtesy and courage, as a moral standard. After Mollie had been emotionally devastated by the death of her three babies, Edward roused himself from his usual lethargy and made an exemplary effort to be a good parent:

> I loved my father—always deep in my subconscious I have referred judgments back to him, to what he would have thought or done. He loved me—and felt a deep responsibility for me. . . . He came from tired old stock with very little left of vitality and mental energy but he managed to raise a little for me. We walked downtown in the summer to have our shoes shined, me in my sailor suit and my father in his always

beautifully cut clothes, and he told me the few things I ever
learned about life until a few years later from a Catholic priest,
Monsignor Fay.[6]

Since Edward lived in Mollie's shadow and eventually became financially dependent on her, he was (unlike his wife) proud of his son's profession and took great vicarious pleasure in his early success.

While Scott was on holiday in Frontenac, Minnesota, in July 1909, his
father—who was always pressed for money and even had to charge his
postage stamps at the local drugstore—sent him a sententious, paradoxical
and possibly playful note, which expected quite a lot from a rather small
sum: "I enclose $1.00. Spend it liberally, generously, carefully, judiciously,
sensibly. Get from it pleasure, wisdom, health and experience."

Edward was preoccupied with money because of his manifest
inability to earn it. The most traumatic incident in Scott's childhood
took place in Buffalo in March 1908, and suddenly transformed his
father from an elegant gentleman into a hopeless wreck:

> One afternoon—I was ten or eleven—the phone rang and my
> mother answered it. I didn't understand what she said but I felt
> that disaster had come to us. My mother, a little while before,
> had given me a quarter to go swimming. I gave the money back
> to her. I knew something terrible had happened and I thought
> she could not spare the money now.
>
> Then I began to pray, "Dear God," I prayed, "please don't
> let us go to the poorhouse." A little while later my father came
> home. I had been right. He had lost his job.
>
> That morning he had gone out a comparatively young man,
> a man full of strength, full of confidence. He came home that
> evening, an old man, a completely broken man. He had lost his
> essential drive, his immaculateness of purpose. He was a
> failure the rest of his days.

Unlike the compassionate Linda Loman in *Death of a Salesman*,
who responds to her husband's failure in business by telling her sons—
"he's a human being, and a terrible thing is happening to him. So attention must be paid. He's not to be allowed to fall into his grave like an
old dog"[7]—Mollie remained locked in her own hysterical world. She
looked down on her husband, who began to drink too much, and fre-

quently asked young Scott: "If it weren't for your Grandfather McQuillan, where would we be now?" The fathers of most of Fitzgerald's fictional heroes are dead before the novels begin.

IV

In July 1908 the defeated Fitzgeralds returned to St. Paul. The children moved in with Grandmother McQuillan on Laurel Avenue, the parents lived with a friend on Summit Avenue, and they were not reunited until the following April. Edward listlessly sold wholesale groceries from his brother-in-law's real estate office, and the Fitzgeralds changed their rented residences, in the neighborhood of Summit Avenue, almost every year. Despite the loss of income, the family made a brave attempt to maintain their social status by providing lessons, arranging dances and sending their children to the right schools.

Scott's swaggering adolescent roles as "actor, athlete, scholar, philatelist and collector of cigar bands" were undermined by his mother's insistence that he demonstrate his "accomplishments" by singing for company. The attractive, egoistic, socially insecure boy now revealed a crucial, lifelong flaw in his character, which would hurt him as a writer. He had a weakness for showing off instead of listening and observing, and was unaware of the effect he had on others. "I didn't know till 15," Fitzgerald said, "that there was anyone in the world except me, and it cost me *plenty*." Two of his closest friends later criticized the narcissistic self-absorption that limited Fitzgerald's understanding of other men and women. Sara Murphy wrote, with some exaggeration: "I have always told you you haven't the faintest idea what anybody else but yourself is like." And Hemingway, who agreed with her, told their editor Max Perkins: "Scott can't invent true characters because he doesn't know anything about people."[8]

Scott did develop a new awareness, however, when he perceived that he was popular with girls (if not with boys) and that they created strangely mixed feelings within him: "For the first time in his life he realized a girl is something opposite and complementary to him, and he was subject to a warm chill of mingled pleasure and pain." His chaste adolescent heroine, Josephine, likes the daring experience of kissing boys, but has no real sexual feeling. And in a potentially lyrical moment in *This Side of Paradise*, when the thirteen-year-old Amory Blaine kisses a girl for the first time, she responds with conventional romantic modesty while he is overwhelmed by nauseous repulsion: "Their lips brushed like young wild flowers in the wind. 'We're awful,' rejoiced Myra gently. She slipped her hand into his, her head drooped against his shoulder. Sudden revulsion seized Amory, disgust, loathing for the whole incident. He desired frantically to be away, never to see Myra again, never to kiss any one."[9]

Scott's sexual revulsion was undoubtedly connected to what his Anglo-Irish friend, Shane Leslie, called the "middle-class, dull, unpoetical and fettering" Catholicism of the Middle West. His mother was fanatical about religion, went to Mass every day and, as he told Sheilah Graham, "believed that Christian boys were killed at Easter and the Jews drank the blood. She was a bigot." He had attended two Catholic schools in Buffalo, and had shocked himself by lying in the confessional and telling the priest that he never told a lie.

When his family, still clinging precariously to the fringe of "good society," returned to Minnesota, the twelve-year-old Scott entered a nonsectarian school, St. Paul Academy, which had forty boys between the ages of ten and eighteen. During his three years there, he energetically began his literary apprenticeship. He would memorize titles in bookstores and confidently discuss works he had not read (the same intellectual pretentiousness would permeate his first novel). He attempted to achieve popularity with his classmates, as he had in Buffalo and at summer camp, but failed abysmally because he observed and criticized their faults. As he would later do at Princeton and in the army, he ignored his studies and "wrote all through every class in school in the back of my geography book and first year Latin and on the margins of themes and declensions and mathematics problems."[10]

He wrote many juvenile adventure stories for the school newspaper and melodramatic plays for the Elizabethan Dramatic Club, which was named after the director, Elizabeth Magoffin. Scott's first published story, "The Mystery of the Raymond Mortgage" (1909), echoed the title and imitated the characters and themes of Poe's "The Murders in the Rue Morgue." Though he neglected to bring the mortgage into the story, no one seemed to notice. "When it came to rewriting," Magoffin recalled, "Fitzgerald was indefatigable, retiring to a corner and tossing off new lines with his ever-facile pen." Scott was also capable of the kind of heroic action that fulfilled his childhood fantasies. The St. Paul *Pioneer Press* reported that in September 1914, during a performance of his fourth play, *Assorted Spirits,* a fuse suddenly exploded and the audience panicked. The young playwright saved the evening by leaping onto the stage and calming the frightened audience with an improvised monologue.

Another incident that made the newspapers took place during a Christmas service at St. John's Episcopal Church the previous year. Scott made a dramatic gesture, drew attention to himself and expressed his defiance of convention and rejection of religion. Though he called it "the most disgraceful thing I ever did," his cocky tone suggests that he welcomed the notorious publicity he had inspired: "I plodded toward the rector. At the very foot of the pulpit a kindly thought struck me— perhaps inspired by the faint odor of sanctity which exuded from the saintly man. I spoke. 'Don't mind me,' I said, 'go on with the sermon.' Then, perhaps unsteadied a bit by my emotion, I passed down the other aisle, followed by a sort of amazed awe, and so out into the street. The papers had an extra out before midnight."[11]

V

Three crucial entries in Scott's autobiographical *Ledger* for his boyhood years from 1901 to 1904 expressed his acute anxiety and shame about his feet, which he associated with fear of exposure, with filth and with perversion. Scott's bizarre obsession with and phobia about his feet were closely connected not only to his childhood guilt about sex and revulsion when kissing girls—the result of what he called "a New England conscience, developed in Minnesota"—but also to adult doubts about his masculinity and fears about his sexual inadequacy:

He went to Atlantic City—where some Freudian complex refused to let him display his *feet,* so he refused to swim, concealing the real reason. They thought he feared the water.

There was a boy named Arnold who went barefooted in his yard and peeled plums. Scott's Freudian shame about his feet kept him from joining in.

He took off John Wylie's shoes. He began to hear "dirty" words. He had this curious dream of perversion.

In a *Smart Set* interview of 1924, Fitzgerald commented on the childhood phobia that had made him so unhappy and falsely claimed that it had suddenly vanished when he reached adolescence: "The sight of his own feet filled him with embarrassment and horror. No amount of persuasion could entice him to permit others to see his naked feet, and up until he was twelve this fear caused him a great deal of misery. . . . This complex suddenly disappeared one day without any reason."[12]

Frances Kroll, Fitzgerald's secretary in Hollywood, observed that he was slightly pigeon-toed, always wore slippers and never went about in bare feet. Sheilah Graham, Fitzgerald's companion during the last years of his life, wrote that he had mentioned his "mysterious shyness" about his feet, and during the years that she knew him always refused to take off his shoes and socks on the beach. When Tony Buttitta, who visited Fitzgerald's hotel room in Asheville in 1935, noticed his "stubby and unattractive feet," Fitzgerald "fumbled for his slippers and hid his feet in them." Most significantly, Lottie, a prostitute who became Fitzgerald's mistress that summer, described his foot fetishism and said that he "caressed her feet, the toes, instep, and heel, and got an odd pleasure out of it. . . . It seems that the sight of women's feet has excited him since he first started thinking about sex."[13]

Early in his career Fitzgerald used his curious obsession to suggest the presence of evil. In *This Side of Paradise*, in a five-page scene called "The Devil," Amory Blaine and a friend pick up two chorus girls in a nightclub, where he notices a pale, middle-aged man dressed in a brown suit. They then go up to the girls' apartment to get drunk and have sex. Just as Amory is tempted by Phoebe, the minatory devil figure from the nightclub mysteriously appears in the apartment: "suddenly, Amory perceived the feet, and with a rush of blood to the head [instead of to the penis] he realized he was afraid. The feet were all wrong . . . with a sort of wrongness that he felt rather than knew. . . . It was like weakness in a good woman, or blood on satin; one of those terrible incongruities that shake little things in the back of the brain." Associating the horrific feet with sexual immorality and sexual violation, Amory rushes out of the sinful apartment and descends in the elevator. As he reaches the lower floor, "the feet came into view in the sickly electric light of the paved hall."

This fictional scene made an emotional impact on Scott's boyhood friend Stephan Parrott, who had attended the same Catholic prep school and had read an early draft of the novel in April 1919. "The farther I got into it the more interested I became," Parrott said, "but when I came to the place where you saw the man with the disgusting feet, I had to stop reading. I know just what you felt. Your mood was exactly like some I have felt, of the worst kind; in fact it started a humour in me that was quite horrible."[14]

Fitzgerald's childhood phobia evolved from his subconscious "Freudian" feelings. Though revolted by his own feet, he was sexually excited by the feet of women. His fearful associations with feet—which stuck out stiffly and were strongly associated with sex—both displaced and expressed his adolescent and adult fears about his masculinity. His deep-rooted insecurity later led him to seek embarrassing reassurance, not only from his mistresses of the 1930s but also from personal friends, about the size and potency of his sexual organ.

VI

Scott's poor performance at St. Paul Academy prompted his parents to send him to a stricter, Eastern, Catholic boarding school. This would, they hoped, provide a more rigorous academic program, expose him to a more sophisticated way of life and increase his chances of gaining admission to a good college. The Newman School in Hackensack, New Jersey (across the Hudson River and about ten miles northwest of midtown Manhattan) had been founded in 1890 by Cardinal Gibbons of Baltimore to attract the sons of "Catholic gentlemen" and taught sixty boys from well-off Catholic families throughout the country. Scott, brought up with the traditional values of his paternal ancestors in Maryland, had always yearned for an Eastern education. Like Basil Duke Lee in "The Freshest Boy," he "had lived with such intensity on so many stories of boarding-school life that, far from being homesick, he had a glad feeling of recognition and familiarity."

Scott's gladness, however, was short lived. As he entered Newman in September 1911, he naively overrated his appearance and athletic ability, social graces and intellectual power, which he felt would lead to success in school, and retrospectively made the honest admission that he lacked the fundamental elements of good character:

> First: Physically—I marked myself handsome; of great athletic possibilities, and an extremely good dancer. . . . Second: Socially . . . I was convinced that I had personality, charm, magnetism, poise, and the ability to dominate others. Also I was sure that I exercised a subtle fascination over women. Third: Mentally . . . I was vain of having so much, of being so talented, ingenious and quick to learn. . . . Generally—I knew that at bottom I lacked the essentials. At the last crisis, I knew I had no real courage, perseverance or self-respect.

Scott attempted to cultivate friendships with several classmates by composing their weekly English essays and enhanced his reputation as an athlete by writing an anonymous account in the Newman News of his "fine running with the ball" during a football game. But these ingenious ploys did not work. One student recalled that he was "eager to be liked by his companions and almost vain in seeking praise." His roommate remembered him as having "the most impenetrable egotism I've ever seen."[15]

"Sap" Donahoe, a popular and well-respected boy from Seattle, and a fine scholar and athlete, traveled with Scott during the long trips home on the holidays and remained his friend at Princeton. Though Sap liked Scott, he explained that "he was unpopular starting out at Newman partly because his good looks prompted classification as a sissy, which was reinforced by what appeared to be a lack of physical courage." He described Scott as "imaginative in temperament, keen in observation, rather critical in taste and sceptical in mind"—traits which made him something of a misfit in the orthodox school and led to a crisis of faith after he left.

Fitzgerald wrote about two wasted school years of "utter and profitless unhappiness" in both This Side of Paradise (in which he called the school St. Regis) and in "The Freshest Boy." In the novel he records that he was resentful of authority and indifferent to his work, that he was considered both conceited and arrogant, and that he was universally detested. In the story he goes into greater detail about the numerous reasons for his extraordinary unpopularity. He mentions that he had received a hostile note that objected to his brash conceit and rudely asserted: "If someone will please poison young Basil, or find some other means to stop his mouth, the school at large and myself will be much obliged." As one of the poorest boys in a rich boys' school, he overcompensated by boasting, pointing out other people's mistakes and showing off his fund of general knowledge. When, in addition to all this, he revealed his cowardice during a football game by avoiding a dangerous tackle, he became "the scapegoat, the immediate villain, the sponge which absorbed all malice and irritability abroad." The lonely outcast was irreparably condemned to the ranks of "the bitter, the selfish, the neurasthenic and the unhappy." Scott's academic work inevitably suffered and he failed four courses during his two years at the school.

Though Scott loved to go on school holidays to the theater in New York, his happiest recollections concerned the exciting train journeys that allowed him to escape from the hateful school for longer periods and return to his adoring parents in the familiar Midwest. In *The Great Gatsby*, one of Nick Carraway's

> most vivid memories is of coming back West from prep school and later from college at Christmas time. Those who went farther than Chicago would gather in the old dim Union Station at six o'clock of a December evening, with a few Chicago friends, already caught up into their own holiday gayeties, to bid them a hasty good-by. . . .
>
> That's my Middle West—not the wheat or the prairies or the lost Swede towns, but the thrilling returning trains of my youth, and the street lamps and sleigh bells in the frosty dark and the shadows of holly wreaths thrown by lighted windows on the snow.[16]

VII

Scott's desperate unhappiness and isolation at Newman made him eagerly receptive to the attention, encouragement and flattery of an unusual Catholic priest and trustee of the school, whom he met during

his second year in November 1912. Father Cyril Sigourney Webster
Fay was born in Philadelphia in 1875, the only son of a wealthy Irish-
American lieutenant-colonel in the United States Army. After graduat-
ing from the University of Pennsylvania in 1897 and the Episcopal
Divinity School in Philadelphia five years later, he taught dogmatic and
moral theology at Nashotah House, the Anglican seminary in Fond du
Lac, northwest of Milwaukee. Though Fay had once started writing a
book to prove the invalidity of Roman orders, he later joined a group of
Anglo-Catholic Episcopal clergymen who seceded to the Roman
Catholic Church in 1908. A hostile Protestant contemporary explained
that "Fay's unstable temperament called for a new thrill. . . . He was
tired of socialism and the mild forms of modernism he had adopted. He
was looking Romeward and the papal condemnation of modernism led
him to declare publicly: 'We must obey the Holy Father.'" Fay was
ordained by his patron, Cardinal Gibbons, in 1910, and taught Sacred
Liturgy and Ecclesiastical Greek from 1910 to 1914 at Catholic University in Washington, D.C. After Scott had left Newman, Fay became
headmaster of the school.

Father Fay, a brilliant intellectual and fascinating talker, was a
strange-looking man. The huge, eunuch-like priest, almost a pure
albino, had a shrill, high-pitched, giggling voice. He was extremely
nearsighted and enormously fat. His thin, pale yellow hair, rising above
a broad forehead, was parted in the middle. A thick pince-nez distorted
his pink, watery eyes. His pudgy nose, round face, triple chins and thick
neck emphasized his porcine appearance and made him look twenty
years older than his actual age.

The absolute antithesis of the dreary German Midwestern priest in
Fitzgerald's story "Absolution," the heavily perfumed and wittily epi-
grammatic Father Fay was a fin-de-siècle aesthete and dandy, who
adored Decadent authors like Huysmans, Swinburne and Oscar Wilde.
Fay's close friend Margaret Chanler emphasized the charming, worldly
aspect of his personality and described him as a rather jolly monk: "He
was a learned man with much of the delightful child about him. He
combined spiritual with temporal gifts, for he preached admirably, and
could bring fire from heaven to kindle the hearts of his hearers, but he
was no ascetic and clearly loved good company, good food and drink."

He also took childish pleasure in ecclesiastical vestments and elaborate liturgy. Fitzgerald's biographers, from Turnbull to Bruccoli, have

stated that Father Fay recited the Mass in Gaelic. But a Gaelic version of the Mass did not exist in Fay's lifetime and the Mass could not be said in any language but Latin until the Vatican II reforms of 1965. Henry Dan Piper was more accurate when he explained that Fay "obtained special dispensation to celebrate the Roman Mass according to the more exotic rites of the Greek Church, which he found more aesthetically satisfying."[17]

Fay took a paternal interest in Scott, strengthening his religious beliefs, recognizing his talent and praising his first novel. He frequently invited Scott to his comfortable home in Washington, brought him into elite circles and introduced him to important men like Shane Leslie and Henry Adams. Fay's influence became even stronger when the older, more appreciative Scott was at Princeton and in the army. After Fay's death in the influenza epidemic of 1919, Fitzgerald idealized him as Monsignor Darcy in *This Side of Paradise* and compared him to an exiled Stuart king, waiting to be called back to rule his country: "Monsignor was forty-four then, and bustling—a trifle too stout for symmetry, with hair the color of spun gold, and a brilliant, enveloping personality. When he came into a room clad in his full purple regalia from thatch to toe, he resembled a Turner sunset, and attracted both admiration and attention."[18]

Scott's other mentor was the dashing, wealthy and well-connected Shane Leslie. The son of an Anglo-Irish baronet and one of the beautiful American Jerome sisters, he was a first cousin of Winston Churchill. Tall, blunt-featured and rugged-looking, he went to Eton, studied at the Sorbonne, where he met Henry Adams, and at King's College, Cambridge, where he rowed for the college and came to know Rupert Brooke. He visited Tolstoy in Russia, studied philosophy at Louvain and converted to Catholicism. He did social work in Wapping, in the East End of London, worked for the Home Rule movement in Ireland and changed his name from John to Shane to emphasize his Celtic origins. He married an American wife in 1912, became acquainted with Yeats and D. H. Lawrence, lived among diplomats in Spain and served with the American Ambulance Corps in France during World War I. Leslie—the friend of two powerful American priests, Archbishop Ireland of St. Paul and Cardinal Gibbons of Baltimore—moved in exalted circles and, as chamberlain to the Pope, became an influential Catholic layman.

Leslie called Fitzgerald "an American Rupert Brooke," recommended his first novel to Scribner's and wrote a favorable review of the book. He encouraged Fitzgerald's courtship and marriage to Zelda Sayre, commenting that "literary men need wives to edit their letters (in two volumes)." He also saw his disciple as the American equivalent of the novelist, priest and son of the Archbishop of Canterbury, who had converted to Catholicism, and told Fitzgerald: "I think you would be happier if you were anchored like Hugh Benson to the priesthood." Fitzgerald admired Leslie, and was grateful for his friendship and generous help. In his review of Leslie's Etonian novel, *The Oppidan* (1922), he called him "the most romantic figure I had ever known" and described the liberating effect of his friendship: "He was a convert to the church of my youth, and he and another, since dead [Father Fay], made of that church a dazzling, golden thing, dispelling its oppressive mugginess and giving the succession of days upon gray days, passing under its plaintive ritual, the romantic glamour of an adolescent dream."[19] Scott's friendships with Fay and Leslie compensated for his disappointment and unhappiness at Newman, and fortified his self-confidence and his Catholic faith as he entered Princeton in the fall of 1913.

Chapter Two

PRINCETON, 1913–1917

I

Fitzgerald's grandmother Louise McQuillan died in the summer of 1913 and left her daughter Mollie $125,000. This legacy rescued Fitzgerald from the lumpenproletariat at the University of Minnesota or a parochial education at Georgetown University (where his father had been a student). It allowed him, instead, to become a gentleman scholar at Princeton.

Fitzgerald chose the image as much as the reality of Princeton. It was in the same state as his prep school and—to a young man who identified with his Maryland ancestors—was more social and "Southern" than Harvard or Yale. Harvard, which he associated with New England puritans and brainy Jews, seemed too "indoors" and intellectual. Yale men, like Tom Buchanan in *The Great Gatsby*, were too brawny and brutal. Even the *Yale Daily News* conceded, in the spring of 1913, that the Yale type dressed correctly and had fine manners but lacked intellectual ability: "Sometimes it has tremendous dumb energy. And it has nearly the mental power of the original Yale Bull Dog." Fitzgerald imagined the Princeton man, by contrast, as lazy, good-looking and aristocratic: "Princeton drew him most, with its atmosphere of bright colors and its alluring reputation as the pleasantest country club in America."

Fitzgerald also imagined himself a great football player and strongly identified with the heroes of the Princeton team. In a draft of his first novel, Fitzgerald said that seeing the Princeton end Sam White block a Harvard field goal and run ninety-five yards for a winning touchdown decided him for Princeton in 1911. This glorious image was reinforced four years later, while Fitzgerald was an undergraduate, when he saw the romantic Buzz Law kicking from behind his goal line with a bloody bandage round his head. Fitzgerald, the mediocre prep school player, always reveled in college football as spectator, statistician and would-be participant.

Most importantly, Fitzgerald—who had been publishing stories and poems in his school newspapers since 1909 and had had four plays produced by the Elizabethan Dramatic Club in St. Paul—was attracted by the Princeton Triangle Club. This undergraduate club wrote and produced a lively if slightly antiquated musical comedy each fall and, during the Christmas vacation, performed it—with chorus, orchestra and scenery—in a dozen large cities across the country. "That was enough for me," Fitzgerald wrote. "From then on the university question was settled. I was bound for Princeton."[1]

Since Fitzgerald's school grades were deficient, he had to take a college entrance examination. The student who staunchly defended the honor system and had never heard of a Princeton man cheating, gained admission by some judicious cribbing and by convincing the examiners that they could not possibly reject him on September 24, his seventeenth birthday. Conditionally admitted to the Class of 1917, he immediately wired his mother for football pads and shoes. Weighing only 138 pounds, he tried out for the freshman team and was cut from the squad on the first day.

Princeton had been founded in 1746 as a Presbyterian college and Jonathan Edwards, the Yale-educated theologian, had been an early president. In the 1770s its students included Aaron Burr, who later killed Alexander Hamilton in a duel; James Madison, who became the fourth president of the United States; the novelist H. H. Brackenridge and the poet Philip Freneau. Booth Tarkington, an influence on Fitzgerald's early work, had founded the Triangle Club in the early

1890s; and Eugene O'Neill had failed out, after a rebellious and dissipated year, in 1907.

The spire-filled college, surrounded by luxurious estates, rose out of the flat midlands of New Jersey. "The loveliest riot of Gothic architecture in America" was modeled on the Oxford quads just as the system of preceptors, founded by Woodrow Wilson (who had been president of the university before becoming governor of New Jersey and then wartime president of the United States), was based on the Oxford tutors. Anglophilia prevailed at Princeton, whose fifteen hundred students cultivated a tradition of gentility, charm and honor that reaffirmed the values of Fitzgerald's old-fashioned father.

After meeting privileged beings like Richard Cleveland (son of former president Grover Cleveland) and David Bruce (son of a United States senator, who himself later became a distinguished ambassador), Fitzgerald soon discovered that there was a vast difference between young men from St. Paul's School and a young man from St. Paul, Minnesota. Surrounded by rich, Eastern, Anglo-Saxon Protestants from the most elite private schools, the poor, provincial Irish Catholic from obscure and undistinguished Newman felt socially and financially inferior. As Fitzgerald later told a friend, he never had the money to sustain the precarious position he had struggled to achieve: "That was always my experience—a poor boy in a rich town; a poor boy in a rich boy's school; a poor boy in a rich man's club at Princeton."[2] He also became, after his fortunes failed in the 1930s, a poor man at a luxurious resort in North Carolina and a poor writer among the fabulously rich film stars in Hollywood.

While Fitzgerald's more polished and self-assured classmates glided through Princeton with apparently effortless ease, the ambitious Midwestern schoolboy threw himself into college life with unusual seriousness and made strenuous efforts to distinguish himself by social and literary—if not athletic and academic—achievements.

Considered deficient in Latin, French, algebra and physics, Fitzgerald (like two-thirds of the 430 freshmen) had to pass examinations in these subjects in December as well as do his ordinary course work. During his freshman year he was required to take an unusually heavy schedule: Latin (Roman historians), survey of French literature, English composition and rhetoric, trigonometry, physics and hygiene, in addition to physical education and an extra course in algebra to prepare for the make-up exam.

Since math and physics were boring and obstructive, and foreign languages remained a mystery, he was most keenly interested in his courses in English literature. Alfred Noyes, a popular conventional poet and author of "The Highwayman," was Murray Professor and gave two lectures a week for half the college year. Fitzgerald naively asked Noyes if he should write for fame or for money (a question that troubled him throughout his life). On another occasion he was permitted to carry the vintage port into the dining room during a formal dinner for John Galsworthy.

The other English teachers were deeply disappointing. His talented classmate John Peale Bishop thought most of them were old boys with a weakness for pedantry. Fitzgerald, even more critical, complained that none of his English teachers ever mentioned contemporary American writers. The surprisingly pallid English department was "top-heavy [and] undistinguished, with an uncanny knack for making literature distasteful to young men." The dead academic hand touched passionate poetry and made it wither: "one of my first discoveries was that some of the professors who were teaching poetry really hated it and didn't know what it was about. I got in a series of endless scrapes with them so that I finally dropped English altogether"[3]—and was left with little else in the classroom that interested him.

The lectures in each course were supplemented by weekly meetings with the preceptors, who were supposed to strengthen the course by teaching small groups of students. But Fitzgerald's English tutor, far from inspiring him, merely offered pedantic analyses. Instead of dutifully paying attention and taking notes, Fitzgerald vented his anger in his copy of Sidney's *Defence of Poesie:* "this man Griffin is terrible. I sit here bored to death and hear him pick English poetry to pieces. Small man, small mind. Snotty, disagreeable. Damn him.... They say Griffin has made more men leave the English department than any other praeceptor in College. The slovenly old fool! *I have the most terrible praeceptors."* Though repeatedly warned about his lateness to class, Fitzgerald refused to change his habits to please his teacher and excused himself by declaring: "Sir—it's absurd to expect me to be on time. I'm a genius!"

Though Fitzgerald's grades were predictably terrible, he managed to survive his freshman year. But he established the disastrous pattern of trying to make up past deficiencies while failing his current courses. Christian Gauss, who taught French Romantic poetry and was one of the few teachers Fitzgerald admired, gave a perceptive analysis of the character, ambitions and defects of his bright but wayward student: "He was impatient of discipline . . . and was fascinated by the operatic pageantry of the pre–World War campus. . . . He yearned rather consistently to dominate the world, become president of the Triangle Club and be a Big Man on the Campus. He possessed a far less solid background of reading than his friends but was deeply interested in the problems of art and its techniques. . . . He pursued his studies only spasmodically."[4]

II

Fitzgerald's Princeton friends, as Gauss suggested, were more intellectual than he was. Sap Donahoe, a serious student who had been a friend at Newman and remained close to Fitzgerald, invited him in the summer of 1915 to his family ranch in White Sulphur Springs, sixty-five miles north of Bozeman, in the highlands of central Montana. Togged in Western clothes, Fitzgerald had a good time drinking with the cowboys and winning fifty dollars in a poker game.

Henry Strater, a pacifist devotee of Tolstoy and Edward Carpenter, was the model for the "fair-haired, silent, and intent" Burne Holiday in *This Side of Paradise*. A popular man who liked to champion unpopular causes, Strater led an influential protest against the discriminatory club system at Princeton and also opposed America's entry into World War I. He later became a mediocre painter, and a hunting and fishing companion of Hemingway.

John Biggs, whose grandfather had been governor of Delaware and whose father was attorney general, had a booming voice and an impressive head and build. Biggs roomed with Fitzgerald in 1917; wrote many issues of the college humor magazine, the Princeton *Tiger*, with him; and collaborated with him on the 1916 Triangle Club play, *Safety First!* Biggs published two novels with Scribner's in the 1920s, and was the youngest judge named to the Third U.S. Circuit Court of Appeals. He remained Fitzgerald's faithful friend and eventually became his literary executor.

Fitzgerald's most literary companions (who also remained lifelong friends) were John Peale Bishop and Edmund Wilson. Born in West Virginia in 1892, Bishop had been an invalid as a child and entered Princeton several years later than his contemporaries. Christian Gauss said that "even as a freshman John had a self-possession and self-mastery which gave him the poise and bearing of a young English lord." Fitzgerald was intrigued by Bishop's scholarly and aesthetic persona, so different from his own boyish enthusiasm, and found him exquisite, anachronistic and decadent. In *This Side of Paradise* he portrayed the cracked-voiced Bishop as Thomas Parke D'Invilliers, "an awful highbrow . . . who signed passionate love-poems in the [*Nassau*] *Lit*. He was perhaps nineteen, with stooped shoulders, pale blue eyes, and . . . without much conception of social competition." Bishop—partly deceived and wholly delighted by Fitzgerald's pretentious talk about books he had not read—directed Fitzgerald's reading, guided his literary taste and, with Wilson, taught him more about poetry than all the teachers at Princeton.

Bishop, who won all the literary prizes as an undergraduate, cultivated his precious persona and later remarked: "As to my tastes, I like to eat and drink, and above all to talk; I am fond of looking at paintings, sculpture, architecture and formal gardens; in a very modest way, I paint and garden myself. In particular, I like the architecture of humanism and the music of the eighteenth century. I prefer the ballet—at its best—to the theatre. I no longer care very much for reading, except for information."[5] Bishop published his first volume of poems in 1917, served overseas during the war, married a rich and rather stuffy wife, and lived mostly in France in the 1920s. Though he turned out novels and poems,. he was weakened by wealth, became desiccated and depressed, and never fulfilled his literary promise. He died on Cape Cod of a heart attack in 1944. Though aware of Bishop's limitations as a writer, Fitzgerald was always eager to earn his praise.

Edmund Wilson, like Bishop, was Fitzgerald's antithesis. Born in New Jersey in 1895, the son of a brilliant Princetonian trial lawyer and sometime attorney general of the state, Wilson was a solid member of the Eastern gentry. Haughty and aloof, he attended the Hill School, graduated from Princeton with an outstanding record in 1916 and served overseas with the ambulance corps in World War I. Plain in appearance, the stocky, auburn-haired Wilson was intellectual and sternly rational, stiff and self-conscious. The dazzlingly handsome

Fitzgerald, by contrast, had an imaginative and intuitive mind, a spontaneous and impetuous approach to experience.

At Princeton Wilson had all the advantages. A year ahead of Fitzgerald and editor of the *Nassau Lit.*, he corrected Fitzgerald's one-act play "Shadow Laurels" and his story "The Ordeal," and published them in the college magazine in 1915. They collaborated that year on a musical comedy for the Triangle Club, Wilson writing the book and Fitzgerald the lyrics for *The Evil Eye*. To Fitzgerald, Wilson seemed self-conscious and pedantic; a well-dressed, withdrawn grind, smug and superior about his intelligence and erudition. It was understood between them that Fitzgerald was the brash, superficial upstart, destined to make a risky splash in the world, while Wilson was the solid intellectual who would set him straight.

Despite their friendship, Wilson and Bishop maintained a rather condescending attitude toward Fitzgerald's considerable literary achievement at Princeton: two dozen pieces for the *Nassau Lit.*, three dozen for the *Tiger* and the lyrics for three absurdly plotted musicals of the Triangle Club—the most powerful organization, outside of athletics, on campus. Some of these early stories were good enough to rewrite and publish in H. L. Mencken's *Smart Set* at the beginning of Fitzgerald's professional career.

Fitzgerald studied the "amazing lyrics" of Gilbert and Sullivan's *Iolanthe* and *Patience* when writing his own songs and modeled his witty dialogue on the plays of Oscar Wilde. In 1924 Fitzgerald recalled: "I spent my entire freshman year writing an operetta for the Triangle Club. I failed in algebra, trigonometry, coordinate geometry and hygiene, but the Triangle Club accepted my show, and by tutoring all through a stuffy August I managed to come back a sophomore and act in it as a chorus girl."

Though Fitzgerald reserved for himself the role of the sexy and seductive show girl, his poor grades made him ineligible to act in the play. He had to be content with dressing up for the part in a blond wig, glamorous hat, tulle shawl and flowered gown, and having his theatrical photograph published in the newspapers of all the cities in the Christmas tour. Fitzgerald was five feet eight inches tall, with blond hair, green eyes, perfect features and a smooth, almost honeyed voice. He was "pretty" without being effeminate (his class poll gave him two votes for handsomest and five for the prettiest man), and had the same Irish beauty as Wilson's future wife Mary McCarthy. In this photograph, with his head tilted fetchingly back, Fitzgerald looks for all the world like a charming drag queen. A St. Paul friend recalled: "He was strikingly good-looking and when his eyes sparkled and his face shone with that powerful interior animation it was truly an exciting experience." And a Princeton contemporary, noting that all the female parts in the musicals were played by male students, agreed that "besides being one of the prettiest girls in the shows, he looked exactly like a beautiful lady and acted like one."[6]

In Minneapolis, Fitzgerald again put on his costume, falsies and make-up. Escorted by a St. Paul friend, he created a sensation by appearing at a fraternity party at the University of Minnesota. He brazenly smoked cigarettes on the dance floor, took a powder compact from the top of his blue stocking and was not unmasked until, after several drinks, he had to use the men's room. His ambitions at the Triangle Club also ended badly, as he later warned his daughter while minimizing his own academic failures: "You are doing [at Vassar] exactly what I did at Princeton. I wore myself out on a musical comedy there for which I wrote the book and lyrics, organized and mostly directed while the president played football. Result: I slipped way back in my work, got T.B., lost a year in college—and, irony of ironies, because of the scholastic slip I wasn't allowed to take the presidency of the Triangle."

Though the football-playing club president took credit for Fitzgerald's book and Scott failed to succeed him in office when forced to leave in the middle of his junior year, he did at least achieve the desired social success. Toward the end of each year the eighteen eating clubs on Prospect Street elected about three-quarters of the second-year students, while the rejected men continued to eat in the university dining halls. The Princeton eating clubs had no other function, Arthur Mizener noted, than "to provide a system of grading people according to social distinction at the middle of the sophomore year."

Fitzgerald was elected to Cottage, which—with Ivy, Tiger, and Cap and Gown—was one of the "big four" clubs. It had been founded in 1887, was the most architecturally sumptuous of the clubs and had a large Southern following from St. Louis and Baltimore. Cottage was "an impressive mélange of brilliant adventurers and well-dressed philanderers,"[7] he wrote in *This Side of Paradise*. Its lavish weekend parties in impressive surroundings, which attracted girls from New York,

Philadelphia and beyond, may well have provided the first grain of inspiration for Fitzgerald's portrayal of Jay Gatsby's fabulous parties on Long Island.

III

Apart from Father Fay, whom he continued to see at the priest's family home on the New Jersey coast, Fitzgerald had no significant social connections in the East and no girlfriends at Princeton. But at a Christmas dance in St. Paul in 1914 (the middle of his sophomore year) he met Ginevra King, who was visiting her roommate from Westover School, and immediately fell in love with the sophisticated sixteen-year-old girl. "I didn't have the top two things—great animal magnetism or money," Fitzgerald later wrote in his *Notebooks*. "I had the two second things, tho', good looks and intelligence. So I always got the top girl." In *This Side of Paradise* Fitzgerald also observed that his autobiographical hero Amory Blaine lacked animal magnetism—the basis of physical attraction—and that Isabelle (based on Ginevra) had this admirable quality: "Flirt smiled from her large black-brown eyes and shone through her intense physical magnetism." It is significant that in his *Notebooks* Fitzgerald valued money more than intelligence, and did not even mention artistic ability. And he did *not* get Ginevra, the top girl. She was too self-absorbed to notice his unusual talent and played an indifferent Fanny Brawne to Fitzgerald's suffering Keats.

Ginevra came from Lake Forest, north of Chicago on Lake Michigan, a suburb which epitomized the zenith of upper-class Midwestern society. She grew up among the country mansions of the Swifts, the Armours and the McCormicks, and impressed the middle-class, socially insecure Fitzgerald with her sense of privilege and innate superiority. Ginevra's sensual, seductive manner (which promised much and gave nothing) had a powerful impact on the older college boy. In a letter to his young sister, Annabel, he recommended Ginevra's languid artifice as an ideal mode of behavior: "Never try to give a boy the [impression] that you're popular—Ginevra always starts by saying that she's a poor unpopular woman without any beaux. . . . A pathetic, appealing look is one every girl ought to have. Sandra and Ginevra are specialists at this. . . . It's best done by opening the eyes wide and drooping the mouth a little, looking upward (hanging the head a little) directly into the eyes of the man you're talking to."[8]

Though Scott was smitten by Ginevra, she considered him an amusing but by no means exclusive suitor. The narcissistic girl was more interested in attracting a series of boyfriends than in restricting herself to only one. She rather callously considered courtship a kind of stock market in which the wise investor bent the rules and bought shares in several promising prospects: "I can't remember even kissing Scott. I imagine I did. But it wasn't exactly a big thing in my life! . . . I guess I was too busy adding to my string to analyze my reaction to one suitor. . . . He was mighty young when we knew each other. I just never singled him out as anything special. . . . I was [later] engaged to two other people. That was very easy during the war because you'd never get caught. It was just covering yourself in case of a loss."[9]

The one-sided romance continued for the next two years during dances, dinners and plays in Lake Forest and New York, at Westover and Princeton. Though doomed in August 1916, when Fitzgerald overheard someone say that poor boys should not think of marrying rich girls, it was kept alive by hundreds of letters from Fitzgerald (some of them, thirty pages long, had to be stuffed into a series of envelopes). Fitzgerald kept Ginevra's letters typed and bound into a 275-page book; she considered his clever but unimportant and destroyed them in 1917.

The following year she sent Fitzgerald an announcement of her marriage to a naval ensign. She had no regrets about rejecting Fitzgerald, and later showed some insight into his youthful character: "As I remember him, he was like a great many truly shy people, who give a feeling of conceit and self-importance as a cover up and an escape. . . . I truly feel that my part in Scott's college life was a detriment to him—I certainly kept him from his work. . . . My attitude didn't help an already supersensitive and sentimental person. . . . Scott's and my temperaments would have clashed dreadfully & I would have undoubtedly driven him to drink a great many years earlier." Ginevra's younger sister, Marjorie Beldon of Santa Barbara, never understood how any girl could have been interested in a nobody like Scott Fitzgerald.[10]

After divorcing her first husband in 1936, Ginevra married the heir to the Carson, Pirie, Scott department store in Chicago. In 1937, just before his apprehensive meeting with Ginevra, who was then between marriages and whom he had not seen for twenty years, Fitzgerald told his daughter, with a mixture of nostalgia and regret: "She was the first girl I ever loved and I have faithfully avoided seeing her up to this moment to keep that illusion perfect, because she ended up by throwing me over with the most supreme boredom and indifference." Though heartbroken at the time, Fitzgerald answered Yeats' crucial question—"Does the imagination dwell the most / Upon a woman lost or a woman won?"[11]—by using his lost love as imaginative inspiration. He re-created Ginevra as Isabelle in *This Side of Paradise* (1920), as Judy Jones in "Winter Dreams" (1922), as Daisy Buchanan in *The Great Gatsby* (1925) and as Josephine in the Basil and Josephine stories (1930–31).

In his first novel Fitzgerald revealed that Ginevra was less a reality than an imaginative construct and gave his own reasons for the end of the affair. There was "nothing at all to her except what I read into her. . . . I convinced her that she was smarter than I was—then she threw me over. [Truly] said I was critical and impractical." But her rejection inspired him much more than if she had surrendered herself to him. As he wrote in "Basil and Cleopatra" (1929) of the character based on the intensely idealized and voraciously virginal Ginevra: "Radiant and glowing, more mysteriously desirable than ever, wearing her very sins like stars, she came down to him in her plain white uniform dress, and his heart turned out at the kindness of her eyes." Acknowledging her colossal vanity and egoism, Ginevra later confessed: "I read with shame the very true portrait of myself in my youth in the Josephine stories."

Fitzgerald's greatest tribute to the elusive, unattainable Ginevra appeared in *The Great Gatsby*, in which he portrayed her as Daisy Fay Buchanan. He punned on Ginevra's name ("High in a white palace [lived] the *king's* daughter, the golden girl") and throughout the novel described her as an almost disembodied voice which, Gatsby realizes at the end, was "full of money." "Her face," Fitzgerald wrote, "was sad and lovely with bright things in it, bright eyes and a bright passionate mouth, but there was an excitement in her voice that men who had cared for her found difficult to forget."[12] Gatsby's ability, like Fitzgerald's, "to keep that illusion perfect" sustains his self-deceptive and ultimately self-destructive quest, with the help of his own fabulous money, to win Daisy back from her husband.

IV

Fitzgerald's emotional upheavals with Ginevra, his devotion to the Triangle Club, his social striving at Cottage Club, his disappointment with the English department and his complete lack of interest in other subjects led to academic disaster in the middle of his junior year. He once remarked that "Princeton is still the hardest institution to get in to and stay in (and leave!) in America." But he got into it with only mediocre qualifications and left it all too easily.

While at Princeton Fitzgerald maintained the careless indifference to academic life that had characterized his years at Newman and would continue during his training in the army. He did not even attempt the minimum work required to pass many of his courses and took the maximum of forty-nine absences allowed during his freshman year. He failed three courses in both his freshman and sophomore years, failed his makeup exams in Latin and chemistry at the beginning of his junior year, which again made him ineligible for Triangle, and barely managed to survive without expulsion. He never even learned how to spell and, despite his training in Latin and French, was hopeless at foreign languages.

In November 1915 Fitzgerald entered the infirmary with a touch of malaria, then endemic in the marshlands around Princeton. Though his illness (which he preferred to call tuberculosis) was real, it also provided an excellent excuse to leave college honorably as an invalid instead of failing out after his midyear exams. "After the curriculum had tied me up," he defensively explained to the president of Princeton in 1920, "taken away the honors I'd wanted, bent my nose over a chemistry book and said, 'No fun, no activities, no offices, no Triangle trips— no, not even a diploma if you can't do chemistry'—after that I retired." He was extremely sensitive about his failure and persuaded the dean to give him a letter stating that he had voluntarily withdrawn "because of ill health and that he was fully at liberty, at that time, to go on with his class, if his health had permitted." At the same time the exasperated dean rubbed salt in the wound by including a caustic note to Fitzgerald: "This is for your sensitive feelings. I hope you will find it soothing."[13]

After idling away the spring of 1916 in St. Paul, he returned to Princeton to repeat his junior year. But his spirit was crushed. He felt it was stupid to spend four hours a day in his tutor's stuffy room enduring the infinite boredom of conic sections. He had been deprived of the recognition he craved and had lost all chance of winning honors during his final years. "After a few months of rest I went back to college," he explained in *The Crack-Up*. "But I had lost certain offices, the chief one was the presidency of the Triangle Club, a musical comedy idea, and also I dropped back a class. To me college would never be the same. There were to be no badges of pride, no medals, after all." If he could not achieve great success at Princeton, Fitzgerald did not see the point of struggling through his courses.

He confessed that when his morale was at its lowest point he had even sought solace from a prostitute. "It seemed on one March afternoon [in 1917] that I had lost every single thing I wanted—and that night was the first time that I hunted down the spectre of womanhood that, for a little while, makes everything else seem unimportant." But this kind of behavior was out of character. On one occasion, when Bishop and another Princeton friend, Alexander McKaig, had gone off to pick up two girls, Scott priggishly told Edmund Wilson: "That's one thing that Fitzgerald's never done."[14]

In 1916 Wilson and Bishop, his fellow highbrow, published a cruel satiric poem that put the popular but cheeky Fitzgerald in his proper place. They contrasted his shallowness to their learning, and deflated his flashy cleverness, superficial reading, derivative cynicism and unworthy ambition by having Fitzgerald exclaim:

> I was always clever enough
> To make the clever upperclassmen notice me;
> I could make one poem by Browning,
> One play by Shaw,
> And part of a novel by Meredith
> Go further than most people
> Could do with the reading of years;
> And I could always be cynically amusing at the expense
> Of those who were cleverer than I
> And from whom I borrowed freely,
> But whose cleverness
> Was not the kind that is effective
> In the February of sophomore year. . . .
> No doubt by senior year
> I would have been on every committee in college,
> But I made one slip:
> I flunked out in the middle of junior year.

In his *Ledger* Fitzgerald honestly characterized 1916 as "a year of terrible disappointments & the end of all college dreams. Everything bad in it was my own fault." But he never completely accepted his share of the blame. In 1937, when Bishop truthfully stated that Fitzgerald had failed out of Princeton and used illness as an excuse for his departure, Fitzgerald became furious and melodramatically claimed that he had been carried out on a stretcher.

Glenway Wescott once observed that "Fitzgerald must have been the worst educated man in the world."[15] It was ironic, Fitzgerald later told his daughter, that he had failed "Buzzer" Hall's course in modern European history, but now owned more than three hundred books on the subject. Aware of his own intellectual limitations, he struggled to improve his mind until the very end of his life.

Fitzgerald dedicated the summer of 1917 to drinking gin and reading Schopenhauer, Bergson and William James. But the gin had a more powerful effect than the philosophy, and he returned to Princeton to await his commission in the army rather than to get his degree. The most famous alumnus of the college never graduated. Though bitter about his failures, he always remained intensely idealistic about and deeply devoted to Princeton.

Chapter Three

THE ARMY AND ZELDA, 1917–1919

I

Fitzgerald, who was extremely self-absorbed, had no serious interest in or understanding of the greatest historical event of his lifetime: World War I. "Beyond a sporting interest in the German dash for Paris," he wrote with studied indifference in *This Side of Paradise*, "the whole affair failed either to thrill or interest him. . . . He hoped it would be long and bloody." When the war bogged down in the trenches after the German invasion of France, he "felt like an irate ticket holder at a prizefight where the principals refused to mix it up." Fitzgerald joined the army for the same reasons that he went to Princeton. It was the fashionable thing to do. He imagined himself as a war hero as he had once pictured himself as a football star and wanted to prove his courage in combat. The army was also a convenient way, as malaria had been in 1916, to escape his recurrent failures in college.

Writing to his cousin Cecilia Taylor and to his mother (who had wanted him to become an army officer) after America had entered the war in April 1917, Fitzgerald emphatically rejected the patriotic motives that had inspired thousands of young men and had been immortalized in Rupert Brooke's "The Soldier": "If I should die, think only this of me: / That there's some corner of a foreign field / That is forever England." Instead, when explaining his voluntary enlistment to these good ladies, he alluded to Ireland's neutrality and stressed his own individuality and deliberate detachment: "Updike of Oxford or Harvard says 'I die for England' or 'I die for America'—not me. I'm too Irish for that—I may get killed for America—but I'm going to die for myself. . . . About the army, please let's not have either tragedy or Heroics because they are equally distasteful to me. I went into this perfectly cold-bloodedly and don't sympathize with the 'Give my son to country' . . . stuff because *I just went* and purely for *social reasons.*"

In July 1917, after his brief bout with Schopenhauer and Bergson, Fitzgerald went to Fort Snelling, near St. Paul, and took the exams required for an appointment as second lieutenant in the regular army. He could not become an officer until he reached the age of twenty-one in September. When he received his commission in the infantry on October 26, he immediately ordered his smart uniforms at Brooks Brothers—just as he had sent for his football equipment as soon as he was admitted to Princeton.

He was sent for three months of training, from November 1917 to February 1918, to Fort Leavenworth, Kansas, on the Missouri River northwest of Kansas City. The captain in charge of training provisional lieutenants in exercises, calisthenics and bayonet drills was Dwight Eisenhower. One of his trainees wrote home enthusiastically about the young captain: "He has given us wonderful bayonet drills. He gets the fellows' imaginations worked up and hollers and yells and makes us shout and stomp until we go tearing into the air as if we meant business."[1]

Fitzgerald, however, was not so keen. He did as badly as an army officer as he had as a college student. Just as classes seemed to interfere with his theatrical career at Princeton, so drills and marches became an irritating interruption of the novel he wanted to write. Though he intended to lead an infantry platoon into battle, he never took his responsibility seriously, never realized that it was vitally important to acquire basic military skills. Like T. E. Lawrence, who would translate Homer's *Odyssey*, with a pad on his knees, in the RAF barracks in India in 1930, Fitzgerald, concealing his pad behind *Small Problems for Infantry*, continued to compose while in the army and "wrote paragraph after paragraph on a somewhat edited history of me and my imagination. The outline of twenty-two chapters, four of them in verse, was made, two chapters were completed; and then I was detected and the game was up. I could write no more during [evening] study period." Undeterred by this interruption, he continued to compose his book amidst noise and distractions: "Every Saturday at one o'clock when the week's work was over, I hurried to the Officers' Club, and there, in a corner of a room full of smoke, conversation and rattling newspapers, I wrote a one hundred and twenty thousand word novel on the consecutive weekends of three months."[2]

Fitzgerald had known Charles Scribner at Princeton; and Christian Gauss suggested that Scott send "The Romantic Egoist" to the venerable firm that published his own works as well as those of such eminent authors as Meredith, James, Stevenson, Barrie, Wharton and Galsworthy. Shane Leslie, another Scribner's author, wrote an encouraging letter to accompany the manuscript. He noted its weaknesses but felt it was worth publishing, and compared Fitzgerald to the handsome and romantic Rupert Brooke, who had died of a fever on a Greek island while on active service in 1915. Fitzgerald used Brooke's poem "Tiare Tahiti" for the title, epigraph and theme (age has nothing to tell the young in this world) of "The Romantic Egoist," which was published as *This Side of Paradise.*

"In spite of its disguises," Leslie wrote, "it has given me a vivid picture of the American generation that is hastening to war. I marvel at its crudity and its cleverness. . . . About a third of the book could be omitted without losing the impression that it is written by an American Rupert Brooke." Since the mortality rate of infantry lieutenants was extremely high, Leslie thought that Fitzgerald, like Brooke, would die in the war. He urged Scribner's to accept the book in order to make Fitzgerald happy during the last few months of his life.

On August 19, 1918—about five months after submitting the novel—Fitzgerald received a constructive response from a young editor at Scribner's, Maxwell Perkins. Perkins saw considerable merit in the book, but felt its innovations were outweighed by its glaring defects: "We have been reading 'The Romantic Egoist' with a very unusual degree of interest;—in fact no ms. novel has come to us for a long time that seemed to display so much originality, and it is therefore hard for us to conclude that we cannot offer to publish it as it stands at present. . . . It seems to us in short that the story does not culminate in anything as it must to justify the reader's interest as he follows it; and that it might be made to do so quite consistently with the characters and with its earlier stages."[3] Perkins asked Fitzgerald to revise the book, changing the narrator from the first to the third person, and then submit it for reconsideration.

Fitzgerald, meanwhile, had become distracted by his military duties and by his frequent shifts around the country prior to embarkation for Europe. In March 1918 he joined the 45th Infantry Regiment in Camp Zachary Taylor, near Louisville, Kentucky—where Jay Gatsby would meet Daisy Fay in Fitzgerald's novel. In April he was sent to Camp Gordon in Augusta, Georgia; in June his unit combined with another regiment and became part of the Ninth Division at Camp Sheridan, near Montgomery, Alabama.

Despite Fitzgerald's three years in the sophisticated male milieu of Princeton, most of his military colleagues considered him weak, spoiled and immature. Devereux Josephs, an older officer and graduate of Harvard, criticized him for concentrating on writing instead of on training. He also felt that Fitzgerald, though incompetent and rebellious in the army, wanted to be admired: "He was eager to be liked by his companions and almost vain in seeking praise. At the same time he was unwilling to conform to the various patterns of dullness and majority opinion which would insure popularity." Major Dana Palmer, an army friend, was more tolerant of his faults, which were balanced by his charm, and anticipated the opinion of many men who met Fitzgerald later on: "Scott abused the kindness and friendship of nearly everyone, but at that time, one could not help liking him very much."

Alonzo Myers, who served with Fitzgerald for most of his military career, concluded that "as an Army officer, Fitzgerald was unusually dispensable." Myers felt he was a ludicrous figure: immature, irresponsible and unfit for command. Fitzgerald was therefore treated by his military companions in much the same way as he had been treated at Newman School: "Nobody took Fitzgerald seriously. His fellow officers generally conceded that he lacked sound judgment. Much of the time he even appeared to lack any independent judgment at all. The result was that we tended to take advantage of him and to perpetrate pranks on him that sometimes could have had quite serious consequences."[4] On one occasion the officers encouraged Fitzgerald to contravene military regulations and force a conscientious objector to pick up a rifle and drill. On another, according to Myers, they persuaded their naive comrade to sleep through reveille instead of turning out for inspection by the commanding general. When Fitzgerald did report for parade he fell off his horse.

After his superiors had reluctantly entrusted him with a command, Fitzgerald got involved in dangerous and absurd misadventures. When directing a mortar company, he mistakenly ordered his men to fire on another unit. And his soldiers, nearly blown up when a shell jammed in a Stokes mortar, were saved at the last moment when Dana Palmer bravely tipped the barrel and spilled out the shell.

Responsible as a supply officer for unloading equipment on the docks of Hoboken, New Jersey, when his unit was on its way to France, Fitzgerald left the train to visit Princeton and allowed thousands of dollars of matériel to be stolen. He falsely claimed to have commandeered a special locomotive to take him to Washington with an urgent message for President Woodrow Wilson. While stationed at Camp Mills on Long Island, Fitzgerald went into New York for a party, borrowed a friend's room at the Hotel Astor and was caught there by the house detective—naked and in bed with a girl. He tried to bribe the detective with a dollar bill folded to look like a hundred, but was caught again and saved from jail only by being put under military arrest in his army camp.

His one redeeming act occurred when a ferry used to get troops across the Tallapoosa River near Montgomery was swamped during maneuvers. Fitzgerald helped save a number of men who had fallen into the water. He described this incident in his story "I Didn't Get Over" (1936)—whose title alludes both to crossing the river and crossing the ocean to fight in Europe—and gives the guilty hero, Hibbing, a name that recalls the president of Princeton in Fitzgerald's time, John Grier Hibben.

Despite his manifest incompetence, Fitzgerald's good looks, well-cut uniform, Princeton charm and Irish-Catholic background (for once, an advantage) attracted the attention of Brigadier General James Augustine Ryan, who in December 1918 appointed him aide-de-camp. Born in Danbury, Connecticut, in 1867, Ryan had graduated from West Point, become a cavalry officer and been put in charge of relations with the civil authorities. He apparently thought Fitzgerald would be useful—or at least harmlessly decorative—in this quasi-diplomatic role.

Fitzgerald's regiment was about to leave for France when the Armistice ended the war on November 11, 1918. He never even got close to making the fatal sacrifice of the twenty-one Princeton boys (five percent of his class) who were killed in the war. He wanted to prove his courage, gain glory and win the acceptance of his comrades, and always considered his lack of combat experience one of the deepest disappointments in his life. He equated athletic with military failure, called himself "the army's worst aide-de-camp," and in *The Crack-Up* said the two greatest regrets of his youth were "not being big enough (or good enough) to play football in college, and not getting overseas during the war." He later suggested that the army was merely a social extension of Princeton and declared: "I can't tell you how I wanted to get over. I wanted to belong to what every other bastard belonged to: the greatest club in history"[5]—a sort of Cottage Club of the trenches. His ludicrous career in the army explains why Hemingway believed that if Scott *had* gone to war he would have been shot for cowardice.

II

While his military life alternated between escapades and disasters, Fitzgerald turned for achievement and recognition to secret diplomacy, love affairs and literature. He had kept in close touch with his kindly benefactor Father Fay and while in the army had corresponded with this "brilliant enveloping personality." Since Stephan Parrott, Fay's other favorite at Newman, seemed ruined by having too much money and had failed to live up to Fay's expectations, the priest—who was the first to perceive Scott's unusual talents—pinned all his hopes on Fitzgerald.

The letters of this physically repulsive but personally enchanting priest express his sublimated homoeroticism and strongly suggest that he was in love with his handsome protégé. Fay drew him into his ambience by mentioning his own connections with great figures in the world of religion and politics, by equating Fitzgerald with himself and by filling his seductive correspondence with outrageous flattery: "We are many other things—we're extraordinary, we're clever, we could be said

I suppose to be brilliant. We can attract people, we can make atmosphere, we can almost always have our own way. . . . I never deny that I need you boys—your companionship and all that—but I am also coming to the conclusion that you both need a little touch of me, and I do hope if you get leave in August you will fly to my paternal arms." Fitzgerald, always eager for admiration, was not fully aware of the intensity of Fay's feelings.

In August 1917, while Fitzgerald was waiting to come of age and obtain his commission, Fay included him in a tremendously exciting scheme. In March 1917 the first revolution had broken out in Russia; and in July the democratic socialist Alexander Kerensky had become prime minister and vigorously pursued the war against Germany. Fay's ambitious plan was to journey via Japan to Russia (where he had traveled in 1915 on an ecclesiastical visit), ostensibly as head of a Red Cross mission but actually, during these turbulent times, to lead the Russian masses back to the Catholic church. Fitzgerald, in the guise of a Red Cross lieutenant, would be Fay's traveling companion and confidential assistant.

On August 22 Fay wrote Fitzgerald, with dramatic exaggeration: "The conversion of Russia has already begun. Several millions of the Russians have already come over to the Catholic Church from the schism in the last month. Whether you look at it from the spiritual or the temporal point of view it is an immense opportunity and will be a help to you all the rest of your life." Fay wisely mentioned the kind of uniform Fitzgerald would wear as well as the expenses that would be paid by the church, and said they would have to work hard on his French—though the idea of Fitzgerald conducting diplomatic negotiations in a foreign tongue seems absurd.

Most importantly, Fay heightened the significance of their expedition by insisting on cloak-and-dagger secrecy: "Do be discreet about what you say to anybody. If anybody asks you, say you are going as secretary to a Red Cross Commission. Do not say anything more than that, and if you show this letter to anybody, show it only in the strictest confidence."[6] But as Fitzgerald was applying for his Japanese and Russian visas, the Bolshevik coup d'état on November 7 (in the Western calendar) extinguished all future hope of a Catholic church in godless Russia.

When the Russian mission failed, Fay immediately came up with another plan, which unfortunately did not include Fitzgerald. Fay joined the Red Cross and was sent to Rome by Cardinal Gibbons to acquaint the pope with the attitude of American Catholics toward the war and to stress their loyal determination to help the Allies (which included Italy) until the very end. In his patriotic essay, "The Genesis of the Super-German," published in the *Dublin Review* in April 1918, Fay also urged the Irish people, for religious and philosophical reasons, to support the Allied cause.

While in Italy Fay also became involved in negotiations to remove a clause from a secret treaty that had excluded the Holy See from participation in the peace conference after the war. Fay's diplomatic visit to Rome was considered valuable and in 1918 he was created a monsignor by Pope Benedict XV. Delighted as a child and camping it up with a vivid simile that Fitzgerald adopted in his first novel, Fay immediately announced: "the Holy Father has made me a Prelate, so that I am the Right Reverend Monsignor now, and my clothes are too gorgeous for words. I look like a Turner sunset when I am in full regalia."

Fay also used this occasion to emphasize the spiritual quality that bound him to Stephan Parrott and to Fitzgerald. Though Fitzgerald's religious beliefs were fading fast (he recorded that 1917 was his last year as a Catholic), Fay exclaimed: "I discovered that if I did not have a good hold on the mystical side of religion the romance [of my success] would have died down considerably. Sometimes I think that in all three of us, the secret of our success is the mystical element in us. Something flows into us that enlarges our personalities."

On August 17, two days before Scribner's rejected "The Romantic Egoist," Fay wrote another conspiratorial letter that ecstatically praised the unpublished work. Shane Leslie and Max Perkins had offered constructive criticism that would enable Fitzgerald to revise his book and get it published; Fay merely flattered his disciple in order to win his gratitude: "I have ten thousand things to say that I cannot write. There are intimacies that cannot be put upon paper. . . . Really the whole thing is most startling; I am keen beyond words to read the rest of that book. I may be frightfully prejudiced but I have never read anything more interesting than that book. . . . The more I see of it the more amazingly good I think it is."[7]

Fay died suddenly of influenza on January 10, 1919 (just before Fitzgerald was demobilized), on the eve of his departure for another

diplomatic mission to London. He would have been even more fascinated by *This Side of Paradise* had he known that Fitzgerald's description of Monsignor Darcy's funeral would be taken nearly verbatim from
Shane Leslie's letter describing the funeral of Monsignor Fay. Shattered by the loss of his friend, Fitzgerald responded to Leslie's account
of the ceremony with heartfelt insincerity: "I can't tell you how I feel
about Monsignor Fay's death.—He was the best friend I had in the
world and last night he seemed so close and so *good* that I was almost
glad—because I think he wanted to die. . . . Your letter seemed to start
a new flow of sorrows in me. I've never wanted so much to die in my
life. Father Fay always thought that if one of us died the other would,
and now how I've hoped so. . . . This has made me nearly sure that I
will become a priest. I feel as if in a way his mantle had descended
upon me."[8] But the momentarily pious Fitzgerald had no more intention of becoming a priest than he did of becoming a professional soldier. Fay's death meant that he would now have to find his own way to
wealth and fame. In any case, he had already come under the powerful
secular influence of Zelda Sayre.

III

Except for a brief time at Camp Mills on Long Island, Fitzgerald was
stationed from June 1918 until February 1919 in Montgomery,
Alabama. In that hot, static little town of forty thousand souls, nothing
much had happened since the Civil War. In "The Ice Palace" (1920)
Fitzgerald described Montgomery as a "languid paradise of dreamy
skies and firefly evenings and noisy, niggery street fairs—and especially
of gracious, soft-voiced girls, who [unlike Ginevra King] were brought
up on memories instead of money."

At a country club dance on one of those "firefly evenings" in July
1918 Fitzgerald met a gracious, soft-voiced girl named Zelda Sayre.
She let her long hair hang down loose and wore a frilly dress that made
her look younger than eighteen. She came from a prominent though
not wealthy family and had just graduated from Sidney Lanier High
School.

The solid respectability of the Sayres disguised the dangerous currents swirling beneath the calm surface of their lives. Zelda's father, Anthony Sayre, son of the editor of the *Montgomery Post,* was born in Tuskegee, Alabama, in 1858, graduated from Roanoke College in Virginia and was admitted to the bar in 1881. He married three years later, and was elected and reelected associate justice of the Supreme Court of Alabama from 1909 until 1931. A man of fanatically regular habits, Judge Sayre always took the streetcar to and from work at exactly the same time every day and always retired for the night at exactly eight o'clock. Cold, humorless and hypercritical, the judge became increasingly unsociable and remote from his family. Zelda considered him inhumanly perfect and desperately tried to penetrate his stony reserve. The first time Fitzgerald was invited to dinner at the Sayres' house at 6 Pleasant Avenue, Zelda goaded her father into such a rage that he picked up a carving knife and, while the rest of the family ignored them, chased her around the dining room table. Fitzgerald, nervous and infatuated, failed to perceive that this was a familiar occurrence, that the judge was not as self-controlled as he appeared to be and that all was not well in the Sayre family.

Zelda's mother, Minnie Machen, the daughter of a Kentucky senator, was born in 1860 and had in her youth cherished hopes of an operatic career. The Sayres had three older daughters—Marjorie, Rosalind and Clothilde—whose ages ranged from nine to eighteen when Zelda was born, and a son, Anthony, who was then six. Minnie nursed Zelda, her youngest and favorite child, till the age of four.

Minnie's mother and sister had both committed suicide. Marjorie had had a mental breakdown and suffered from nervous illness throughout her life. Young Anthony became notorious for his dissolute behavior and left Auburn University without earning his degree. In 1933, after recurrent nightmares about killing his mother, he would also commit suicide by leaping from the window of his hospital room in Mobile. No one ever told Fitzgerald, when he was courting Zelda, about the terrifying history of insanity and suicide in her family.

Four years younger than Scott, Zelda was born on July 24, 1900, and named for the romantic gypsy heroine in Robert Edward Francillon's *Zelda's Fortune* (1874). In this popular novel, Zelda—who "could have been placed in no imaginable situation without drawing upon herself a hundred stares"—foresees that she will find a fortune of gold treasure and fall in love with the handsome Dr. Vaughan. Zelda Sayre had no close friends in girlhood or in later life, but was always close to her mother. Protected by the respectability and prestige of her family, Zelda was known for her striking beauty, her unconventional behavior and her sexual promiscuity. As she wrote in the opening sentence of her novel *Save Me the Waltz* (1932): "'Those girls,' people said, 'think they can do anything and get away with it.' That was because of the sense of security they felt in their father. He was a living fortress."[9]

Zelda had a perfect peaches-and-cream complexion and honey-golden hair. In *This Side of Paradise* Fitzgerald portrayed her as Rosalind Connage and gave a delightful account of her physical attributes: "There was the eternally kissable mouth, small, slightly sensual, and utterly disturbing. There were gray eyes and an unimpeachable skin with two spots of vanishing color. She was slender and athletic, without underdevelopment, and it was a delight to watch her move about a room. . . . Her vivid, instant personality escaped that conscious, theatrical quality that Amory had found in Isabelle [Ginevra]."

Fitzgerald was also keenly aware of the flaws in Zelda's character—her rudeness, selfishness and lack of restraint—but found them quite provocative and exciting: "She treats men terribly. She abuses them and cuts them and breaks dates with them and yawns in their faces—and they [like Scott himself] come back for more. . . . [She] smokes sometimes, drinks [alcoholic] punch, frequently kissed. . . . She is prone to make every one around her pretty miserable when she doesn't get [her way. . . . She believed] the only excuse for women was the necessity for a disturbing element among men." She was, to Scott's delight, an inspiring example of the postwar modern girl.

Zelda's notorious reputation in Montgomery began in childhood. When she was only ten she called the fire department (a recurrent ploy), climbed onto the roof and waited to be rescued. Unlike her self-effacing father, she scorned convention, liked to attract attention to herself and exploited the dramatic possibilities of the scene. She always gave a good public performance. Virginia Foster Durr, who went to dances with Zelda and later became a leader in the civil rights movement, confirmed Zelda's powerful impact on her contemporaries: "Zelda always did things to shock people. . . . She used to come up to the dances in Birmingham and she was just gorgeous. She had a glow around her. When she came into a ballroom, all the other girls would want to go home because they knew the boys were going to be concentrating on Zelda. The boys would line up the whole length of the ball-room to dance with her for one minute. She was pre-eminent and we recognized it."

Mrs. Durr later elaborated her view of Zelda's character and explained how her glorious youth left her especially vulnerable:

Zelda was like a vision of beauty dancing by. She was funny, amusing, the most popular girl; envied by all others, worshipped and adored, besieged by all the boys. She *did* try to shock. At a dance she pinned mistletoe on the back of her skirt, as if to challenge the young men to kiss her bottom.

In the South women were not supposed to *do* anything. It was sufficient to be beautiful and charming. Zelda, a spoiled baby just out of high school, never even learned to read or sew. She was always treated like a visiting film star: radiant, glowing, desired by all. Since she had absolutely nothing to do and no personal resources to draw on, she later bothered Scott when he was trying to write. She had no ability to suffer adversity, and was unprepared for it when it came.

Fitzgerald would have agreed with this analysis. He later told his daughter that Zelda had burnt herself out by refusing to accept ordinary norms of behavior: "She had no education—not from lack of opportunity because she could have learned with me—but from some inner stubbornness. She was a great original in her way, with perhaps a more intense flame at its highest than I ever had, but she tried and is still trying to solve all ethical and moral problems on her own."[10]

Despite the contrast in their backgrounds—a lower-middle-class Irish Catholic from the Upper Midwest, who had lived in five different towns and had been to college, and an upper-middle-class Anglo-Protestant from the Deep South, who had spent her entire life in Montgomery and had just completed a patchy high school education—Scott and Zelda had a great deal in common. They were both spoiled children of older parents. They had the same blond hair, fair skin, straight nose and thin lips, and looked enough alike to be brother and sister. They even wore matching jackets and knickerbockers on their drive from Connecticut to Montgomery in the summer of 1920. Both liked to exchange sexual roles. Scott dressed up as a show girl for the Triangle Club. Zelda put on men's clothing and went to the movies with a group of boys. Scott—who had a weak father, strong mother, younger sister and eventually a wife, daughter and several mistresses—was always surrounded by women. He believed: "I am half feminine—that is, my mind is." Zelda told a friend: "I have always been inclined toward masculinity."[11] Both spent extravagantly, drank heavily, behaved irresponsibly and did not care what people thought of them.

Zelda's volatile mixture of beauty and daring was fatally attractive to men. Officers gathered on her sagging veranda, which resembled an army recruiting station, and gladly surrendered their military insignia to express their esteem. Flyers from Camp Sheridan performed aerial stunts over her house and two planes crashed during these daring exhibitions. Admirers at Auburn University, where she was tremendously popular, founded a fraternity based on her initials, Zeta Sigma. To be admitted, potential members had to pledge their devotion to Zelda and offer proof that they had had at least one date with her in Montgomery. Fitzgerald was excited—and sometimes tormented—by other men's love for Zelda, which enhanced her value in his eyes. And having lost Ginevra, he was determined to win Zelda from her Southern halfbacks and golfing beaux.

During their parabolic courtship Zelda used her power over men to make Scott unbearably jealous. She once grabbed a boy and started kissing him just as Fitzgerald approached; and later "regretted having flirted so much with other men and never telling Scott how far she'd gone with them, letting him guess the worst and neither denying nor correcting his suspicions." "But selfishness in women had an irresistible appeal to Fitzgerald, and their fights (like those of Frieda and D. H. Lawrence) were a form of sexual foreplay that made their reconciliations and lovemaking even sweeter. "I love your tenderness—when I've hurt you," Zelda confessed. "That's one of the reasons I could never be sorry for our quarrels."[12] The intensely romantic Fitzgerald had a Proustian impulse to construct an ideal image of the woman he loved— first Ginevra, then Zelda—to compensate for any defects in reality.

Fitzgerald often pondered the differences between the woman lost and the woman won. Ginevra's family was wealthy and socially prominent, Zelda's was more intellectual and artistic. Ginevra was cool and distant, Zelda spontaneous and sensual; Ginevra poised and self-assured, Zelda vivacious and impulsive. Though Ginevra was more worldly and sophisticated, Zelda was more beautiful and exciting. Zelda was much closer to Scott in temperament and, though pursued by legions of young men, soon fell in love with *him*. Ginevra was sexually unattainable, Zelda willing to sleep with him. He had nothing to give Ginevra that she did not already have, but could offer Zelda something she really wanted: an escape from constrictive provincial life into the glamorous world of New York.

IV

The "unusually dispensable" Fitzgerald, one of the first officers to be discharged from his unit in February 1919, returned that month to New York. While still an undergraduate in 1916, he had looked up Edmund Wilson, who shared an apartment on West Eighth Street in Greenwich Village, worked for the *Evening Sun* and seemed to embody the ideal literary life. Fitzgerald discovered that "the shy little scholar of Holder Court" in Princeton had been transformed into a promising symbol of cosmopolitan sophistication. "That night, in Bunny's apartment," Fitzgerald recalled, "life was mellow and safe, a finer distillation of all that I had come to love at Princeton . . . and I began wondering about the rent of such apartments."[13]

Fitzgerald now assumed he could easily adopt Wilson's attractive way of life and earn enough money to marry Zelda. But he lacked his friend's discipline and found it difficult to break into commercial or literary life in New York. Instead of a congenial flat in the Village, shortage of money forced him into a remote and depressing room at 200 Claremont Avenue, near Columbia University in uptown Manhattan. After a fruitless search for work on a newspaper, he took an unappealing job with the Barron Collier advertising agency at thirty-five dollars a week. For several stupefying months he wrote ads for signs on streetcars. His best slogan, composed for a steam laundry in Iowa, was "We keep you clean in Muscatine."

When not working Fitzgerald got drunk with his college friends and self-consciously indulged in the kind of sophomoric pranks that would become tediously familiar to friends throughout his life. He threatened to jump out of the window of the Yale Club and was disappointed when nobody tried to stop him. He celebrated May Day in the

Childs' restaurant on Fifty-Ninth Street by carefully mixing hash, eggs and ketchup in a friend's hat.

His attempts to write were as depressing as his work and his drinking bouts. He wrote film scenarios, sketches, jokes and nineteen stories, and decorated his room with a frieze of 122 rejection slips. Near the end of June Wilson helped him get started by introducing him to George Jean Nathan, who paid thirty dollars for a trivial story, "Babes in the Woods" (which he had written at Princeton for the *Nassau Lit.*), and published it in the sophisticated *Smart Set*.

In the spring of 1919, while struggling to make his way in New York, Fitzgerald made three trips to Montgomery. In April he became engaged to Zelda and slept with her for the first time. One of her provocative and reassuring letters, written that spring, alludes to their sexual intimacy: "Sweetheart, I love you most of all the earth—and I want to be married soon—soon—Lover—Don't say I'm not enthusiastic—You ought to know."

Though Fitzgerald was undoubtedly thrilled that Zelda was willing to sleep with him, he was also shocked by her behavior. At Princeton he had discovered that half his classmates admitted they had never even kissed a girl. Girls of his class were not expected to grant sexual favors or express enthusiasm for sexual pleasure. Zelda had in fact lost her virginity at fifteen and openly flaunted her defiance of these conventions. He was also surprised and hurt to realize, despite her sexual responsiveness, that she would not marry him before he had achieved financial success.

His portrait of Rosalind in *This Side of Paradise* captures this impulsive yet calculating side of Zelda. It reveals that he was well aware of her desire to remain young and irresponsible forever, and have wealth to comfort and protect her. As his heroine ingenuously exclaims: "I'm just a little girl. I like sunshine and pretty things and cheerfulness—and I dread responsibility. I don't want to think about pots and kitchens and brooms. I want to worry whether my legs will get slick and brown when I swim in the summer."

Fitzgerald also resented her family's opposition to the marriage. They felt (with good reason) that she needed a strong, reliable husband who could control rather than encourage her wild behavior. In their view, he was an unstable Irish Catholic who had not graduated from college, had no career and drank too much. Zelda claimed that Scott was the sweetest person in the world when sober, to which Judge Sayre sternly replied: "He's never sober." In 1927, long after his marriage but still eager for acceptance, Fitzgerald would rather pathetically kneel beside the judge's sick bed and plead: "Tell me you believe in me." "Scott," the judge grudgingly conceded, "I think you will always pay your bills."[14] This prediction proved accurate. Though often in debt, Scott *did* pay his bills.

Fitzgerald tried to persuade Zelda to marry him immediately by threatening, pleading and overwhelming her with kisses. But in June, impatient with his failures, she broke off their engagement and ended their sexual relations. In his plan for the "Count of Darkness" stories, Fitzgerald noted that his heroine, "after yielding, holds Philippe at bay like Zelda and me in [early] Summer 1919."

Fitzgerald felt he had foolishly allowed himself to be dominated by mentally inferior "authorities," first at St. Paul's Academy, Newman and Princeton, then in his regiment and in advertising. Clearly unsuited to a regular office job, he loathed business as much as he had hated academic and army life. He was fearful of losing Zelda to a prosperous local rival and determined to win her by writing a successful novel. He would express his love by including her diaries and portraying her character. Haunted by his drab room and by the crowded subway, obsessed by his shabby clothes, his poverty and his hopeless love, he quit his job: "I was a failure—mediocre at advertising work and unable to get started as a writer. Hating the city, I got roaring, weeping drunk on my last penny and went home."[15]

V

While estranged from Zelda and working hard on his novel in the top-floor room of the family house at 599 Summit Avenue in St. Paul, Fitzgerald met a kindred spirit: the lively and witty Donald Ogden Stewart. The tall, balding, bespectacled Stewart was born in Columbus, Ohio, in 1894, the son of an improvident lawyer. After attending Exeter and Yale, he spent a few years working for the telephone company in St. Paul. He started his literary career as a popular writer of humorous and satiric fiction—*Parody Outline of History* (1921) and *Mr. and Mrs.*

Haddock Abroad (1925)—and then became a successful novelist, dramatist and screenwriter.

Though Fitzgerald and Stewart interested each other, especially at the beginning of their careers, and later traveled in the same social circles, they never became intimate companions. Stewart felt that Fitzgerald's "note-taking watchfulness . . . kept me from ever feeling that he was really a friend." Fitzgerald called him "an intellectual simpleton" and criticized his ingratiating manner: "He pleases you not by direct design but because his desire to please is so intense that it is disarming. He pleases you most perhaps when his very words are irritants."

In early September Fitzgerald completed the second version of his novel, sent the manuscript back to Perkins and—eager to work outdoors—took a job repairing train roofs for James J. Hill's Northern Pacific Railroad. Instructed to wear old clothes, Fitzgerald turned up in elegant white flannels, irritated the foreman by sitting down when he tried to hammer in nails and—despite his experience in dealing with ordinary soldiers—complained that he was unable to talk to the working men.

Fitzgerald lasted no longer as a rude mechanical than he did as a writer of slogans. On September 16, 1919, Perkins freed him from his job with an enthusiastic letter: "I am very glad, personally, to be able to write to you that we are all for publishing your book, *This Side of Paradise*. . . . I think you have improved it enormously. As the first manuscript did, it abounds in energy and life and it seems to me to be in much better proportion. . . . The book is so different that it is hard to prophesy how it will sell but we are all for taking a chance and supporting it with vigor."[16] Fitzgerald rushed up and down the streets of St. Paul, stopping friends and strangers on foot and in cars to announce his good fortune. He then returned to New York to await success.

VI

Fitzgerald's period of concentrated work, when he revised and improved his novel in the summer of 1919, transformed him from an unemployed amateur into a professional writer. During that time he discovered his subject, his voice and his style. When he returned to

New York, he began to turn out amusing, cleverly plotted and sometimes absurd tales about the innocent adventures of bright upper-class teenagers and young people. Instead of the massive series of rejections he had suffered in the spring, he now found that his stories were accepted as fast as he could produce them. Slight pieces like "The Debutante," "Porcelain and Pink," "Dalrymple Goes Wrong" and "Benediction" (one of his few overtly Catholic works) were gobbled up by the *Smart Set* in the fall of 1919. And *Scribner's Magazine* paid $150 each for more didactic pieces—"The Cut-Glass Bowl" and "The Four Fists"—from their firm's new author.

Fitzgerald also sold "Head and Shoulders"—in which a prodigy marries a chorus girl and they exchange roles: he becomes a trapeze artist and she a successful author—to the *Saturday Evening Post* for $400 and made his first appearance in a mass circulation magazine when it was published in February 1920. He energetically poured out five other stories between November 1919 and February 1920—including the more substantial "Ice Palace," which effectively portrays a Southern girl's horrified response to a frozen Northern city—and sold every one of them to the *Post*. Proud of his rapid composition, he boasted to Perkins that he had written and revised twelve thousand words of "The Camel's Back"—in which a suitor with a marriage license goes to a costume ball dressed as a camel and is accidentally married by a Negro waiter-minister to his irate and then pacified girl—in twenty-one straight hours of work.

VII

When Fitzgerald returned to New York he resumed his uneasy friendship with Edmund Wilson. Soon after they left college Fitzgerald had presumptuously declared: "I want to be one of the greatest writers who ever lived, don't you?" Looking back on this period twenty-five years later and assuming his familiar Johnsonian persona with the Boswellian Fitzgerald, Wilson contrasted (as he had done in his satiric undergraduate poem) his own high intellectual standards with those of his bumbling disciple, who would take a long time to mature: "I had not myself quite entertained this fantasy because I had been reading Plato and

Dante. Scott had been reading Booth Tarkington, Compton Mackenzie, H. G. Wells [all of whom influenced his early novels] and [the
intoxicating rhythms of] Swinburne; but when he later got to better
writers, his standards and his achievement went sharply up, and he
would always have pitted himself against the very best in his own line
that he knew." Wilson failed to acknowledge that Fitzgerald, despite his
naïveté, had actually achieved his fantasy by learning from his older
contemporaries instead of pitting himself (as Wilson had done) against
impossible standards.

In August 1919 Fitzgerald had sharply defined the difference in
their talents and future careers by presciently warning Wilson, who
would become an accomplished anthologist: "For God's sake, Bunny,
write a novel and don't waste your time editing collections [of war sto-
ries]. It'll get to be a habit."[17] Wilson longed to be an imaginative
writer, but his knowledge and appreciation of the literature of the past
inhibited his creative urge. He was making a living as a journalist and in
time would become the most influential literary critic of his day. But
now, like Fitzgerald, he aspired to be a novelist, and assumed that fiction was an altogether higher and more valuable kind of writing than
literary criticism.

In college Wilson had been the older, wiser and more sophisticated
student, and, with Bishop, a scornful critic who punctured Fitzgerald's
illusions. Now he became Fitzgerald's literary mentor, discussing the art
of the novel with him, urging him to pay more attention to form.
Fitzgerald eagerly sought his comments on the manuscript of *This Side
of Paradise*. On November 21, 1919, Wilson responded with his usual
mixture of friendly derision, backhanded compliments and faint praise.
He compared Fitzgerald's novel to the trivial current bestseller by the
preadolescent Daisy Ashford, spotted the influence of the hero of
Mackenzie's *Sinister Street*, mocked Fitzgerald's intellectual pretensions
and warned him about preferring popularity to serious art—a question
Fitzgerald had raised with Alfred Noyes: "I have just read your novel
with more delight than I can well tell you. It ought to be a classic in a
class with *The Young Visiters*. . . . Your hero is an unreal imitation of
Michael Fane, who was himself unreal. . . . As an intellectual [Amory] is
a fake of the first water and I read his views on art, politics, religion and
society with more riotous mirth than I should care to have you know."
At the same time he offered sound criticism, and warned him against

adopting the cheap effects of commercial stories instead of doing the serious work needed to achieve high art: "It would all be better if you would tighten up your artistic conscience and pay a little more attention to form. . . . I feel called upon to give you this advice because I believe you might become a very popular trashy novelist without much difficulty."[18]

In the years to come Wilson often read Fitzgerald's work before publication and also wrote reviews for public consumption. Wilson's private and public comments helped Fitzgerald define and develop his art. Fitzgerald constantly deferred to Wilson's literary judgment, appeared to surrender his intellectual conscience to him and retained him as mentor long after establishing himself as a serious novelist. (He later called Hemingway his "artistic conscience.") Wilson, however, clearly resented Fitzgerald's creative talent, and envied his enormous, apparently arbitrary financial success. In his view, Fitzgerald wasted his talent and sacrificed his integrity by publishing trashy stories in popular magazines.

In November, the month he received Wilson's letter, between the acceptance of the novel and his marriage to Zelda, Fitzgerald had a brief love affair with the English actress Rosalinde Fuller. Her picture had appeared in *Vanity Fair*, and she had also had an affair with her brother-in-law, the author Max Eastman. Fitzgerald may have wanted to retaliate for Zelda's promiscuous adventures or to have one final fling before committing himself to her. In her diary, Rosalinde provocatively described riding through the city—like Emma Bovary and Léon Dupuis—in a closed carriage that aroused their sexual appetites: "The clip-clop of the horse's hoofs made a background to our discovery of each other's bodies. Eager hands [were] feeling in warm secret places under the old rug, while the bouncing of the horse's bottom was our only contact with the outside world. 'You have Egyptian ears,' whispered Scott" (who could resist his "Egyptian ears"?) "'and the look of a naughty boy.'"[19]

The money earned from his copious flow of stories enabled Fitzgerald, who had exhausted himself and was afraid of developing tuberculosis, to leave the harsh New York winter for the gentler climate of New Orleans. He rented a room in a boarding house at 2900 Prytania Street, but disliked the city and remained for only a month. While living in New Orleans he visited Zelda twice, finally persuaded her to marry him and became engaged for the second time. She knew she had inspired his novel and told him: "It's so nice to know you really *can* do things—*anything*—and I love to feel that maybe I can help just a little."

In February 1920 Zelda mistakenly thought she was pregnant, and Fitzgerald sent her some pills to induce an abortion. But she refused to take them, emphasizing that she did not regret their lovemaking and wanted above all to preserve her integrity:

> I wanted to for your sake, because I know what a mess I'm making and how inconvenient it's all going to be—but I simply *can't* and *won't* take those awful pills—so I've thrown them away. I'd rather take carbolic acid. You see, as long as I feel that I had the right, I don't much mind what happens—and besides, I'd rather have a *whole family* than sacrifice my self-respect. They just seem to place everything on the wrong basis—and I'd feel like a damn whore if I took even one.

A few days later, Fitzgerald repeated the key phrase from Zelda's brave letter and, acknowledging her delicious faults to a friend's sister, explained why he wanted to marry her: "Any girl who gets stewed in public, who frankly enjoys and tells shocking stories, who smokes constantly and makes the remark that she has 'kissed thousands of men and intends to kiss thousands more,' cannot be considered beyond reproach. . . . [But] I fell in love with her courage, her sincerity and her flaming self-respect."[20] Zelda's courage to oppose conventional behavior, her sincere defiance of hypocrisy and the self-respect that made her want to have the baby impressed Fitzgerald tremendously. That same month, when he sold the movie rights of "Head and Shoulders" for the vast sum of $2,500, he expressed his generosity and love, and tried to assuage her wounded feelings, by spending the money on gifts for Zelda.

Just before their Catholic wedding Mrs. Sayre, who had always been fond of Fitzgerald, gave a lighthearted warning that deliberately obscured the darker side of Zelda's character: "It will take more than the Pope to make Zelda good: you will have to call on God Almighty direct. . . . She is not amiable and she is given to *yelping*" when she does not get her own way. In the late 1930s, during bitter recriminations about the failure of their marriage, Scott, with retrospective

insight, reminded Zelda that he had been deceived by Mrs. Sayre and
by Zelda herself. Despite his admiration of her defiant courage, they
had had serious sexual problems from the very beginning of their marriage:

> [Your mother] chose me—and she did—and you submitted at
> the moment of our marriage when your passion for me was at
> as low ebb as mine for you—because she thought romantically
> that her projection of herself in you could best be shown
> through me. I never wanted the Zelda I married. I didn't love
> you again till after you became pregnant [in 1921]. . . . You
> were the drunk—at *seventeen,* before I knew you—already
> notorious. . . . The assumption [was] that you were a great
> prize package—by your own admission many years after (and
> for which I have never reproached you) you had been seduced
> and provincially outcast. I sensed this the night we slept
> together first, for you're a poor bluffer.

He also told his daughter that he had soon regretted his foolish decision: "I decided to marry your mother after all, even though I knew she
was spoiled and meant no good to me. I was sorry immediately I had
married her."[21] Despite his misgivings, their wedding was scheduled to
take place a week after his novel came out. His book and his wife were
bound in a common destiny.

Chapter Four

THIS SIDE OF PARADISE AND
MARRIAGE, 1920–1922

I

This Side of Paradise was published on March 26, 1920, received considerable acclaim and made Fitzgerald instantly famous. It is (to use Orwell's term) a "good-bad book"—superficial and immature, but still lively and readable, and valuable both as autobiography and as social history. The novel's defiant tone had the same powerful impact on rebellious postwar youth as Salinger's *The Catcher in the Rye* did in 1951, and it became a bible and guidebook as the Twenties began to roar. Like Eliot's *Poems*, Owen's *Poems*, Huxley's *Limbo* and Lawrence's *Women in Love* (all of which appeared in 1920), Fitzgerald's novel captures the spirit of disillusionment that followed the Great War. The overt and somewhat naive theme echoes Woodrow Wilson's "war to end wars" and portrays the hero of the new generation "grown up to find all Gods dead, all wars fought, all faiths in man shaken."

Book One of the novel, "The Romantic Egoist," recounts the life of Amory Blaine from his wealthy and pampered childhood through prep school to Princeton. A weak "Interlude" alludes to but does not actually describe his wartime service. The book is loosely structured by Amory's three unhappy romantic attachments with Isabelle Borgé, Rosalind Connage and Eleanor Savage. Isabelle rejects Amory because he is too egoistic, analytical and critical. Rosalind, who feels that marrying him would ruin both their lives, jilts him for a rich and reliable rival. Eleanor, who comes from a mentally unstable family, discourages him by attempting suicide. After breaking with Eleanor, Amory finds himself in Atlantic City. In a scene based on Fitzgerald's wartime contretemps with the detective in the Hotel Astor, Amory gallantly takes the blame when hotel detectives discover Rosalind's brother in bed with a prostitute.

The title of Book Two of this *Bildungsroman*, "The Education of a Personage," echoes *The Education of Henry Adams* (1907). This phrase also alludes to the pedantic distinction made by Amory's mentor, Father Darcy. In his view, the inconsequential "personality" is merely a false sense of self while the significant "personage" is a man with intellectual purpose and a definite goal: "Personality is a physical matter almost entirely; it lowers the people it acts on—I've seen it vanish in a long sickness. But while a personality is active, it overrides 'the next thing.' Now a personage, on the other hand, gathers. He is never thought of apart from what he's done. He's a bar on which a thousand things have been hung—glittering things sometimes, as ours are, but he uses those things with a cold mentality back of them."

In the last chapter of the novel, in which "The Egotist Becomes a Personage," Amory is picked up on the road to Princeton by the wealthy father of a college friend who has been killed in the war. Having cornered his host in his own car, Amory gives him a long and unwelcome lecture on the virtues of socialism. In the final sentence, following the Socratic dictum, Amory proclaims: "I know myself . . . but that is all"—though there is no evidence in the novel to suggest that he has moved beyond egotism to self-awareness or done anything at all significant.

The novel, dedicated to the recently deceased Father Sigourney Fay (the model for Father Darcy), incorporated extracts from Fay's letters to Fitzgerald, Shane Leslie's description of Fay's funeral and Zelda's diary. After reading the striking scene in which the devil appears with horrible feet and warns Amory not to sleep with a girl he had picked up at a nightclub, Fay had observed: "What a tremendous role the actual and cold fear of Satan does play in our make-up." But it is more likely that this scene (which had horrified Scott's friend Stephan Parrott) was influenced by Ivan's chilling encounter with the devil in *The Brothers Karamazov* (1880) than by Fay's discussions with his young disciples about the nature of evil. As early as January 1918 Bishop, in a letter to Fitzgerald, cited examples from Dostoyevsky's *Crime and Punishment* to show that novels should be written in scenes "with successive climaxes." And Fitzgerald must have heard about the famous diabolic scene in *Karamazov* from Christian Gauss, who remarked that at Princeton, Fitzgerald reminded him of all the Karamazov brothers at once.

In a letter of August 1920 Fitzgerald called Leslie "my first literary sponsor, godfather to this book." He told Leslie that he had originally intended to dedicate the novel to him as well as to Fay, ingenuously explained that he had used Leslie's account of the funeral because "I didn't see it myself and had to describe it" and joyfully announced: "I married the Rosalind of the novel, the southern girl I was so attached to, after a grand reconciliation."[1]

In *This Side of Paradise* (as we have seen) Fitzgerald exploited the dramatic possibilities of Father Fay, Ginevra King, Zelda Sayre, Henry Strater and John Peale Bishop (whose fictional name, Thomas D'Invilliers, was probably suggested by that of the nineteenth-century French writer Villiers de l'Isle-Adam). He also put other real-life models into the book. Thornton Hancock was based on the distinguished historian Henry Adams, whom Fitzgerald had met through Fay and Leslie; Mrs. Lawrence on Mrs. Margaret Chanler, whose memoirs included a vivid description of Fay; Allenby (the name of a triumphant British general in the Great War) on the Princeton football star Hobey Baker; Eleanor Savage on Bishop's friend Elizabeth Beckwith, with whom Fitzgerald had gone horseback riding in Charlestown, West Virginia, while waiting to enter the army in the summer of 1917; and the idealized Clara Page on his attractive widowed cousin, Cecilia Taylor, who lived in Norfolk, Virginia.

Clara "was alone in the world, with two small children, little money, and, worst of all, a host of friends," Fitzgerald wrote. "What a twist Clara had to her mind! She could make fascinating and almost brilliant conversation out of the thinnest air that ever floated through a drawing-room." Cecilia's daughter Sally Abeles "remembered Scott from his Princeton days as being very good-looking and, to his young female cousins, very glamorous." She explained that "my mother was quite beautiful and the relationship with Scott was based on the family connection and the fact that she was sixteen years older than he and (as he matured) more his kind of person than his parents were."[2]

This Side of Paradise was written with facile cleverness in a series of short episodic scenes and in an unusual mixture of prose, poetry, drama, letters, book lists and quotations. Though flippant, it contains flashes of insight on a number of serious subjects: wealth, class, sex, mores, fame, romance, glamour, success, vanity, egoism, politics and religion. The potentially sensational chapter on "Petting" is in fact about kissing: "None of the Victorian mothers . . . had any idea how casually their daughters were accustomed to be kissed." And none of the passionless kissing scenes—"HE: Rosalind, I really *want* to kiss you. SHE: So do I. (*They kiss—definitely and thoroughly*)"—stimulates Amory to engage in more daring sexual acts. The originality of the novel lies in its *attitude* toward sex rather than in its descriptions of sexual behavior. At a time when twelve percent of Fitzgerald's Princeton class regarded casual kissing as morally wrong, and when a serious kiss meant that a proposal was expected, This Side of Paradise seemed daring in recognizing the sexual impulses of young men and women and in celebrating—just after Prohibition had been enacted—the freedom of drinking and sex.

"I'm sick of the sexless animals writers have been giving us," Fitzgerald told an interviewer in January 1921. "Personally, I prefer this sort of [modern] girl. Indeed, I married the heroine of my stories. I would not be interested in any other sort of woman."[3] Fitzgerald persuaded Scribner's to advertise the book as "A Novel About Flappers Written for Philosophers." And with Zelda in mind, he popularized the term "flapper" (originally derived from a "wild duck"). The word had evolved from meaning a young harlot in the early nineteenth century, and then an immoral girl in her early teens at the turn of the twentieth century, to a young girl with her hair not yet put up in 1905, and finally to an unconventional young woman with short hair in the 1920s. The novel had an immense social as well as literary impact. Amory and his girlfriends—freed by wealth, alcohol and automobiles—became models for unconstrained behavior. Fitzgerald's book expressed the current revolt against prewar respectability and alarmed protective parents. It both baptized the Jazz Age and glorified its fashionable hedonism.

Most reviewers were surprisingly enthusiastic and generous about the flawed but vibrant novel, which seemed to fit Fitzgerald's own description of similar works by his young rivals Floyd Dell and Stephen Vincent Benét: "This writing of a young man's novel consists chiefly in dumping all your youthful adventures into the reader's lap with a profound air of importance, keeping carefully within the formulas of Wells and James Joyce." Fitzgerald himself was influenced by the social context of Wells' *The History of Mr. Polly* and closely paraphrased ("He was . . . preserved to help in building up the living consciousness of the race") the famous words about the rebellious hero in Joyce's *Portrait of the Artist*.

Franklin P. Adams criticized *This Side of Paradise* as "sloppy and cocky; impudent instead of confident; and verbose," but most critics were favorably impressed by its originality, its vitality and its style. The anonymous reviewer in the *New York Times Book Review* admired "the glorious spirit of abounding youth [that] glows throughout this fascinating tale." Burton Rascoe of the *Chicago Tribune* exclaimed: "It is sincere, it is honest, it is intelligent, it is handled in an individual manner, it bears the impress, it seems to me, of genius." And the influential, frequently harsh H. L. Mencken, who had with George Jean Nathan published Fitzgerald's first stories in the *Smart Set* and would soon become his friend, pronounced it "a truly amazing first novel—original in structure, extremely sophisticated in manner, and adorned with a brilliancy that is as rare in American writing as honesty is in American statecraft."[4]

Bishop, Wilson, Fitzgerald himself, as well as students and faculty at Princeton, all commented on the provocative book. After reading the manuscript, Bishop called it "damn good, brilliant in places, and sins chiefly through exuberance and lack of development." Later on, Bishop tried to account for its astonishing popularity by observing: "Sincerity for hypocrisy, spontaneity in the place of control, freedom from repression—who could resist such a program? The response was prodigious. Success, as we know, was only less immediate. The faults of the program were not so soon apparent."[5]

In the *Bookman* of March 1922 Wilson (who was supposed to be a friend) opened his review of the novel with his usual put-down. He repeated some of the points he had made in his letter about the as-yet-unpublished novel and authoritatively established the line of criticism about Fitzgerald's work that would be repeated throughout his lifetime: "He has been given imagination without intellectual control of it; he has been given the desire for beauty without an aesthetic ideal; and he has been given a gift for expression without very many ideas to express." Though Wilson clearly had the intellectual control, aesthetic ideals and abundant ideas, it was Fitzgerald who had somehow blundered into the creation of a phenomenally popular novel. Trying, like Bishop, to account for its surprising critical success, Wilson praised the book's vitality: "I have said that *This Side of Paradise* commits almost every sin that a novel can possibly commit: but it does not commit the unpardonable sin: it does not fail to live. The whole preposterous farrago is animated with life."

In 1920 Fitzgerald, riding high on his new-found wealth and fame as spokesman for the postwar generation, had fulfilled Wilson's prediction that his shallowness would make him a popular success. Still toiling as an obscure journalist, Wilson found other ways to attack Fitzgerald and now became as critical of his personal faults as he was of his literary failings. Wilson and Bishop, whose thin volume of poems had also been eclipsed by Fitzgerald, drew up, after seeing the novel piled high in his publisher's handsome shop window on Fifth Avenue, a satiric catalogue for a "Proposed exhibit of Fitzgeraldiana for Chas. Scribner's Sons." These items—which reflected Fitzgerald's immaturity, vanity, narcissism, shallowness and undistinguished military career (Wilson and Bishop had both served in France)—consisted of three double malted milks, a bottle of hair tonic, a yellow silk shirt, a mirror, his entire seven-book library (including a notebook and two scrapbooks) and an "overseas cap never worn overseas."[6] The yellow shirt anticipated Jay Gatsby's exhibition of his wardrobe; the overseas cap would be cunningly adopted by Fitzgerald in "The Crack-Up." Though emotionally vulnerable, Fitzgerald tolerated this sharp criticism with humility and good-natured resignation.

Fitzgerald had good reason to put up with Wilson's spiteful attacks. He was being exceptionally well paid for his work and could understand Wilson's manifest envy. He knew that he was not an intellectual novelist and, though his commercial stories were hastily composed, that his style and subject matter were his own. He instinctively perceived that his work evolved from his personal faults and emotional crises. His role as passive target was, moreover, fundamental to his relationship with

Wilson. Had he become angry and broken with his friend, he would have lost the benefit of Wilson's harsh but stimulating criticism.

In the 1930s Fitzgerald retrospectively agreed with Wilson's criticism, but also defended his cheeky novel. Comparing it to a work by Oscar Wilde that had provided one of the epigraphs, he told Max Perkins: "I think it is now one of the funniest books since *Dorian Gray* in its utter spuriousness—and then, here and there, I find a page that is very real and living." Referring to Wilson in "Early Success," Fitzgerald remarked: "A lot of people thought it was a fake, and perhaps it was, and a lot of others thought it was a lie, which it was not."[7] Its intellectual pretensions were fake, Fitzgerald conceded, since he had brashly discussed books and issues about which he knew very little. But his descriptions of experiences and feelings were real and sincere.

The Princeton bookstore was stampeded on the day of publication. Five days later, on March 31, 1920, Fitzgerald gave Cottage Club an inscribed copy of the novel (which is still there) to mark his visit to Princeton a few days before his wedding. *This Side of Paradise*—which portrayed the undergraduates as social climbers, arrogant snobs, energetic hedonists and political windbags—was a direct and deliberate assault on Woodrow Wilson's staunch Presbyterian values. H. L. Mencken, delighted by its wild iconoclasm, remarked that if a new Fitzgerald escaped from Princeton, he would be "received with a cordiality (both spiritual and spiritous) that the president of his university might envy."

But John Grier Hibben, Wilson's successor as president of the university, was angered and upset by the portrayal of Princeton as "the pleasantest country club in America." Rejecting Fitzgerald's emphasis on frivolity, Hibben frankly told him "that your characterization of Princeton has grieved me. I cannot bear to think that our young men are merely living for four years in a country club and spending their lives wholly in a spirit of calculation and snobbishness." Humbly deferring to authority, Fitzgerald admitted that the novel "does overaccentuate the gayety and country club atmosphere of Princeton."[8] He did not mention, however, that his notorious phrase had been lifted from Wilson's predecessor, President Patton, who had reigned at Princeton until 1902 and "was heard to boast that he was head of the finest country club in America." Though the book offended Hibben's ideal vision of Princeton, it conveyed a romantic aura to succeeding generations. The young George Kennan, later a diplomat and Soviet specialist, was drawn to Princeton by the novel; and Adlai Stevenson called it "a great human document."[9]

II

Fitzgerald was fortunate, at the beginning of his literary career, to win the loyal friendship and generous support of two remarkably similar men: his editor, Maxwell Perkins, and his agent, Harold Ober. Both gentlemen were reserved, respectable, reliable New Englanders, who had graduated from Harvard and led a conventional family life in the New York suburbs. Perkins came from a distinguished background. One of his ancestors had signed the Declaration of Independence; his grandfather had been attorney general under Andrew Johnson and secretary of state under Rutherford Hayes. Born in New York in 1884, the son of a lawyer, Perkins grew up in Windsor, Vermont, and attended St. Paul's School in New Hampshire. After college he worked in a Boston welfare house and became a reporter on the *New York Times*. He married an extremely proper wife just after becoming an editor at Scribner's in 1910, had five proper daughters and lived properly in New Canaan, Connecticut. He also maintained a platonic friendship with another woman for twenty-five years. In the summer of 1916 Perkins unexpectedly joined the U.S. Cavalry, was sent to the Mexican border and chased but never found the revolutionary, Pancho Villa.

Rather stuffy and correct, but uncommonly generous, Perkins had, according to the Canadian author Morley Callaghan, "a talent for diplomacy in difficult human situations, and a kind of nobility of spirit and a fine sense of fairness." Hemingway liked the strange way Perkins moved his lips and his reporter's habit of keeping his hat on in the office. He admired Perkins' kindness, modesty and tact, but criticized his deep-rooted puritanism, which made him abandon any pursuit that gave him pleasure.

Perkins gave excellent literary advice to authors who needed it. He helped Thomas Wolfe—who portrayed him unsympathetically as Foxhall Edwards in *The Web and the Rock* (1939)—to assemble his unwieldy tomes from a mass of disordered fragments. But he did not edit Hemingway, a careful author, beyond excising passages that were libelous and obscene. He merely accepted Hemingway's typescripts, praised them and published them as expeditiously as possible.

Perkins was more intimate with Fitzgerald than with Hemingway and did much more for Scott. As Fitzgerald's editor Perkins had to be as encouraging as possible. In contrast to Father Fay's flattery and Edmund Wilson's mockery, Perkins provided a constructive response that enabled Fitzgerald to improve his work. But Perkins could not spell and was absolutely useless at correcting, copy-editing and proof-reading a text. As a result of both the author's and the editor's careless-ness, Fitzgerald's novels—from the first editions to the present time—are filled with hundreds of ludicrous orthographical, grammatical and factual errors. Though both Fitzgerald and Scribner's looked foolish when Franklin P. Adams' newspaper column listed scores of errors in *This Side of Paradise,* Perkins continued to be grossly negligent. In October 1921 he offered some typically bad advice when preparing the proofs of Fitzgerald's second novel, *The Beautiful and Damned:* "I shall send them on to you but you will not need to read them very carefully unless you wish to. Just look them over."[10]

As Fitzgerald's career progressed, Perkins assumed the additional roles of substitute parent, father confessor, secret sharer, social worker, medical mentor, psychiatric adviser, intermediary to Hemingway and rather reckless banker. He was one of the few people who maintained his friendship with Fitzgerald until the very end. Fitzgerald—like Ford and Pound—was generous with fellow authors. He repaid Perkins by recommending to Scribner's many little-known and extremely promis-ing writers, whom he had met or heard about in Princeton, St. Paul, New York and Paris: John Biggs, John Peale Bishop, Thomas Boyd, Ring Lardner, Gertrude Stein, Ernest Hemingway, Morley Callaghan, André Chamson, Raymond Radiguet, Erskine Caldwell and Franz Kafka. Through Fitzgerald's good offices, Hemingway and Caldwell became two of Scribner's most profitable authors.

Harold Ober was born near Lake Winnipesaukee in 1881 and grew up in New Ipswich, New Hampshire, on the Massachusetts border. He worked his way through Harvard as a tutor, rowed for the varsity crew and graduated in 1905. Eager to become an author, he spent the next two years in Europe; and he returned to France with the Red Cross in 1917. Ober joined the Paul Reynolds literary agency in 1907, became a partner in 1919 and opened his own agency, just before the Wall Street Crash, in 1929. "He was tall and lean," wrote Catherine Drinker Bowen, one of his satisfied clients, "with deep-set, serious blue eyes, a big nose, a high color, and . . . a head of handsome grey hair which he wore parted on one side and carefully brushed down." But he also had overgrown eyebrows, a pendulous lower lip and a weak chin.

Ober had two sons, and was interested in dogs, gardening, music and skiing. Like Perkins, he was generous with advice and money, and always behaved with old-fashioned courtesy and extreme reserve. After some difficult negotiations, one editor remarked: "That New Hampshireman can say nothing for longer periods than the great Buddha." Fitzgerald's daughter Scottie, who became part of the Ober family during her years in high school and college, called him "a man of TOTAL integrity."[11]

Fitzgerald dealt directly with Perkins at Scribner's. Ober handled only his magazine stories, but was instrumental in his financial success. "In 1919," Fitzgerald wrote, "I had made $800 by writing, in 1920 I had made $18,000, stories, picture rights and book. My story price had gone from $30 to $1,000"—and would continue to rise until it reached $4,000 from the *Saturday Evening Post* in 1929. No longer a poor boy in a rich boy's world, Fitzgerald now revealed a vulgar streak and seemed to illustrate Thorstein Veblen's concept of conspicuous consumption. Intoxicated by the excitement of money and eager to advertise his success, he would prepare for parties by prominently displaying hundred dollar bills in his vest pockets.

This Side of Paradise, which had sold out in twenty-four hours, required twelve more printings by the end of 1921 and by then had sold more than 49,000 copies. Fitzgerald, who naively expected all his books to achieve a similar success, lived up to what he imagined his future income would be. He spent his money and his talent as if they would last forever. "All big men have spent money freely," he told his mother. "I hate avarice or even caution."[12] He did make one attempt to provide for the future by buying two bonds, but they lost value and he was unable to sell them. When he tried to abandon them in the subway, they were always returned to him.

Fitzgerald's lavish expenditure of money indelibly marked him as nouveau riche. Once he developed luxurious tastes, he preferred to sacrifice his independence and go deeper into debt rather than reduce his standard of living to match his diminished income. Like Joseph Conrad, he felt he had to live like a gentleman and (even when pressed for money) provide his family with maids, governesses, nannies, nurses, expensive hotels, luxurious cars, private schools and the finest hospitals. Forced to borrow from his publisher and agent to get what he needed, he became as financially dependent on Ober as Conrad had been on his agent, J. B. Pinker.

Fitzgerald's sudden wealth and fame created emotional and intellectual problems. He felt guilty because he did not deserve these blessings. Having reached the peak of financial and critical success, he found it extremely difficult to surpass his first achievement. He could do this only by writing a more serious and ambitious novel, which would inevitably earn less money than a popular one. This would force him once again to turn out commercial stories in order to pay for his lavish way of life.

At the same time that he began his friendship with Perkins and Ober, Fitzgerald met the editors of the *Smart Set*, H. L. Mencken and George Jean Nathan. The *Smart Set: A Magazine of Cleverness* was satiric and avant-garde, snobbish and stylish, witty and iconoclastic. It published Somerset Maugham's "Rain," fiction by Willa Cather, James Branch Cabell and Sinclair Lewis as well as more experimental works by Lawrence, Joyce and Pound. It also took stories by Fitzgerald that were too serious or too highbrow for the *Saturday Evening Post*.

Nathan—a short, dark, well-dressed and melancholy man—was born in Indiana in 1882. After graduating from Cornell, he made his reputation as a cynical and sophisticated drama critic and literary editor. In *The Beautiful and Damned*, Fitzgerald portrayed him as Maury Noble and compared him to "a large, slender and imposing cat. His eyes are narrow and full of incessant, protracted blinks. His hair is smooth and flat, as though it had been licked by a . . . mother-cat." Like Nathan, Noble was considered a brilliant and original figure—"smart, quiet and among the saved."

Henry Louis Mencken, a Baltimore-born journalist and critic, was two years older than Nathan. An intensely Germanic, beer-drinking, cigar-chomping man, he had a squat proletarian face with a pudgy nose and plastered hair divided down the middle of his head. Though notorious for his aggressive iconoclasm and savage satires on philistine life in America, Mencken was enthusiastic about Fitzgerald's work. Scott thought Mencken had done more for American letters than any man alive and called him one of the greatest men in the country. After Father Fay's death in 1919, his spiritual influence on Fitzgerald was replaced by Mencken's violent hostility to Christianity. Scott called Mencken "The Baltimore Anti-Christ" and in letters addressed him ironically (as he had once addressed Fay respectfully) as "the Right Reverend HLM." Mencken was enchanted by Zelda; Nathan conducted a dangerous flirtation with her. But Mencken also told Cabell that Zelda's extravagance fueled Scott's desire for money and pulled him away from serious art: "His wife talks too much about money. His danger lies in trying to get it too rapidly. A very amiable pair, innocent and charming."[13]

III

Though Zelda was Protestant and Scott no longer a practicing Catholic, they were married on April 3, 1920—eight days after the publication of his first novel—in the rectory of St. Patrick's Cathedral on Fifth Avenue. Zelda, who later became a model for fashionable women in the 1920s, had no taste or style when she first came north. She was even considered a bit cheap and "tacky." Horrified by her Southern frills and furbelows, Fitzgerald anxiously asked Marie Hersey—his St. Paul friend, Ginevra King's roommate at Westover School and a graduate of Vassar—to buy Zelda the proper clothes for New York.

As if to emphasize the break the young couple had made with their backgrounds, neither Scott's nor Zelda's parents attended the wedding. The only witnesses were Scott's Princeton friend and best man, Ludlow Fowler, and Zelda's three older sisters, who were by then married and living in New York. Scott, who was nervous, insisted the ceremony begin before Clothilde arrived. There was no lunch or party after the wedding, which Rosalind considered rude and never forgave, and the couple promptly left for their honeymoon at the Biltmore Hotel.

Though absorbed by the sensations of the moment, Fitzgerald was also keenly aware of the ephemeral nature of happiness. In *This Side of Paradise*, as Amory Blaine put in his collar studs before a party on Long Island, "he realized that he was enjoying life as he would probably never enjoy it again." When Fitzgerald and his friends left Princeton for the war in June 1917, "some of us wept because we knew we'd never be quite so young any more as we had been here." And in "My Lost City" he recaptured the manic-depressive emotions of Wordsworth's "Resolution and Independence"—

> But, as it sometimes chanceth, from the might
> Of joy in minds that can no further go,
> As high as we have mounted in delight
> In our dejection do we sink as low—

and remembered that "riding in a taxi one afternoon between very tall buildings under a mauve and rosy sky [which represents his extreme variations of mood]; I began to bawl because I had everything I wanted and knew I would never be so happy again."[14]

Zelda had spent her entire life with her family in Montgomery but, like Sally Carrol Happer in "The Ice Palace," wanted "to live where things happen on a big scale." Suddenly thrown into a chaotic existence in New York, she managed to conquer the city. But her life from then on was always rootless and unstable. Scott, whose childhood had been marked by frequent moves, continued to live a nomadic life. The catalogue of temporary rooms in her article "Show Mr. and Mrs. F. to Number———" describes how they hopped nervously from place to place. They never owned a house of their own, never settled anywhere for very long and were often expelled from the places they rented.

Fitzgerald confused immaturity with youthfulness and boasted to a former St. Paul girlfriend about their weaknesses: Zelda is "very beautiful and very wise and very brave as you can imagine—but she's a perfect baby and a more irresponsible pair than we'll be will be hard to imagine." He immediately set the tone of his marriage by taking his teenage bride to an April weekend at Cottage Club and introducing her to everyone as his mistress. He got a black eye (the first of many) at a rowdy Princeton party, and took it badly when his self-righteous club suspended him for drunken behavior.

Their wild and well-publicized pranks soon became notorious. Watching a comedy in the front row of a theater, they annoyed the actors by laughing appreciatively in all the wrong places. Kicked out of the Biltmore for disturbing other guests, they celebrated their move to the Commodore by spinning through the revolving doors for half an hour. Looking like a figurehead on the prow of a ship, Zelda paid a surcharge to catch the breeze on the hood of a taxi. Out of sheer exuberance they jumped into the fountain in Union Square and into the fountain near the Plaza, and achieved instant fame at the Greenwich Village Follies, whose curtain by Reginald Marsh included a picture of Zelda splashing in these urban pools. During a Hawaiian pageant in Montgomery (which they visited in March 1921), Zelda bent over, lifted her grass skirt and wriggled her pert behind. In May 1920 they rented a house on Compo Road in suburban Westport and hired a Japanese servant. Bored by the suburbs, Zelda summoned the firemen (as she had done as a child in Montgomery). When asked where the blaze was, she struck her breast and exclaimed: "Here!" Like the autobiographical heroine of *Save Me the Waltz*, Zelda lived impulsively: "You took what you wanted from life, if you could get it, and you did without the rest."

In July 1920 they bought an unreliable second-hand Marmon automobile and had a series of mechanical breakdowns, absurd mishaps and unpleasant confrontations when their twin knickerbockers scandalized small Southern towns en route to Montgomery. Fitzgerald later chronicled this journey in "The Cruise of the Rolling Junk" (1924). He was one of the first writers to use the automobile for dramatic scenes in fiction. In *This Side of Paradise* Amory's college friend Dick Humbird is killed in a car crash. In *The Great Gatsby* Daisy Buchanan kills her husband's mistress with her lover's car. In *Tender is the Night* Nicole Diver, enraged by jealousy while driving on the Riviera with her husband and children, tries to force their car off a steep, dangerous road. And a key chapter on Fitzgerald in Hemingway's *A Moveable Feast* describes a disastrous trip from Lyons to Paris in a Renault whose top had been cut off.

The familiar catalogue of infantile pleasures has been admired by the chroniclers of the Fitzgeralds' legend and accepted as an expression of their youthful vitality. But it also suggests a tiresome self-absorption, self-importance and striving for irresponsibility as well as a rather desperate hedonism that threatened to burn itself out and lapse into boring repetition (five minutes in the revolving door would have sufficed to make the point).

Alcohol fueled most of these uninhibited episodes, which changed from high-spirited to malicious as Fitzgerald's drinking intensified. David Bruce, the Princeton friend who became an eminent diplomat, was ambivalent about Zelda and reported that she "can drink more than any other woman he has ever seen, and is a trifle ordinary and Alabamian, but has brains." Scott admitted that he could never get sufficiently sober to endure being sober, but he could get into dangerous trouble even when he was not drunk. In April 1921 (a year after Fitzgerald got the black eye at Princeton) the writer Carl Van Vechten stopped by Scott's apartment in New York and found him "with two black eyes, one a bleeding mass, discreetly covered by a towel. He had hopefully attacked the bouncer in the Jungle, a New York cabaret, on the previous Friday. When he was completely sober: an unheard of occurrence."[15] Van Vechten does not mention that Zelda, to test or punish Scott, had urged him to take on the bouncer.

Their wild behavior was also inspired by more rational, even calculated motives. Fitzgerald had a strong and nervous craving to be liked, and tried to make people happy—even if it meant making a fool of himself. Immense vitality and charm flowed out of him and made the most commonplace encounter seem like a real adventure. The actress Carmel Myers felt that "it required the special quality of Scott's personality to infuse such sophomoric behavior with an atmosphere of explosive gaiety." Both Scott and Zelda had a need for drama—or farce. Their public performances, which resembled the Marx Brothers at a debutantes' cotillion, expressed their desire to act up to their reputation, be seen to lead the revolt against boring conventions and transform a dull experience into a lively occasion. Zelda had few inhibitions and would do almost anything. She had always been the star performer in Montgomery, and her shocking pranks in the North, which she called "exploring her abysses in public," were meant to compete with Scott, who had stolen top billing, and refocus attention on herself. Like Nicole Diver in *Tender is the Night*, Zelda believed "we should do something spectacular . . . all our lives have been too restrained."

Scott had been in the advertising business and knew how to create an attractive public image. Like Hemingway, he exploited his good looks, wit and charm. He would not have been nearly as successful if he had called himself Francis, been as ugly as Dreiser and as bald as Dos Passos, and had a dowdy wife who looked and dressed like Gertrude Stein. His outrageous acts were often quite deliberate. He misbehaved to arouse attention and gain publicity. And he was very successful (as his scrapbooks of press cuttings indicate) in getting into the newspapers, keeping his name in the public eye and helping to sell his books. In contrast to disillusioned and embittered writers like Hemingway, Robert Graves, Richard Aldington and Erich Maria Remarque, all of whom published their war books in 1929, Fitzgerald helped his generation recover from the war by emphasizing and embodying the joyous and hopeful possibilities at the beginning of the 1920s. Zelda felt that Scott's greatest contribution, in both his life and works, was to endow "a heart-broken and despairing era" with a "sense of tragic courage."[16]

Scott deliberately encouraged Zelda's madcap role so that he could write about the bizarre things she had done. He was attracted by the qualities that were at first essential to his work and later helped to destroy it. Writing about what had happened to them seemed to define— or recover—their real selves, which were hidden beneath their self-conscious role-playing and image making. As he ingenuously observed: "I don't know whether Zelda and I are real or whether we are characters in one of my novels." After he had created the public personae which he and Zelda felt obliged to imitate, and which revealed the disparity between their projected and actual lives, he admitted: "we scarcely knew any more who we were and we hadn't a notion what we were."[17]

Though Fitzgerald's literary image was daring, nonconformist and unconventional, he could never quite extinguish his provincial, puritanical streak. He told one friend: "Parties are a form of suicide. I love them, but the old Catholic in me secretly disapproves." Another friend agreed that Fitzgerald had to make a deliberate effort to misbehave: "Poor Scott, he never really enjoyed his dissipation because he disapproved intensely of himself all the time it was going on."[18] His corruption was always tempered by innocence.

As they whirled from party to party their chaotic and dissipated mode of life seemed to sustain them in a cataclysmic sort of way. But it put an enormous strain on their marriage. Zelda's extravagance and flirtations, which had once seemed so delightful, soon became intolerable. Zelda resembled the spoiled wife in Hemingway's story "Cat in the Rain," though she craved much more expensive things: "And I want to eat at a table with my own silver and I want candles. And I want it to be spring and I want to brush my hair out in front of a mirror and I want a kitty and I want some new clothes." The spoiled and acquisitive Zelda, who had to be courted with feather fans and expensive jewelry, believed "having things, just things, objects, makes a woman happy.

The right kind of perfume, the smart pair of shoes. They are great comforts to the feminine soul." Dorothy Parker agreed with Zelda's mother that she had a petulant streak and would begin to sulk if something displeased her. Zelda's craving for luxuries (as Mencken had noted) kept Fitzgerald turning out poor stories for good money.

Like Leopold Bloom in Joyce's *Ulysses*, Fitzgerald was sexually excited by Zelda's flirtations with other men and liked to possess a woman who was universally admired. The first fault in the unstable landscape of their marriage occurred when Zelda, who still needed to exert her sexual power and remain the center of attention, began to embrace and kiss his friends in public. When she rushed into John Peale Bishop's room as he was going to bed and said she wanted to spend the night with him, when she lured Townsend Martin into the bathroom and insisted he give her a bath, Fitzgerald became disturbed by her seductive behavior. It made his friends uncomfortable and put everyone in a compromising position.

The dapper George Jean Nathan, a well-known ladies' man, fell so deeply in love with Zelda, after months of apparently innocent flirtation, that Scott felt obliged to terminate their friendship. Zelda, much more unconventional than Scott, evoked hedonism to justify her daring behavior and define the new morality of the flapper: "She flirted because it was fun to flirt and wore a one-piece bathing suit because she had a good figure; she covered her face with paint and powder because she didn't need it and she refused to be bored chiefly because she wasn't boring."[19]

The most intimate view of the troubled early months of their marriage appeared in the diary of Scott's Princeton friend Alexander McKaig, who saw the Fitzgeralds regularly in the summer of 1920 when they were living in Westport and coming down to New York for parties. On September 15, for example, they started to fight in Westport and, after Scott had hastily pursued her on the train to Manhattan, resumed their quarrel (for they liked to have an audience) in front of McKaig: "In the evening Zelda—drunk—having decided to leave Fitz & having nearly been killed walking down RR track, blew in. Fitz came shortly after. He had caught same train with no money or ticket. They threatened to put him off but finally let him stay on—Zelda refusing to give him any money. They continued their fight while here." After describing the fight, McKaig recorded the advice he may have given Fitzgerald as well as the difficulty of following it, and noted that she had the dominant personality: "Fitz should let Zelda go & not run after her. Like all husbands he is afraid of what she might do in a moment of caprice. . . . Trouble is, Fitz [is] absorbed in Zelda's personality—she is the stronger of the two. She has supplied him with all his copy for women."

A month later McKaig noted that their flat at 38 West 59th Street (which they had rented, when they tired of Westport, from October 1920 until April 1921) was "a pig sty." Zelda had kept her promise not to think about "pots and kitchens and brooms." McKaig also stated their insoluble dilemma: "If she's there Fitz can't work—she bothers him—if she's not there he can't work—worried of what she might do. . . . Zelda increasingly restless—says frankly she wants to be amused and is only good for useless, pleasure-giving pursuits; great problem—what is she to do?" Smitten by Zelda, like most of Scott's friends, McKaig rather incongruously concluded: "She is without doubt the most brilliant & most beautiful young woman I've ever known." Though deeply disturbed by Zelda's refusal to restrain herself, Scott remained infatuated. In a letter to Edmund Wilson, he expressed his admiration for "the complete, fine and full-hearted selfishness and chillmindedness of Zelda."[20]

IV

In February 1921 Zelda discovered she was pregnant, and they decided to take their first trip to Europe while she could still travel. They sailed on the *Aquitania* and docked in Southampton in May 1921. While staying at the Hotel Cecil on the Strand in London, they dined at the Hampstead home of John Galsworthy, a Scribner's author whom Fitzgerald had met through Alfred Noyes at Princeton. "Tall, austere looking, with a Roman profile and tightly closed lips, always correctly dressed, Galsworthy would not have looked out of place in Downing Street." In contrast to the easy-going Fitzgerald, Galsworthy was correct, formal and stiff.

During dinner Fitzgerald, who habitually adopted a self-conscious and self-abasing attitude when encountering established writers, suddenly burst out with: "Mr. Galsworthy, you are one of the three living writers I admire most in the world: you and [Galsworthy's friend] Joseph Conrad and Anatole France!" He later admitted to Edmund Wilson that Galsworthy had not "liked it much. He knew he wasn't that good." But Galsworthy, who was easily as good as Anatole France and later won the Nobel Prize, was probably more embarrassed by Fitzgerald's gauche flattery than dismayed (as Fitzgerald suggested) by his own sad estimation of his work. Though Galsworthy was kind, the host and guest seemed temperamentally at odds with each other and the evening was not a success. Fitzgerald told Shane Leslie that he was rather disappointed in the older writer and unfavorably compared him to Conrad: "I can't stand pessimism with neither irony nor bitterness."

On this visit to England, Fitzgerald observed the poor and was entertained by the rich. Leslie, who had done social work in Wapping, took them on a nighttime tour of the London docks (with Zelda, in that rough district, protectively dressed in men's clothing). He also invited them to dinner with his half-American first cousin Winston Churchill, who was then head of the Colonial Office. Like Gatsby, Fitzgerald ordered quantities of English suits and shirts. And he was tremendously impressed by Oxford, "the most beautiful spot in the world," and by its evocative associations with Compton Mackenzie, Max Beerbohm and Thomas Hardy. But when he returned there two months later, after visiting Paris and Rome, he was fearful that the once-impressive English, exhausted by the war, might soon become a dying breed: "We'd been to Oxford before—after Italy we went back there, arriving gorgeously at twilight when the place was fully peopled for us by the ghosts of ghosts—the characters, romantic, absurd or melancholy, of *Sinister Street, Zuleika Dobson* and *Jude the Obscure*. But something was wrong now—something that would never be right again. . . . In how many years would our descendants approach this ruin with supercilious eyes to buy postcards from men of a short, inferior race—a race that once were Englishmen."[21]

The Fitzgeralds had scant interest in museums and monuments. They knew no one in France and Italy, quickly grew weary of sightseeing and rejected Edmund Wilson's sober advice to "settle down and learn French and apply a little French leisure and measure to that restless and jumpy nervous system." Instead, they waited outside Anatole France's house, hoping to see and perhaps speak to the distinguished author, but were disappointed when he failed to appear. And they were asked to leave the Hôtel de Saint-James et d'Albany because Zelda repeatedly tied up the cage-style elevator with her belt so that it would always be ready when she had dressed for dinner.

Impelled by piety—or by mere curiosity—Fitzgerald had asked Archbishop Dowling of St. Paul to arrange an audience with the Holy Father in Rome. The archbishop, acceding to Fitzgerald's request and remembering the family's beneficence, told a Vatican official that "none have merited more of the Church in this city than [the Fitzgeralds] have through several generations—staunch, devout, generous." Though Fitzgerald noted "women weeping in Vatican" and "the loot of 20 centuries,"[22] he did not mention seeing the pope, who by late June may have moved to his summer residence outside Rome.

Fitzgerald enjoyed himself hugely in Venice, but had a "rotten time" in France. Influenced by Mencken's pro-German attitudes and bitterly disillusioned by the decadent state of postwar Europe, he assumed a superior attitude and (in a letter to the Francophile Edmund Wilson) condemned Latin culture with an uneasy ferocity that anticipated the rantings of Tom Buchanan in *The Great Gatsby*:

> God damn the continent of Europe. It is of merely antiquarian interest. Rome is only a few years behind Tyre and Babylon. The negroid streak creeps northward to defile the nordic race. Already the Italians have the souls of blackamoors. . . . France made me sick. . . . I think it's a shame that England and America didn't let Germany conquer Europe. It's the only thing that would have saved the fleet of tottering old wrecks. My reactions were all philistine, anti-socialistic, provincial and racially snobbish. I believe at last in the white man's burden. We are as far above the modern Frenchman as he is above the Negro.

Proud of his philistine thought and bohemian behavior, Fitzgerald told Robert Bridges, the editor of *Scribner's Magazine*, when they returned from Europe, that "there were legends enough current to supply three biographers."[23]

The Fitzgeralds sailed home on the *Celtic* in early July and made a brief visit to Montgomery. They then rented a house in Dellwood, on White Bear Lake, about ten miles northeast of St. Paul. They had contracted to stay for a year, but were asked to leave in November (as they had been asked to leave the Biltmore, Cottage Club and the Hôtel de Saint-James). They had carelessly allowed a pipe to freeze and burst, which had caused severe water damage. The following summer their rambunctious parties led to expulsion from the White Bear Yacht Club. The Fitzgeralds never seemed troubled by all these evictions and merely shifted their chaotic household to the next convenient place.

In the summer of 1921 Zelda met Fitzgerald's parents for the first time, and settled down to await the birth of their first child. Zelda, who loved swimming and sunbathing, evoked the Minnesota scene with an image that suggested both protection and entrapment: "When summer came, all the people who liked summertime moved out to the huge, clear lake not far from town, and lived there in long, flat cottages surrounded with dank shrubbery and pine trees, and so covered by screened verandas that they made you think of small pieces of cheese under large meat safes." A childhood friend of Fitzgerald vividly recalled how Zelda had loathed and mocked St. Paul.

Fitzgerald made two new friends that summer. He spent many hours drinking and arguing with Thomas Boyd, the owner of the Kilmarnock Book Shop in St. Paul and the literary editor of the *St. Paul Daily News*. Born in Ohio two years after Scott, Boyd had been a marine hero, and was then working on his war novel *Through the Wheat* (1923). He favorably reviewed three of Fitzgerald's books and interviewed him twice. Xandra Kalman, an old friend and contemporary of Scott, had a summer place in Dellwood and had found a house for him. Though Catholic, in 1917 she had married a divorced banker, Oscar Kalman, a wealthy and generous man who was twenty-five years her senior. Since Zelda had made no preparations for the baby, the practical Xandra bought all the necessary clothing and supplies.

Frances Scott Fitzgerald, at first called Patricia but always known as Scottie, was born in St. Paul on October 26, 1921. When Zelda first saw the new baby she exclaimed: "I hope it's beautiful and a fool—a beautiful little fool"—a sentence attributed to Daisy Buchanan in *The Great Gatsby*. Fitzgerald's telegram to the Sayres hyperbolically announced that their baby daughter had already eclipsed the most dazzling silent film stars: "Lillian Gish is in mourning; Constance Talmadge is a back number; and a second Mary Pickford has arrived." Nick Carraway responds in the same witty tone as this telegram when

Daisy asks him if they miss her in Chicago: "The whole town is desolate. All the cars have the left rear wheel painted black as a mourning wreath, and there's a persistent wail all night long along the north shore."[24]

In January 1922 Zelda became pregnant again, but decided not to have another child just after Scottie. Though she had refused to take pills to terminate her pregnancy *before* she was married, Zelda decided in March to have the first of her three abortions in New York. A cryptic, undated entry in Fitzgerald's *Notebooks* grimly states: "His son went down the toilet of the XXXX hotel after Dr. X—Pills."

In Rome, in the fall of 1924, an operation to help Zelda conceive caused a lingering infection. By the fall of 1930, when this infection had damaged her reproductive organs, she had abandoned hope of more children and despairingly told Fitzgerald: "Dr. Gros said there was no use trying to save my ovaries. I was always sick and having *piqûres* [injections]."[25] It is not surprising, in view of her medical history, that Zelda greatly admired Hemingway's fine story "Hills Like White Elephants," in which a selfish man bullies his reluctant girlfriend into having an abortion.

V

All Fitzgerald's friends recounted his mad escapades. But very few of them remembered him actually writing, which was done in spurts and completely absorbed him for weeks at a time. His daughter Scottie, stressing his dedication to his craft, recalled that "my father was always sitting at his desk in his bathrobe and slippers, writing, or reading Keats or Shelley—although there was often a faint aroma of gin in the air to dispel too romantic a picture."

Sinclair Lewis had predicted as early as 1920 that "Fitzgerald is going to be a writer the equal of any young European." Shane Leslie had compared him to the sacrificial and mythic Rupert Brooke. And the English critic Cyril Connolly, writing in 1951, observed that the legendary rise and fall of Fitzgerald's literary career and reputation seemed to epitomize both the celebration of the Twenties and the gloom of the Thirties: "Fitzgerald is now firmly established as a myth, an American version of the dying God, an Adonis of letters born with the century, flowering in the 'twenties, the Jazz Age which he perfectly expressed and almost created, and then quietly wilting away through the 'thirties to expire—as a deity of spring and summer should—on December 21st, 1940, at the winter solstice and the end of an epoch."

The difference in quality between Fitzgerald's best and worst work is exceptionally wide. He wrote two of the best novels in American literature and some of the most memorable stories. He also, like most authors, pursued a number of unfortunate dead ends: his unsuccessful play *The Vegetable*, the abandoned versions of *Tender is the Night*, his absurd and lifeless "Philippe, Count of Darkness" stories, his scores of trashy tales for commercial magazines, and virtually all the Hollywood scenarios and screenplays.

Despite his dissipation, Fitzgerald was a very hard worker. During his lifetime he published four novels (another remained unfinished and appeared posthumously), four volumes of short fiction, a play, and three hundred stories, articles and poems in magazines. He wrote in pencil with his left hand and had a large, loopy handwriting that looked like a child's. He often composed in the evenings, clouded by the smoke of Chesterfields and propelled (according to whether or not he was drinking) by astonishing quantities of gin or Coca-Cola. He made several drafts, depending on the importance of the work, before sending it out to a secretary to be typed. In 1922 his St. Paul friend Thomas Boyd reported that Fitzgerald's original drafts were (like his character) spontaneous and impulsive:

> [Fitzgerald's] writing is never thought out. He creates his characters and they are likely to lead him into almost any situation. His phrasing is done in the same way. It is rare that he searches for a word. Most of the time words come to his mind and they spill themselves in a riotous frenzy of song and color all over the page. Some days he writes as many as 7,000 or 8,000 words; and then, with a small *Roget's Thesaurus*, he carefully goes over his work, substituting synonyms for any unusual words that appear more than once in seven or eight consecutive pages.[26]

Fitzgerald's art, like the phoenix, was nourished and consumed by the same source. His only material was his own life, so he meticulously observed and recorded his family and friends, and created his fiction out of his personal experience. He repeatedly stressed the autobiographical nature of his fiction. His most powerful works—"Babylon Revisited," *Tender is the Night* and "The Crack-Up"—were searingly confessional. But he was often limited as a writer by his inability to get outside or beyond himself. "I never did anything but live the life I wrote about," he declared. "My characters are all Scott Fitzgerald. Even the feminine characters are feminine Scott Fitzgeralds. . . . Mostly, we authors must repeat ourselves—that's the truth. We have two or three great and moving experiences in our lives. . . . Whether it's something that happened twenty years ago or only yesterday, I must start out with an emotion—one that's close to me and that I can understand."[27]

Fitzgerald's best stories were hard to write and hard to sell. His trivial work could be cranked out mechanically, once he had invented the formula, and easily placed in the *Saturday Evening Post*. This magazine could well afford to pay him high fees, for every issue had nearly three million readers and earned five million dollars from advertising. His typical stories have a glittering surface, are fanciful and fantastic, comic and mildly satirical, and portray the sophisticated manners and mores of well-off, usually idle and always attractive youths in bars and balls, sleek cars and swimming pools.

"The Popular Girl," published in the *Saturday Evening Post* in February 1922 and never reprinted in his lifetime, contains many elements of his characteristic stories: a Minnesota setting, a contrast between Midwestern and Eastern values, a country club dance, a handsome and well-dressed young hero with charming manners, who has been elected to Bones at Yale and has inherited great wealth, another poor but worthy suitor, a seventeen-year-old girl of exquisite beauty and (to add pathos and drama) her drunken father. The girl practices familiar and rather transparent deceits to capture the hero. But there are complications and sudden reversals. Her father dies, leaving her penniless; she is forced to spend her very last cent; and she is predictably rescued, just in time to avert disaster, by the wealthy heir.

Fitzgerald tried to justify such stories by claiming that the high fees they earned bought him time to concentrate on the ambitious novels that would establish his reputation as a serious artist. Though his fees continued to soar, they never bought quite enough money or time. He published three novels between 1920 and 1925, then took nine years to complete *Tender is the Night* and was unable to finish *The Last Tycoon*.

His older friends, well aware of the insoluble conflict between money and art that had obsessed Fitzgerald since his Princeton days, tried to warn him about the danger of corruption. In a letter of April 1920 to George Jean Nathan, the critic Burton Rascoe presciently remarked: "I hope you are able at all events to dissuade Fitzgerald from writing *too many Saturday Evening Post* stories. Since writing you I have read one of his yarns in the *Post:* it is not to be differentiated from the stories of Nina Wilcox Putnam, Mrs. [Mary Roberts] Rinehart or any of a half dozen others. Clever enough but that's all. Trouble is that he is likely to begin, with the money rolling in, to think that *that* is literature." The following year Charles Norris, whose novel *Brass* Fitzgerald had favorably reviewed in the *Bookman,* warned him directly that catering to the trivial taste of the *Post* would destroy him as a writer: "You can re-christen that worthy periodical 'The Grave-Yard of the Genius of F. Scott Fitzgerald' if you go on contributing to it until [the editor George Horace] Lorimer sucks you dry and tosses you into the discard where nobody will care to find you."[28] Despite these salutary warnings Fitzgerald—extravagant in the Twenties and desperate in the Thirties—continued to write for the *Post* until it began to reject his work in 1937.

Fitzgerald wrote two of his best stories, "The Ice Palace" (*Post,* May 1920) and "May Day" (*Smart Set,* July 1920), at the same time that he was turning out weak commercial stuff.[29] In "The Ice Palace," he imaginatively portrayed Zelda's negative reaction to St. Paul—before she had ever been there. The story opens with a luminous description of Montgomery (called Tarleton, Georgia), which immediately establishes the languorous mood, and uses military metaphors to suggest that the South will be placed in opposition to the North: "The sunlight dripped over the house like golden paint over an art jar, and the freckling shadows here and there only intensified the rigor of the bath of light. The Butterworth and Larkin houses flanking were intrenched behind great stodgy trees; only the Happer house took the full sun, and all day long faced the dusty road-street with a tolerant kindly patience."

After the scene is effectively established, Sally Carrol Happer talks to her visiting fiancé, Harry Bellamy, in a Confederate cemetery, which for Fitzgerald had strong historical and personal associations. It represents courtliness and chivalry, tradition and dignity, and a glorious past. Scott had proposed to Zelda in a Montgomery cemetery. Its atmosphere was evoked in one of her most romantic letters, which influenced his portrayal of Sally Carrol's feelings about the South:

> I've spent to-day in the grave-yard—It really isn't a cemetery, you know—trying to unlock a rusty iron vault built in the side of the hill. It's all washed and covered with weepy, watery blue flowers that might have grown from dead eyes—sticky to touch with a sickening odor. . . . Why should graves make people feel in vain? . . . All the broken columns and clasped hands and doves and angels mean romances. . . . Isn't it funny how, out of a row of Confederate soldiers, two or three will make you think of dead lovers and dead loves.

When Sally Carrol travels to the unnamed northern city (clearly based on St. Paul, which actually had a palace made of ice), Harry boasts about John J. Fishburn (i.e., James J. Hill), the "greatest wheat man in the Northwest, and one of the greatest financiers in the country." Zelda had complained that Scott repeatedly said she should be locked in a tower like a princess. And Harry proudly shows Sally Carrol the frozen palace, built like a fortified castle, out of blocks of the clearest ice: "It was three stories in the air, with battlements and embrasures and narrow icicled windows, and the innumerable electric lights inside made a gorgeous transparency of the great central hall." But to Sally Carrol, it is merely a depressing pagan altar to the God of Snow.

She finds the town dismal; misses the affectionate flattery that a young lady expects to receive in the South; feels hostile to the women in Harry's family, who disapprove of her smoking and bobbed hair. And she is repelled by the thoroughly repressed, "righteous, narrow, and cheerless [people], without infinite possibilities for great sorrow and joy." While visiting the ice palace, which she thinks is far more morbid than the cemetery, she gets lost and is terrified to find herself utterly "alone with this presence that came out of the North, the dreary loneliness that rose from ice-bound whalers in the Arctic seas, from smokeless, trackless wastes where were strewn the whitened bones of adventure."[30] Though safely rescued, Sally Carrol realizes that she can never marry Harry Bellamy, who has something of the ice palace in his heart. So she breaks her engagement and returns to the drowsy heat of the South.

"May Day," a more complex and ambitious story, has a tragic ending that disqualified it for the *Post*. It had to be sold for a much lower fee. The story takes place in New York on May 1, 1919, a few months after Fitzgerald had left the army and was trying to start a career in advertising and in writing. The shifting, episodic scenes in this long work capture the chaotic celebration of this holiday as the déclassé hero and his proletarian mistress become involved with a series of upper- and lower-class characters. The dominant themes, which emerge as the mood changes from idealism to disillusionment, are betrayal and violence, moral and financial bankruptcy.

"May Day," whose title puns on the international signal for distress, charts the tragic decline of Gordon Sterrett. He has lost his job and, desperate for cash, attempts to borrow money from a rich Yale friend, Philip Dean, so he can pay off a girl who is blackmailing him and begin his career as an artist. The two college friends present a striking contrast in dress, wealth, health and moral well-being, and their mutual embarrassment makes them hate each other. When Philip finally refuses the loan, Gordon, observing him closely, suddenly notices how much his upper teeth project.

At this point the focus shifts to two proletarian soldiers, Gus Rose and Carrol Key (who has the middle names of Sally Happer and of Scott Fitzgerald). Just back from the war in Europe, they are trying to get some bootleg liquor from Key's brother, a waiter at Delmonico's, where the major characters converge. At this restaurant Edith Bradin, a former girlfriend of Gordon, has come to a Yale prom. As Edith admires herself and dances with her many beaux, her drunken date Peter Himmel talks to the two soldiers. Hearing about Edith from Philip Dean, the gloomy Gordon seeks her out, confesses his troubles and is rejected by her as brusquely as he had been by Dean. Edith then decides to visit her brother Henry, the editor of a Socialist newspaper, and Gordon is taken away from the party by his blackmailing girlfriend Jewel Hudson. While Edith is in the newspaper office, a mob of soldiers, who dislike the pacifistic and (in their eyes) pro-German Socialists, charge in, break Henry's leg and kill Key by pushing him out of a high window.

In yet another shift of mood, from tragedy to farce, Gus Rose, Peter Himmel, Philip Dean, Gordon Sterrett and Jewel Hudson, after drunken all-night parties, turn up the next morning at Childs'. Dean and Himmel, who has replaced Sterrett as Dean's friend, are ejected from the restaurant for throwing hash at the customers—as Fitzgerald sometimes did. They then go to the Biltmore for breakfast, remove the signs from the coatroom doors and adopt the vaudevillian roles of Mr. In and Mr. Out. In this unreal "segment of a whirring, spinning world," they practice their comic routine on the elevator man and conclude their surrealistic dialogue with Fitzgerald's rare bilingual pun on Himmel's German name:

> "What floor, please?" said the elevator man.
> "Any floor," said Mr. In.
> "Top floor," said Mr. Out.
> "This is the top floor," said the elevator man.
> "Have another floor put on," said Mr. Out.
> "Higher," said Mr. In.
> "Heaven," said Mr. Out.

In ironic counterpoint to this witty dialogue, Gordon Sterrett wakes up in a cheap hotel room with a hangover and realizes that he has been trapped into marriage with Jewel. He buys a gun and—leaning on his drawing materials—shoots himself.

Though the ending is rather forced and unconvincing, "May Day" remains an impressive story with a great number of carefully delineated characters. The subtly complicated plot is effectively placed in the social and political context of the May Day riots of 1919 when, Fitzgerald wrote, "the police rode down the demobilized country boys gaping at the orators in Madison Square."[31] But the story is personal as well as political. It conveys a powerful sense of loneliness and alienation, and poignantly describes what might have happened to Fitzgerald if he had failed to write his novel, lost his girl and succumbed to despair.

Flappers and Philosophers, his first collection of stories, was dedicated to Zelda and appeared in September 1920 to capitalize on the tremendous success of *This Side of Paradise.* It contained "The Ice Palace" but not "May Day," which was published too late to be included. The reviewers, slightly puzzled by this extremely uneven volume, were not nearly as enthusiastic as they had been about the novel. The *New York Times* complained that the "blatant tone of levity" almost drowned out "the perception of the literary substance" of Fitzgerald's work, but acknowledged that he "is working out an idiom, and it is an idiom at once universal, American and individual." The Chicago *Sunday Tribune* identified Fitzgerald as the laureate of the high-spirited younger generation: "There is something far more important than his popularity about Scott Fitzgerald. It is youth, uncompromising, unclothed, but not, as youth often is, dour and morbid. It is youth conscious of its powers and joyous in them." But the New York *Herald* perceived the superficiality beneath Fitzgerald's snappy dialogue and slick technique. His "faculty of characterizing people in a sentence in a way to make one thank Heaven one is not related to them; his facility in the use of the limited but pungent vocabulary of his type; his ingenuity in the hatching of unusual plots, all point to a case of cleverness in its most uncompromising form."[32] The next few years would test Fitzgerald's ability to go beyond mere cleverness and prove that he could fulfill his potential as a serious writer.

Chapter Five

THE BEAUTIFUL AND DAMNED AND
GREAT NECK, 1922–1924

I

In November 1921 the Fitzgeralds moved from their water-damaged summer home in Dellwood to a late-Victorian house at 626 Goodrich Avenue, three blocks south of Summit Avenue, in St. Paul. While awaiting the appearance of his new novel, Fitzgerald worked on his play, *The Vegetable*. The winter was long, cold and melancholy. Sobered by the repressive atmosphere and by the responsibility of caring for a new baby, Zelda was not in the mood for parties and discouraged visitors. Both she and Scott found provincial life very boring. In early March 1922 they made a brief visit to New York for the publication of Scott's novel.

The Beautiful and Damned was gratefully dedicated to three early mentors—Shane Leslie, George Jean Nathan and Maxwell Perkins—"in appreciation of much literary help and encouragement." The book covers the same prewar to postwar period (approximately 1910 to 1920) as *This Side of Paradise,* and also describes the personal history and genteel Romanticism of a wealthy and attractive young man. But while the earlier novel is witty, flippant and lighthearted, the later is ponderous and tragic, twice as long, less "literary" and more static. Its title suggests the protagonists' movement from the pampered life of the beautiful to the suffering of the damned.

The damnation (such as it is) is mainly caused by alcohol. Toward the end of the book the broken, debt-ridden hero, Anthony Patch, "awoke in the morning so nervous that Gloria [his wife] could feel him trembling in the bed before he could muster enough vitality to stumble into the pantry for a drink. He was intolerable now except under the influence of liquor, and as he seemed to decay and coarsen under her eyes, Gloria's soul and body shrank away from him." Anthony's drunken decline and unhappy marriage reflect Fitzgerald's personal problems and anticipate those of Dick Diver in *Tender is the Night*.

Money plays as dominant a role in this novel as it does in the Naturalistic works of Dreiser and Norris, whom Fitzgerald greatly admired. Anthony's relentless pursuit of money is very different from Amory Blaine's long denunciation of capitalism in *This Side of Paradise*. The middle name of the cynical, decadent and potentially wealthy hero, Anthony Comstock Patch, ironically alludes both to Anthony Comstock, a fierce contemporary crusader against vice, and to the Comstock Lode, the most valuable silver deposit in America, found near Virginia City, Nevada, in 1859. Anthony is born into a wealthy family, graduates from Harvard and lives on the expectation of a multi-million-dollar fortune. He is ruined, however, by having sufficient income so that he does not have to work, but not quite enough to maintain his luxurious way of life. The word "clean" recurs throughout the novel to describe beautiful or elegant women and mornings of hard work. But at the very end of the book, when the Patches are corrupted by inheriting thirty million dollars, Anthony overhears a fellow passenger describing the luxuriously dressed Gloria as "*unclean.*"

Wealth—or the promise of wealth—turns Anthony into a facile mediocrity. He believes nothing is worth doing and refuses to work, dabbles with a medieval essay and rejects his grandfather's offer to make him a war correspondent. As friends succeed in their own careers, Anthony dissipates himself in wild and finally repulsive parties during which "people broke things; people became sick in Gloria's bathroom; people spilled wine; people made unbelievable messes of the kitchenette." When his rich, priggish grandfather sees Anthony at one of these parties, he is horrified at his deterioration and disinherits him. After failing as a salesman, Anthony becomes seedy and unhealthy, and—like Gordon Sterrett in "May Day"—is cruelly rejected when he tries to borrow money from his old friend Maury Noble.

Before his precipitous decline, Anthony courts and marries the beautiful, vain, selfish and stupid Gloria Gilbert, who "took all the things of life to choose from and apportion, as though she were continually picking out presents for herself from an inexhaustible counter."[1] She hates staying home in the evening, always eclipses other women at parties and wants to marry a lover rather than a husband. Her marriage to Anthony is predictably wrecked by boredom and wastefulness, futile fighting and joyless parties.

Gloria's unhappy marriage makes her responsive to Joseph Bloeckman, the vice president of a film company, who does business with her father and who rises in the course of the novel as the more genteel characters decline. Like Samuel Goldwyn, Louis Mayer and most other movie executives of Fitzgerald's time, Bloeckman was a Jewish immigrant who started life in the humblest circumstances. After managing a side-show and owning a vaudeville house, he entered the film industry, in which his ambition, money and knowledge of show business propelled him to the top. When first introduced in the novel, he is insensitive, ingratiating and self-assured—and hopelessly in love with the wealthy and stylish Gloria.

Later in the novel, as Anthony becomes bored and Gloria disillusioned, Bloeckman reappears—now "infinitesimally improved, of subtler intonation, of more convincing ease"—and tempts her with a screen test. At the end of the long novel, the impoverished and humiliated Anthony has been rejected by all his friends. In a desperate attempt at blackmail, he impulsively phones Bloeckman (now called Joseph Black), who has usurped Anthony's rightful place in society and tried to steal his wife. He finds Bloeckman in a nightclub and falsely accuses him of keeping Gloria out of the movies. When Anthony calls him a "Goddamn Jew," Bloeckman beats him up and has him thrown into the gutter.

The Beautiful and Damned, like most of Fitzgerald's fiction, is extremely autobiographical. The Fitzgeralds' house in Westport, their servant Tana (who also appears in *Save Me the Waltz*) provided by the "Japanese Reliable Employment Agency," their extravagance, quarrels and drinking all appear in the novel. The long-awaited fortune is based on the sudden wealth acquired after the publication of *This Side of Paradise*, Gloria's movie test on an offer made to Scott and Zelda to star in the film version of that novel, Bloeckman's courtship of Gloria on Nathan's of Zelda, the laconic discussion about whether or not the pregnant Gloria should have a child ("If you have it I'll probably be glad. If you don't—well, that's all right too") on Zelda's decision to have her first abortion. Anthony has the same name as Zelda's father; and Gloria seems to have all Zelda's worst features without any of her redeeming qualities. As Scott later told their daughter: "Gloria was a much more trivial and vulgar person than your mother. I can't really say there was any resemblance except in the beauty and certain terms of expression she used, and also I naturally used many circumstantial events of our early married life. . . . We had a much better time than Anthony and Gloria had."[2]

The novel powerfully expresses Fitzgerald's fear of failure, sense of lost happiness and feeling of imminent collapse. Anthony's friend Richard Caramel, who publishes a decent novel and then becomes a contemptible example of a commercial and Hollywood hack, prefigures Fitzgerald's career as a compromised writer. Fitzgerald clearly saw Zelda's threat to his future as a writer, but could neither change his domestic life nor stop writing about it. Confused at times between his imaginative and his real existence, he behaved like his own fictional characters and would eventually be overcome by the very doom he had foreshadowed in *The Beautiful and Damned*.

The reviewers were kind to the novel and felt it represented a considerable improvement on *This Side of Paradise*. The liveliest notice, "Friend Husband's Latest" in the *New York Tribune* of April 2, 1922, was written by Zelda. In her first published work, she wittily urged readers to buy the book because Scott needed a winter overcoat and she craved an expensive cloth-of-gold dress and platinum ring with a complete circlet. She revealed, for the first time, that Scott—with her permission—had absorbed bits of her writing into his novel: "On one page I recognized a portion of an old diary of mine which mysteriously disappeared shortly after my marriage, and also scraps of letters which, though considerably edited, sound to me vaguely familiar. In fact, Mr. Fitzgerald—I believe that is how he spells his name—seems to believe that plagiarism begins at home." Two years later, after Zelda had published two articles, an interviewer in the *Smart Set* emphasized her idiosyncratic style and exaggerated his use of her material: "Mrs. Fitzgerald writes also. She has a queer, decadent style, luminous in its imagination, and very often Scott incorporates whole chapters of his wife's writing into his own books. He steals all her ideas for short stories and writes them as his own." Critics realized, early in Fitzgerald's career, that his novels ruthlessly exposed their emotional conflicts and made Zelda a participant in his fiction as well as a partner in his marriage.

Writing more seriously about *The Beautiful and Damned* in the *Nation,* Carl Van Doren concluded that "its excellence lies in the rendering not of the ordinary moral universe but of that detached, largely invented region where glittering youth plays at wit and love." In the *Smart Set,* the normally acerbic H. L. Mencken provided loyal praise: "Fitzgerald discharges his unaccustomed and difficult business with ingenuity and dignity. . . . If the result is not a complete success, it is nevertheless near enough to success to be worthy of respect. There is fine observation in it, and much penetrating detail, and the writing is solid and sound. . . . [With this novel] Fitzgerald ceases to be a *Wunderkind* and begins to come into his maturity."

Eager as always for honest criticism that would help him as a writer, Scott was particularly interested in the responses of Bishop and Wilson. In the New York *Herald,* Bishop emphasized the art and the vitality of the novel: "the book represents both in plan and execution an advance on *This Side of Paradise.* If, stylistically speaking, it is not so well written, neither is it so carelessly written. . . . Fitzgerald is at the moment of announcing the meaninglessness of life [one of the themes of the novel] magnificently alive."[3]

In 1921 Fitzgerald had solicited Wilson's comments on the typescript of the novel, just as he had done with the typescript of *This Side of Paradise* in 1919. Wilson, who would eventually supplant Mencken as the most influential critic in America, must have been pleased by his brief but flattering appearance in *The Beautiful and Damned* as Eugene Bronson, "whose articles in The New Democracy [*The New Republic*] were stamping him as a man with ideas transcending both vulgar timeliness and popular hysteria." In February 1921 Wilson had told a friend that he was impressed by Fitzgerald's ability to describe the seeds of destruction in his own marriage: "I am editing [not merely reading] the ms of Fitz's new novel, and, though I thought it was rather silly at first, I find it developing a genuine emotional power which he has scarcely displayed before. . . . It is all about him and Zelda." Wilson also reported that alcohol had aged Fitzgerald's handsome profile at the same time that experience had tempered his mind: "He looks like John Barrymore on the brink of the grave . . . but also, somehow, more intelligent than he used to."[4]

Wilson served as both private editor and public critic. He showed Fitzgerald his rather cruel composite review of the first two novels (to be published in the *Bookman* of March 1922) when it was still in typescript. Appreciating the serious analysis, Fitzgerald modestly accepted his comments on the unconvincing characters, the "lack of discipline and poverty of aesthetic ideas," and even told George Jean Nathan that he had enjoyed reading Wilson's criticism. Though he asked Wilson to delete references to his drinking and his criticism of the war, which would have offended Zelda's parents and hurt his reputation, he told him: "It is, of course, the only intelligible and intelligent thing of any length which has been written about me and my stuff—and like everything you write it seems to me pretty generally true. I am guilty of its every stricture and I take an extraordinary delight in its considered approbation. I don't see how I could possibly be offended at anything in it"—though Wilson clearly felt he well might be. Less confident and resilient authors might have been discouraged by the review, but Fitzgerald, mining the scrap of praise, was particularly pleased by Wilson's conclusion that "*The Beautiful and Damned,* imperfect though it is, makes an advance over *This Side of Paradise:* the style is more nearly mature and the subject more solidly unified, and there are scenes that are more convincing than any in his previous fiction."

The financial success matched the critical approval of the novel. It sold fifty thousand copies in the first few months and Fitzgerald earned another $2,500 by selling the film rights to Warner Brothers. But he was extremely unhappy when he saw the film in 1922 and told Oscar Kalman: "it's by *far* the worst movie I've ever seen in my life—cheap, vulgar, ill-constructed and shoddy. We were utterly ashamed of it."[5]

II

After a few months in St. Paul, the Fitzgeralds moved out to the lake for the summer season of 1922 and stayed at the White Bear Yacht Club, which relieved Zelda of her tedious household duties. Following the pattern established in 1920 by the publication of a novel and then a volume of stories, Fitzgerald capitalized on the success of *The Beautiful and Damned* by publishing his second collection of stories, *Tales of the Jazz Age*, in September 1922. In a letter to Max Perkins, written two months before publication, Fitzgerald used a culinary metaphor to comment on the disparate elements in the book: "I don't suppose such an assorted bill-of-fare as these eleven stories, novelettes, plays & 1 burlesque has ever been served up in one book before in the history of publishing."

In fact, he had had a difficult time finding sufficient material to round out his menu. He threw into the stew every story he had written since *Flappers and Philosophers*, except two extremely trivial pieces, and included three early works—"The Camel's Back," "Porcelain and Pink" and "Mr. Icky"—which he had excluded from his previous collection. The most innovative aspect of the book was the introduction to each story in the table of contents. Fitzgerald revealed that "The Curious Case of Benjamin Button" (which echoes the title of several Sherlock Holmes stories) "was inspired by a remark of Mark Twain's to the effect that it was a pity that the best part of life came at the beginning and the worst part at the end." In this fantasy, the hero is born an old man of seventy, gets progressively younger instead of older and finally becomes an infant. Fitzgerald also boasted that in January 1920 he had rapidly dashed off "The Camel's Back": "it was written during one day in the city of New Orleans, with the express purpose of buying a platinum and diamond wristwatch which cost six hundred dollars. I began it at seven in the morning and finished it at two o'clock the same night."[6]

Fitzgerald's note seems to confirm the idea expressed in Zelda's review that his writing had to be justified, even validated, by rapid composition and bountiful payment. It promoted an image of a hasty, superficially brilliant and calculating artist who controls the form as he dominates the commercial market. His self-created image of the story writer is very different from the author of the novels. The real Fitzgerald used the intimate details of his life in his work, struggled to find a form that would express his ideas and would spend years perfecting his novels.

Later on, Fitzgerald took a more serious view of *Tales of the Jazz Age*, which included two of his best stories: "May Day" and "The Diamond as Big as the Ritz." In his essay "Early Success" he emphasized the tragic aspect of his work and compared his doomed characters to those of a far more pessimistic English novelist. There was "a touch of disaster in them—the lovely young creatures in my novels went to ruin, the diamond mountains of my short stories blew up, my millionaires were as beautiful and damned as Thomas Hardy's peasants." In his *Notebooks* of the 1930s, he stressed his devotion to his craft, and his emotional and artistic exhaustion, punning on the double meaning of "price"—both the payment he received for the stories and the personal cost of writing them: "I have asked a lot of my emotions—one hundred and twenty stories. The price was high, right up with Kipling, because there was one little drop of something, not blood, not a tear, not my seed, but me more intimately than these, in every story, it was the extra I had. Now it is gone."[7]

Though it is impossible to reconcile this Romantic view of the artist, wringing his works out of his heart, with the many formulaic pieces he turned out, his best stories express the same themes as the novels. Though not as intimately self-revealing as in *The Beautiful and Damned*, in "The Diamond as Big as the Ritz" (1922) Fitzgerald does something more interesting: he deliberately imitates and parodies Edgar Poe's most famous story, "The Fall of the House of Usher" (1839).

Distancing himself from his youthful hero's obsession with the rich and disillusion with money, Fitzgerald cast his fable in the form of a fantasy—an extremely odd mixture of fairy tale, social satire, conventional romance and gothic horror. Poe characteristically emphasizes the decay and horror, Fitzgerald the glamour and luxury of the house; Poe's heroine is diseased and moribund, Fitzgerald's "the incarnation of physical perfection"; Poe has a tragic, Fitzgerald an ambiguously happy ending, but the numerous parallels, once perceived, are as clever and amusing as they are unmistakable.

Fitzgerald echoes the name of Poe's Usher by calling his hero

Unger. In both stories a young man, Poe's narrator and Fitzgerald's naive schoolboy, is invited to visit an "intimate" boyhood friend. The neurasthenic Roderick Usher comes from an ancient family, and Percy Washington boasts to the provincial Unger that his father is the richest man in the world. Both visitors represent a conventional ordinariness, a certain norm of behavior that helps to define the bizarre nature of the events they observe.

The narrator in Poe and the naive hero in Fitzgerald see their friends as part of a doomed family in a cursed house. Both mansions have intricate subterranean passages and are remote, isolated and unreal. Situated near a tarn, or lake, the monstrous houses contain an oppressive secret, and reflect the fearful mood of their inhabitants. Poe rolls out his familiar rhetoric and creaky gothic paraphernalia when describing the gloomy landscape and the decrepit building, with its barely perceptible fissure zigzagging down the facade from the roof to the watery foundation:

> [I looked] upon the mere house, and the simple landscape features of the domain—upon the bleak walls—upon the vacant eye-like windows—upon a few rank sedges—and upon a · few white trunks of decayed trees—with an utter depression of soul.

Fitzgerald adjusts his Babylonian fairyland style to match the pathological menace and corrupt attraction evoked by Poe:

> The Montana sunset lay between two mountains like a gigantic bruise from which dark arteries spread themselves over a poisoned sky. . . . After half an hour, the twilight had coagulated into dark.

Poe's hothouse rhetoric: "What was it—I paused to think—what was it that so unnerved me in the contemplation of the House of Usher?" is echoed in John Unger's troubled questions when he first arrives at the mountain house: "What desperate transaction lay hidden here? What moral expedient of a bizarre Croesus? What terrible and golden mystery?" Poe mentions the sentience of vegetable matter—the proliferating fungi that overspread and the decayed trees that surround the house—which reflects the doom of the family. Fitzgerald imitates the idea of the house as prison by describing an old family trapped, stupefied and corrupted by its selfish accumulation of useless wealth and by the enormous diamond that cannot be sold lest it destroy the economic foundations of the world.

Roderick Usher's dissipated artistic endeavors—his dreary dirges, phantasmagoric paintings and morbid poetry—are parodied in Fitzgerald by a kidnapped "landscape gardener, an architect, a designer of stage settings, and a French decadent poet" who fail to create as expected, go mad and are confined to a mental asylum. Only a crude "moving picture fella" from Hollywood succeeds in designing the lavish reception rooms and luxurious baths.

Both visitors briefly glimpse their host's sister as she passes through the house. Madeline Usher is cursed by the secret sexual guilt she shares with her brother. Kismine Washington (Unger's girlfriend and *kismet,* or fate) is cursed by the murder of the friends who had visited her in the past, could not be permitted to betray the secret wealth to the outside world, and were sacrificed after they had provided distraction and pleasure for the family.

Fitzgerald echoes the premature entombment of Madeline in one of the numerous vaults beneath the House of Usher in Braddock Washington's incarceration of the captured aviators in a deep, Poe-like pit, covered by an iron grating. Both young men are suddenly awakened in the middle of the night by a strange, frightening noise. Poe's familiar physiological description of fear when Usher realizes he has entombed the living Madeline:

> there came a strong shudder over his whole person; a sickly smile quivered about his lips; and I saw that he spoke in a low, hurried, and gibbering manner,

is equaled by Fitzgerald's fantastic simile when Unger perceives that the Washingtons have murdered their guests:

> Stunned with the horror of this revelation, John sat there open-mouthed, feeling the nerves of his body twitter like so many sparrows perched upon his spinal column.

In Poe, Usher throws back the ebony jaws of the huge antique panels to reveal his vengeful, blood-stained sister. In Fitzgerald, the ebony panel of one wall slides aside to reveal a uniformed manservant who assists Unger with his bath. Madeline murders her brother; Percy

Washington's grandfather was also compelled to murder his brother, who had the unfortunate Poe-and-Fitzgerald-like habit "of drinking himself into an indiscreet stupor." At the end of both stories the evil houses are completely destroyed, but the visitors manage to escape.

If the Ushers' sin is incest (a dominant theme in *Tender is the Night*), the Washingtons' is greed; and both sins lead to the final destruction of their family, dynasty and class. Building on Poe's story, Fitzgerald shows his hero moving from sheer enjoyment of the overwhelming luxury to an awareness of evil in the House of Washington and to a condemnation of its perverse corruption. Fitzgerald indicates, by the name of the family, that his purpose is allegorical and satirical. The House of Washington represents a vulgar, greedy America where everything—freedom, human values, art and culture—is sacrificed to gross wealth.

In "The Diamond as Big as the Ritz" Fitzgerald adds some witty remarks ("There go fifty thousand dollars' worth of slaves at prewar prices," cries Kismine, when the servants' quarters are destroyed by an aerial bombardment. "So few Americans have any respect for property") and he invents a brilliant scene in which Kismine's father, like Satan tempting Christ, offers a futile bribe to God. Unlike her father, Kismine has so slight a respect for property that she innocently carries away rhinestones instead of diamonds, and leaves herself and Unger penniless but virtuous at the end of the story. Fitzgerald's tale is a caustic warning about the American Dream. It reveals the illusory power of great wealth and the impossibility of being both rich and happy.

Fitzgerald's story, like Poe's, ends on a disillusioned and despairing note. John Unger realizes that without the diamonds to sustain him he will not be able to love Kismine for more than a few years. In "The Crack-Up" Fitzgerald returned to the bitter conclusion and the dominant symbol of his early Poesque story in order to illustrate the difference between authentic and meretricious experience: "In thirty-nine years an observant eye has learned to detect where the milk is watered and the sugar is sanded, the rhinestone passed for diamond and the stucco for stone."[8]

III

When the Minnesota summer had ended and they had been asked to leave the White Bear Yacht Club, the Fitzgeralds became utterly weary of wholesome provincial life and unable to face another dreary season of arctic winds and ice floes. In mid-October 1922 they eagerly returned to the Plaza Hotel, the center of their legendary life in New York. They soon found a comfortable place to rent at 6 Gateway Drive in Great Neck, an affluent town on the north shore of Long Island, about an hour from Manhattan. Alluding to Sinclair Lewis' bestselling satire on the American businessman, Zelda called it our "nifty little Babbitt-house."

In the early 1920s, before the film industry moved to Hollywood, many millionaires and celebrities from show business—Sam Goldwyn, Eddie Cantor, Ed Wynn, the actress Mae Murray and the songwriter Gene Buck as well as General John Pershing and Herbert Swope, the editor of the *New York World,* whose lavish parties inspired Jay Gatsby's—lived in Great Neck. At one party that October, Fitzgerald proudly told his cousin Cecilia Taylor, he met the English novelist Hugh Walpole, the columnist Franklin P. Adams, the Irish tenor John McCormack, the composers Rudolf Friml and Deems Taylor. His neighbors also included the popular actor Ernest Truex, who would star in Fitzgerald's play *The Vegetable,* and the sportswriter Ring Lardner, who became Scott's close friend.

Born in Niles, Michigan, in 1885, Lardner had been a journalist in Chicago and New York. He had written baseball stories in *You Know Me, Al* (1916), and had also published books of verse, satirical stories and a comic novel. "A tall sallow mournful man with a high-arched nose . . . dark hollow eyes and hollow cheeks," Lardner had a long, somber face that resembled Buster Keaton's. His son recalled that Ring, a puritan in his attitudes, found Zelda quite different from anyone he had ever known. He was impressed by her unconstrained speech and behavior, intrigued by her startling eyes and her pure complexion. Ring flattered Zelda with witty poems just as Nathan had done with seductive letters. But the courtly tributes of the married Lardner, unlike those of the bachelor Nathan, seemed harmless. Zelda found Ring less interesting than Nathan and, in a letter to Xandra Kalman, dismissed him as "a typical newspaper man whom I don't find very amusing." She probably thought Ring was a bad influence on her husband.

Ring found Scott a stimulating and responsive friend as well as a great admirer of his work. They shared a Midwestern background, an interest in sports, a dedication to the craft of writing and an addiction to drink. But they were affected very differently by alcohol. While Ring remained solemn and dignified, Scott became aggressive and vulgar. An alcoholic who could hold his drink, Ring became a model for the kind of drinker Scott would have liked to be. But he was also the mirror image of the doomed drinker that Scott feared he might become. The two congenial neighbors would stay up all night, talking and drinking gin, until Ring staggered to his feet and announced: "Well, I guess the children have left for school by this time—I might as well go home."[9] His son recalled that his father would often arrive home in a taxi as he was leaving for school and would have to be helped into the house.

In May 1923 Scott heard that Joseph Conrad, on a visit to America, was staying at the estate of his publisher, Frank Doubleday, in nearby Oyster Bay. Scott, who had kept a vigil outside Anatole France's house in 1921, now got drunk with Ring and, in a typically high-spirited but childish episode, danced on Doubleday's lawn in order to pay homage to the great novelist. But they were apprehended by a vigilant caretaker and thrown off the grounds for trespassing before they could gate-crash the house and attract Conrad's attention. Too timid to arrange a serious conversation, Scott did not seem to realize that a drunken dance was not the best way to impress the formal old sea captain, who always insisted on correct behavior.

Fascinated by the Fitzgeralds' personalities, Ring portrayed them in his work. In *What of It?* (1925) he said: "Mr. Fitzgerald is a novelist and Mrs. Fitzgerald is a novelty." In his burlesque of a popular fairy tale, he portrayed Scott as Prince Charming and colloquially wrote: "Her name was Zelda but they called her Cinderella on account of how the ashes and clinkers clung to her when she got up noons." And, exaggerating Scott's precocious literary debut, Ring remarked: "Mr. Fitzgerald sprung into fame with his novel *This Side of Paradise* which he turned out when only three years old and wrote the entire book with one hand. Mr. Fitzgerald never shaves while at work on his novels and looks very funny along towards the last five or six chapters."[10]

During the Christmas season of 1923 the two friends exchanged witty poems that expressed their mutual affection. Parodying the spirit of Christmas giving, Ring wrote:

We combed Fifth Avenue this last month
A hundred times if we combed it onth,
In search of something we thought would do
To give a person as nice as you.

We had no trouble selecting gifts
For the Ogden Armours and Louie Swifts,
The Otto Kahns and the George F. Bakers,
The Munns and the Rodman Wanamakers.

It's a simple matter to pick things out
For people one isn't wild about,
But you, you wonderful pal and friend, you!
We couldn't find anything fit to send you.

Parodying Ring's parody, Scott revealed their similarity of style and taste. Shifting the venue to the distinctly less elegant Third Avenue, he varied Ring's catalogue of millionaires (including the transportation executive Teddy Shonts) and imitated his "down-hoem" diction:

You combed Third Avenue last year
    For some small gift that was not too dear
—Like a candy cane or a worn out truss—
    To give to a loving friend like us
You'd found gold eggs for such wealthy hicks
    As the Edsel Fords and the Pittsburgh Fricks
The Andy Mellons, the Teddy Shonts
    The Coleman T. and Pierre du Ponts
But not one gift to brighten our hoem
—So I'm sending you back your Goddamn poem.

After the Fitzgeralds had settled on the Riviera in May 1924, Ring sent Zelda a mock-serious love poem in which he tried to steal her away from her unworthy husband and lure her back to Prohibition-damned America:

So, dearie, when your tender heart
Of all his coarseness tires,
Just cable me and I will start
Immediately for Hyères.

To hell with Scott Fitzgerald then!
To hell with Scott, his daughter!
It's you and I back home again,
To Great Neck where the men are men
And booze is ¾ water.[11]

Scott, who kept a careful record of his publications and was eager
for literary fame, was shocked by Ring's indifference to—even scorn
for—his own work. Ring Lardner, Jr., reporting a characteristic incident, wrote that "getting into a taxi with a friend, Ring dropped a
manuscript and the pages scattered in the street. The friend gathered
what he could, but there were two pages missing. 'Makes no difference,
it's for *Cosmopolitan*,' Ring said." In 1923 Fitzgerald collected a dozen
of Ring's best stories by photographing old issues of magazines in the
public library and persuaded Max Perkins to publish them under the
catchy but misleading title, *How to Write Short Stories* (1924). Ring's
parodic introduction to his stories in this volume was influenced by
Scott's flippant introduction in *Tales of the Jazz Age* (1922). Scott's
patronage helped arouse interest in the book, which first attracted serious critical attention to Ring's sardonic humor.

Ernest Hemingway had once admired and imitated Lardner. But
he was unimpressed by this volume and jealous of Scott's admiration for
Ring's work. In April 1926, just after Scott had dedicated *All the Sad
Young Men* "To Ring and Ellis Lardner," Hemingway rather harshly
wrote: "Your friend Ring is hampered by lack of intelligence, lack of
any aesthetic appreciation, terrible repressions and bitterness." But
Scott reaffirmed his admiration and tried to explain the reasons for this
bitterness in one of his finest and most revealing essays—the obituary
memoir of Ring Lardner in 1933.

Scott idealized his old friend as "Proud, shy, solemn, shrewd, polite,
brave, kind, merciful, honorable," and added that these qualities
aroused people's affection as well as their awe. He poignantly recalled
his last visit to Ring, when alcohol had undermined his health and

made him seem like a *memento mori:* "it was terribly sad to see that six feet three inches of kindness stretched out ineffectual in the hospital room. His fingers trembled with a match, the tight skin on his handsome skull was marked as a mask of misery and nervous pain," and he seemed pursued by impenetrable despair. In a self-reflective passage, Scott wrote that Ring "had, long before his death, ceased to find amusement in dissipation." Thinking of Ring's minatory example and of his own sell-out to Hollywood and the *Post,* Scott declared: "whatever Ring's achievement was, it fell short of the achievement he was capable of, and this because of a cynical attitude toward his work."[12]

Scott paid his final tribute to Ring by portraying him as the alcoholic composer Abe North in *Tender is the Night* (1934). "His voice was slow and shy," Scott wrote, "he had one of the saddest faces [she] had ever seen, the high cheekbones of an Indian, a long upper lip, and enormous deep-set dark golden eyes." Though physically and intellectually impressive, Abe is also weak, self-indulgent and bitter. His friends are aware of his talent, but frightened by his urge to self-destruction: "All of them were conscious of the solemn dignity that flowed from him, of his achievement, fragmentary, suggestive and surpassed. But they were frightened at his survivant will, once a will to live, now become a will to die."[13]

IV

Fitzgerald's move from St. Paul to New York placed him in the center of literary life, enabling him to keep in touch with old friends and meet a number of new writers: John Dos Passos, P. G. Wodehouse, Van Wyck Brooks, Carl Van Vechten, Theodore Dreiser and Rebecca West. The nearsighted and introspective Dos Passos was the grandson of an immigrant cobbler from Portuguese Madeira and the illegitimate son of a successful New York lawyer. Born in Chicago in 1896, he had been educated in Europe and at the Choate School. After graduating from Harvard, he drove ambulances during the war in France and Italy. He had traveled widely in Spain and the Middle East; and his war novel, *Three Soldiers* (1921), had been favorably reviewed by Fitzgerald in the *St. Paul Daily News.*

Dos Passos first met Scott and Zelda at the Plaza Hotel in October

1922. They introduced him to Sherwood Anderson, gave him cocktails and champagne, and then asked the shy writer embarrassing questions about his sex life. Anderson left after a lunch of lobster croquettes, and Dos Passos drove out to Great Neck in their chauffeured red touring car to help them search for a house. They had plenty of time to talk that day and Dos Passos found Fitzgerald interesting, despite his intellectual limitations: "When he talked about writing his mind, which seemed to me full of preposterous notions about most things, became clear and hard as a diamond. He didn't look at landscape, he had no taste for food or wine or painting, little ear for music except for the most rudimentary popular songs, but about writing he was a born professional."

After searching in vain for a suitable house, they visited Ring Lardner, who was completely drunk. On the way back to the city, they stopped at an amusement park. Dos Passos and Zelda rode together on a Ferris wheel, and an alarming gulf opened between them when he realized that she was emotionally disturbed: "I had come up against that basic fissure in her mental processes that was to have such tragic consequences. Though she was so very lovely, I had come upon something that frightened and repelled me, even physically." Zelda sulked and Scott drank during the rest of the trip, and Dos Passos was glad to part with them in front of the Plaza.

Though most writers emphasized Fitzgerald's drunkenness and bizarre behavior, the English humorist P. G. Wodehouse found Scott sober and charming, though rather seedy, when he ran into him at the village train station. As Wodehouse wrote to a friend: "I have also met Scott Fitzgerald. In fact I met him again this morning. He was off to New York with Truex, who is doing his play *The Vegetable*. I believe these stories you hear about his drinking are exaggerated. He seems quite normal, and a very nice chap indeed. You would like him. The thing is he goes to New York with a scrubby chin, looking foul. I suppose he gets a shave when he arrives, but it doesn't show him at his best in Great Neck. I would like to see more of him."[14]

In contrast to Wodehouse, the wealthy, Harvard-educated critic and biographer Van Wyck Brooks remarked on Fitzgerald's unconventional behavior and conspicuous extravagance. After arriving late for a Manhattan dinner party in 1923, the Fitzgeralds promptly fell asleep at the table. Scott went to lie down more comfortably in the living room, but woke up suddenly to take command of the festivities and "telephone an order for two cases of champagne, together with a fleet of taxis to take us to a night club."

The following year, Edmund Wilson used Brooks in his dialogue, "Imaginary Conversations: Mr. Van Wyck Brooks and Mr. Scott Fitzgerald," to contrast the two men. Continuing his critical debate with Fitzgerald, Wilson attributed his *own* ideas to the thorough, learned and scholarly Brooks, who "knows far more about American literature than anybody else in the world," and gave Brooks all the best lines. In this conversation, Brooks, the mouthpiece for Wilson, freely censured Fitzgerald for haste, superficiality and commercialism; for writing too much and too fast; and for allowing himself to be corrupted by high-paying magazines like the *Post.* This influential and frequently reprinted essay contained some useful admonitions, and portrayed Fitzgerald as foolish, shallow and outclassed by the heavyweight critic.

The sophisticated aesthete and novelist Carl Van Vechten first met Fitzgerald at a New York party in 1923, saw him socially in Hollywood and Delaware, and photographed him in 1937. Like Dos Passos and Brooks, Van Vechten usually saw Scott when he was getting drunk and quarreling with Zelda. He closely observed the Fitzgeralds, who were trying to live up to their dashing reputation, and portrayed them as David and Rilda Westlake in his novel *Parties* (1930). In this work Rilda influences most of David's behavior. He does everything either to please or to annoy her, and they torture each other because they love each other. But, Rilda complains, with considerable insight: "Our damned faithfulness, as you call it, our clean 'fidelity,' doesn't get us very far. We follow each other around in circles, loving and hating and wounding. We're both so sadistic. It's really too bad one of us isn't a masochist."[15]

Van Vechten was present—along with Mencken, Sherwood Anderson, Burton Rascoe and the novelist Llewelyn Powys—at a deadly party given by Theodore Dreiser. The dour novelist had no idea how to entertain his guests, lined them up in straight-backed chairs, did not introduce them to one another and failed to provide any drink. At this point Fitzgerald staggered in drunk, clutching a bottle of excellent champagne. In an attempt to enliven the proceedings, he generously declared: "Mr. Dreiser, I get a great kick out of your books," and handed over the precious bottle. Instead of offering it to his thirsty guests, Dreiser carefully placed it in the icebox, and the party sank back into its torpor.

Another social mishap occurred just after Fitzgerald told Thomas Boyd, early in 1924, that the young English novelist "Rebecca West and a rather (not *too*) literary crowd are coming out Sunday for a rather formal party and Zelda's scared." Fitzgerald told Rebecca West, the guest of honor, that someone would pick her up and drive her from Manhattan out to Great Neck. Due to a typical misunderstanding, she was not picked up. Since she did not know Fitzgerald's address, she spent the entire evening waiting for his call in her hotel room. Insulted by her failure to appear, Fitzgerald made fun of her at dinner. When they were finally reconciled on the French Riviera in the summer of 1925 Zelda, always uncomfortable with intellectuals, cattily said that West looked "like an advertisement for cauliflower ears and [was] entirely surrounded by fairies—male."[16]

Apart from Lardner, Fitzgerald's most important friend during the Great Neck years was the patrician war hero and polo star, Tommy Hitchcock, whom he often saw playing in championship matches at the Meadow Brook Club on Long Island. Born into a wealthy, upper-class family in 1900, Tommy attended the Fay School and St. Paul's. During the war, while still in his teens, he joined the legendary Lafayette Corps of flyers. Shot down and wounded in German territory, he escaped to Switzerland by jumping off a moving train. His bravery earned him the Croix de Guerre with three palms.

After the war Tommy attended Harvard and (like Jay Gatsby) spent a term or two at Oxford. He married a steel heiress, became a successful investment banker with Lehman Brothers and dominated the international polo scene as a ten-goal player from 1919 to 1939. Tommy's biographer writes that "he was deficient in the graces, as 'country' aristocrats often are, sloppy in dress and awkward in manner; but he possessed in full measure the virtues valued by his class: modesty, loyalty, and magnanimity. . . . [Scott's Princeton friend] David Bruce, who shared an apartment with Hitchcock during World War II, went so far as to call him the only 'perfect' man he'd ever met."[17]

Fitzgerald idolized Tommy, who had many of the qualities he himself desired. Tommy had the great wealth, social class and fine breeding of Gerald Murphy (whom Scott would meet in 1925) combined with the good looks, athletic ability and heroic war record of Ernest Hemingway. In April 1929 Scott told Perkins that a French book was about to appear that would describe Tommy's daring escape from the German train. In his *Notebooks,* Scott contrasted two of his personal heroes and suggested how they would become models for the fictional characters in *Tender is the Night:* "Difference in conversation between Gerald Murphy and Tommy Hitchcock. Tommy doesn't answer foolish questions or trivial questions [from Fitzgerald]. . . . Trace a character who once was like Gerald and who now tends toward Tommy Hitchcock's impatience with fools." Toward the end of his life, Scott used Tommy's career to inspire his daughter to take her college studies more seriously: "Tommy Hitchcock, who came back from England in 1919 already a newspaper hero in his escapes from Germany and the greatest polo player in the world—went up to Harvard in the same year to become *a freshman*—because he had the humility to ask himself 'Do I know anything?' That combination is what forever will put him in my pantheon of heroes."

Tommy Hitchcock inspired Scott's portrait of both Tom Buchanan in *The Great Gatsby* and Tommy Barban in *Tender is the Night.* Hitchcock was an exceptionally powerful man with wide shoulders and big arms. Sensing in the urbane, charming and greatly admired Tommy a ruthlessness, even brutality, which had enabled him to become "the greatest polo player in the world," Scott attributed these qualities to his fictional characters. Like Tommy Hitchcock, Tom Buchanan came from an enormously wealthy family, was a nationally known sports figure and was seen "wherever people played polo and were rich together." Buchanan's clothes could not "hide the enormous power of that body—he seemed to fill those glistening boots until he strained the top lacing, and you could see a great pack of muscle shifting when his shoulder moved under his thin coat. It was a body capable of enormous leverage—a cruel body."

In *Tender is the Night,* as in *The Great Gatsby,* the rather delicate Fitzgerald stresses Tommy's physical power. He writes of the tough soldier of fortune, Tommy Barban: "He was tall and his body was hard but overspare save for the bunched force gathered in his shoulders and upper arms."[18] Like Hitchcock, Barban has the Harvard manner and intimidates men with his overwhelming courage.

V

Fitzgerald had always been keenly interested in the theater. He had written and acted in four plays in St. Paul, had written the lyrics for three Triangle Club musicals at Princeton, and had included theatrical scenes and dramatic dialogue in his first two novels. All this potentially valuable experience led directly to the failure of *The Vegetable*. Like Henry James and Joseph Conrad, Fitzgerald was a fine novelist but an unsuccessful dramatist. His failure in the theater foreshadowed his consistently unhappy experiences as a Hollywood screenwriter.

The Vegetable, or From President to Postman was inspired by the pervasive stupidity, gross cronyism and rampant corruption—in the Veterans Bureau, the Departments of Justice and the Interior—during the administration of the philistine president, Warren Harding, in the early 1920s. While working on the play in March 1922 Fitzgerald, who had advocated Socialism in *This Side of Paradise* and portrayed the Socialists sympathetically in "May Day," seemed to be wavering in his egalitarian beliefs. In a letter to Perkins, he expressed fear of the masses and denounced mob rule: "freedom has produced the greatest tyranny under the sun. I'm still a socialist but sometimes I dread that things will grow worse and worse the more the people nominally rule."

The odd and unappealing title of the play came from Mencken's satiric essay "On Being an American," which attacked the Babbitt-like conformity of America: "Here is a country in which it is an axiom that a businessman shall be a member of the Chamber of Commerce, an admirer of [the steel magnate] Charles M. Schwab, a reader of the *Saturday Evening Post*, a golfer—in brief, a vegetable." The fantastic and satiric plot reverses the log cabin to White House myth. In the first act, on the eve of Warren Harding's nomination, Jerry Frost, an unhappily married railroad clerk who aspires to be a postman, gets drunk and is surprised to discover that he has become the Republican candidate for president. In the dream sequence of the second act, Frost suddenly finds himself and his small-town family in the White House. But his tenure of office is a predictable series of disasters. He suffers threats of impeachment from Idaho senators, incitements to war from a belligerent general, bankruptcy of the Treasury by his Bible-thumping father and self-righteous lectures from the Supreme Court. In the final act

Frost wakes up to find it has all been a dream. He finds his true calling as a postman and sorts out the problems of his marriage. An unintentionally funny line occurs at the end of the play when Charlotte, his once estranged but now reconciled wife, tells Frost, who has been absent for some time: "I'll be waiting. [*Quickly.*] . . . Stop by a store and get some rubbers."[19]

Edmund Wilson, who had admired Fitzgerald's fantasy and humor when they collaborated on an undergraduate musical comedy, showed real enthusiasm when he read *The Vegetable* in typescript. In a critical misjudgment, he told Fitzgerald that the play was "one of the best things you ever wrote" and "the best American comedy ever written." Inflating the merits of Fitzgerald's worst full-length work and encouraging the weakest aspect of his talent, he urged Fitzgerald "to go on writing plays." Wilson, then married to the actress Mary Blair, also tried to place the play in New York. In gratitude for his support, Fitzgerald dedicated the work to his childhood friend Katherine Tighe and to "Edmund Wilson, Jr. / Who deleted many absurdities / From my first two novels I recommend / The absurdities set down here." When the play was published in April 1923, Wilson opposed the generally negative response, stuck to his earlier judgment and called it "a fantastic and satiric comedy carried off with exhilarating humor. . . . I do not know of any dialogue by an American which is lighter, more graceful or more witty."

After the publication of the play had attracted some backers, Fitzgerald persuaded his Great Neck neighbor Ernest Truex to take the role of Jerry Frost. A well-known actor, six years older than Scott, Truex had been on stage from early childhood. He played the impish hero with Mary Pickford in silent films and later became a typically henpecked husband in the talkies.

The Vegetable opened on November 10, 1923, at Nixon's Apollo Theater, not far from Princeton, in Atlantic City, New Jersey. Zelda told Xandra Kalman that "the first act went fine but Ernest says he has *never* had an experience on stage like the second. I *heard* one woman hit the roof when the bible was mentioned. They seemed to think it was sacrilegious or something. People were so obviously bored!" Shocked and disappointed by the hostile reception, Fitzgerald agreed with Zelda's account and described the event with a pun on his hero's name: "It was a colossal frost. People left their seats and walked out, people rustled their programs and talked audibly in bored impatient whispers. After the second act I wanted to stop the show and say it was all a mistake but the actors struggled heroically on."[20] Though he desperately tried to repair the defects, the tryout closed after only one week.

When a director expressed interest in reviving the play in 1936, Fitzgerald frankly mentioned its flaws and warned him away from it: "It reads well, but there is some difference between the first and second acts that is so disparate that every time a Little Theatre has produced it (and many of them have tried it), it has been a failure in a big way." The drama critic Martin Esslin, who had a higher opinion of the play than Fitzgerald, thought the experimental second act "must be regarded as an early example of the Theatre of the Absurd, at least in the middle part, which gives a grotesque nonsense version of life at the White House." But he agreed with the author that its "attempt to leave the naturalistic convention fails by remaining firmly anchored within it" during the first and third acts.[21]

The failure of *The Vegetable*, Fitzgerald's first professional setback, made him realize that he could no longer count on the success of every book, or continue to drink and spend without suffering the consequences. In a confessional letter to Perkins he criticized his dependence on Zelda and his lack of self-confidence, and accused himself of "Laziness; Referring everything to Zelda—a terrible habit, nothing ought to be referred to anybody till it's finished; Word consciousness—self doubt." He suddenly "realized how much I've—well, almost *deteriorated* in the three years since I've finished *The Beautiful and Damned*," and vowed to change his habits and become more serious: "If I'd spent this time reading or travelling or doing anything—even staying healthy—it'd be different but I spent it uselessly, neither in study nor in contemplation but only in drinking and raising hell generally." On one chaotic occasion, for example, the drunken Scott had suddenly stood up at his dinner party, torn the cloth off the table and stormed out of the room amid the clatter of broken glass. Zelda, maintaining her sang-froid, turned to her guests and politely asked: "Shall we have our coffee in the next room?"

Fitzgerald was unable to control his enormous expenses and live on the extraordinarily high income of $36,000 a year—about twenty times more than the average American earned. Perkins (like Mencken) blamed Zelda and wrote: "Scott was extravagant, but not like her; money went through her fingers like water; she wanted everything; she kept him writing for the magazines." Fitzgerald had counted on *The Vegetable* to bring in a small fortune. When it failed, he was forced to go on the wagon and write himself out of debt. Working in a large, bare, badly heated room over the garage on Gateway Drive, he took two days to turn out a seven-thousand-word story that paid the rent and the most pressing bills. He then worked "twelve hours a day for five weeks to rise from abject poverty back into the middle class."[22] By March 1924 he had earned $16,500 from magazine stories, paid off his debt to Harold Ober and financed a trip to Europe. The Riviera would provide a stimulating change, cost less than Great Neck and be more conducive to work. Though he had told Wilson that "France made me sick," he sailed there in early May to write *The Great Gatsby*.

Chapter Six

EUROPE AND
THE GREAT GATSBY, 1924–1925

I

Scott and Zelda stopped in Paris en route to the Riviera in May 1924 and saw his old Princeton friend John Peale Bishop. He had married a wealthy but pretentious, talkative and boring Chicago socialite, and had not been stimulated by expatriate life in France. Archibald MacLeish, who had an affair with Margaret Bishop that year, called her a misplaced clubwoman whose money had emasculated her husband. And Fitzgerald, whose career had taken off while Bishop's remained stagnant, criticized in a letter to Edmund Wilson the dullness and weakness of his former mentor: "Yes, John seemed to us a beaten man—with his tiny frail mustache—but perhaps only morally. Whether or no he still echoes the opinions of others I don't know—to me he said nothing at all. In fact, I remember not a line (I was drunk and voluble myself though)." Fitzgerald continued to see his friend for nostalgic reasons and remarked two years later that Bishop "was here with his unspeakably awful wife. He seems anemic and washed out, a memory of the past so far as I'm concerned." Scott did not help matters on this occasion by getting drunk and writing on Margaret's expensive dress with a lipstick.

After about ten days in Paris, the Fitzgeralds traveled south and pitched up at Grimm's Park Hotel in Hyères. This staid establishment featured goat meat every evening and was populated by elderly English invalids who treated the brash Americans with icy hostility. Despite his dislike of these people, Fitzgerald hired a bossy English nanny, Lillian Maddock, to live with the family and look after their small daughter. According to Hemingway, Miss Maddock taught Scottie to speak with a Cockney accent.

After searching eastward along the coast for several weeks, they finally found Villa Marie, a clean, cool house set on a hill above St.-Raphaël. "It was a red little town," Scott wrote, "built close to the sea, with gay red-roofed houses and an air of repressed carnival about it."[1] The charming villa had a winding gravel driveway, a large terraced garden filled with exotic plants and tiled balconies overlooking the glistening Mediterranean. They bought a small Renault and settled down with their cook, maid and nanny to a more orderly way of life.

The Fitzgeralds seemed to live in France without having any significant contact with the country. The only French people they knew were their servants (who grew rich by constantly cheating them). They met very few French writers and ignored the avant-garde. Uninterested, as Dos Passos had noted, in museums and churches, art and music, good food and wine, and unable to understand an alien culture, the Fitzgeralds inhabited a Europe of hotels and nightclubs, bars and beaches that catered to wealthy Americans.

Despite his French courses at Princeton, Fitzgerald had no knowledge of the language. He never bothered to learn more than taxi-cab French nor made the slightest effort to pronounce it correctly. Even Scottie, who soon mastered the tongue, later remarked on "his really horrendous French" and "his atrocious accent." Fitzgerald gave an accurate and self-mocking example of his franglais when he quoted: "'Je suis a stranger here,' I said in flawless French. 'Je veux aller to le best hotel dans le town.'"[2] If pushed, his eloquent French could rise to: "*Très bien,* you son-of-a-bitch!"

The Fitzgeralds' closest friends in Europe, Gerald and Sara Murphy, were, culturally speaking, their exact antithesis. They first met this Jamesian couple in Paris in May 1924 through Gerald's sister, Esther, who was a Great Neck friend. Gerald's father owned the Fifth Avenue leather goods shop, Mark Cross, which was worth two million dollars

when Gerald inherited it in 1931. Eight years older than Scott, a dandy
in dress and manner, he had graduated from Yale and come to Europe
in 1921. But Gerald's looks were somewhat spoiled by premature bald-
ness and rather thick lips. His beautiful wife Sara, five years older than
Gerald, was a warm, motherly, solid and sensible woman. The daughter
of a wealthy ink manufacturer in Cincinnati, Ohio, she owned twenty-
seven substantial acres in East Hampton, Long Island, and had a fortune of two hundred thousand dollars. The Murphys were among the
first to discover that the South of France could be pleasant in the summer and to make it fashionable to remain there (instead of traveling
north to Deauville or west to Biarritz) during the long hot season. In
the summer of 1924 the Murphys were staying in the Hôtel du Cap in
Antibes while their new house, the Villa America, was being renovated.

The Murphys lived in hedonistic luxury and tended to dissipate
their energy in the perfection of trivialities: Gerald's Zen-like ritual of
raking the beach and Sara's absorption with objects to furnish their
house. As Gerald confessed, "we did nothing notable except enjoy ourselves." But he was also a kind, cultured and exquisitely civilized man,
with a serious interest in the arts and a minor talent as a painter. Instead
of using his wealth selfishly for himself and his family, he used it generously for his friends and provided lavish hospitality for many of the leading French and American artists of the 1920s. Gerald was a good husband and father, and a loyal friend. When struck by tragedy, he endured
it with great courage. To companions like Dos Passos, the elegant couple
seemed to be the essence of perfection: "The Murphys were rich. They
were goodlooking. They dressed brilliantly. They were canny about the
arts. They had a knack for entertaining. They had lovely children."

In contrast to the Princeton bachelors who had swarmed around
Zelda in New York, most of the Fitzgeralds' friends on the Riviera were
married. Scott and Zelda soon became absorbed into the Murphys'
social circle, which included a core of Yale friends: Archibald
MacLeish, Cole Porter, the playwrights Philip Barry and Donald
Ogden Stewart (whom Fitzgerald had known in St. Paul); expatriate
writers like Dos Passos and Hemingway; dancers and designers from
the Russian Ballet; and abstract painters like Picasso, Miró and Juan
Gris. Scottie remembered the small Braque and Picasso drawings that
her parents bought, with the Murphys' encouragement, and carried
with them on their travels through Europe.

The Murphys also introduced them to another lively and cultured couple, Dick and Alice Lee Myers. Dick was a large, jolly, humorous man, an amateur musician who had studied piano with Nadia Boulanger and composed songs, a bon viveur who enjoyed the good things of life. Both Dick and Alice Lee had graduated from the University of Chicago. He had been a soldier during the war, she a nurse; and after a nine-year engagement, they had finally married in 1920. Dick worked for American Express in Paris, had a country house in Normandy, lived comfortably on his American salary and stayed on in France until 1932.

Their daughter Fanny (a lifelong friend of Scottie) remembers Scott ringing their doorbell during lunchtime and staggering into their Paris flat while drunk. When Fanny finished eating and went to her bedroom, she was surprised to find Scott in her bed. Alice, sitting next to him, tactfully explained that he was "having a little lie down." When Scott recovered, he told Fanny that she was very pretty and she turned bright red upon receiving her first compliment.

Scott's easy intimacy with the Myers allowed free expression of his bizarre sense of humor. In 1928 he annotated a clipping of the murderer Ruth Snyder, strapped into the electric chair, with a touching inscription, ostensibly written by Snyder but actually by Scott. In a similar vein, he gave the Myers an *enlarged* edition of Marie Stopes' *Contraception* (1928), with a witty and flirtatious inscription to Alice Lee: "I felt you should have this. So that Dick should never have an awful surprise—he is too nice a fellow. Yours in Sin, but, I hope, *sincere* sin. F. Scott Fitzgerald."[3]

The Fitzgeralds and Murphys had little in common apart from the men's Irish background and love of literature, but they had an abiding affection for each other. In contrast to the spontaneous and chaotic Fitzgeralds, the Murphys (who appear as the Cornings in Zelda's unpublished novel *Caesar's Things*) carefully planned every detail of their life and turned every event into a theatrical occasion: "All of the Cornings' parties have the air of having been rehearsed. . . . He perfects 'his garden, his gadgets, his graces, his retainers, his dependents, his children.'"

. Scott was genuinely interested in the Murphys' three children and named the child in "Babylon Revisited" after their daughter Honoria, who was three years older than Scottie. Noticing Honoria's favorite red

1. EDWARD FITZGERALD WITH
SCOTT, BUFFALO, CHRISTMAS 1899:
A small, inarticulate, ineffectual
man with well-cut clothes and fine
Southern manners. *(Princeton
University Library)*

2. MOLLIE FITZGERALD, C. 1905:
"The most awkward and the
homeliest woman I ever saw."
(Princeton University Library)

13. RING LARDNER, CHICAGO, C. 1910:

"A tall sallow mournful man with a higharched nose . . . dark hollow eyes and hollow cheeks." *(Ring Lardner, Jr.)*

14. TOMMY HITCHCOCK, C. 1933:

"He was tall and his body was hard but overspare save for the bunched force gathered in his shoulders and upper arms." *(Mrs. Thomas Hitchcock)*

dress and favorite red flowers in her mother's garden, and curious about her tastes, Scott sweetly asked her: "Why do you like red?" He was full of imagination at Scottie's birthday party, for which Zelda made elaborate papier-mâché costumes and Scott—down on the floor and playing with the children—conducted a complicated war with armies of toy soldiers and used a large real beetle to play the part of an evil dragon.[4]

Both Murphys were attracted to Zelda, who shared their passion for swimming and sunbathing, and who would pronounce "Say-reh" to make it sound like her own maiden name. Impressed by Zelda's intensity and gracefulness, Gerald said "she had a rather powerful, hawk-like expression, very beautiful features, not classic, and extremely penetrating eyes, and a very beautiful figure, and she moved beautifully." Like most other friends, he was struck by Zelda's defiant behavior. At the Casino in Juan-les Pins the exhibitionistic Zelda, who had exposed her bottom during the Hawaiian pageant in Montgomery, suddenly got up from their table, lifted her skirt above her waist and danced like Salomé before a startled audience.

Sara noticed that Zelda, who became upset if Scott was criticized, loyally came to his defense and backed him up in everything. She still quarreled with Scott. But, in contrast to their violent early rows (which were recorded in Alex McKaig's diary), they now closed ranks and no longer fought in public. Philip Barry's wife, Ellen, thought they managed to conceal their marriage problems, but competed openly to attract their friends' attention. Scott would slip into the pantry to throw down a secret gin, then reappear to exclaim, "you all like Zelda better than me" and express self-pity by rolling in the dust of the garden. Ellen found Scott rather pathetic and desperately in need of reassurance.

Gerald, at times exasperated with Fitzgerald, frankly declared: "I don't think we could have taken Scott alone." Scott's childish insecurity and desire to be the center of interest led him, during the 1920s, to abuse the kindness and test the friendship of the Murphys just as he had done with his fellow officers in the army. But Gerald, amazingly tolerant of Scott's drunken antics and deeply concerned about him, was more worried than angry about his behavior. Once, when they were leaving the dance floor at the Casino, Scott deliberately fell down and expected Gerald to pick him up. But Gerald, adopting the role of a strict father with a naughty child, told him: "We're not at Princeton, I'm not your roommate, get up yourself." On another occasion, irritated by the formality of the Murphys' dinner party, Scott provocatively threw a soft fig at the bare back of a titled guest and became furious when she and everyone else ignored his boorish behavior.

Scott's worst offense, which stretched Gerald's tolerance to the breaking point, led to temporary banishment from the Villa America. It seemed to justify Gerald's angry statement that "he really had the most appalling sense of humor, sophomoric and—well, trashy." Feeling that his fellow guests were not paying sufficient attention to him, Scott seemed determined to destroy the formal dinner party. He "began throwing Sara's gold-flecked Venetian wineglasses over the garden wall. He had smashed three of them this way before Gerald stopped him. As the party was breaking up, Gerald went up to Scott (among the last to leave) and told him that he would not be welcome in their house for three weeks."[5] While exiled from their parties, Scott made his presence felt by throwing a can of garbage onto the patio as the Murphys were dining.

Scott had another extremely irritating habit, which led the gentle Sara to censure him. To compensate for his lack of insight and satisfy his curiosity, he would grill friends—even when sober—with tedious and often embarrassing personal questions. Both Donald Stewart and Dos Passos had objected to this habit, which Zelda described as "nagging and asking and third-degreeing his acquaintances." Sara, in a frank, exasperated yet sympathetic and well-intentioned letter, also criticized his naive interrogation, and used the same word as Gerald to describe his intolerable behavior: "You can't expect anyone to like or stand a *Continual* feeling of analysis & sub-analysis, & criticism—on the whole unfriendly—such as we have felt for quite a while. It is definitely in the air,—& quite unpleasant.—It certainly detracts from any gathering. . . . We *Cannot*—Gerald & I—at our age—& stage in life— *be bothered* with Sophomoric situations—like last night."

Sara later connected the selfishness and insensitivity in Scott's character to a defect in his work, and bluntly told him: "consideration for other people's feelings, opinions or even time is *Completely* left out of your makeup.—I have always told you you haven't the faintest idea what anybody else but yourself is like. . . . Why,—for instance *should* you trample on other people's feelings continually with things you permit yourself to say & do—owing partly to the self-indulgence of drinking too much." Confronted with this harsh truth, Scott was forced to agree that he only knew himself: "My characters are all Scott Fitzgerald."[6]

Scott severely tested the Murphys' patience. He had to prove to himself, again and again, that they would, no matter how badly he behaved, always forgive him and love him. As Gerald, moved by Scott's charming and good-natured apologies, generously wrote in 1928: "we are very fond of you both. The fact that we don't get on always has nothing to do with it." Scott, who valued Gerald's forgiveness and treasured his friendship, later praised his social charm and paid tribute to him along with his intellectual, moral and artistic mentors, Edmund Wilson, Sap Donahoe and Ernest Hemingway: "a fourth man had come to dictate my relations with other people when these relations were successful: how to do, what to say. How to make people at least momentarily happy." In a simple, honest and moving statement, Scott told Gerald, "as a friend you have never failed me."[7]

In the 1920s, however, offended by the heavy drinking and bad manners that spoiled many of their fêtes, the Murphys did not recognize either Scott's genius or his problems with Zelda. "The one we took seriously was Ernest, not Scott," Gerald said. "I suppose it was because Ernest's work seemed contemporary and new, and Scott's didn't." Yet Scott's work, not Ernest's, influenced Gerald. Gerald loved giant eyes and in the late 1920s absorbed a central symbol of *The Great Gatsby,* the gigantic eyes of Doctor T. J. Eckleburg, into his own life and art. Gerald "designed a flag for his custom-made schooner, *Weatherbird,* with a schematic eye that appeared to blink as it flapped in the wind, and in 1928 he included a large human eye in his painting, *Portrait.*"[8]

II

Minimizing the marriage problems he had portrayed in *The Beautiful and Damned* and ignoring the exemplary harmony of the Murphys, Fitzgerald told Bishop, with an odd mixture of candor and concealment: "Zelda and I sometimes indulge in terrible four-day rows that always start with a drinking party but we're still enormously in love and about the only truly happily married people I know." In the summer of 1924, when Scott was absorbed in *The Great Gatsby* and Zelda was bored and restless, they experienced the severest crisis of their crisis-filled marriage and forced the Murphys to witness the agonizing aftermath of Zelda's infidelity.

In June 1924, on the beach at St.-Raphaël, Zelda met a handsome French naval aviator, Édouard Jozan. The son of a middle-class family in Nîmes with a long military tradition, he was a year and two days older than her. The antithesis of Fitzgerald, Jozan was a dark, romantic man with curly black hair and a Latin profile. He wore a smart uniform (as Scott had done when he first courted her), was muscular and athletic, and led the small group of officers who surrounded Zelda. He regretted having missed the war, longed to smoke opium in Indochina and wrote a few things for his own pleasure.

Attracted at first to both Scott and Zelda, Jozan found them "brimming over with life. Rich and free, they brought into our little provincial circle brilliance, imagination and familiarity with a Parisian and international world to which we had no access." But he soon focused his attention on the vibrant Zelda, "a creature who overflowed with activity, [and was] radiant with desire to take from life every chance her charm, youth and intelligence provided so abundantly."

With no friends in St.-Raphaël, Scott was eager as always for a bit of social life. Behaving like a man of the world, he invited Jozan to dine with them and met him at cafés in the evenings. Scott was excited and flattered when men fell in love with his wife—as long as she did not reciprocate their feelings. Left alone, with nothing to amuse her, Zelda went to the beach with Jozan while Scott stayed at home and worked on his novel.

After five years of marriage and the experience of motherhood, Zelda feared she had passed the peak of her beauty and had to prove that she was still attractive to men. She felt her life was empty, resented Scott's successful career, wanted to make him jealous and, as *Save Me the Waltz* makes clear (Scott considered the novel proof of her adultery), was overwhelmed by the courageous Frenchman. Like the American pilots in wartime Montgomery, Jozan made daredevil flights over her luxurious villa.

Zelda took the chance that life—or Jozan—provided. A masochistic and sensual passage in her novel describes how "he drew her body against him till she felt the blades of his bones carving her own. He was bronze and smelled of the sand and sun; she felt him naked underneath the starched linen." In her unpublished novel, *Caesar's Things*,

Zelda explains that the heroine is drawn to the Frenchman not only because he is attractive but also because she is afraid of love, and must confront and overcome her fear. "She told her husband she loved the French officer and her husband locked her up in the villa"[9]—just as the anxious Scott, during their turbulent courtship, kept repeating (to Zelda's annoyance) that he now understood why they always locked up princesses in towers.

Scott had good reason to fear Zelda's infidelity—both before and after he married her. Writing of his superior sexual rivals in "The Crack-Up," he confessed that he could not "stop thinking that at one time a sort of *droit de seigneur* might have been exercised to give one of them my girl." Jozan, using his French charm and aeronautic daring, exercised this right. He invited Zelda to his apartment and seduced her. "There was Jozan," she later admitted, "and you were justifiably angry." The crisis peaked on July 13 when Zelda told Scott that she loved Jozan and asked for a divorce.

But Jozan—just beginning his career and without any money—wanted a mistress, not a wife. Though he found Zelda a delightful lover, she did not touch his deepest feelings and meant no more to him than a brief fling on the beach. His transfer to Hyères (where the Fitzgeralds had begun the summer) put an end to their relations. But Zelda, more emotionally involved than Jozan, was deeply hurt by his rejection. When Jozan abandoned her, she tried to kill herself with an overdose of sleeping pills. Honoria Murphy remembers a disturbance one night at the Hôtel du Cap. Scott sought help from her parents, and Zelda had to be walked up and down in the hallway and kept awake until the effect of the pills wore off. "That September 1924," Scott wrote, "I knew something had happened that could never be repaired."[10] He now realized that he would have to test himself against Zelda's lover, that she was not absolutely committed to him (as he was to her) and that he could no longer trust his wife to be faithful. The purity of their marriage had been tainted, their innocence lost.

Jozan went on to have a distinguished naval career. He became a vice admiral, commanded France's Far Eastern fleet and was decorated with the Legion of Honor. If Zelda had left him for Jozan in 1924, Scott would have had another lost love to inspire his work and been spared the horrors of her insanity in the 1930s.

III

Zelda's affair with Jozan had spoiled the Riviera for Scott. Their expenses, even in the off-season, were much higher than expected and they had not been able to save any money. As soon as he finished his novel, they had to find a place to heal the wounds of their marriage and attempt to restore their old intimacy. Though they had disliked Italy on their previous trip to Europe, Zelda's reading of James' *Roderick Hudson* inspired them to spend the winter in Rome. But the cold weather and rampant dishonesty made Italy an even greater disappointment than France, where servants had drained their resources and driven them out of the Villa Marie. "What at first seemed a secluded villa just right for us to live in quietly," Zelda said, with amused exasperation, "had a habit of developing into a sort of charity institution, owing to the mysterious complaints by which the domestic personnel was stricken down, necessitating the presence of their relations, sometimes down to the third and fourth generations."

Instead of renting a villa in Italy, they moved into an expensive but uncomfortable thin-walled hotel on the Piazza di Spagna. They ate simple meals and—as Scott revised the novel he had completed in France—gradually found their way to the romantic sights of the city:

> In the Hôtel des Princes at Rome [Zelda wrote] we lived on Bel Paese cheese and [Sicilian] Corvo wine and made friends with a delicate spinster who intended to stop there until she finished a three-volume history of the Borgias. The sheets were damp and the nights were perforated by the snores of the people next door, but we didn't mind because we could always come home down the stairs to the Via Sistina, and there were jonquils and beggars along that way. We were too superior at that time to use the guide books and wanted to discover the ruins for ourselves, which we did when we had exhausted the night-life and the market places and the campagna. We liked the Castel Sant'Angelo because of its round mysterious unity and the river and the debris about its base. It was exciting being lost between centuries in the Roman dusk and taking your sense of direction from the Colosseum.

Their principal distraction in Rome was watching the filming of the spectacular, expensive and accident-prone *Ben-Hur*, and forming a friendship with one of its stars, Carmel Myers. The bright and attractive actress, who was the same age as Scott, was the daughter of a San Francisco rabbi. She began her film career in 1916 as the protégée of D. W. Griffith; starred as a vamp with Rudolph Valentino, Douglas Fairbanks, John Barrymore and John Gilbert; and would retire, shortly after talkies began, in the early 1930s. Scott, who would meet Carmel again when he first went to Hollywood in 1927, told a friend that "she is the most exquisite thing I have met yet, and is just as nice as she is beautiful."[11]

Fitzgerald's humorous but bitter account of his winter in Rome during 1924–25, "The High Cost of Macaroni," is—like D. H. Lawrence's *Aaron's Rod* (1922), Hemingway's "Che Ti Dice La Patria?" (1927) and Thomas Mann's "Mario and the Magician" (1929)—a disillusioned and dispirited response to oppressive life in Fascist Italy. The conclusion of this essay describes a humiliating reprise to his black eye at Princeton in 1920 and his savage beating at the Jungle Club the following year. Fitzgerald's petty midnight quarrel with some extortionate taxi drivers about the fare back to their hotel ended, when he refused to be cheated, in a brutal street fight:

First there was *one* taxi driver, and I had a little the best of it; then there were two and I was having a little the worst of it. But I didn't think I was, and when the meddlesome stranger stepped between us I was in no mood to have it stop there, and I pushed him impatiently out of the way. He came back persistently, lurching in between us, talking in a stream of Italian, doing his best, it seemed to me, to interrupt my offensives—and to the advantage of the taximan. Once too often he caught at my arm. Blind with anger I turned on him quickly and (with more success than I had so far had with the others) caught him under the point of the chin; whereupon, rather to my surprise, he sat down.

The unfortunate interloper turned out to be a plainclothes policeman. Fitzgerald was arrested for assaulting an officer, taken to a police station and savagely beaten.

Fitzgerald called this degrading experience "just about the rottenest thing that ever happened to me in my life." It aroused his hostility, provoked his prejudices and inspired his violent fantasies about the country, the politics and the people. "I hate Italians," he told Carmel Myers. "They live in tenements and don't have bathtubs!" When Harold Ober asked him to write a piece about his travels for the *Post*, he rather childishly replied that he could not write anything acceptable to that audience unless they wanted an article on "Pope Syphilis the Sixth and his Morons." He imagined filling a theater with the flower of Italy, coming on stage with a machine gun and murdering the entire audience. He thought Italy was trying to live on its glorious past and saw through the histrionic absurdities of Fascism. "Italy depressed us both beyond measure," he wrote to an editor at Scribner's, "a dead land where everything that could be done or said was done long ago (for whoever is deceived by the pseudo activity under Mussolini is deceived by the spasmodic last jerk of a corpse)."[12]

The unexpected cold, Zelda's painful ovarian infection and Scott's brutal encounter with the police drove them out of Rome. In February 1925 they crossed the Bay of Naples and settled in the fashionable Hotel Tiberio on Capri. Fitzgerald's hero Joseph Conrad, who had visited the highly praised island in 1905, said the air was too stimulating for consumptives and complained of hot winds, violent contrasts and sexual scandals: "Too much ozone they say: too exciting and that's why no lung patients are allowed to come here. . . . This place here, this climate, this sirocco, this transmontana, these flat roofs, these sheer rocks, this blue sea—are impossible. . . . The scandals of Capri—atrocious, unspeakable, amusing, scandals international, cosmopolitan and biblical." In February 1920 D. H. Lawrence, more succinctly, condemned Capri as "a stewpot of semi-literary cats." Fitzgerald, repelled by the thriving colony of English homosexuals—including Norman Douglas, Somerset Maugham and E. F. Benson—agreed that "this place is full of fairies."

Fitzgerald was also disappointed by his former literary hero, Compton Mackenzie, whose *Sinister Street* had influenced *This Side of Paradise*. He sat up half the night talking to the good-looking and extremely successful Scottish novelist, who wore striking clothes and owned two luxurious villas on the island. Though Mackenzie would go on to write his finest work, he now seemed exhausted as an author. "I found him cordial, attractive and pleasantly mundane," Scott told Bishop. "You get no sense from him that he feels his work has gone to pieces. He's not pompous about his present output. I think he's just tired. The war [in which Mackenzie had had a distinguished career in the Secret Service] wrecked him as it did Wells and many of that generation."[13]

IV

In late October 1924, just before he left St.-Raphaël for Rome, Fitzgerald had sent Perkins the typescript of *The Great Gatsby*, which he continued to revise throughout his stay in Italy. Three weeks later Perkins, recognizing its greatness, enthusiastically praised its themes, narrative technique, symbolism, characters, drama, style and art:

> I think you have every kind of right to be proud of this book. It is an extraordinary book, suggestive of all sorts of thoughts and moods. You adopted exactly the right method of telling it, that of employing a narrator who is more of a spectator than an actor: that puts the reader upon a point of observation on a higher level than that on which the characters stand and at a distance that gives perspective. In no other way could your irony have been so immensely effective, nor the reader have been enabled so strongly to feel at times the strangeness of human circumstance in a vast heedless universe. In the eyes of Dr. Eckleburg various readers will see different significances; but their presence gives a superb touch to the whole thing: great unblinking eyes, expressionless, looking down upon the human scene. It's magnificent! . . .
>
> The presentation of Tom, his place, Daisy and Jordan, and the unfolding of their characters is unequalled so far as I know. The description of the valley of ashes adjacent to the lovely country, the conversation and the action in Myrtle's apartment, the marvelous catalogue of those who came to Gatsby's house,—these are such things as make a man famous. And all these things, the whole pathetic episode, you have given a place in time and space, for with the help of T. J. Eckleburg and by an occasional glance at the sky, or the sea, or the city, you have imparted a sort of sense of eternity. You once told me

you were not a *natural* writer—my God! You have plainly
mastered the craft, of course; but you needed far more than
craftsmanship for this.[14]

Ring Lardner, aware of the carelessness of both Fitzgerald and
Perkins, and eager to repay Scott for his generous help with *How to
Write Short Stories*, volunteered to read the proofs. His experienced
eye caught a number of minor errors about the levels in Penn Station,
the elevated train in Queens, the "tides" in Lake Superior and the rail-
roads that ran out of the La Salle Street station in Chicago.

The Great Gatsby, as both Perkins and Lardner perceived, is
Fitzgerald's most perfectly realized work of art. The novel reveals a
new and confident mastery of his material, a fascinating if sensational
plot, a Keatsian ability to evoke a romantic atmosphere, a set of memorable and deeply interesting characters, a witty and incisive social
satire, a surprisingly effective use of allusions, an ambitious theme and
a silken style that seems as fresh today as it did seventy years ago.

In 1925—the year Dreiser published *An American Tragedy*, Dos
Passos *Manhattan Transfer* and Hemingway *In Our Time*—Fitzgerald
made an impressive leap from his deeply flawed early novels to his first
masterpiece. Unlike his previous novels, *The Great Gatsby* is imaginative rather than autobiographical, unified rather than episodic. In place
of the loosely constructed story of a young man's life, influenced by
Compton Mackenzie and H. G. Wells, Fitzgerald set out to capture a
social scene and satirize a social class in the manner of Henry James
and Edith Wharton. As John Dos Passos noted, in the three years since
his early success Fitzgerald had thought seriously about his art. His
careful study of the works of Joseph Conrad—who died in August 1924
while Fitzgerald was writing his novel—was mainly responsible for his
astonishing technical and intellectual advance.

In June 1925 Fitzgerald told H. L. Mencken that he had "learned a
lot" from Conrad and had consciously imitated him in *The Great
Gatsby*. Conrad's influence can be seen in Fitzgerald's evocative symbolism (the green light at the end of Daisy's dock, the desolate waste land
of the Valley of Ashes, the God-like judgment of the eyes of Doctor T. J.
Eckleburg), in his resonant style, revelation of the story by moving forward and backward in time, themes of romantic illusion and corrupted
idealism. Fitzgerald's confidential narrator Nick Carraway, like Conrad's

Charlie Marlow in *Heart of Darkness* (1899) and *Lord Jim* (1900), provides distance and credibility by retrospectively telling a story that he, a character in the novel, has personally observed. He combines disapproval of and sympathy for Gatsby just as Marlow does for Lord Jim.

Gatsby's attempt to reinvent himself, move into the upper class and win Daisy from Tom is heroic but doomed. But Gatsby's effort is also treated satirically because he is (or has been) a liar and a crook. Yet his lies are sad because they are all meant for Daisy, who is really "hollow at the core" and unworthy of his sacrificial quest. And Gatsby becomes as disillusioned with Daisy as Marlow does with the hollow Kurtz. In *The Great Gatsby* Fitzgerald still uses fiction to tell his own story— reflecting on the superior and brutal qualities of the rich and on the impossibility of becoming one of them—but it is now truly *invented* fiction, not something carelessly cobbled together from diaries and letters and clever remarks.

Fitzgerald takes his themes as well as his narrator from Conrad and alludes to his master at three crucial points in the novel. In Conrad's "The Secret Sharer" (1910), the young captain wonders "how far I should turn out faithful to that ideal conception of one's own personality." Carraway also considers this important question and explains the hero's transformation from the poor, provincial James Gatz into the buoyantly successful Jay Gatsby by observing that he "sprang from his Platonic [that is, his ideal and self-created] conception of himself" and "invented just the sort of Jay Gatsby that a seventeen-year-old boy would be likely to invent, and to this conception [of his personality] he was faithful to the end."[15]

Lord Jim, which Fitzgerald called "a great book," concerns the tragic loss of self-esteem and, Conrad writes, "those struggles of an individual trying to save from the fire his idea of what his moral identity should be." Jim's mentor Stein anticipates Gatsby's idealistic trajectory by urging Jim "To follow the dream, and again to follow the dream." And when Carraway warns Gatsby: "You can't repeat the past," Gatsby naively cries: "Can't repeat the past? . . . Why of course you can!" Like Jim, Jay is crippled by a past he cannot escape; and Nick gathers that, like Jim, "he wanted to recover something, some idea of himself."

Fitzgerald also learned from Conrad to use a more subtle and suggestive conclusion to his fiction. As he remarked to Bishop: "It was Ernest Hemingway who developed to me, in conversation, that the dying fall was preferable to the dramatic ending under certain conditions, and I think we both got the germ of the idea from Conrad." Fitzgerald also told Hemingway that Conrad's Preface to *The Nigger of the "Narcissus"* (1897), which he had reread while writing *The Great Gatsby,* had taught him that fiction must "appeal to the lingering after-effects in the reader's mind."[16]

Conrad had concluded his African novella *Heart of Darkness* by connecting the Thames to the primitive past of mankind, symbolized by the Congo: "The tranquil waterway leading to the uttermost ends of the earth flowed sombre under an overcast sky—seemed to lead into the heart of an immense darkness." Adopting the psychological suggestiveness of the riverine metaphor and alluding to Gatsby's hopeless attempt to repeat the past, Fitzgerald imitated Conrad's "appeal to the lingering after-effects" in his own concluding sentence: "So we beat on, boats against the current, borne back ceaselessly into the past."

After *The Great Gatsby* had been published in April 1925, Fitzgerald acknowledged two major flaws in the novel. He admitted that he himself did not know what Gatsby looked like or what criminal activities he was engaged in, and told Bishop that the composite origins of his hero made Gatsby blurred and patchy: "I never at any one time saw him clear myself—for he started as one man I knew and then changed into myself—the amalgam was never complete in my mind." Another radical fault in the book, he confided to Mencken, was "the lack of an emotional presentment of Daisy's attitude toward Gatsby after their reunion (and the consequent lack of logic or importance in her throwing him over)."[17] Fitzgerald had always been aware of these faults and had disguised them with consummate skill. The elusive ambiguity of Gatsby actually enhances his mysterious character. At the beginning of the novel he vanishes as suddenly as he had appeared, leaving Nick "alone again in the unquiet darkness"—as Kurtz had left Marlow alone in the moral darkness of the Congo.

Gatsby's vague connection with Oxford, which Fitzgerald had visited twice in 1921, is an important part of his ambiguous persona. But it is based on rumor, lies, misleading evidence, dubious endorsement, intense scepticism and, finally, on his own rather unsatisfactory explanation. Daisy's friend Jordan Baker tells Nick that Gatsby once told her he was an Oxford man. Gatsby, who comes from humble origins, tells Nick, with wild exaggeration: "I was brought up in America but educated at Oxford, because all my ancestors have been educated there for many years. It is a family tradition." And he actually produces a souvenir photograph, taken in Trinity Quad with the Earl of Doncaster, to prove his assertion. The gambler Meyer Wolfsheim dubiously calls Gatsby "an Oggsford man," but Tom Buchanan, who is incredulous, contemptuously associates the man who wears pink suits with "Oxford, New Mexico." When Tom questions Gatsby directly in order to discredit him in front of Daisy, Gatsby (contradicting his earlier statement to Nick) uneasily explains: "It was in nineteen nineteen. I only stayed five months. That's why I can't really call myself an Oxford man. . . . It was an opportunity they gave to some of the officers after the Armistice. . . . We could go to any of the universities in England or France." Later on, we learn that Daisy's letter, announcing her marriage to Tom and inspiring Gatsby's impossible dream to win her back, reached him while he was at Oxford. Gatsby's claim to Oxford, commented on by all the major characters in the novel, emphasizes his obsessive need to change as well as to repeat the past.

Gatsby's shadowy character is placed against a realistic background and setting. *The Great Gatsby* captures, better than any other novel about the 1920s, not only the lavish house parties on Long Island but also what one historian has called "the bootleggers and the speakeasies, the corruption of police and judiciary, the highjackers and their machine guns, the gang wars, the multimillionaire booze barons, the murders and assassinations, the national breakdown of morals and manners."[18] The corruption in the novel is exemplified by Meyer Wolfsheim, who is based on the notorious New York gambler Arnold Rothstein. Rothstein was closely involved with Edward Fuller (Fitzgerald's neighbor in Great Neck) who, with his brokerage partner William McGee, declared bankruptcy and left their firm with a debt of six million dollars. They were convicted and jailed, after four sensational trials during 1922–23, for fraudulently gambling away their clients' money. Rothstein—who was also behind the Black Sox scandal, when gamblers bribed the Chicago White Sox to lose the World Series in 1919—was killed by anonymous gunmen in 1928.

In the novel Meyer Wolfsheim is both physically and morally repulsive. He has a strong Jewish accent, and offers Carraway a dishonest and dangerous business "gonnegtion." He recounts the brutal murder of another gangster and shows off his barbaric cuff links, made of "the

finest specimens of human molars." Like his name, these teeth—an
allusion to the human skulls on Kurtz's fence posts in *Heart of Darkness*—suggest his rapacious, even cannibalistic traits. When Wolfsheim
leaves, Gatsby explains that the gambler had fixed the World Series.
Nick, alluding to the maiden name of Daisy Fay and evoking the pervasive theme of bitter disillusionment, thinks: "It never occurred to me
that one man could start to play with the *faith* of fifty million people—
with the single-mindedness of a burglar blowing a safe." After Gatsby
has been murdered by Wilson, Nick goes into New York to tell Wolfsheim that the funeral of his friend will take place that day. But Wolfsheim refuses to attend the ceremony and confirms the worst rumors
about Gatsby's character and background, and the source of his wealth,
by claiming that he had "made" Gatsby: "I raised him up out of nothing, right out of the gutter."

Other real-life models also contributed to the characters in the
novel. Daisy Fay has the surname of the Catholic priest, Sigourney
Webster Fay. She is based partly on the Chicago debutante Ginevra
King and partly on Zelda. While writing *The Great Gatsby* Scott
learned of her affair with Jozan, just as Tom learns of Daisy's love for
and affair with Gatsby. Tom reclaims Daisy from Gatsby just as Scott
reclaimed Zelda from Jozan. Nick's girlfriend Jordan Baker (whose
aunt, Mrs. Sigourney Howard, recalls the first name of Father Fay) was
modeled on a close school friend of Ginevra, Edith Cummings, who
once won the women's national golf championship. And (as we have
seen) Tommy Hitchcock was the model for Tom Buchanan.

Great Neck, where Fitzgerald lived during 1922–24, inspired the
setting of the novel. Andrew Turnbull notes that while he was living
there Fitzgerald's "magic word was 'egg.' People he liked were 'good
eggs,' or 'colossal eggs,' and people he didn't like were 'bad eggs' or
'unspeakable eggs.'"[19] Edmund Wilson was "an incomparable egg."
Fitzgerald's favorite slang expressions were transmuted in the novel
into the more affluent East Egg (based on Manhasset) where Tom and
Daisy live, and the generally more modest West Egg (based on Great
Neck) where Nick lives in a cottage on Gatsby's estate. Even today, if
you stand at night on King's Point on the tip of Great Neck peninsula,
and look across Manhasset Bay, you can still see—as Gatsby did—the
promising lights winking on the opposite shore.

Fitzgerald's *Ledger* and *Notebooks* reveal that he was a habitual maker of lists, and the catalogue of the names of people who came to Gatsby's West Egg mansion in the summer of 1922, which opens Chapter IV and is one of the wittiest sections of the novel, is the greatest list he ever made. Many of the bizarre names suggest animals, incongruously yoke the exotic and the banal, and indicate the kind of corrupt people who were attracted to Gatsby's parties. At least four of the guests have disastrous experiences: Webster Civet (yet another allusion to Father Fay) is drowned, Ripley Snell goes to the penitentiary, Henry L. Palmetto kills himself and young Brewster has had his nose shot off in the war.

The strange, suggestive names of the guests—whom Tom rightly calls "crazy fish" in Gatsby's "menagerie"—were influenced by two of the most important writers of the century. T. S. Eliot, whom Fitzgerald described as "the greatest living poet in any language," gave the characters in "Gerontion" (1920) equally peculiar names: Mr. Silvero, "Hakagawa, bowing among the Titians; / Madame de Tornquist, in the dark room / Shifting the candles; Fräulein von Kulp / Who turned in the hall, one hand on the door." And James Joyce assembled a comically named diplomatic corps to witness the execution scene in the "Cyclops" chapter of *Ulysses* (1922). Fitzgerald lifted the most obscene name in his own novel—Vladimir Tostoff—from Joyce's double pun on the name of a character in an imaginary play by Buck Mulligan. This unregenerate masturbator, who habitually "tossed off" and destroyed his own sexual organ, was named "Toby Tostoff (a ruined Pole)."

The scene in which Gatsby shows Daisy his house (on one of the rare occasions when it is not filled with intrusive guests), and in which his nearly but never-to-be realized dream reaches "an inconceivable pitch of intensity," is perhaps the greatest in the novel. Gatsby displays his luxurious pile of shirts, reveals his intense materialism and offers his things as well as his love. Daisy, frequently characterized (and made unreal) as a disembodied voice, "full of money," begins to sob as she realizes that his entire ostentatious life has been created solely to impress her. But even on that exalted afternoon, Nick explains, expressing one of the major themes of the novel in a resonant Conradian phrase, Daisy inevitably "tumbled short of his dreams—not through her own fault, but because of the colossal vitality of his illusion."[20] No reality can ever match Gatsby's elaborate fantasy.

But winning Daisy's love is not enough for Gatsby. He must also change and remake reality by eliminating her past love for and sexual relations with Tom, and by transforming Daisy into the innocent girl she was when he first met and took her. In an agonizing, inquisitorial scene, Gatsby arrogantly tells Tom: "Your wife doesn't love you. . . . In her heart she has never loved anyone except me!" But Tom, with surprising tenderness, persuades Daisy to deny Gatsby's solipsistic reconstruction of their emotional history: "'Oh, you want too much!' she cried to Gatsby. 'I love you now—isn't that enough? I can't help what's past.' She began to sob helplessly. 'I did love him once—but I loved you too.'" Daisy may even have stayed with Tom because she knew that Gatsby would demand the impossible from her. Gatsby's romantic illusions are shattered by Tom, who possesses the much-desired Daisy (better perhaps as an ideal than as a real wife) but is unfaithful to her with the vulgar Myrtle Wilson. And the self-made, worldly, criminally connected but idealistic Gatsby is easily unmasked, betrayed and destroyed by the brutal playboy, who calls him "a common swindler who'd have to steal the ring he put on her finger."

The climax of the novel is as ambiguous as Gatsby's character. Daisy—who went into New York in Tom's car but is driving Gatsby's car on the way back to Long Island—kills Tom's mistress and flees the scene of the accident. Tom tells Wilson, Myrtle's husband, what he subjectively calls the "truth": that Gatsby "ran over Myrtle like you'd run over a dog and never even stopped his car." And Wilson (whose dream is an ironic reflection of Gatsby's and who wants to buy a car like the one that killed his wife) mindlessly murders Gatsby before killing himself.

Nick sharply observes that Tom's statement "wasn't true." Fitzgerald is deliberately unclear about whether Daisy lied to Tom and told him Gatsby was driving or whether Tom knew Daisy was driving and tried to protect her by blaming Gatsby. In any case, Gatsby saves Daisy from scandal, is rejected by her and is killed for her crime. The Buchanans are both murderers. As Nick observes: "They were careless people, Tom and Daisy—they smashed up things and creatures and then retreated back into their money."[21]

The Great Gatsby transcends Fitzgerald's personal life and brilliantly expresses some of the dominant themes in American literature: the idealism and morality of the West (where most of the characters originate and where Nick returns at the end of the novel) in contrast to the complexity and corruption of the East (where the novel takes place); the frontier myth of the independent self-made man; the attempt to escape the materialistic present and recapture the innocent past; the predatory power of rich and beautiful women; the limited possibilities of love in the modern world; the heightened sensitivity to the promises of life; the doomed attempt to sustain illusions and recapture the American dream.

V

Fitzgerald sent *The Great Gatsby* to a number of eminent literary friends, and had the benefit of both a private and public response. On April 11, 1925, the day after the novel was published, Edmund Wilson wrote Fitzgerald, who was then on Capri, with his usual qualifications: "It is undoubtedly in some ways the best thing you have done—the best planned, the best sustained, the best written." Four years later, in a crucial letter to the novelist Hamilton Basso, Wilson, with uncommon modesty, unfavorably contrasted his own recently published novel, *I Thought of Daisy* (their fictional heroines had the same name), to Fitzgerald's best work of fiction. For the first time, but privately, he acknowledged Fitzgerald's superiority, and placed his achievement on a national rather than on a merely personal level: "[I've been] thinking with depression how much better Scott Fitzgerald's prose and dramatic sense were than mine. If only I'd been able to give my book the vividness and excitement, the technical accuracy, of his! Have you ever read *Gatsby*? I think it's one of the best novels that any American of his age has done."

Five days later Mencken agreed with Perkins' judgment about the fine craftsmanship, but found the plot insubstantial: "*The Great Gatsby* fills me with pleasant sentiments. I think it is incomparably the best piece of work you have done. Evidences of careful workmanship are on every page. The thing is well managed, and has a fine surface. My one complaint is that the basic story is somewhat trivial—that it reduces itself, in the end, to a sort of anecdote. But God will forgive you for that."

The following month Gertrude Stein, who had by then met Fitzgerald in Paris, offered, in her characteristically precious mode, generous praise of his extraordinary sensitivity and style: "Here we are and have read your book and it is a good book. I like the melody of your dedication ["Once Again, To Zelda"] and it shows that you have a back-

ground of beauty and tenderness and that is a comfort. The next good
thing is that you write naturally in sentences and that too is a comfort.
You write naturally in sentences and one can read all of them and that
among other things is a comfort. You are creating the contemporary
world much as Thackeray did his in *Pendennis* and *Vanity Fair* and this
isn't a bad compliment."[22]

In June, Edith Wharton, a Scribner's author whom Fitzgerald
greatly admired, agreed with her colleagues that he had made a notable
advance on his previous work. But, like Mencken, she had a serious
reservation about the incomplete characterization of Gatsby: "My present quarrel with you is only this: that to make Gatsby really Great, you
ought to have given us his early career (not from the cradle—but from
his first visit to the yacht, if not before) instead of a short résumé of it.
That would have *situated* him & made his final tragedy a tragedy
instead of a 'fait divers' [news item] for the morning papers."

Hemingway, who rarely praised his contemporaries, called it "an
absolutely first rate book." And T. S. Eliot, whose *Waste Land* had
influenced the desolate Valley of Ashes, provided the finest tribute in
the chorus of praise: "it has interested and excited me more than any
new novel I have seen, either English or American, for a number of
years. . . . It seems to me to be the first step that American fiction has
taken since Henry James."[23]

All the finest authors and critics of the time had admired *The
Great Gatsby*, believed that Fitzgerald had fulfilled his artistic potential and agreed that he had finally produced a great novel. But the sale
of about 25,000 copies (far less than his first two novels) did not match
his expectations and barely paid off his advance. The dramatic adapta-
tion of the novel by Owen Davis opened in New York in February
1926, ran for 112 performances and earned an unexpected $18,000. It
also led to the sale of the film rights for another $17,000. But after *The
Great Gatsby* Fitzgerald, who found it difficult to live on $36,000 a
year, realized that he could no longer count on his novels to pay his
considerable expenses. Two weeks after the book was published, he
admitted to Perkins that he was trapped by his own extravagance. He
mentioned the old conflict between art and money, and said he might
have to sacrifice his career and sell out to the movies: "If [*Gatsby*] will
support me with no more intervals of trash I'll go on as a novelist. If
not, I'm going to quit, come home [from Europe], go to Hollywood and

learn the movie business. I can't reduce our scale of living and I can't stand this financial insecurity."

When *The Great Gatsby* failed to bring in what he thought he needed, he was once again forced to return to lucrative stories until he had banked enough money to devote himself to his novels. In April 1925, the month his novel was published, he reviewed the work he had done since completing his book the previous October, regretted his wasted talent and disgustedly told Bishop, as if self-condemnation would justify his sell-out: "I now get $2,000 a story and they grow worse and worse and my ambition is to get where I need write no more but only novels. . . . I've done about 10 pieces of horrible junk in the last year that I can never republish or bear to look at—cheap and without the spontaneity of my first work." Since his fees for stories sold to the *Post* seemed to rise in inverse proportion to their merit, he now became embarrassed about publishing them. Though he always needed money, he actually asked Ober not to push the price up any higher. "I've gotten self-conscious," he told his agent, "and don't think my stuff is worth half what I get now."

Most writers could not devote themselves to great art and to popular trash at the same time. If they did, they would have to improve or reject their inferior work. But Fitzgerald, knowing it was trash, published it for the money and condemned himself for doing so. Untroubled by Scott's conflict and glad to see the money rolling in from any source, Zelda naively remarked: "I don't see why Scott objected so to those *Post* stories when he got such wonderful prices for them."[24]

The novelist who had written *The Great Gatsby* at the age of twenty-eight and had published seven books between 1920 and 1926 would seem to have a great career before him. But Fitzgerald succumbed to the temptation of easy money. He scarcely considered trying to live on the modest royalties of a serious novelist. Though he had earned a great deal, he and Zelda spent more than he made. Trapped in an increasingly hand-to-mouth existence, he never broke loose from the short story market and brought out only two more books during the last fourteen years of his life.

Chapter Seven

PARIS AND HEMINGWAY, 1925–1926

I

Exalted by the critical success of *The Great Gatsby* but not yet aware of the disappointing sales, the Fitzgeralds left Capri in early April 1925 and joined the thirty thousand Americans who were then living in Paris. They rented a fifth-floor walk-up flat at 14 rue de Tilsitt, near the Arc de Triomphe, until the end of the year. A photograph taken at Christmas showed an elegantly dressed and apparently happy family in front of an elaborately decorated tree, a pile of presents, a low chandelier and an overflowing bookcase. Scott wore a three-piece suit and thick-soled shoes, Zelda (with slender legs but now wider at the hips) was burdened by a huge corsage, and the beribboned four-year-old Scottie, nervous about the pose, bit her lower lip and showed her knickers as they all did a chorus-line kick.

In reality the Fitzgeralds were not the secure and happy family they appeared to be. The novelist Louis Bromfield, who visited them that year, found their place ornate and pretentious: "It represented to some degree the old aspirations and a yearning for stability, but somehow it got only halfway and was neither one thing nor the other. . . .

The furniture was gilt Louis XVI but a suite from the Galeries Lafayette [department store]. The wallpaper was the usual striped stuff in dull colors that went with that sort of flat. It was all rather like a furniture shop window and I always had the impression that the Fitzgeralds were camping there between two worlds." Zelda, noting their inability to escape the wounds inflicted by her affair with Jozan, recalled that the stale flat "smelled of a church chancery because it was impossible to ventilate" and became "a perfect breeding place for the germs of bitterness they brought with them from the Riviera." Scottie also remembered that the "apartments were always rather dark and unprepossessing, with their only redeeming feature the views over the rooftops which so fascinated my mother. The elevators were always 'en panne' [out of order] and I can feel the heavy chains, suspended from the ceiling, that caused such an uproarious commotion in all our toilets."[1]

Coming to Paris allowed the Fitzgeralds to escape the scene of their unhappiness on the Riviera and the oppressive atmosphere of Fascist Italy, and to enter the world of American expatriates in this lively and stimulating city. They could sit in cafés, drink in bars, eat in restaurants, see their friends and visit literary salons. Paris enabled many American artists to escape Prohibition as well as the moral and intellectual confinement of American society, and to breathe the freer air of continental culture. But the very freedom of the city, where they could live inexpensively and create their own social roles, did not help the Fitzgeralds. This time in France deepened the rift between them, made Zelda more insecure and propelled her toward her future mental crisis. Scott continued to waste money and drink heavily, spending his time at parties, dances and nightclubs instead of concentrating on his work. His friendship with Ernest Hemingway accentuated Fitzgerald's personal crises. But Ernest's harsh yet truthful criticism helped Scott to define his ideas about art and to recognize that his way of life was destructive.

In October 1924, six months before the Fitzgeralds settled in Paris, Edmund Wilson had reviewed Hemingway's pamphlet *in our time*. He told Fitzgerald about the young writer who had begun to publish his strikingly original stories and poems with small private presses in Paris. Fitzgerald's meeting with Hemingway in the Dingo Bar in late April 1925, two weeks after the publication of *The Great Gatsby* and six months before the enlarged trade edition of *In Our Time*, led to the most important friendship of Scott's life. He was then writing for the three million readers of the *Saturday Evening Post* while Hemingway's work was still confined to little magazines. Fitzgerald was three years older, had gone to Princeton, published three successful novels and made a great deal of money. But Hemingway—an athlete, war veteran and foreign correspondent who had established a reputation as a dedicated writer before he had actually published anything—became his heroic and artistic ideal.

Six inches taller and forty pounds heavier than Fitzgerald, Hemingway was a literary version of the bloodied and bandaged football heroes Scott had worshiped in college. Hemingway later told Arthur Mizener, to exemplify Fitzgerald's immaturity and naïveté, that he remembered "one time in N.Y. we were walking down Fifth Avenue and [Scott] said, 'if only I could play foot-ball again with everything I know about it now.'" But Hemingway, who did not meet Fitzgerald in New York until after he had published *The Sun Also Rises* in 1926, actually attributed to Fitzgerald a statement made by his own fictional anti-hero, Robert Cohn: "I think I'd rather play football again with what I know about handling myself, now." Hemingway was so fond of this phrase that he recycled it in *Across the River and into the Trees* (1950), published the same year as his letter to Mizener, when his hero Richard Cantwell thinks about the war: "I wish I could fight it again, he thought. Knowing what I know now."[2]

Hemingway had the masculine strength, capacity for drink, athletic prowess and experience in battle that Fitzgerald sadly lacked and desperately desired. And his impressive achievements seemed to magnify Fitzgerald's failures. Both writers were fascinated by the war. Hemingway had suffered a traumatic wound when serving with the Red Cross in Italy while Fitzgerald had merely experienced "noncombatant's shell shock." Fitzgerald owned a bloodcurdling collection of photograph albums of horribly mutilated soldiers, stereopticon slides of executions and roasted aviators, and lavishly illustrated French tomes of living men whose faces had been chewed away by shrapnel. In a remarkably morbid letter of December 1927, he told Hemingway: "I have a new German war book, *Die Krieg Against Krieg*, which shows men who mislaid their faces in Picardy and the Caucasus—you can imagine how I thumb it over, my mouth fairly slathering with fascination." The photographs in

Ernst Friedrich's *Krieg dem Kriege!* (Berlin, 1924) stimulated his pathological curiosity about the war—a subject he had ignored at Princeton
and evaded in his first two novels—and allowed him to confront in his
imagination scenes of violence, mutilation and death. Hemingway also
took perverse pleasure in emphasizing the grisly details of war wounds
in works like "The Natural History of the Dead" (1932). He too was fascinated by gruesome photos of maimed bodies. In 1935 he took and collected pictures of bloated corpses after the Matecumbe hurricane in the
Florida Keys, and during the Spanish Civil War reproduced some astonishing horrors in "Dying, Well or Badly" (1938).

But the two writers had very different ideas about the use of violent experience in art. In December 1925 Hemingway defined his
attraction to the intensity of war by telling Fitzgerald: "the reason you
are so sore you missed the war is because war is the best subject of all.
It groups the maximum of material and speeds up the action and brings
out all sorts of stuff that normally you would have to wait a lifetime to
get." Hemingway believed you had to live the actual experience before
you could write about it honestly. Fitzgerald believed (as he had to,
given his lack of experience in war) that imagination could serve the
artist's purpose just as well, that "if you weren't able to function in
action you might at least be able to tell about it, because you felt the
same intensity—it was a back door way out of facing reality."

There were also considerable differences in their characters and
way of life. Janet Flanner, the Paris correspondent for the *New Yorker,*
found Fitzgerald's manner "remote" and thought he was "set apart by
his elegance."[3] Fitzgerald always stayed in luxurious hotels; and his
expensive apartment in Paris isolated him from ordinary life and placed
him among the rich American tourists of the Right Bank. Hemingway
preferred small pensions and modest flats, which in Paris put him in
touch with local people on the more bohemian Left Bank. Fitzgerald
had an English nanny for his daughter; Hemingway had a French peasant to look after his son. In the summers, Fitzgerald went to the Riviera
to lie on the beach; Hemingway went to Spain to see the bullfights and
live the experience he would write about in *The Sun Also Rises.*
Fitzgerald could compete with Hemingway as a writer but not as a
sportsman. Unlike the Murphys, Dos Passos, Don Stewart and Max
Perkins, Fitzgerald never followed Hemingway to Spain or went fishing
with him in Key West.

But Fitzgerald, who emphasized his extravagance, seemed wealthier than he actually was while Hemingway, who exaggerated his poverty, was not as poor as he claimed to be. Though his wife had a comfortable trust fund, Hemingway said he had to catch pigeons in the public park so they could have some food for dinner. When they first met, Hemingway must have envied and desired Fitzgerald's literary fame, material success and luxurious way of life, which provided a striking contrast to his own obscurity and rather pinched existence. But he made a virtue of this difference, compared his own frugality to Fitzgerald's wastefulness and ironically offered to send all his royalties to his friend's villa on the Riviera.

Fitzgerald lived lavishly and squandered his talent; Hemingway (who lectured him about this, as Fitzgerald had lectured Lardner) lived in relative poverty so that he could dedicate himself to art. Hemingway was absolutely sure of himself; Fitzgerald was full of self-doubts. While Fitzgerald had unbounded admiration for Hemingway's talent, Ernest (like Edmund Wilson) was extremely critical of Scott's faults. Though Fitzgerald seemed to toss off stories while Hemingway struggled to perfect every word, Scott contrasted his own plodding struggle to Ernest's natural ability. As he later wrote Perkins: "I told [Hemingway], against all the logic that was then current, that I was the tortoise and he was the hare, and that's the truth of the matter, that everything I have ever attained has been through long and persistent struggle while it is Ernest who has a touch of genius which enables him to bring off extraordinary things with facility."

Fitzgerald seemed to have a much weaker character, but he was actually more courageous than Hemingway when faced with adversity. Hemingway was ruthless with anyone who interfered with his work or his wishes. When his marriages went bad, he selfishly discarded a series of sometimes rich and always devoted wives. Ill equipped to deal with disease and depression, he finally shot himself. Fitzgerald, by contrast, endured poverty and neglect during the 1930s and remained loyal to Zelda in her madness.

II

Despite these significant differences, Fitzgerald and Hemingway initially had a good deal in common. Both writers came from a middle-class Midwestern background, had a strong mother and weak father, were close in age, were married, had one small child, lived an expatriate life in Paris and were devoted to the craft of writing. They traveled in the same social circles and, through mutual introductions, shared many of the same friends. Ezra Pound had introduced Hemingway to Scott's Princeton classmate Henry Strater. Don Stewart ran with Hemingway and the bulls in Pamplona and went trout fishing in Burguete, was instrumental in getting *In Our Time* published in New York and was a model for Bill Gorton in *The Sun Also Rises*. After Hemingway joined Scribner's, Max Perkins also became his close friend, and often acted as intermediary between the two writers. Both Hemingway and Fitzgerald sat at the feet of Gertrude Stein and—along with Dos Passos and Dorothy Parker—enjoyed the hospitality of the Murphys. In the late 1920s both writers became friendly with the Canadian novelist Morley Callaghan.

Shortly after they met, Fitzgerald persuaded Hemingway to accompany him on a trip to Lyon to recover the Renault he and Zelda had abandoned on the way to Paris. Under the heading "Most Pleasant Trips" in his *Notebooks*, Scott listed "Auto Ernest and I North." And in June 1925 Hemingway told Perkins: "Scott Fitzgerald is living here now and we see quite a lot of him. We had a great trip together driving his car up from Lyon through the Côte d'Or." Thirty years later, in *A Moveable Feast*, Hemingway, who had no tolerance for weakness or for behavior he considered unmanly, gave a radically revised and contemptuously affectionate account of that ludicrous car trip. In his posthumous time bomb he portrayed Fitzgerald as hostile to the French, childish and gauche, wasteful and irresponsible, quarrelsome and irritating, hypochondriac and insecure, dependent upon and dominated by Zelda, a complacent and self-confessed cuckold, a drunkard, an artistic whore, a destroyer of his own talent.

Fitzgerald, however, at that time and later on, had nothing but admiration for Hemingway's integrity and fiction, and adopted him as his artistic conscience. After their drive through Burgundy, he told

Gertrude Stein: "He's a peach of a fellow and absolutely first-rate" and called himself (with a characteristic sense of inferiority in relation to Hemingway) "a very second-rate person compared to first-rate people." When Booth Tarkington met the traveling companions in Paris that year, he thought they got on splendidly—though Hemingway (in his eyes) lacked the Princeton polish: "My impression was of a Kansas University football beef; but I rather liked him. Fitzgerald brought him up and was a little tight—took him away because Hemingway was to have a [boxing] fight that afternoon at three o'clock, though I gathered they'd both been up all night."[4]

Fitzgerald liked to tell admiring stories of Hemingway and invest his life with a special touch of glamour. The hero of his four absurd "Count of Darkness" stories was modeled on Hemingway as he might have existed in the Middle Ages. In these tales Fitzgerald portrayed Hemingway as a medieval knight; in *A Moveable Feast* Ernest portrayed the sickly Scott as "a little dead crusader." Fitzgerald said that he "had always longed to absorb into himself some of the qualities that made Ernest attractive, and to lean on him like a sturdy crutch in times of psychological distress." The novelist Glenway Wescott, who would soon be satirized as the homosexual Robert Prentiss in *The Sun Also Rises*, exaggerated Fitzgerald's artistic irresponsibility and personal abasement when he claimed that Scott cared more about Hemingway's work than about his own. But there is no doubt that Fitzgerald (like Murphy and Archibald MacLeish) hero-worshiped Hemingway. According to Wescott, Fitzgerald "honestly felt that Hemingway was inimitably, essentially superior. From the moment Hemingway began to appear in print, perhaps it did not matter what he himself produced or failed to produce. He felt free to write just for profit, and to live for fun, if possible. Hemingway could be entrusted with the graver responsibilities and higher rewards such as glory, immortality. This extreme of admiration—this excuse for a morbid belittlement and abandonment of himself—was bad for Fitzgerald."

Fitzgerald took several practical steps to advance Hemingway's career and introduced him to Scribner's just as Shane Leslie had once introduced him to that firm. In October 1924, six months before he met Hemingway and while living in St.-Raphaël, Fitzgerald (still vague about details) told Perkins about the first *in our time*. It had been published, with Pound's help, by William Bird's Three Mountains Press in the spring of 1924. "This is to tell you," Fitzgerald wrote, "about a young man named Ernest Hemingway, who lives in Paris, (an American) writes for the *transatlantic review* & has a brilliant future. Ezra Pound published a collection of his short pieces in Paris, at some place like the Egoist Press. I haven't it here now but it's remarkable & I'd look him up right away. He's the real thing."[5]

Fitzgerald had urged Wescott to write a laudatory essay to launch Hemingway. When Wescott (more concerned about his own career) refused, Fitzgerald wrote an enthusiastic review of *In Our Time* in the *Bookman* of March 1926. He had been tremendously impressed by the autobiographical revelations and the high art of these violent tales about bullfighting, criminals, war, politics and executions, "felt a sort of renewal of excitement at these stories" and, in a notable tribute, said he had read them "with the most breathless unwilling interest I have experienced since Conrad first bent my reluctant eyes upon the sea."

On Fitzgerald's early recommendation Perkins had expressed serious interest in the second *In Our Time* before he even read the book. But his letter reached Hemingway ten days after he had accepted Boni & Liveright's offer, which gave them an option on his next three books. In late November 1925 Hemingway rapidly wrote *The Torrents of Spring: A Romantic Novel in Honor of the Passing of a Great Race*, whose subtitle echoed *The Passing of the Idle Rich* (1911) by Frederick Townsend Martin, the father of Fitzgerald's Princeton friend Townsend Martin. *The Torrents of Spring* was a satire on *Dark Laughter* (1925), the latest book by Hemingway's friend Sherwood Anderson. Then at the height of his reputation, Anderson was Boni & Liveright's best-selling author.

Fitzgerald knew that if Boni & Liveright rejected the book, Hemingway would be free to follow him to Scribner's. He could then publish his nearly completed *The Sun Also Rises* with a more commercially successful firm, acquire a first-rate editor and have an outlet for his stories in *Scribner's Magazine*. But Fitzgerald, whose loyalty to Hemingway was even greater than to Scribner's, thought *The Torrents of Spring* was a funny and a salutary book. On December 30 he urged Horace Liveright to publish it: "It seems about the best comic book ever written by an American. It is simply devastating to about seven-eighths of the work of imitation Andersons, to facile and 'correct' culture." On the same day, in a letter to Perkins (who was equally eager to capture Hemingway) Fitzgerald expressed his belief that Anderson's feeble fiction provoked and deserved Hemingway's witty and well-executed condemnation: "I agree with Ernest that Anderson's last two books have let everybody down who believed in him—I think they're cheap, faked, obscurantic and awful." Two weeks later, when Liveright (as expected) had rejected the attack on his star author, Fitzgerald emphasized Hemingway's inexperience with publishers and urged Perkins to take the satire in order to get the new novel: "To hear him talk you'd think Liveright had broken up his home and robbed him of millions—but that's because he knows nothing of publishing, except in the cuckoo magazines, and is very young and feels helpless so far away [in Paris]. You won't be able to help liking him—he's one of the nicest fellows I ever knew."[6]

Fitzgerald's enthusiasm about the humor in *The Torrents of Spring* was rather surprising because Hemingway (remembering Scott's drunken visits to his Paris flat) had also satirized *him* as an alcoholic clown: "Mr. F. Scott Fitzgerald came to our home one afternoon, and after remaining for quite a while suddenly sat down in the fireplace and would not (or was it could not, reader?) get up and let the fire burn something else. . . . I have the utmost respect for Mr. Fitzgerald and let anybody else attack him and I would be the first to spring to his defense!" In an interview published in April 1927 Fitzgerald alluded to Hemingway's subtitle and his Indian themes, and despondently declared: "There is now no mind of the race, there is now no great old man of the tribe, there are no longer any feet to sit at."[7]

Fitzgerald later recalled that his devotion to Hemingway had—like Anderson's—been repaid with hostility. Scott sadly observed that he, and especially Ernest, had hardened their carapaces and turned against their friends: "People like Ernest and me were very sensitive once and saw so much that it agonized us to give pain. People like Ernest and me love to make people very happy, caring desperately about their happiness. And then people like Ernest and me had reactions and punished people for being stupid." Scott and Zelda had not yet begun their fatal decline when Hemingway first met them, but he was able to perceive the warning signs. Unusually vindictive to benefactors, Hemingway felt superior to Fitzgerald (in Oak Park the Irish were usually servants) and tended to bully him, "like a tough little boy sneering at a delicate but talented little boy." In his retrospective recollection of Fitzgerald, the tough Hemingway uses the words "pretty," "delicate," "girl," "beauty" and "beautiful" to emphasize Scott's effeminate, even decadent good looks: "Scott was a man then who looked like a boy with a face between handsome and pretty. He had very fair wavy hair, a high forehead, excited and friendly eyes and a delicate long-lipped Irish mouth that, on a girl, would have been the mouth of a beauty. His chin was well built and he had good ears and a handsome, almost beautiful unmarked nose. . . . The mouth worried you until you knew him and then it worried you more."[8]

As this passage suggests, Hemingway was drawn to Fitzgerald's attractiveness and charm. But, unerringly perceptive about human weakness, he also despised Fitzgerald's worship of youth, his sexual naïveté, attraction to money, alcoholism, self-pity and lack of dedication to his art. Paraphrasing Georges Clemenceau and Henry Adams on American society, Hemingway felt Fitzgerald put so much value on youth that he confused growing up with growing old, never achieved maturity and "jumped straight from youth to senility" without going through manhood.[9] Fitzgerald also irritated Hemingway (who misunderstood Scott's motives) by asking if he had slept with his wife, Hadley, before they were married. By posing this awkward question, Fitzgerald was not prying into Hemingway's sex life, but trying to understand his own. He really wanted to know if Zelda, who had recently had an affair with Jozan, had been unusual—and immoral—by sleeping with him (and others) before *they* were married.

III

Some of Fitzgerald's Paris friends found him sympathetic and convivial when in his cups, but most of them could not tolerate his alcoholism. The humorist James Thurber first met him in the summer of 1925. Imitating Fitzgerald's series of adjectives in his obituary of Ring Lardner, Thurber affectionately described Scott with a string of contradictory words: "witty, forlorn, pathetic, romantic, worried, hopeful and despondent." And the composer Deems Taylor, Fitzgerald's Great Neck friend, joined him in some lively, Lardner-like pranks in a Paris nightclub. Taylor's daughter recalled that "my father did mention several

drinking sprees with Scott in Paris, and what he considered Scott's outrageous sense of humor. I remember he said that once they were
together at Zelli's, surrounded by *poules* [whores], and Scott said, 'Let's
get rid of these girls.' 'Fine,' said my father. So Scott turned to the
ladies and said, 'I like only men. And this is my friend.' The girls went
away, all right."[10]

But Hemingway, unlike Fitzgerald, did not drink until after his
daily stint of writing was completed and never allowed alcohol to interfere with his work. Much of the trouble between them came from
Fitzgerald's attempts to keep up with Hemingway's drinking. Fitzgerald's worst qualities, Hemingway thought, were his inability to hold his
liquor—a crucial test of manhood—and his compulsion to humiliate
himself and others when he inevitably got drunk. Fitzgerald passed out
on the very first evening they spent together, and the memory of Scott's
waxen death's-head remained rooted in Hemingway's mind.

Writing from Minnesota in August 1921, Fitzgerald had gloomily
told Perkins: "I should like to sit down with ½ dozen chosen companions and drink myself to death." Three years later, in his "Imaginary
Conversation" between Fitzgerald and Van Wyck Brooks, Edmund
Wilson had the enthusiastic Fitzgerald, then living in Great Neck, say:
"Think of being able to give a stupendous house party that would go on
for days and days, with everything that anybody could want to drink
and a medical staff in attendance and the biggest jazz orchestras in the
city alternating night and day!" Fitzgerald must have also said something like this to Hemingway, who wrote from Spain in July 1925 defin-
ing the differences in their tastes and values. He portrayed Fitzgerald
as empty, faithful, snobbish and alcoholic; himself as experienced, athletic, fantastically adulterous and sober: "I wonder what your idea of
heaven would be—A beautiful vacuum filled with wealthy monog-
amists, all powerful and members of the best families, all drinking
themselves to death. . . . To me heaven would be a bull ring with me
holding two *barrera* [front-row] seats and a trout stream outside that
no one else was allowed to fish in and two lovely houses in the town;
one where I would have my wife and children . . . the other where I
would have my nine beautiful mistresses."[11]

Hemingway thought it bad enough that Fitzgerald's drinking was
ruining his life, but found it absolutely intolerable when it began to
interfere with his own sleep and work. Hemingway felt Fitzgerald did

not know how to behave—either socially or morally. He would come drunk to Hemingway's flat (as he had come to the Myers') at any time of the day or night and insult anyone he considered inferior. When little Scottie had to pee and Hemingway's landlord directed them to the toilet, Fitzgerald, angered by his intrusion, exclaimed: "Yes, and I'll put your head in it too, if you're not careful." Though Hemingway hated Fitzgerald's late-night visits, he used the opportunity to observe his alcoholic behavior. Later on, however, he became intensely irritated with Fitzgerald's pranks and their friendship began to cool. He refused to tell Scott his address, lest his drunken antics endanger Hemingway's lease, and insisted they meet only in cafés and restaurants.

Fitzgerald sometimes seemed to welcome the chance to display the worst side of his character. He was particularly unpleasant in June 1926 when he broke up an elegant party the Murphys gave to welcome the Hemingways to Antibes. Jealous of the attention paid to Hemingway, Fitzgerald threw ashtrays at the other tables, laughed hilariously and drove the disgusted Gerald away from his own festivities. In January 1933, after Hemingway had achieved great success with *A Farewell to Arms* and Fitzgerald's career was stagnant, Scott turned up drunk in New York for a dinner with Hemingway and Edmund Wilson. Fitzgerald's behavior shocked the two hardened drinkers, who would never have used liquor as an excuse to degrade themselves in public. Wilson thought this incident illustrated Fitzgerald's habitual self-humiliation, his combination of childishness and cunning, which enabled him to excuse his own failings and attack others without provoking retaliation: "The last time I ever saw [Hemingway]," Wilson wrote, "I had dinner with him and Scott Fitzgerald. Hemingway was now a great man and Scott was so much overcome by his greatness that he embarrassed me by his self-abasement, and he finally lay down on the restaurant floor, pretending to be unconscious but actually listening in on the conversation and from time to time needling his hero, whose weaknesses he had studied intently, with malicious little interpolations." At regular intervals, Hemingway and Wilson would take Scott to the toilet and hold his head while he vomited. When he recovered, Scott insulted his friends and then asked if they still liked him.

Fitzgerald apologized in a letter to Wilson the following month. He completely agreed with Wilson's interpretation of his behavior, and tried to explain how his admiration for and resentment of Hemingway brought out his self-destructive impulse: "I came to New York to get drunk and swinish and I shouldn't have looked up you and Ernest in such a humor of impotent desperation: I assume all responsibility for all unpleasantness—with Ernest I seem to have reached a state where when we drink together I half bait, half truckle to him."[12]

Unlike Hemingway, Fitzgerald was both boring and boorish when drunk. Hemingway vaguely remembered an awful night in New York when he had to bribe the doorman at the Plaza Hotel to compensate for Scott's terrible behavior. He then told Fitzgerald that he would not dine out with him unless he stopped insulting the waiters. Writing in a confessional mood in September 1929, Fitzgerald innocently emphasized the maudlin aspect of his character that Hemingway so despised: "My latest tendency is to collapse about 11:00 and, with the tears flowing from my eyes or the gin rising to their level and leaking over, tell interested friends or acquaintances that I haven't a friend in the world."

Four years later Fitzgerald told Perkins, who often received Scott's confidences and Ernest's condemnations, that he felt compelled to live up to the defensive persona he had established with Hemingway. Ernest "has long convinced himself that I am an incurable alcoholic, due to the fact that we almost always meet at parties. I am *his* alcoholic just like Ring is mine and do not want to disillusion him." Yet alcohol had formed a bond between Scott and Ring (a "good" drinker) that never existed with Ernest. Fitzgerald later tried to equate his drinking with Hemingway's: "An inferiority complex comes simply from not feeling you're doing the best you can—and Ernest's 'drink' was simply a form of this." But their tolerance for alcohol was very different. Fitzgerald got drunk and passed out after only a few drinks; Hemingway could down several bottles of wine without showing the effects. Their striking similarities (which Fitzgerald hinted at) did not emerge until the end of Hemingway's life, when he began to drink and damage himself as much as Fitzgerald had done. In 1930 Fitzgerald told Zelda's doctor: "Give up strong drink permanently I will. Bind myself to forswear wine forever I cannot." In 1957 Hemingway told MacLeish: "Wine I never thought anybody could take away from you. But they can."[13]

Fitzgerald's alcoholism not only alienated his friends and interfered with his writing, but also limited his understanding and choked off his lifeline to fictional material. "How could he know people except on the surface," Hemingway (repeating Sara Murphy's criticism) asked the critic Malcolm Cowley, "when he never fucked anybody, nobody told him anything except as an answer to a question and he was always too drunk late at night to remember what anybody really said." He believed that Fitzgerald's troubles were self-inflicted and that he almost took pride in his shameless defeat. In his gloomier moments of self-analysis, Scott agreed with Ernest and admitted: "At the last crisis, I knew I had no real courage, perseverance or self-respect."

Though Fitzgerald ruthlessly observed and accurately portrayed his own alcoholism in Tender is the Night, "The Crack-Up," the Pat Hobby stories and "The Lost Decade," he never convincingly explained what compelled him to drink. He never found the cause of his addiction and never (until the last year of his life) brought it under control. Though his alcoholism got worse after Zelda's mental breakdown in 1930, she was also partly responsible for his drinking before she became ill. Instead of restraining him for his own good, Zelda encouraged him for her own pleasure. She was, Hemingway believed, insanely jealous of Scott's work. Whenever Fitzgerald decided to write instead of drink, she treated him as if he were a killjoy or spoilsport. "He would start to work," Hemingway wrote, "and as soon as he was working well Zelda would begin complaining about how bored she was and get him off on another drunken party."[14]

Fitzgerald drank to heighten his feelings and put himself in the proper mood for a party; to attract attention, charm, upset, disrupt and shock. As William James observed: "Sobriety diminishes, discriminates, and says no; drunkenness expands, unites, and says yes. . . . It brings its votary from the chill periphery of things to the radiant core." Liquor inspired Fitzgerald's conviviality, extinguished his remorse and compensated for his feelings of inferiority. It prolonged his state of irresponsibility, provided useful if temporary comfort and gave the illusion of happiness. "Drink made past happy things contemporary with the present," he explained in Tender is the Night, "as if they were still going on, contemporary even with the future as if they were about to happen again." The best explanation of the social motives for drinking and of the futile attempt to transform himself into a pleasure-giving Gerald Murphy appeared in "A New Leaf," a minor story of 1931: "I found that with a few drinks I got expansive and somehow had the ability to please people, and the idea turned my head. Then I began to take a

whole lot of drinks to keep going and have everybody think I was wonderful. Well, I got plastered a lot and quarreled with most of my
friends."[15]

Alcohol prevented Fitzgerald from writing. But it also helped compensate for physical and emotional exhaustion, gave him courage to
return to his work and enhanced the power of his imagination. "Drink
heightens feeling," he declared. "When I drink it heightens my emotions and I put them in a story." He found liquor a relief from the
oppressive strain of writing as well as an anodyne from the even greater
torments of creative sterility.

Most often, however, Fitzgerald sought relief in alcoholic binges
during times of emotional stress. He drank to keep up morale—to
shield himself from torturing memories, from insupportable loneliness
and from a dread of impending doom. During the 1930s alcohol
allowed him to forget for a time his guilt about Zelda, his wasted potential, disappointing expeditions to Hollywood, weakening powers,
declining sales, lack of money and psychological depression. Like
William Styron, Fitzgerald used alcohol both "as the magical conduit to
fantasy and euphoria and . . . as a means to calm the anxiety and incipient dread that I had hidden away for so long."

Well aware of the terrible effects of drink, Fitzgerald was unable to
control his addiction and saw himself in the tradition of self-destructive
American writers that had been initiated by Poe. When Scottie was in
college he gave her dire warnings about liquor and threatened to go on
his greatest nonstop binge if she ever touched a drink before she was
twenty. When on the wagon, he would give his friends little lectures.
"Drinking is slow death," he warned Robert Benchley, who promptly
replied: "who's in a hurry?"[16] Fitzgerald even collected photographs put
out by a temperance society that showed the terrible effects of alcohol
on the inner organs, and would morbidly study them—as he had pored
over the ghastly photos of the war wounded—and joke about them in a
menacing fashion.

Fitzgerald's alcoholism led to self-deception, violence and change
of personality. His habit of needling people while drunk became a way
to test how much Dos Passos, the Murphys, Hemingway and Edmund
Wilson really liked him. If they could tolerate his worst behavior, then
they were truly his friends. But most people were not very tolerant; and
Fitzgerald kept a list of "Snubs," many of which occurred when he was

drunk, that stretched over two decades. Scottie, whose childhood was dominated by alcoholic scenes, called him a boring, megalomaniacal and *mean* drunk. Liquor also loosened his tongue and released his sexual inhibitions. "When he was drunk," Sheilah Graham remarked, "he would have had an affair with a tree." Louis Bromfield gave a vivid account of Fitzgerald's alcoholic transformation and terrible behavior, which continued until he suddenly collapsed and passed out: "Like many others who got the name of being drunkards, Scott simply couldn't drink. One cocktail and he was off. It seemed to affect him as much as five or six drinks affected Hemingway and myself. Immediately he was out of control and there was only one end ... that he became thoroughly drunk, and like many Irishmen, when he became drunk he usually became very disagreeable and rude and quarrelsome, as if all his resentments were released at once."

With Fitzgerald, as with Poe, there was a medical explanation for his alcoholism. Both writers suffered from hypoglycemia, or lack of sugar in the blood, which interfered with the supply of glucose to the brain and gave Fitzgerald an abnormal craving, when he was not drinking, for chocolate and Coca-Cola. This disease made it difficult for him to metabolize and tolerate alcohol, which always had an immediate and catastrophic effect on his system. Fitzgerald manifested many of the symptoms of hypoglycemia: insomnia, pallor and fatigue as well as aggressive speech, excessive sweating, visual blurring, muscular tremor, a sense of uncertainty, increasing confusion and, finally, unconsciousness.[17] Hemingway might have been more compassionate about Fitzgerald's alcoholism had he known that it had a physical cause.

IV

Like most of Fitzgerald's friends, Hemingway was physically attracted to Zelda. Describing their first meeting in *A Moveable Feast,* he praised her creamy complexion and gave her the same penetrating eyes he had attributed to his father in "Fathers and Sons": "Zelda was very beautiful and was tanned a lovely gold color and her hair was a beautiful dark gold and she was very friendly. Her hawk's eyes were clear and calm." But Zelda did not remain friendly for very long. Always wary of writers,

Zelda became jealous of her husband's boyish enthusiasm for his hard-boiled new friend. In contrast to Scott, she sensed Hemingway's disapproval, instinctively disliked him and considered him a threat to her marriage. Hemingway's self-conscious display of virility both irritated and menaced her. Attracted to more genteel, polished and deferential men, she provoked Hemingway's hostility by questioning his sexual power. She thought Hemingway was bogus and told him "no one is as masculine as you pretend to be." She tauntingly called him "a phony," "a sort of materialist mystic," "a professional he-man," "a pansy with hair on his chest."[18] According to Zelda, *The Sun Also Rises* was about "bullfighting, bullslinging, and bullshitting."

Like Dos Passos, Hemingway realized that Zelda's intelligence was streaked with madness after she shocked him by declaring, with strange intensity: "Ernest, don't you think Al Jolson is greater than Jesus?" Hemingway agreed with Mencken that "Scott will never amount to a hoot in hell till he gets rid of his wife." He believed that Zelda encouraged him to waste his talent, and undermined his confidence as a man and writer. He saw Fitzgerald's energy and creativity dissipated in bursts of self-destruction.

In 1934, after Zelda had broken down and begun her long series of ineffectual treatments, and Fitzgerald's career seemed to be in decline, Hemingway told him, with brutal honesty: "Of all people on earth you needed discipline in your work and instead you marry someone who is jealous of your work, wants to compete with you and ruins you." At the same time Hemingway recognized Fitzgerald's responsibility for his drinking, his desperate love for Zelda and the overwhelming power of her personality: "It is not as simple as that and I thought Zelda was crazy the first time I met her and you complicated it even more by being in love with her and, of course, you're a rummy."[19] Zelda may have contributed to Hemingway's hostile portrait of the beautiful, dominant and destructive Margot Macomber. There was a hardness beneath Zelda's soft exterior, and underneath that hardness a more vulnerable inner core.

Scott and Zelda's sexual problems, inherent from the beginning of their relationship, came glaringly to the surface during her affair with Jozan and intensified during the late 1920s. Though temperamentally attracted and emotionally attached to each other, they were sexually incompatible. Zelda was sensual; Scott, inhibited by Midwestern puritanism, was not. Other women Scott courted recalled that he could be a witty lover, especially when drink had loosened his tongue, but that he was not especially virile. Elizabeth Beckwith McKie (whom he had known in West Virginia) remembered him cheekily asking: "Are your breasts standing up like that for me?" But she unfavorably compared him to her more aggressive and more physically satisfying Southern beaux, and regretfully reported: "In 1917, I'm afraid, Scott just wasn't a very lively male animal."[20]

During the winter of 1926 the Fitzgeralds, who wanted to have a son, tried in vain to conceive another child. This failure, probably caused by the after-effects of her abortions, made Zelda increasingly unhappy, and provoked her to lash out at her husband's inadequacies. Comparing Scott unfavorably with Jozan, she began to complain that his penis was too small to give her sexual satisfaction. It was naive to blame the size of his organ for her lack of sexual orgasm, which was more likely to have had an emotional cause. But Scott's alcoholism undoubtedly affected his sexual capacity and may even have caused occasional impotence. Later on, as Zelda became obsessed with and exhausted by ballet dancing, their sexual relations gradually petered out and she began to accuse him of homosexuality.

Zelda also repeated the malicious charge of the homosexual expatriate writer Robert McAlmon, who called Fitzgerald and Hemingway a couple of queers. Though this charge was absurd, it wounded Scott and hurt his comradeship with men. One drunken night he took Morley Callaghan's arm and then dropped it. "It was like holding on to a cold fish," Scott told Callaghan. "You thought I was a fairy, didn't you?" Acknowledging in his *Notebooks* the effectiveness of McAlmon's malice, Fitzgerald sadly wrote of Hemingway: "I really loved him, but of course it wore out like a love affair. The fairies have spoiled all that."

Fitzgerald had (as Hemingway remarked) "pretty" feminine looks and once posed as an attractive girl in a Princeton musical. But he had failed as an athlete, soldier, drinker, brawler and sexual partner to his wife, was cruelly hurt by Zelda's accusations and became deeply worried about his masculinity. Edmund Wilson's diary of 1932 contains the earliest account of Fitzgerald's and Hemingway's response to Zelda's attempt at psychological castration, and of Scott's habit of asking strangers: "Do women like a man's private parts large or small?" Wilson recorded: "Hemingway said, Scott thinks that his penis is too small.

(John Bishop had told me this and said that Scott was in the habit of making this assertion to anyone he met—to the lady who sat next to him at dinner and who might be meeting him for the first time.) I explained to him, Hemingway continued, that it only seemed to him small because he looked at it from above. You have to look at it in a mirror."[21]

In a notorious passage in Hemingway's *A Moveable Feast* (set during a lunch in Paris that probably took place in September 1931), Fitzgerald naively confessed: "You know I never slept with anyone except Zelda. . . . Zelda said that the way I was built I could never make any woman happy and that was what upset her." After a personal inspection in the toilet (where the two men spent a surprising amount of time together), the patronizing Ernest reassured the pathetic Scott about his physical equipment: "'You're perfectly fine,' I said. 'You are O.K. There's nothing wrong with you.'" When Fitzgerald asked: "But why would she say it?" Hemingway responded: "To put you out of business." Their exchange ended as Fitzgerald gratefully replied: "I wanted you to tell me truly," and Hemingway told the terrible truth: "Forget what Zelda said. . . . Zelda is crazy. . . . Zelda just wants to destroy you."

But Hemingway's account is highly suspect. Fitzgerald may have felt the need to humiliate himself before the intimidating Hemingway, but it is very doubtful that he would risk the possibility of a devastating confirmation of Zelda's charges. Fitzgerald's convincing statement in "The Crack-Up" that he slept with prostitutes at Princeton in 1917 and his affair with the English actress Rosalinde Fuller two years later cast serious doubt on Hemingway's assertion that Fitzgerald told him he had "never slept with anyone except Zelda." The phrase "tell me truly" sounds much more like Hemingway than like Fitzgerald. The "Matter of Measurements," as Hemingway called it, was rather meaningless without an erection. And if Fitzgerald was unwilling to hold Callaghan's arm, it is extremely unlikely that he would expose and arouse himself in front of Hemingway. In 1935 Fitzgerald told Lottie, a prostitute of mixed race in Asheville, North Carolina, that he had discussed the size of his penis with Hemingway. In Hemingway's version, they began with Scott examining Ernest's manuscripts and ended with Ernest examining Scott's cock. But there is a more plausible scenario. Hemingway, with characteristic exaggeration, probably transformed talking about Fitzgerald's small member at the table into actually showing it in the toilet. Hemingway may have magnified Fitzgerald's sexual innocence. But he was telling the truth about Zelda, who had undoubtedly attacked Scott's sexual capacity.

There is a surprising amount of evidence about Fitzgerald's sexual organ and sexual performance. The *Esquire* editor Arnold Gingrich, Fitzgerald's mistress Sheilah Graham and the prostitute Lottie all saw Fitzgerald's penis and agreed that it was adequate, perfectly normal and like that of other men.[22] His problem was therefore more psychological than physical. He told Edmund Wilson that after Zelda's breakdown he had affairs with other women and worried because he "didn't get very excited by them." And he told another friend that he disliked those casual affairs and could not enjoy sex unless he was emotionally involved with the woman.

Lottie, in an unusual revelation, both described and explained the reasons for Scott's premature ejaculation, which had provoked Zelda's complaints:

> He was nervous and I thought maybe that was why he was so quick about it. I asked him if that was his usual way and he said, yes. . . . I remember him telling me that he only made love to help him write [through excitement and release]. No wonder he was so quick. He might know how to write but he sure doesn't know about this other thing. . . . He believed the real reason for his hasty climax was fear and guilt, both going back to his boyish years of masturbating, a time when he thought sex was dirty and sinful.

Fitzgerald's perceptive St. Paul friend Oscar Kalman (in an interview with Arthur Mizener) confirmed Scott's puritanical inhibitions, lack of a powerful sexual urge and belief—which extended from adolescence into adult life—that sex was "dirty and sinful":

> Scott was at bottom a very conventional man who shocked rather easily, who had some compulsion to shock, and who shocked himself more than he did others. He did things, or liked Zelda to do things, which *did* shock him. Scott had told [Kalman] about Zelda's living with him before they were married; a common enough thing, but Scott never got over being impressed by it. Scott liked the idea of sex, for its

romance and daring, but was not strongly sexed and told
Kalman—and a number of friends of his, including females—
about his anxiety over the shortness of his penis. Kalman said
that Scott was inclined to feel the actual act of sex was messy.[23]

V

Fitzgerald's flaws of character and sexual problems were not fully
apparent in 1925, when Hemingway still trusted him as craftsman and
critic, and deferred to him as the more experienced writer. They read
and revised each other's work, and the passionate discussions about the
art of fiction transcended their differences and drew them together. In
A Moveable Feast Hemingway misleadingly stated that Fitzgerald "was
upset because I would not show him the manuscript of the first draft of
The Sun Also Rises." In fact, Fitzgerald read and corrected the novel.
He had deleted what became his story "Absolution" from the original
opening of The Great Gatsby and shrewdly advised Hemingway, who
followed his advice, to delete the first two chapters of his new novel
before sending it to the printer.

Their first novels, This Side of Paradise and The Sun Also Rises
(1926), had much in common. Fitzgerald called his somewhat pretentious novel "A Romance and a Reading List," and characterized Hemingway's novel, which takes place in France and Spain, "A Romance
and a Guide Book." Both books had bold heroines who defied moral
conventions and influenced the social behavior of the postwar generation. But Hemingway's Brett Ashley—who lives from hand to mouth,
cuts her hair like a boy's, gets drunk, has several adulterous affairs and
loves a sexually incapacitated man—is, unlike Fitzgerald's flirtatious
but chaste debutantes, a truly wild and reckless bohemian. In "Homage
to Switzerland" (1933), Hemingway gently mocked Fitzgerald's sexless
preppy girls when a traveling American asks a Swiss waitress, who has
been to language school: "Were the Berlitz undergraduates a wild lot?
What about all this necking and petting? Were there many smoothies?
Did you ever run into Scott Fitzgerald?"[24]

Fitzgerald's suggestions about Hemingway's later work were less successful than his ideas about *The Sun Also Rises*. Hemingway also took his advice about cutting the opening anecdote of "Fifty Grand" (1927), though he later quoted the passage and regretted the deletion of "that lovely revelation of the metaphysics of boxing." But he rejected Fitzgerald's ludicrous recommendations about how to improve the ending of *A Farewell to Arms* (1929). Fitzgerald thought the novel would be more popular if Hemingway brought in the U.S. Marines and suggested that Frederic Henry read about their victory at Belleau Wood as Catherine Barkley is dying. Hemingway said that he had revised the ending of this novel thirty-two times, but he did not mention that a sentence from *The Great Gatsby*—"Then I went out of the room and down the marble steps into the rain"—directly inspired the famous conclusion of *A Farewell to Arms:* "After a while I went out and left the hospital and walked back to the hotel in the rain." Hemingway acknowledged, however, as Glenway Wescott later observed, that Fitzgerald, a loyal and devoted friend, "was truly more interested in my career at this point than in his own."[25]

Hemingway, who admired *The Great Gatsby*, tried to repay Fitzgerald by encouraging him during the long, difficult nine years between the publication of that novel and *Tender is the Night:* "You just have to *go on* when it is worst and most [hopeless]—there is only one thing to do with a novel and that is go straight on through to the end of the damn thing." Hemingway, with much less money than Fitzgerald, had recently given up a salaried job on the *Toronto Star* in order to concentrate on serious art. He doubted Fitzgerald's claim that he wrote for eight hours a day, and thought the real problem was that Scott wasted his talent on stories for the *Post* and had nothing left over for his novel. Fitzgerald accepted Hemingway's idealistic belief that you had to worship at the altar of art "on your knees" and "with a pure heart," and told Perkins: "there's no point in trying to be an artist if you can't do your best." But he found it difficult to live up to these ideals and in 1929 confessed to Hemingway that he had sold out for money: "the *Post* now pays the old whore $4,000 a screw. But now it's because she's mastered the 40 positions—in her youth one was enough." Genuinely shocked by Fitzgerald's changing good stories to make them more salable (as he had suggested Hemingway do with the ending of *A Farewell to Arms*), Hemingway adopted Fitzgerald's word and called it "whoring." When Hemingway collected his stories in 1938 he rightly felt that all of them were worth reprinting. Fitzgerald, by contrast, deliberately included inferior stories to fill out his collections and, even then, reprinted less than one-third of the ones he had written. Hemingway's stories were not all first rate, but his standard was much higher than Fitzgerald's.

Hemingway felt that Fitzgerald was uneducated, unaware of the immutable laws of fiction and "did everything wrong," but managed to succeed because of his great natural talent. When *Tender is the Night* finally appeared in 1934, Hemingway thought it was too autobiographical, too full of self-pity about Zelda's breakdown and madness, Scott's alcoholism and deterioration. The following year, in *Green Hills of Africa*, Hemingway used the unnamed Fitzgerald to exemplify an author who had declined and dried up: "Our writers when they have made some money increase their standard of living and they are caught. They have to write to keep up their establishments, their wives, and so on, and they write slop. . . . Or else they read the critics. . . . At present we have two good writers [Fitzgerald and Anderson] who cannot write because they have lost confidence through reading critics."[26]

VI

Fitzgerald also met two important women writers when he moved to Paris in the spring of 1925. Hemingway introduced him to Gertrude Stein, who had studied with William James while at Radcliffe and had been trained as a doctor at Johns Hopkins, though she did not complete her medical degree. Rich and domineering, she weighed two hundred pounds, was one of the leading lesbians of the Left Bank and was still struggling to establish her literary reputation. Hemingway's description compared her Jewish features to those of an Italian and concentrated on her sensual hair: "Miss Stein was very big but not tall and was heavily built like a peasant woman. She had beautiful eyes and a strong German Jewish face that could also have been Friulano and reminded me of a northern Italian peasant woman with her clothes, her mobile face and her lovely, thick, alive immigrant hair." Stein's companion, Alice Toklas, an amiable gargoyle, resembled (according to Hadley Hemingway) "a little piece of electric wire, small and fine and very Spanish looking, very dark, with piercing dark eyes." Emphasizing Fitzgerald's rather appealing lack of self-confidence, Toklas remembered Stein's "unfailing appreciation of his work and belief in his gift— which he would not believe. I mean he did neither believe in his gift nor believe she meant what she told him about his work." The less tolerant Hemingway was actually annoyed about Fitzgerald's perverse refusal to accept Stein's sincere compliment and his attempt to distort her praise into a slighting remark.

At that time Stein, who had praised *The Great Gatsby*, admired Fitzgerald's work as much as she did Hemingway's. She was then preoccupied with generations, lost and new. In her third-person narrative *The Autobiography of Alice B. Toklas*—written after she had quarreled with Hemingway, who refused to remain her disciple—she demoted Hemingway and placed Fitzgerald above him: "Gertrude Stein had been very much impressed by *This Side of Paradise*. . . . She said of it that it was this book that really created for the public the new generation. She has never changed her opinion about this. She thinks this equally true of *The Great Gatsby*. She thinks Fitzgerald will be read when many of his well-known contemporaries [i.e., Hemingway] are forgotten."[27] Toklas herself adored Fitzgerald, considered him her favorite young American writer and declared that "his intelligence, sensibility, distinction, wit and charm made his contemporaries [i.e., Hemingway] appear commonplace and lifeless."

Zelda, however, disliked Stein as much as she disliked Hemingway, and thought her involuted conversation was "sententious gibberish." Zelda irreverently told Edmund Wilson, who would write perceptively about the portentous mandarin in *Axel's Castle* (1931): "We went to Gertrude Stein's where a young poet vomited from sheer emotion and the atmosphere was hazy and oracular." Though Zelda avoided Stein in Paris, she received her in Baltimore in December 1934. Andrew Turnbull, then living in Baltimore, gave a dramatic account of Scott's attempt to dominate Zelda, her lively resistance to his demands and Stein's tactful acquiescence to Zelda's wishes:

> During the visit, Zelda came in with some of her paintings, and Fitzgerald asked Miss Stein to take any ones she pleased. She chose two which Zelda had promised her doctor.
>
> "But dear," said Fitzgerald, "you don't understand. Gertrude

will hang them in her salon in Paris and you will be famous. She's been kinder to me than almost anyone and I'd like to give her something."

"If she has been as kind to you as my doctor has been to me," said Zelda, "you should give her everything you own but she can't have those paintings." In the end Miss Stein chose two others.

Turnbull also mentioned Stein's characteristically regal demeanor: "When Scottie appeared, Miss Stein drew from the pocket of her homespun skirt a handful of hazel nuts which she had gathered on her afternoon walk. She gave one to Scottie, who wanted it autographed. 'That would be appropriate,' said Miss Stein, inscribing it."[28]

The bohemian Stein, though a formidable personality, was less intimidating than Edith Wharton, who was then a much grander figure in the world of letters. While the egoistic Stein felt Fitzgerald's deferential reverence was entirely appropriate, the respectable and autocratic Wharton was embarrassed by his awkward and self-abasing homage. His behavior was intended to express his youthful admiration and respect for her art. But Fitzgerald could never quite bridge the gulf between himself and his artistic heroes. Instead of living up to the dramatic occasion, he nervously erupted in gaucherie with Galsworthy, Dreiser, Conrad and Wharton just as it later would with Isadora Duncan and James Joyce.

When Fitzgerald first met Wharton in Charles Scribner's office, just after his first novel was published in the spring of 1920, he impulsively threw himself at her feet and exclaimed: "Could I let the author of *Ethan Frome* pass through New York without paying my respects?" In July 1925, after receiving *The Great Gatsby* and complimenting him on the novel, Wharton invited the Fitzgeralds to tea at her home outside Paris. Zelda, remembering the boredom at Stein's salon and fearing she would be patronized by the grande dame, refused to go. So Scott took the young American composer Theodore Chanler. They had a few drinks on the way; and, as Zelda later wrote, "the nights, smelling of honeysuckle and army leather, staggered up the mountain side and settled upon Mrs. Edith Wharton's garden."

Their conversation was slow and awkward. Swaying against the mantelpiece, Fitzgerald proposed to enliven the dull tea party by telling a couple of "rather rough stories." After Wharton, by no means as stuffy as Fitzgerald imagined, had encouraged him to proceed (writes Wharton's biographer), he "got entangled in an anecdote about an American couple [perhaps himself and Zelda] who by mistake spent a night in a Paris bordello. His hostess, listening attentively, commented at last that the story 'lacks data'—the kind of rounded realistic information and description that the flustered Fitzgerald was unable to provide."[29]

Wharton made no effort to put her nervous guest at ease, deliberately led him into an awkward situation, which he was not quite drunk enough to ignore or to brazen out, and seemed to enjoy his discomfort. Though he certainly had the necessary "data," he felt he could not, under the circumstances, provide it. So his performance fell completely flat. After he left, Wharton remarked: "there must be something peculiar about that young man." But, according to Janet Flanner, Wharton maintained her admiration of his work and later spoke appreciatively of Fitzgerald.

VII

In August 1925 the Fitzgeralds rejoined the Murphys, who had completed the Villa America, and moved into the Hôtel du Cap in Antibes. Fitzgerald celebrated this idyllic place and its devout sun worshipers in the alluring, chromatic opening paragraphs of *Tender is the Night:* "The hotel and its bright tan prayer rug of a beach were one. In the early morning the distant image of Cannes, the pink and cream of the old fortifications, the purple Alp that bounded Italy, were cast across the water." He sent Bishop a characteristically sparkling list of celebrities who gathered in Antibes that summer and who seemed to re-create the Great Neck parties in a more exotic setting: Esther, Gerald and Sara Murphy, Dos Passos, MacLeish, Max Eastman, Floyd Dell, the screenwriter Charlie Brackett, the mystery writer E. Phillips Oppenheim, Rudolph Valentino, the French singer Mistinguett, the actress Alice Terry and her husband, the film director Rex Ingram, the violinist David Mannes, the soprano Marguerite Namara, ex-premier Vittorio Orlando of Italy and the art connoisseur Count Étienne de Beaumont.

A real place to rough it, he added, and escape from the world. The Fitzgeralds almost made their escape complete one drunken evening when their car stalled and they fell asleep on some dangerous trolley tracks. Early the next morning, a peasant awakened them minutes before a trolley smashed their car to pieces. Fitzgerald described their life during this pleasant but wasteful period as "1,000 parties and no work."

In November 1925 the Fitzgeralds returned to England, once again equipped with useful introductions to well-placed people. Through Tallulah Bankhead, a girlhood friend of Zelda, they went to some "high tone" parties with the Mountbattens and the Marchioness of Milford Haven. "Very impressed, but not very," Fitzgerald told Perkins, with newly acquired English nonchalance, "as I furnished most of the amusement myself." Fitzgerald's visit to his new London publisher, Chatto & Windus, without first making an appointment, was more significant. The novelist Frank Swinnerton, who received him, recalled:

> I went from my office to the waiting-room, where a young man sat, with his hat on, at a small table. He did not rise or remove his hat, and he did not answer my greeting, so I took another chair, expressing regret that no partner was available, and asking if there was anything I could do. Assuming, I suppose, that I was some base hireling, he continued brusque to the point of truculence; but we spoke of the purpose of his visit, and after a few moments he silently removed his hat. Two minutes later, looking rather puzzled, he rose. I did the same. I spoke warmly of *The Great Gatsby;* and his manner softened. He became an agreeable boy, quite ingenuous and inoffensive, and finally asked my name. I told him. If I had said "The Devil" he could not have been more horrified. Snatching up his hat in consternation, he cried: "Oh, my God! *Nocturne's* one of my favorite books!" and dashed out of the premises.[30]

In this encounter between a poised Englishman and a bumbling American, Swinnerton, completely in control of the situation, brought Fitzgerald round from rudeness to adoration. Their meeting revealed the uncomfortably defensive and effusive aspects of Fitzgerald's character, and suggested that far from being at ease in English society, he got on with Swinnerton no better than he had with Galsworthy, Mackenzie and Rebecca West. In the end, he had to rush out of the room in acute embarrassment.

Fitzgerald, to his intense irritation, had much less of a reputation in England than in America. He was virtually ignored by the critics from the early 1920s until after World War II and none of his books sold well there during his lifetime. Though Thomas Hardy, shortly before his death, said he "had read and been greatly impressed by *This Side of Paradise*" and that Fitzgerald "was one of the few younger American writers whose work he followed with any interest," the *Times Literary Supplement* correctly stated that "when Fitzgerald died in 1940 his work, outside a small circle, was hardly known in this country."

Fitzgerald had been in London when William Collins brought out *This Side of Paradise* in May 1921 and had told an editor friend that the book was "having a checkered career in England." The *Manchester Guardian* dismissively concluded: "But what people! What a set! They are well lost." And the *Times Literary Supplement* disagreed with the American critics who had found the novel original and exuberant. Setting the critical tone for the next twenty years, its anonymous reviewer rejected the novel as trivial, unconvincing and "rather tiresome; its values are less human than literary, and its characters . . . with hardly an exception, a set of exasperating *poseurs,* whose conversation, devoted largely to minute self-analysis, is artificial beyond belief."[31] The novel, which had required twelve printings and sold 49,000 copies during its first year in America, bombed in England with a sale of only 700.

Flappers and Philosophers, The Beautiful and Damned and *Tales of the Jazz Age,* also published by Collins, did not receive serious critical attention. When Scribner's sent Fitzgerald's masterpiece, *The Great Gatsby,* to Collins, he invented a rather absurd reason to reject an author whose books had been losing money for the firm. "We do not at all like to part with Scott Fitzgerald, but we feel very strongly that to publish *The Great Gatsby* would be to reduce the number of his readers rather than to increase them," he explained to Perkins, who passed the bad news on to Fitzgerald in October 1925. "The point is, that the atmosphere of the book is extraordinarily foreign to the English reader, and he simply would not believe in it, and therefore I am regretfully returning it to you." Fitzgerald justly complained that the publisher had rejected his serious and encouraged his frivolous work: "Collins never believed in me. (He always wanted me to write [another] 'Offshore Pirate.') I know my public in England is small—but I have had enough enthusiastic letters to know it exists." Though Chatto & Windus published *The Great Gatsby* in 1926, his last two collections of stories, *All the Sad Young Men* and *Taps at Reveille*, have never appeared in England.

The Great Gatsby received excellent notices from two American critics, Gilbert Seldes and Conrad Aiken, in T. S. Eliot's magazine, *The Criterion*. Eliot himself, an editor at Faber, had been enthusiastic about the novel and hoped his firm would publish it. But the English reviewers were much less keen. The *Times Literary Supplement* acknowledged that it was "undoubtedly a work of art and of great promise"—though its promise had surely been fulfilled—but complained about the unpleasantness of the characters. And the novelist L. P. Hartley offered a condescending admonition: "Mr. Scott Fitzgerald deserves a good shaking. Here is an unmistakable talent unashamed of making itself a motley to the view. *The Great Gatsby* is an absurd story, whether considered as romance, melodrama, or plain record of New York high life." Fitzgerald, perhaps unduly touchy, as he had been with Swinnerton, continued to feel that Chatto & Windus was snubbing him. In January 1930 he complained to Perkins about a commonplace business reply: "they answered a letter of mine on the publication of [*The Great Gatsby*] with the signature (Chatto & Windus, per Q), undoubtedly an English method of showing real interest in one's work."[32] Though Fitzgerald admired Oxford, which had played a prominent role in *The Great Gatsby*, he lost interest in England after Collins dropped him. He never returned there after his second visit and was consistently hostile to the English in his work.

Two months after their visit to England, in January 1926, the Fitzgeralds left Paris again. Zelda had been suffering from colitis and persistent gynecological problems; and they decided to spend a cold and restful winter in the western Pyrenees between Bayonne and Pau. In January Fitzgerald wrote to Harold Ober: "We have come to a lost little village called Salies-de-Béarn in the Pyrenees where my wife is to take a special treatment of baths for eleven months for an illness that has run now for almost a year. Here they have the strongest salt springs in the world—and out of season nothing much else—we are two of the seven guests in the only open hotel." After the excitement of Paris and

London, however, the place was too boring to endure. Scott told a friend that the other inhabitants were two goats and a paralytic, and Zelda's rest cure was reduced from eleven months to only one. In June 1926 Zelda, on a quick trip to Paris, had her appendix out at the American Hospital, but continued to feel unwell.

In March they returned to the Riviera for a nine-month stay in Juan-les Pins, just next to Antibes. They spent the first two months in the Villa Paquita, which Fitzgerald found too damp and uncomfortable. When the Hemingways arrived for the summer, Fitzgerald generously gave them the villa and moved to the more suitable Villa St. Louis. The large house was wonderfully situated on the coast, with the beach and the Casino nearby, and they looked forward to a marvelous summer.

At a farewell party for the critic Alexander Woollcott and other friends, Zelda (chirpy again) did her by-now-familiar but always welcome striptease. After speeches had been made, she daringly declared: "I have been so touched by all these kind words. But what are words? Nobody has offered our departing heroes any gifts to take with them. I'll start off"—and she stepped out of her black lace panties and threw them at the grateful men. Not content with her own performance, Zelda also dared Scott (as she had dared him to fight the bouncer in the Jungle Club) to make some dangerous high dives from the cliffs into the sea—and forced him to accept her challenge.

One evening when the Fitzgeralds were dining outdoors with the Murphys at the Colombe d'Or in Vence, a lovely village in the Maritime Alps above Juan-les Pins, Zelda took an even more dramatic dive. "Isadora Duncan was giving one of her last parties at the next table," Zelda wrote. "She had got too old and fat to care whether people accepted her theories of life and art, and she gallantly toasted the world's obliviousness in lukewarm champagne. There were village dogs baying at a premature white exhausted August moon and there were long dark shadows folded accordion-like along the steps of the steep streets of Saint-Paul."[33] Zelda portrayed the dancer who provoked the scene as unattractive and described the fateful evening as if nothing extraordinary had occurred. But the steep stone steps and the long dark shadows suggest an ominous event. Isadora, reputed to be free with her favors, had summoned Fitzgerald to her table. He sat at her feet while she ran her jeweled fingers through his blond hair and called him "my centurion." Zelda, who liked to be the center of attention and resented this seductive behavior, suddenly got up from the table and—in her second attempt at self-destruction—threw herself down a long flight of steps. Though cut and bleeding, she was not badly hurt and offered no explanation for her bizarre act. The Murphys knew something was seriously wrong with Zelda, but did not suspect that she was mentally ill.

Though Fitzgerald was nearly thirty, he continued his heavy drinking and ludicrous pranks. During the summer of 1926 Scott and his Riviera friends lured a hotel orchestra to his villa, locked them in a room with a bottle of whiskey and sat down outside the closed door for a private concert of their favorite music. They made an amateur silent film, with an incestuous Japanese hero, on the grounds of the Hôtel du Cap, and painted the obscene titles on the walls of a friend's villa. Some of these high-spirited adventures found their way into *Tender is the Night*. Abe North, for example, kidnaps a waiter from a café in Cannes in order to saw him in two and find out what is inside. "'Old menus,' suggested Nicole with a short laugh. 'Pieces of broken china and tips and pencil stubs.' 'Exactly [said Abe]—but the thing was to prove it scientifically. And of course doing it with that musical saw would have eliminated any sordidness.'"

But the pranks that had once been playful and innocent now became menacing and malicious. They raided a restaurant in Cannes, captured the owner and waiters, and threatened to push them off a cliff. One late night outside the Casino at Juan-les Pins an old lady offered them a tray of daintily arranged nuts and candies. As they stopped to admire the display, Fitzgerald made an ugly scene by kicking the tray and sending all the sweetmeats into the street. He was repentant, Sara Murphy recalled, and immediately tried "to make amends by offering her his apologies and hundreds of francs. He *always* realized when he had gone too far, & was very sorry & mortified." But the damage had been done—both to the old lady and to his reputation. Fitzgerald certainly helped create the image of the rich and vulgar American in France.

The Murphys could apparently take anything: practical jokes, figs down backs, broken stemware, flying ashtrays, thrown garbage, kicked trays, drunken brawls, passing out and tedious analytical questions as well as Zelda's public disrobing and attempts at suicide. No matter what the Fitzgeralds did, they were always forgiven by their devoted friends. Gerald's moving letter of farewell, for example, echoed the second chapter of the Song of Solomon to express the intensity of their affection for the Fitzgeralds and—though the hush and emptiness must have been a welcome relief—the genuine sorrow they felt when their friends had left the Riviera:

> There *really* was a great sound of tearing heard in the land as your train pulled out that day. Sara and I rode back together saying things about you both to each other which only partly expressed what we felt separately. Ultimately, I suppose, one must judge the degree of one's love for a person by the hush and the emptiness that descends upon the day,—after the departure. We heard the tearing because it was there,—and because we weren't able to talk much about how much we do love you two. We agreed that it made us very sad, and sort of hurt a little—for a "summer holiday."[34]

VIII

Fitzgerald's third volume of stories, *All the Sad Young Men,* was published in February 1926, ten months after *The Great Gatsby.* There was a striking difference between the three best stories—"Absolution" (1924), "Winter Dreams" (1922) and "The Rich Boy" (1926)—and the six mediocre ones that filled out the collection. It is significant that none of his best works was published in the *Saturday Evening Post.*

"Absolution," Fitzgerald's most Catholic story, was originally intended to explain Jay Gatz's background, but was deleted from the novel because Fitzgerald wished to preserve a sense of mystery about his hero. This story—with its disillusioned, ironic tone; its pure, detached style; its oblique, suggestive technique; and its subtle, elusive themes—is deeply indebted to Joyce's *Dubliners* (1914). The homosexual temptation and death of the priest, in fact, evolve directly from "An Encounter" and "The Sisters" in that volume, just as the prurient priest and the insincere confession of sexual offenses derive from Molly Bloom's soliloquy in the last chapter of *Ulysses.*

The opening paragraph of "Absolution" is brilliantly evocative:

There was once a priest with cold, watery eyes, who, in the still of the night, wept cold tears. He wept because the afternoons were warm and long, and he was unable to attain a complete mystical union with our Lord. Sometimes, near four o'clock, there was a rustle of Swede girls along the path by his window, and in their shrill laughter he found a terrible dissonance that made him pray aloud for the twilight to come. . . . He had found the scent of cheap toilet soap desperately sweet upon the air. He passed that way when he returned from hearing confessions on Saturday nights, and he grew careful to walk on the other side of the street so that the smell of the soap would float upward before it reached his nostrils as it drifted, rather like incense, toward the summer moon.

The cold eyes of the tormented Father Schwartz contrast with the warm night of the town and intensify the irony of his impossible desire to attain *complete* mystical union with Jesus. In a similar fashion, the scent of the cheap toilet soap undermines the ironic comparison to incense as the priest, aroused by the sexual secrets of the confessional, is torn between spiritual yearning and sensual desire. The summer moon, which symbolizes his temptation at the beginning of the story, concludes the tale by shining on the scented Swede girls, lying amidst the wheat with their young farmboys and achieving the physical gratification denied to the priest.

The priest's vague but powerful desire immediately focuses on the beautiful, blue-eyed, eleven-year-old Rudolph Miller. In a flashback at the end of section I, to three days earlier, Rudolph dutifully confesses seven sins. But he then lies in the confessional by stating that he never tells lies. Like the young Fitzgerald, Rudolph considers himself too good to be his parents' son and invents a suave alter ego, with the absurd name of Blatchford Sarnemington, which allows him to escape from sin and from the need to deceive God. Rudolph plans to evade communion, while in a state of sin, by drinking a glass of water before church. But when his father catches him in the act, he tells the truth (when he could easily have lied, as he had lied to the priest) by admitting that he has not yet tasted the water.

After being beaten by his father (like the innocent child in Joyce's "Counterparts"), Rudolph goes to a second confession. But he does not admit that he lied in the first one, and takes communion in a state of sin. When the story returns to the present in the final section, Father Schwartz, instead of providing discipline and giving penance, tells Rudolph about "the glimmering places," which the priest associates with amusement parks (like the one in Joyce's "Araby"). But the priest also brings himself back to reality by warning the boy: "don't get up close . . . because if you do you'll only feel the heat and the sweat and the life." This lesson conveyed, Father Schwartz collapses into death. Unable to live up to his religious ideals, the priest cannot provide the necessary comfort during the spiritual crisis of a confused, guilt-ridden boy. Both fathers, natural and spiritual, have failed Rudolph, who never receives the long-sought absolution.

The plots and themes of "Winter Dreams" and "The Rich Boy" are similar. In the former, a poor boy, Dexter Green, falls in love with a rich girl, Judy Jones. He loses her, becomes engaged to and then abandons a poor substitute for his true love. At the end of the story, he discovers that Judy is unhappily married and that her looks have faded. Dexter is shattered by this news because he too has lost his illusions of beauty and perfection: "He had thought that having nothing else to lose he was invulnerable at last—but he knew that he had just lost something more, as surely as if he had married Judy Jones and seen her fade away before his eyes. The dream was gone. Something had been taken from him. . . . Even the grief he could have borne was left behind in the country of illusion, of youth, of the richness of life, where his winter dreams had flourished."

In the latter story, a rich boy, Anson Hunter, loves a rich girl, Paula Legendre, but loses her and becomes involved with an inferior girl, Dolly Karger. Hunter retaliates for his own emotional vacuity by abandoning Dolly and by driving his aunt's lover to suicide. Later on, he encounters Paula, who has had an unhappy first marriage but is now contentedly pregnant by her second husband. At the end of the story, Hunter learns that Paula has died in childbirth.

In one story differences in money and class are the obstacles to love; in the other, the obstacles are great egoism and great wealth. Both works describe the hero's life from boyhood to his early thirties. Both stories portray the destructive power of beautiful women, ephemeral happiness, the reluctance to abandon illusory dreams, the sense of loss and the impossibility of achieving true love. But Anson Hunter is a more fully developed character than Dexter Green and is portrayed in a more substantial social context. Like the Patches in *The Beautiful and Damned*, the Buchanans in *The Great Gatsby* and the Warrens in *Tender is the Night*, Hunter expresses Fitzgerald's fascination with the superiority, the selfishness and the emptiness of the rich. "They are different from you and me," he writes at the beginning of the story. "They possess and enjoy early, and it does something to them, makes them soft where we are hard, and cynical where we are trustful, in a way that, unless you were born rich, it is very difficult to understand."[35] Hunter also shows that money can fatally weaken the will and lead to a meaningless life.

Dexter Green is cruelly manipulated by Judy Jones (based on Ginevra King) who "treated him with interest, with encouragement, with malice, with indifference, with contempt." Though Anson Hunter dominates his women, he is incapable of emotional commitment and deprives himself of a married life and a settled—rather than a dissipated—existence. Fitzgerald based "The Rich Boy" on the confidential revelations of his hard-drinking Princeton friend, Ludlow Fowler. Though Hunter is portrayed negatively, Fitzgerald somehow thought Fowler would be pleased by the tale. "It is in a large measure the story of your life," he wrote Fowler in 1925, "toned down here and there and simplified. Also many gaps had to come out of my imagination. It is frank, unsparing but sympathetic and I think you will like it—it is one of the best things I have ever done." When Hemingway read the story, Fitzgerald told Fowler, he said the real Anson *would* have raped Dolly instead of abandoning the seduction. And, Fitzgerald added, "I hadn't the privilege of telling him that, in life, he *did!*"[36]

The reviews of *All the Sad Young Men* were generally favorable. In Fitzgerald's hometown paper, the Minneapolis *Journal*, Thomas Boyd loyally wrote that "Absolution" reveals a "perfection of mood, of form and implication.... Everything that Scott Fitzgerald writes contains something that is worth reading." Harry Hansen, in the Chicago *Daily News*, was enthusiastic about Fitzgerald's versatility and style, but rightly thought the deeper meaning and greater art made *In Our Time* superior to Fitzgerald's collection. The stories give, he wrote, "excellent proof of his ability to write well in half a dozen manners. It is a joy to read these tales. They lack sameness; they are ironical, and sad, and jolly good fun by turns; they scintillate." And in the *Saturday Review*,

William Rose Benét, more perceptive than the other critics, admired Fitzgerald's originality, but saw that he was torn by the conflict between money and art: "His ingenuity at evolving marketable ideas is extraordinary. But one naturally feels, behind most of the writing in this book, the pressure of living conditions rather than the demand of the spirit. As a writer of short stories the author more displays his astonishing facility than the compulsions of his true nature." The positive reviews helped to sell more than 16,000 copies in 1926, and the collection earned nearly four thousand dollars.

Fitzgerald had completed *The Great Gatsby* in Europe in 1924. But he had become blocked on an early—and subsequently rejected—draft of *Tender is the Night* and had done no serious work since then. He had squandered his money, his life was chaotic, his marriage was disintegrating and he was drinking heavily. Just before he sailed from Genoa in December 1926 on the *Conte Biancamano*—with the familiar intention to save money and devote himself to fiction—he wrote Hemingway (as Murphy had written him): "I can't tell you how much our friendship has meant to me during this year and a half—it is the brightest thing in our trip to Europe for me."[37] For the rest of his life Hemingway was his ideal reader. Scott always sought and respected his good opinion, and was desperately eager to know if Ernest approved of his work.

Chapter Eight

ELLERSLIE AND FRANCE, 1927–1930

I

The Fitzgeralds barely had time to visit his parents, who had moved to Washington, D.C., and hers in Montgomery, when he received an offer from United Artists in Hollywood. They wanted a modern flapper story for the popular and vivacious comedy star Constance Talmadge, whom Fitzgerald had jokingly called "a back number" in the telegram that announced Scottie's birth. He was offered an advance of $3,500, and $12,500 more if the film story was accepted. Movies had been made from two of his stories ("Head and Shoulders" and "The Offshore Pirate") and two of his novels (an awful *The Beautiful and Damned* and an equally awful version of *The Great Gatsby*); and he had done titles (to convey dialogue), a scenario and a screenplay for three silent movies in 1923–24. With his flair for dialogue and facility as a writer, he felt confident that he could easily master the art of screenwriting. Always in need of money and eager to explore a social scene that had even more celebrities than the French Riviera, he decided to carry out his earlier plan to "go to Hollywood and learn the movie business." In January 1927 the Fitzgeralds left Scottie with his parents and took a train across the country on their first, two-month trip to Hollywood.

Enthusiastically received by the film community, the Fitzgeralds were immediately caught up in the swirl of parties. They shared a four-apartment "bungalow" on the grounds of the luxurious Ambassador Hotel on Wilshire Boulevard with the actress Carmel Myers, their friend since Rome; with the novelist Carl Van Vechten, whom they had met in Great Neck; and with the handsome and hard-drinking actor John Barrymore. Fitzgerald gave a copy of *The Great Gatsby* to Barrymore, who had read his earlier work and wrote an unusually perceptive letter about the novel. "The advance on *The Beautiful and Damned* seems to me enormous in all respects," Barrymore wrote. "Your new book has a cohesion and unity—somewhat lacking in the other. You have hit upon a style admirably suited to your subject—; your own style, that is, your own personality. . . . I had not expected you could *write so well.*"

The Fitzgeralds attempted to live up to their glamorous legend, but instead got drunk and acted outrageously. They turned up uninvited at Sam Goldwyn's party, got down on their hands and knees outside the front door, and barked like dogs until they were reluctantly admitted to the house. Armed with a huge sewing shears, they made a late-night visit to the screenwriter and ladies' man John Monk Saunders and threatened to solve all his romantic problems by castration. During the 1919 May Day celebrations Fitzgerald had mixed ketchup and eggs in a friend's hat. In 1927, during tea with Carmel Myers, Scott went even further and boiled a couple of watches and assorted jewelry belonging to several of the guests in a can of tomato soup. No one could understand why he behaved in this bizarre fashion, and none of the guests dared to taste the expensive stew. Ronald Colman was particularly annoyed, but no one else seemed to object to the destruction of valuable property. "Of course they behaved badly," the actress Lois Moran observed, "but they were never mean or cruel or unkind." Nevertheless, these pranks must have angered and alienated many people besides Ronald Colman. They reinforced Fitzgerald's reputation as an alcoholic, hurt his professional standing in Hollywood and made it more difficult for him to get lucrative film work.

While in Hollywood Fitzgerald met and fell in love with the extraordinary eighteen-year-old Lois Moran, who became the model for Helen Avery in "Magnetism" (1928) and for Rosemary Hoyt in *Ten-*

der is the Night (1934). Born in Pittsburgh in 1908, Lois, as an infant, had moved to Paris with her mother, who was (as in Fitzgerald's novel) a doctor's widow. Lois soon fulfilled her mother's own ambition to become an actress. She joined the Paris Opera Corps de Ballet as a professional ballerina at the age of thirteen, acted in her first film in France at fourteen, starred with Ronald Colman as the daughter in *Stella Dallas* (1925) and made four films for Fox before she was twenty. In the 1930s she starred in several Broadway musicals, including George S. Kaufman's *Of Thee I Sing*. Unlike most film stars, Lois was a cultured and refined young lady with a cosmopolitan background. She had spent many years in Europe and spoke fluent French. In 1922 Scott and Zelda had discussed the possibility of starring in a film version of *This Side of Paradise*. In 1927 Lois, who wanted Scott to be the leading man in her next picture, arranged a screen test—which he failed.

Lois' virginal, blond, blue-eyed Irish beauty, Fitzgerald wrote in "Princeton" (1927), inspired the stags to line up for a hundred years to cut in on her dances. In his plan for *Tender is the Night*, he emphasized that the character based on Lois "differs from most actresses by being a lady, simply reeking of vitality, health, sensuality." And he conveyed these qualities in his romantic exaltation of Rosemary at the beginning of the novel: "Her fine forehead sloped gently up to where her hair, bordering it like an armorial shield, burst into lovelocks and waves and curlicues of ash blonde and gold. Her eyes were bright, big, clear, wet, and shining, the color of her cheeks was real, breaking close to the surface from the strong young pump of her heart. Her body hovered delicately on the last edge of childhood—she was almost eighteen, nearly complete, but the dew still on her."[1]

Lois, who had absolutely no idea that Zelda was jealous of her, used to worry because all the attractive men she knew were married. Zelda complained that Scott would not allow her to go anywhere without him while he himself "engaged in flagrantly sentimental relations with a child." But Zelda undermined, while Lois strengthened, his self-esteem. Scott, whose self-confidence was also eroded by failure in Hollywood, defended his friendship with Lois by explaining that he would do "anything to be liked, to be reassured not that I was a man of a little genius but that I was a great man of the world. . . . Anybody [who] could make me believe that, like Lois Moran did, was precious to me."

The telegram Lois sent Scott after he had left Hollywood in mid-March 1927 closely imitated the sophisticated style of *The Great Gatsby*. In the novel, when Daisy asks Nick if people miss her in Chicago, he replies with flattering exaggeration: "The whole town is desolate. All the cars have the left rear wheel painted black as a mourning wreath, and there's a persistent wail all night along the north shore." In real life Lois, referring to Scott's drinking and adopting Nick's mournful tone, exclaimed: HOLLYWOOD COMPLETELY DISRUPTED SINCE YOU LEFT. BOOTLEGGERS GONE OUT OF BUSINESS. COTTON CLUB CLOSED. ALL FLAGS AT HALF MAST. . . . BOTTLES OF LOVE TO YOU BOTH. In a letter that followed this telegram, Lois aroused his jealousy by being both playful and seductive, disclaiming interest in her now-dull life while mentioning that she was sexually attracted to her handsome leading man: "Darling Scott—I miss you enormously—Life is exceedingly dull out here now—Have just been bumming around the studios and seeing people I am not in the least interested in—Maybe I will play with William Haines in his next picture—I rather hope so because I admire him enormously and he gives very satisfactory kisses."[2]

There is conflicting evidence about Scott's relations with Lois. In a letter of October 1937 he mentioned an "AFFAIR (unconsummated) with ACTRESS (1927)." But he was apparently eager to advertise as well as to conceal his liaison with Lois. The illustrator Arthur Brown, who was then living at the Ambassador Hotel, reported that one morning Fitzgerald burst into his room, woke him up and said: "'Say hello to Zelda.' But it was Lois Moran, and not Zelda, on his arm. Scott asked Brown to cover for him [while he secretly spent time with Lois]. If any questions were asked, Brown was to say that they'd spent the day together at First National Studios."

More significantly, Fitzgerald told Zelda's psychiatrist in 1932, when he was trying to justify his past behavior and diminish his responsibility for her breakdown, about "her affair with Edouard Jozan in 1925 and mine with Lois Moran in 1927, which was a sort of revenge." And Zelda told the same doctor: "When I knew my husband had another woman in California I was upset." Scott's powerful attraction to Lois, his description of her as "sensual," his emotional and sexual estrangement from Zelda, his desire to retaliate for her affair with Jozan, his need to restore his manly self-confidence as well as Lois' provocative letters and Zelda's intense jealousy of a beautiful younger rival, all suggest that Fitzgerald had a brief affair with Lois Moran in 1927.

Scott not only fell in love with and slept with Lois, but also used her impressive career to disparage Zelda's idleness. Zelda responded to Scott's infatuation with two self-destructive acts that—like her reckless reaction to his dalliance with Isadora Duncan—were meant to punish him by hurting herself. In February she burned in the bathtub of their Hollywood bungalow all the clothes she had designed for herself. The following month, on the eastbound train, Zelda, who could no longer conceive a child, threw from the train window the valuable platinum watch that Scott had bought her in 1920 when trying to persuade her to have an abortion. To Zelda, the destruction of the watch was equated with Scott's attempt to destroy their child.

When Lois visited the Fitzgeralds in Delaware later that year, Zelda wrote a perceptive but caustic description of the actress's strange mixture of wholesomeness, vacuity and hysteria, which precisely matched Scott's emotional needs: "a young actress like a breakfast food that many men identified with whatever they missed from life since she had no definite characteristics of her own save a slight ebullient hysteria about romance. She walked in the moon by the river. Her hair was tight about her head and she was lush and like a milkmaid."

Lois' later meetings with Scott in the early 1930s, when he was drinking, depressed about Zelda's illness and apparently beyond redemption, were tortured and miserable. "When I saw him in '33, '34 and '35 he was so different from the man I'd known before, and I was still too young to cope with him," she uneasily explained to Mizener. "With a little more maturity and wisdom, perhaps I could have helped him. Instead, I just wanted to run."[3]

There were other anxieties and frustrations, besides Lois Moran, on Fitzgerald's first trip to Hollywood. *Lipstick,* the weak story of Princeton boys and modern flappers he had written for Constance Talmadge, was—after he had quarreled with the actress—rejected by the studio. He never received the additional payment of $12,500 and spent far more in Hollywood than he had earned. Though this failure set the pattern for all his later film work, he could never resist the lure of glamour and money. He returned to Hollywood for six weeks in 1931, and spent the last three and a half years of his life struggling unsuccessfully as a screenwriter.

II

Fitzgerald wanted to keep a safe distance from the parties in New York in order to concentrate on his novel, and Max Perkins suggested he might like to live in the relative tranquility of Wilmington, Delaware. When Scott and Zelda returned from Hollywood in March 1927, his Princeton friend John Biggs helped them find Ellerslie, in the village of Edgemoor, on the west bank of the Delaware River, a few miles north of Wilmington. Impressed by the thirty large rooms and by the low rent of $150 a month, the Fitzgeralds signed a two-year lease. Ellerslie, a square, three-story, white-and-green, shuttered Greek revival mansion, had been built in 1842. (It was demolished about twenty-five years ago.) It had extensive gardens, and was shaded by ancient oaks and blooming chestnut trees. Its imposing front portico, supported by four massive white columns, had a commanding view of the river. There were fifteen high-ceilinged bedrooms, with iron balconies, a walnut-paneled drawing room nearly a hundred feet long and a steep, twisting staircase. Fitzgerald believed there was also a resident ghost.

The Fitzgeralds hoped the squareness of the rooms and the sweep of the columns would bring "a judicious tranquility." But instead of bringing peace, the house inspired their riotous and protracted week-end parties, which featured black jazz bands imported for the occasion. The weekends at Ellerslie revived and recreated—in a much grander setting and on a more elaborate scale—their wasteful and often unpleasant parties in Westport and Great Neck. Scott, who could not focus on his writing, encouraged everyone he knew to come down for a visit, and told a boyhood friend: "We have taken an old place on the Delaware River where we live in splendor surrounded by a nubian guard of sling throwers, eunuchs, back-slappers and concubines." Fitzgerald's parties parodied both the Murphys' elegant entertainments and Tommy Hitchcock's athletic exploits. The playwright Charles MacArthur and other wild guests shot his dinner plates to pieces during target practice on the front lawn, and tried to play polo with croquet mallets and heavy plough horses.

Fitzgerald made strenuous efforts to please his numerous guests: his cousin Cecilia Taylor, Lois Moran, the Irish critic Ernest Boyd, John Dos Passos, Thornton Wilder, Edmund Wilson, Carl Van Vechten, his

Princeton classmate Thomas Linneaweaver, John Biggs and Hemingway. But they all found the forced hilarity, the heavy drinking and the
chaotic atmosphere distinctly disappointing, and were relieved when
the exhausting weekends came to an end. Despite the frequent catas-
trophes at Ellerslie, Fitzgerald managed to retain the friendship of all
these people, who tolerated his faults when drunk because he was so
extraordinarily attractive when sober.

Ernest Boyd, the heavy-drinking Irish critic, told Mencken that the
pace was too hot for him. Dos Passos, who visited Ellerslie in September 1927, had memories of acute starvation: "Those delirious parties of
theirs; one dreaded going. At Wilmington, for instance, dinner was
never served. Oh, a complete mess. I remember going into Wilmington—they lived some miles out, trying to find a sandwich, something to
eat. A wild time." Thornton Wilder's fan letter about The Great Gatsby
led to an invitation in February 1928 and to a life-threatening incident
with one of the guns that had been used to destroy the dinner plates.
Mentioning that he had something to show Wilder, the drunken
Fitzgerald invited him up to the attic, where he picked up a gun and
waved it around. He then fired an accidental shot that narrowly missed
Wilder and tore into the wall. When Wilder mentioned the accident
the next morning Fitzgerald, who had completely forgotten it, was
appalled by his own behavior.[4]

The fullest account of a weekend at Ellerslie was written by
Edmund Wilson, who visited the mansion at the same time as Wilder.
Fitzgerald and Wilson had not seen much of each other since Scott's
trip to Europe in 1924. Their relations had suffered a certain chill
when Wilson began to inquire about the progress of his novel and
Fitzgerald wanted appreciation more than harsh advice. Eager to
revive the friendship, he sent Wilson an invitation that began: "All is
prepared for February 25th. The stomach pumps are polished and set
out in rows, stale old enthusiasms are being burnished." Wilson arrived
at the station with Wilder and the two writers had a lively discussion
about the latest novel by Proust. When they reached the house Fitzgerald, who loved to play the squire of the manor, proudly took them on a
tour. The butler, hiding behind doors, obediently groaned like a ghost.
Fitzgerald then offered his guests the strange choice of either listening
to records of Stravinsky's The Rite of Spring or examining a photograph
album of horribly mutilated soldiers.

The other visitors that weekend included Esther Murphy, Gilbert Seldes, who had previously visited Fitzgerald in St.-Raphaël and had enthusiastically praised *The Great Gatsby,* John Biggs, who was about to publish his second novel with Scribner's, the dramatist Zoë Akins and several actors in her new play, which was trying out in Wilmington. When Fitzgerald asked Seldes to criticize his character frankly, Seldes told him that "if he had a fault, it was making life seem rather dull." Scott, missing the joke, seemed annoyed by the remark.

Like Gerald Murphy, Wilson was completely charmed by Zelda's sparkling but incoherent talk: "She had the waywardness of a Southern belle and the lack of inhibitions of a child. She talked with so spontaneous a color and wit—almost exactly in the way she wrote—that I very soon ceased to be troubled by the fact that the conversation was in the nature of a 'free association' of ideas and one could never follow up anything. I have rarely known a woman who expressed herself so delightfully and so freshly." But when Zelda ambiguously told the designer of Akins' play: "You're just homogeneous!," he took offense and left with his companions.

Wilson was impressed when Fitzgerald read a dazzling passage from the manuscript of *Tender is the Night.* But he was embarrassed when Fitzgerald asked his chauffeur to report the hostile remarks his guests had made about him on the way to the train station. "It's only very seldom," Scott insisted, "that you get a real opportunity to hear what people say about you behind your back." "The aftermath of a Fitzgerald evening was notoriously a painful experience," Wilson concluded in his lively memoir. "Nonsense and inspiration, reckless idealism and childish irresponsibility," he wrote, "were mingled in so queer a way."[5] Wilson found the weekend, which did nothing to revive their friendship, intensely irritating.

The "notoriously painful" festivities were invariably followed by abject letters of apology from both Zelda and Scott. "From the depths of my polluted soul," she wrote Van Vechten, "I am sorry that the weekend was such a mess. Do forgive my iniquities and my putrid drunkenness." And Scott (in a letter to a college friend) tried to palliate his offensiveness, which he only vaguely remembered, with a labored attempt at humor: "I'm afraid I was the world's greatest bore last night. I was in the insistent mood—you know the insistent mood? I'm afraid I irritated both you and Eleanor, and I wanted to please you more than anyone there. It's all very dim to me but I remember a lot of talk about fairies and the managing kind of American woman, whatever that means. It's possible that I may be apologizing to the wrong people— anyway if I was lousy, please forgive me and tell Eleanor I can be almost human when sober."

When the Fitzgeralds went up to New York for the weekend to escape the daily boredom and the exhausting parties at Wilmington, they would wake up in a stupor on Thursday to find they had wasted an entire week. When they stayed at home, they would sometimes have violent fights. In February 1928 (the month of Wilson's visit), Scott returned home late at night in one of the weeping moods he had described to Hemingway. Scott and Zelda began to argue, he hurled her favorite blue vase into the fireplace, and when she called his father an Irish cop, he slapped her face and made her nose bleed. Zelda's sister Rosalind witnessed this scene, which intensified her hatred of Fitzgerald. When he became violent outside the house, the police sometimes had to be summoned. Scott was held in custody, his chauffeur was thrown into a cell and John Biggs was called on at least two occasions to get him out of jail. In Delaware as in France, their life of noisy desperation could be described as "1,000 parties and no work."

Fitzgerald's proximity to Princeton revived his interest in the college. He wrote a nostalgic essay about Princeton in 1927 and began to attend the football games. In January 1928 he accepted an invitation from Cottage Club to lecture in a series by distinguished alumni. Despite a number of fortifying drinks, he was intimidated by the academic audience. After stumbling through a few sentences on "Gallantry," he audibly anticipated the response of the audience by exclaiming, "God, I'm a rotten speaker," and abandoned the lecture soon after he began. Though Dean Christian Gauss had witnessed this debacle, Fitzgerald later asked him to sponsor an official lecture at Princeton— just as, when an undergraduate, he had asked the dean for a letter of recommendation after he had failed out of college.

After a wasted and often destructive year in Ellerslie, the Fitzgeralds traveled to Europe for the third time in April 1928. "We want to go," Zelda wittily explained to Van Vechten, "because Wilmington has turned out to be the black hole of Calcutta and I simply must have some Chablis and curry and *fraises du bois* [wild strawberries] with peaches in champagne for dessert. Also I want to feel a sense of

intrigue which is only in Paris." But there were also more serious reasons. Provoked by the comparison of herself and Lois Moran and by
Scott's criticism that she did not *do* anything with her life, Zelda, at the
late age of twenty-six, had begun ballet lessons in Philadelphia. She
intended to become a professional dancer, and was keen to study in
Paris with the Russian Ballet. The increasingly restless Fitzgeralds, who
also thought that constant travel and change of scene would cure their
problems, adopted D. H. Lawrence's maxim: "When in doubt, *move*."[6]

III

In April 1928 the Fitzgeralds began a five-month stay at 58 rue Vaugirard, opposite the Luxembourg Gardens and around the corner from
Gertrude Stein on the rue de Fleurus. As usual, they chose a dreary
apartment, which Zelda thought would make a good setting for
Madame Tussaud's waxwork figures. Through Sylvia Beach, a charming
and generous American who owned the Shakespeare and Company
bookshop on the rue de l'Odéon, Fitzgerald made two new literary
friends: André Chamson and James Joyce.

Chamson, born into a Protestant family in Nîmes, wrote novels
about austere rural life in the Cévennes. Just starting his literary career,
he worked as a reporter in the Chamber of Deputies and was very poor.
(Later on, he was elected to the French Academy.) When Chamson,
the only French writer who became Scott's friend, visited the Fitzgeralds on the rue Vaugirard, Scott, like Gatsby, rather tactlessly exhibited
their luxurious possessions—drawers full of lingerie, monogrammed
handkerchiefs and silk ties—and insisted that Chamson accept some of
them as gifts. Chamson also remembered receiving antialcohol postcards from Fitzgerald, which had "on one side the liver of a healthy
man, and on the other side the liver of an alcoholic. On the liver of the
healthy man, he wrote 'yours,' and on the liver of the alcoholic he wrote
'mine.'" Fitzgerald convinced Perkins to translate and publish Chamson's *The Road* (1929), but the French writer never became popular in
America.

Fitzgerald was desperately eager to meet the Irishman James
Joyce, whom he revered and whose works had had a significant impact

on his own fiction. *Ulysses* had influenced *The Great Gatsby, Dubliners* had influenced "Absolution." In "A Night at the Fair" (1928), which has the same setting as Joyce's "Araby," the inscription in the boy's history textbook—"Basil Duke Lee, Holly Avenue, St. Paul, Minnesota, United States, North America, Western Hemisphere, the World, the Universe"—imitates the address in Stephen Dedalus' geography textbook in the first chapter of *A Portrait of the Artist as a Young Man* (1916).

Fitzgerald behaved as foolishly with Joyce in July 1928 as he had in all his would-be or actual encounters with great artists. Fitzgerald, who did not know how to express his adulation, was extremely awkward and embarrassed the rather reserved James Joyce. While drunk, Fitzgerald had threatened to jump out the window of the Yale Club in 1919. He had recently climbed on the iron window railing of Chamson's seventh-floor flat and, struggling to keep his balance, had screamed out: "I am Voltaire! I am Rousseau!"

In a similar fashion, according to Joyce's biographer Herbert Gorman who was present at the time, Fitzgerald rushed forward to greet Joyce, sank down on one knee, kissed Joyce's hand as if he were a bishop and declared: "How does it feel to be a great genius, Sir? I am so excited at seeing you, Sir, that I could weep." Instead of weeping, Fitzgerald "enlarged upon Nora Joyce's beauty, and, finally, darted through an open window to the stone balcony outside, jumped on to the eighteen-inch-wide parapet and threatened to fling himself to the cobbled thoroughfare below unless Nora declared that she loved him." Fitzgerald, who felt that ordinary conversation would not sustain so momentous a meeting, had to resort to more dramatic devices. Just as Edith Wharton had said: "There must be something peculiar about that young man," so the bewildered Joyce observed: "I think he must be mad. . . . He'll do himself an injury some day."[7]

In the late 1920s Zelda (who was not impressed by Joyce) began to publish talented and amusing stories and sketches. With her permission, Scott usually signed these pieces as his own. She thus earned infinitely higher fees than if she had sold them as her own work. Zelda used this money to establish her independence and to pay for her ballet lessons. Her ambition to succeed as a dancer, despite her late start, partly accounted for her extreme touchiness about both Isadora Duncan and Lois Moran.

Zelda took lessons from the head of the Diaghilev ballet school,

Lubov Egorova, a lovely little figure whose fine hair was tied in a chignon. Egorova was born in St. Petersburg in 1880, graduated from the Imperial School at the age of eighteen, was created a ballerina in 1914 and danced many of the leading roles, including *Sleeping Beauty* with Nijinsky, for the next seven years. She had married Prince Trubetskoy, begun teaching in Paris in 1923 and replaced Zelda's father as the presiding deity in her life. In *Save Me the Waltz* Zelda described her teacher's appearance—and inner strength—with deep affection: "The eyes . . . were round and sad and Russian, a dreamy consciousness of its own white dramatic beauty gave the face weight and purpose as if the features were held together by spiritual will." Zelda would throw herself at her teacher's feet (as Scott did with Joyce), and forced the six-year-old Scottie to take ballet lessons with Egorova "until Daddy put a stop to it."

Zelda's obsession with dancing led to a reversal of roles in her marriage as she became ascetic and Scott plunged deeper into dissipation. In *Save Me the Waltz*—which recalls the Fitzgeralds on the Riviera in 1925 and in Paris a few years later—David Knight works on his frescoes while his wife Alabama is left alone. When she asks: "What'll we *do*, David . . . with ourselves?" (just as the bored Daisy does in *The Great Gatsby*), David replies that "she couldn't always be a child and have things provided for her to do." But when Alabama vigorously takes up dancing and is absolutely exhausted at night, David, as eager for distraction as Alabama had once been, complains when she will not go out with him.

In her novel Zelda, with considerable insight, equated dancing with exorcism and tried to control her wild emotions by disciplining her body: "It seemed to Alabama that, reaching her goal, she would drive the devils that had driven her—that, in proving herself, she would achieve that peace which she imagined went only in surety of one's self—that she would be able, through the medium of the dance, to command her emotions."[8] Zelda had hoped to join the Diaghilev troupe; Egorova said she was capable of secondary roles in the Massine Ballet in New York; and she was asked—and refused—to join the San Carlo Opera Ballet in Naples. But most of the emissaries who came to Egorova's studio, on the top floor above the Olympia Music Hall on the rue Caumartin, were from the Folies-Bergère. They all wanted to make Zelda into an American shimmy dancer.

Like Zelda, the wife in Fitzgerald's story "Two Wrongs" (1930) is bravely but hopelessly struggling to succeed against younger competitors and impossible obstacles: "she plunged into her work like a girl of sixteen—four hours a day at barre exercises, attitudes, *sauts*, arabesques and pirouettes. It became the realest part of her life, and her only worry was whether or not she was too old. At twenty-six she had ten years to make up, but she was a natural dancer with a fine body—and that lovely face." Watching Zelda dance in 1929, the Murphys—who sympathized with her ambitions but were embarrassed by her efforts—felt she would never achieve her goal: "Zelda was awkward, her legs were too muscular, there was something about her intensity when she danced that made her look grotesque." The distorted legs and tortured feet in Zelda's painting *Ballerinas* (1938), which evoke the suffering of a crucifixion, suggest that she was pushing her mind and body far beyond what they could bear. Looking back on the sad history of their marriage, Fitzgerald later told Sheilah Graham that Zelda, temperamentally unsuited to be his wife, was jealous of his success and destroyed herself by trying to compete with him:

> Zelda and I never should have married. We were wrong for each other. She would have been happier married to almost anyone else. She was beautiful and talented. It was her tragedy that she could not bear to be overshadowed by the attention I received from my early books. For instance, she hated it when Gertrude Stein talked only to me, while her companion Alice B. Toklas talked to her. She had a compulsion to compete with me. She could not as a writer, so she decided to be a famous ballerina and studied with the Russian ballet in Paris. But it was too late for her. And when she realized this, instead of accepting the fact and bending with it, she broke.[9]

IV

In September 1928, after five months in Paris, the Fitzgeralds returned to Ellerslie to complete their two-year lease. In a grand gesture, Fitzgerald brought back to America a former boxer and taxi driver, Philippe, as his butler, chauffeur, sparring partner and drinking companion. Scott would summon Philippe from the distant kitchen with a blast from a brass automobile horn. But Zelda disliked Philippe, and found him disrespectful and intimidating. Their French nanny added to the chaos by falling in love with and becoming hysterical about Philippe, whose name Fitzgerald borrowed for the hero of his "Count of Darkness" stories. The second stay at Ellerslie was a reprise of the first. Zelda set up a bar in front of a "whorehouse" mirror, played "The March of the Toy Soldiers" over and over and over again, and practiced dancing all day long. Scott did very little work, took long solitary walks and, according to his neighbors, looked lonely and miserable.

In mid-November 1928 Francis Godolphin, Hemingway's Oak Park friend, saw Ernest with Scott in New York before the Princeton-Yale football game. Godolphin described their comradely contentment in much the same way as Booth Tarkington had portrayed them in Paris in 1925: "On that particular morning when they landed in our apartment together they were both a bit tight and very cheerful, very pleasant and very happy. They both seemed very harmonious, enjoying each other and having a hell of a fine time. They were at the apartment for a time, then they went off to the Cottage Club and to the game."

When they returned to Ellerslie, which Hemingway found surprisingly impressive, Fitzgerald uncorked *six* bottles of expensive Burgundy just for his friend. Ernest was flattered by his generosity but found the gesture wasteful. Content to be in Hemingway's company, Fitzgerald had behaved well all day. But he got drunk that evening and made Hemingway uncomfortable by insulting the attractive black maid who served dinner. According to A. E. Hotchner, who heard the story from Hemingway, Fitzgerald, imitating what he took to be Ernest's manly swagger, exclaimed: "'Aren't you the best piece of tail I ever had? Tell Mr. Hemingway.' The girl never answered him and kept her composure. He must have said it to her ten times. 'Tell him what a grand piece of pussy you are.' Like that, over and over." Hemingway felt bullfights were sedatives compared to weekends with Fitzgerald.

Fitzgerald redeemed himself the following month when Hemingway, traveling south on a train from New York to Florida, received a telegram announcing his father's death (by suicide) and asking him to go west to Oak Park. Hemingway asked Fitzgerald for a hundred-dollar loan, which he delivered in person to the North Philadelphia station. And Hemingway praised him for his prompt response: "You were damned good and also bloody effective to get me that money."[10]

When the two-year lease on Ellerslie ended in March 1929 the Fitzgeralds—still restless and undecided about where to live—took their fourth and final trip to Europe. They sailed to Genoa, traveled along the Riviera to Paris, and spent April and May in an apartment on the rue Palatine, on the Left Bank, near Saint-Sulpice and their old flat on the rue Vaugirard. They had spent the previous summer in Paris, but from June to October 1929 they rented the Villa Fleur des Bois in Cannes. They returned to Paris in October, when the weather began to turn cold, and rented their last apartment at 10 rue Pergolèse, off the avenue de la Grande Armée, near their first flat on the rue de Tilsitt.

In the spring of 1929, following Max Perkins' suggestion, Fitzgerald looked up the young Canadian novelist Morley Callaghan, who shared his Irish Catholic background and had published his first novel with Scribner's the previous year. Callaghan liked Fitzgerald's "shrewd opinions, quick fine intelligence, extraordinary perception and tireless interest." But he thought Scott was reckless and prodigal when straining to live up to his legend. Fitzgerald loved the vicarious excitement of glamorously recounting Hemingway's exploits, prowess and courage (which were so unlike his own): Ernest's war, his wound and the time Ernest thought he was dead. But Fitzgerald, as Edmund Wilson noted, had also carefully studied Hemingway's weaknesses. In 1929 he made one of the most perceptive and accurate predictions about his friend, who in 1927 had divorced Hadley and married Pauline Pfeiffer: "I have a theory that Ernest needs a new woman for each big book. There was one for the stories and *The Sun Also Rises*. Now there's Pauline. *A Farewell to Arms* is a big book. If there's another big book I think we'll find Ernest has another wife." Following the pattern Fitzgerald had predicted, Hemingway acquired a third wife, Martha Gellhorn, for his next big book, *For Whom the Bell Tolls,* as well as a fourth, Mary Welsh, for *Across the River and into the Trees,* which he hoped would be his big book about World War II.

Fitzgerald's occasional sparring with his chauffeur, Philippe, revived his interest in boxing. There was no question of the delicate Fitzgerald actually getting into the ring with Hemingway, who disdainfully declared: "There's no distinction in punching Scott on his ["almost beautiful, unmarked"] nose. Every taxi driver in Paris has done it." In June 1929 Hemingway used to box at the gym of the American Club with Callaghan, whom he had first met at the *Toronto Star* in 1923. After a lunch together at Prunier's, Scott decided to participate vicariously in their combat by assuming the grave responsibility of timekeeper.

The powerful Hemingway was not troubled by his friends' fear that he would "hurt his brains" in boxing. Callaghan noted that Hemingway had thought a good deal about boxing while he himself had actually worked out with fast college fighters. Hemingway took the sport seriously, was extremely aggressive and hated to lose. When Callaghan punched Hemingway's lip, he retaliated by spitting a mouthful of blood in his opponent's face and solemnly exclaiming: "That's what bullfighters do when they're wounded. It's a way of showing contempt."[11]

There were several versions of the notorious incident involving Fitzgerald and Hemingway. According to Callaghan, Fitzgerald, supposed to be keeping time, became so absorbed in the action that he unintentionally allowed the round to go well past the prescribed one-minute period. After Callaghan knocked Hemingway down, Fitzgerald woke up and screamed: "'Oh, my God! . . . I let the round go four minutes.' . . . 'All right Scott,' Ernest said savagely, 'If you want to see me getting the shit knocked out of me, just say so. Only don't say you made a mistake.' . . . 'Don't you see I got fascinated watching? [Fitzgerald said]. I forgot all about the watch. My God, he thinks I did it on purpose. Why would I do it on purpose?'" Hemingway believed Fitzgerald was using Callaghan as a surrogate to punish him for his superiority in athletics, drinking, war and art. But it is unlikely that Fitzgerald, who genuinely admired Hemingway, wanted to see him hurt. He probably was distracted from his duties by seeing his hero unexpectedly beaten by the smaller Callaghan.

In Hemingway's version, which he related to Perkins (no doubt alarmed about the battering of his literary properties), he was drunk at the time, lost his wind, was beaten by Callaghan and prevented by pride from asking the time. He was convinced that Fitzgerald had been motivated by hidden animosity and had acted with deliberate malice:

> I couldn't see him hardly—had a couple of whiskeys en route. Scott was to keep time and we were to box 1 minute rounds with 2 minute rests on acct. of my condition. I knew I could go a minute at a time and went fast and used all my wind—then Morley commenced to pop me and cut my mouth, mushed up my face in general. I was pooped as could be and thought I had

never known such a long round but couldn't ask about it or
Morley would think I was quitting. Finally Scott called time.
Said he was very sorry and ashamed and would I forgive him.
He had let the round go three minutes and 45 seconds—so
interested to see if I was going to hit the floor!

The matter would have ended with Callaghan victorious, Hemingway embittered and Fitzgerald guilt-stricken. But a journalist—either
Pierre Loving or Caroline Bancroft—heard about the incident from
either Callaghan or Fitzgerald and belatedly sent a grossly distorted
version of the story to the *Denver Post*. The "amusing encounter" was
then reprinted by Isabel Paterson in the *New York Herald Tribune* of
November 24, 1929:

> One night at the [Café] Dôme Callaghan's name was mentioned
> and Hemingway said: "Oh, you can easily see he hasn't any
> practical background for his fight stories—shouldn't think he
> knew anything about boxing." Callaghan, hearing of it, chal-
> lenged Hemingway. After arranging for rounds and a consider-
> able audience, they entered the arena. Not many seconds
> afterward Callaghan knocked Hemingway out cold. The
> [unnamed] amateur timekeeper was so excited that he forgot to
> count and the deflated critic [Hemingway] had to stagger up
> and finish the round.

When Callaghan read this piece two days later, he sent a denial to
Isabel Paterson. He then received an "arrogant" collect cable from
Fitzgerald (under considerable pressure from Hemingway, who was
sensitive about his reputation as a boxer and furious that one of his
friends had spread this damaging story): HAVE SEEN STORY IN HERALD
TRIBUNE. ERNEST AND I AWAIT YOUR CORRECTION. SCOTT FITZGERALD. A
correction duly appeared on December 8; and Hemingway, in a letter to
Callaghan on January 4, 1930, blamed the story—though not the lapse
in timekeeping that had inspired it—on the Paris-based Pierre Loving.
But the real loser in this boxing match was Fitzgerald. Hemingway had
compelled him to send the telegram and, as Callaghan wrote, Scott,
"having been insulted by Ernest that day in the American Club, was
now insulted by me because he had acted to please Ernest."[12]

V

The estrangement from Hemingway and Callaghan was compounded by drunken quarrels with many other friends, few of whom were as tolerant as the Murphys. The summary in Fitzgerald's *Ledger* for 1929, when he and Zelda began their precipitous slide into alcoholism and madness, was extremely grim: *"Ominous. No Real Progress in ANY way and wrecked myself with dozens of people."* Worst of all were the increasingly frequent and bitter arguments with Zelda. Robert Penn Warren, who met them in Paris that year, remembered "the frightful hissing quarrel, well laced with obscenities, which went on between them."

Both somewhat spoiled egoists needed precisely what the other could not give—sympathy, support, love. In the mid-1920s Zelda had recovered from nearly two years of colitis, appendicitis and gynecological problems resulting from her abortions. Since then, driven by demonic intensity, she had desperately tried to make up for lost time in her ballet career. John Biggs compared her frenzied obsession, which both frustrated and tormented her, to "the dancing madness of the middle ages." As Zelda withdrew into an unreal, hypersensitive world of her own, Scott drank more than ever. Louis Bromfield, always perceptive about the Fitzgeralds, contrasted their drinking habits and revealed that Scott's responsibility for her alcoholism was a source of profound guilt: "Of the two Zelda drank better and had, I think, the stronger character, and I have sometimes thought that she could have given it up without any great difficulty and that she was led on to a tragic end only because he could not stop and in despair she followed him. I have sometimes suspected that Scott was aware of this and that it caused remorse which did nothing to help his situation as it grew more tragic."[13]

Scott drank when Zelda was ill and when she danced away her life; he drank to stimulate his work and compensate for his idleness, to prepare for parties and keep them going, to soothe his loneliness and eradicate his guilt. And he had to pay all the penalties for getting drunk: quarrels with friends, terrible hangovers, blurred memory, poor health and inability to write. Zelda bitterly rejected his friends, whom she felt had exploited her. She also ignored her family and—determined to create an independent life—cared about no one but her dance teacher. "As for my friends," she told Scott, "first, I have none; by that I mean that all our associates have always taken me for granted, sought your stimulus and fame, eaten my dinners and invited [themselves to] 'the Fitzgeralds" place."

They also had sexual problems, which were exacerbated by growing disaffection and hostility, by Zelda's physical weariness and Scott's inability to satisfy her, by her complaints about his physical inadequacy and by his wounded pride. With caustic clarity, Zelda told him: "You made no advances toward me and complained that I was un-responsive. You were literally eternally drunk the whole summer. I got so I couldn't sleep and I had asthma again. . . . You didn't want me. Twice you left my bed saying 'I can't. Don't you understand'—I didn't." Fitzgerald was hurt in the same way as Saul Bellow's fictional hero: "Herzog himself had no small amount of charm. But his sexual powers had been damaged by Madeleine. And without the ability to attract women, how was he to recover?"[14]

Despite domestic chaos, dissipation, frustration and compromise, Fitzgerald continued to—had to—write. Between 1924 and 1934 he worked on seven different versions of Tender is the Night but, after many broken promises, had managed to send only two chapters to Max Perkins. In 1929, he had not touched his novel for a year. But he eventually abandoned the theme of matricide, which had blocked him, changed the focus to Zelda's mental illness and finally managed to complete the novel during 1932–34. Meanwhile, to support his extravagant way of life, he turned out increasingly lucrative stories for the Saturday Evening Post and reached a peak payment of $4,000 per story in 1929. In this fashion, he earned nearly $30,000 in 1927, $31,500 for nine Basil Duke Lee stories about his childhood and prep school years in 1928, and $27,000 in 1929.

During this time, amidst much mediocre work, Fitzgerald wrote two first-rate stories: "The Swimmers" in 1929 and "One Trip Abroad" in 1930. These stories portray unhappy marriages and are linked, both thematically and by specific passages, to Tender is the Night. The second paragraph of "The Swimmers," which describes a series of signs in French in order to create the melancholy atmosphere of Paris and to juxtapose "Life and Death" ironically, is repeated almost verbatim on page 91 of the novel. Similarly, the symbolic invasion of locusts, which the chauffeur euphemistically calls bumblebees, the naked Ouled Naïl dancers, the vivid evocation of the noises of Algeria and the allusion to "the Sepoys at the gate" in "One Trip Abroad" all reappear—contrary to Fitzgerald's usual practice—on pages 160–161 and 271 of the novel.

In "The Swimmers" Henry Clay Marston, who has an unfaithful French wife and is recuperating from an illness in St. Jean-de-Luz, helps rescue a drowning American girl, who teaches him how to swim. When his wife is unfaithful again, in America, they quarrel about the custody of the children. He eventually gains custody by threatening to let his wife and her lover drift out to sea in a stalled motorboat. On the ship back to Europe, he meets the young girl who had taught him to swim. Fitzgerald may have adopted the idea of regeneration through swimming from the last chapter of *The Sun Also Rises* when Jake Barnes—to cleanse himself of his friends' sordid behavior during the bullfight festival—achieves purification and self-knowledge during a solitary swim at La Concha beach in San Sebastián. Hemingway suggestively writes: "As a roller came I dove, swam out under water, and came to the surface with all the chill gone. . . . Then I tried several dives. I dove deep once, swimming down to the bottom. I swam with my eyes open and it was green and dark." In "The Swimmers" the unnamed but regenerative American girl swims "to get clean." She helps Marston to find "refuge" in the water and to shed the symbolic odor of gasoline exhaust that foreshadowed the "black horror" of his nervous breakdown in Paris.

"The Swimmers," like "One Trip Abroad," sacrifices intensity by portraying events that occur over a period of several years. The three accidental meetings with the American girl (who may have been based on Lois Moran) and the contrived happy ending are rather implausible. Fitzgerald forfeits dramatic potential by not describing Marston's sons, by not developing the character of the American girl (who is merely the symbol of a happier life), by not portraying the emotional confrontation when he discovers his wife's first lover and, most importantly, by not explaining why Marston tolerates his wife's infidelity or if he is in any way responsible for it. Despite these considerable flaws, "The Swimmers" effectively contrasts the European and American settings, describes the failing marriage and—through the metaphor of swimming—convincingly suggests the possibility of a "clean" new life.

"One Trip Abroad" has a darker mood and a different pattern. In "The Swimmers" Marston moves from breakdown to health, from an adulterous wife to a revitalized existence. "One Trip Abroad" follows a downward curve as Nelson and Nicole Kelly move from happiness and health to decline and drink. The story charts the degeneration of their marriage as the Kellys travel to Algeria, Italy, France and Switzerland. Adopting the theme of the double that had been used from Hoffmann and Poe to Dostoyevsky and Stevenson, Fitzgerald has the Kellys see their own doom reflected in another shadowy but recurrent couple. But (like the Fitzgeralds) they are powerless to avoid it. The biblical plague of locusts at the beginning of the story, and the storm at the end, are—like the odor of gasoline at the beginning of "The Swimmers"—an ominous symbol of the characters' fate.

Fitzgerald's brief evocations of the various locales of the story are quite brilliant: from the suggestive sounds of the Algerian oasis: "drums from Senegal, a native flute, the selfish, effeminate whine of a camel, the Arabs pattering past in shoes made of old automobile tires, the wail of Magian prayer," to the dreary sanatoriums incongruously placed amidst the natural splendors of Switzerland: "a backdrop of mountains and waters of postcard blue, waters that are a little sinister beneath the surface with all the misery that has dragged itself here from every corner of Europe."

Fitzgerald also portrays incisive incidents that reveal the Kellys' differences, disappointments and dissipations. Nelson wants to watch the naked Algerian dancers, Nicole is repelled by them. He stays, she leaves, they both become anxious and angry, and "were suddenly in a quarrel." In Sorrento they have an unpleasant encounter with General Sir Evelyne and Lady Fragelle, who object to Nelson playing the electric piano and rudely unplug it without asking his permission. In Monte Carlo they join a crowd of drunks and parasites; and when Nicole discovers Nelson kissing another woman, they fight and he gives her a black eye. In Paris their drinking increases, and they are exploited by a Hungarian count who steals Nicole's jewel box and tries to make Nelson pay a huge bill for the count's boat party. On Lake Geneva, where Nicole has two operations and Nelson suffers an attack of jaundice, they are finally overcome by "the unlucky destiny that had pursued their affairs." They now need "half a dozen drinks really to open the eyes and stiffen the mouth up to normal."[15] They do not understand why they have lost peace, love and health. But they finally begin to comprehend their fate when they recognize themselves in the elusive but persistent doubles, who have followed them through Europe.

VI

In October 1929, as Zelda headed for her breakdown, Scottie, an exceptionally beautiful child, was eight years old. She had been largely raised by nurses and nannies, both English and French. She had been carried from house to house, state to state, country to country. And she had been left with family or servants, paid to take care of her, when her parents took off on their travels. The Fitzgeralds loved their child and rose to grand occasions like birthdays and Christmas, but they had very little to do with Scottie's day-to-day life.

In Paris Scottie attended catechism classes, took dancing lessons and became fluent in French. Fitzgerald complained that during the fall and winter of 1929–30 Zelda had lost interest in the child. Zelda agreed that she hardly saw Scottie because she hated her nurse, who snored and was mean. Yet she feared that Scottie "was growing away from her before she had ever known her, that she no longer had any voice in her daughter's life." When asked, later on, what she thought of her mother, Scottie replied: "I didn't know her very well."

Though Scottie's relations with her father were also rather "remote," Fitzgerald supervised her schoolwork and disciplined her when necessary. After Zelda's breakdown, he tried to protect Scottie from the effects of that illness, and became both father and mother to her. Fitzgerald's subtle and sensitive story, "Outside the Cabinet-Maker's" (1928), illuminates his relations with the young Scottie.

In the story, while the mother is ordering a doll's house for the child, the father and daughter are left alone in the car. The father tells a fairy story to pass the time, to exercise his imagination, to amuse the child and, most significantly, to express his intense love for her. But the little girl is naturally more interested in the fairy tale (which she continues when he leaves off) than in her father's feelings. When he declares his love openly instead of through the tale he invents for her, she responds dutifully rather than emotionally:

> "Listen," said the man to the little girl, "I love you."
> "I love you too," said the little girl, smiling politely. . . .
> "Oh, I love you," he said.
> "I know, Daddy," she answered, abstractedly.[16]

These two brief but telling exchanges, in which the adverbs are crucial, express Fitzgerald's fear that he could not reach his daughter's deepest feelings, and emphasize the fragility—and possible loss—of her love.

In February 1930 the Fitzgeralds crossed the Mediterranean to Algiers and traveled 250 miles southeast to the desert oases of Bou Saada and Biskra—the setting of André Gide's *The Immoralist* (1902). This journey, during which they saw the naked Arab dancers, provided the background for "One Trip Abroad"' and was mentioned in *Tender is the Night*. Zelda also described the Arabian Nights setting, which reminded her of Valentino's *The Sheik,* in an essay of 1934:

> The Hôtel de l'Oasis was laced together by Moorish grills; and the bar was an outpost of civilization with people accentuating their eccentricities. Beggars in white sheets were propped against the walls, and the dash of colonial uniforms gave the cafés a desperate swashbuckling air. . . . The streets crept through the town like streams of hot white lava. Arabs sold nougat and cakes of poisonous pink under the flare of open gas jets. . . . In the steep cobbled alleys we flinched at the brightness of mutton carcases swung from the butchers' booths.

This journey was meant to help them forget the bad times and perhaps avert the impending crisis. But Zelda was seasick on the way home, and the trip merely delayed the inevitable tragedy.

Many of Fitzgerald's friends—besides Dos Passos, Hemingway and the Murphys—had observed Zelda's increasingly strange and disturbing behavior. Ellen Barry, a Riviera friend, said: "Zelda was thought to be outrageous, like a child, but not crazy." Morley Callaghan noticed that she was extremely restless and had the unnerving habit of laughing to herself for no apparent reason. One evening she came down the stairs in a lovely gown, stood staring at John Biggs, stepped out of her evening slippers and "asked in indescribably ghastly tones: 'John, aren't you sorry you weren't killed in the war?'" And Rebecca West, an acute observer, recalled: "There was something very appealing about her. But frightening. Not that one was frightened from one's own point of view, only from hers."[17]

Sometimes, however, she did frighten others and put their lives in danger. In September 1929, driving on the steep and curving Grand Corniche near Cannes, Zelda suddenly exclaimed: "'I think I'll turn off here,' and had to be physically restrained from veering over a cliff."

This terrifying incident inspired one of the greatest scenes in *Tender is the Night* when Nicole, after riding on a ferris wheel (as Zelda had done with Dos Passos), cracks up and tries to drive the car, with Dick and their children, off a high road. On another occasion, Zelda "lay down in front of a parked car and said, 'Scott, drive over me.'" Fitzgerald, drunk and angry enough to call her bluff, "started the engine and had actually released the brake when someone slammed it on again."

Zelda's breakdown finally occurred in April 1930 when they were living in the rue Pergolèse. Early that month, when she began to panic about being late for her dancing lesson, Oscar Kalman, who was lunching with them, offered to take her to the studio in a cab. But she remained extremely anxious, shook uncontrollably and tried to change into her ballet costume in the narrow taxi. As they ran into a traffic jam, she leapt out of the cab and started running toward the distant studio. Fitzgerald persuaded her to stop the lessons and rest for a while. But she soon returned to them and, at the end of April 1930, broke down completely.

A few months later, as Scott and Zelda struggled to understand what had happened to them, he recounted, in a poignant letter to her, the events that seemed to mark their mutual self-destruction. He refused to attach blame, however, and felt they had to take responsibility for their own behavior:

> The apartments that were rotten, the maids that stank—the ballet before my eyes, spoiling a story to take the Trubetskoys to dinner, poisoning a trip to [North] Africa. You were going crazy and calling it genius—I was going to ruin and calling it anything that came to hand. And I think everyone far enough away to see us outside of our glib presentation of ourselves guessed at your almost megalomaniacal selfishness and my insane indulgence in drink. Toward the end nothing much mattered. The nearest I ever came to leaving you was when you told me you thought I was a fairy in the rue Palatine. . . . I wish *The Beautiful and Damned* had been a maturely written book because it was all true. We ruined ourselves—I never honestly thought that we ruined each other.[18]

Chapter Nine

MADNESS, 1930–1932

I

The Fitzgeralds married in April 1920, Scott published *The Great Gatsby* in April 1925 and Zelda—following this momentous five-year pattern—had her first mental breakdown in April 1930. Fitzgerald identified himself with the Jazz Age, which he helped to define and called "the most expensive orgy in history." If, as Arthur Miller observed, "the 30s were the price that had to be paid for the 20s," then that decade was much more costly than Fitzgerald had ever imagined. Just as his literary career spanned the Twenties and Thirties, so his personal life—which began to collapse at the same time as Zelda's breakdown, soon after the Wall Street Crash of October 1929—ran precisely parallel to the boom and bust phases of the decades between the wars.

Fitzgerald felt partly responsible for Zelda's illness and was intimately involved in her treatment. He was inextricably connected to her by bonds of love and guilt; by the hope that she would recover and they could resume their life together; by his fear that she would remain ill and he would continue to suffer with her. Scott's artistic career was also bound up with Zelda, who had provided inspiration for so much of his work. His unfinished novel would soon focus on her insanity and his stories would be written to pay for her treatment. All paths seemed to lead to Zelda: the destructiveness of their past, the sterility of their present, the uncertainty of their future.

No matter how close to or far away from Zelda he might be during the next ten years, Fitzgerald lived in the phases of her madness and remained deeply involved in the specifics of her treatment: the individual doctors, the different psychiatric approaches, the particular setting and atmosphere of each clinic. Zelda—whose apparent recovery was always followed by another breakdown and who constantly sought a way back to sanity—was treated in seven different hospitals in only six years. She repeatedly had to adjust to new people and strange surroundings while suffering hallucinations, depression and suicidal impulses.

Fitzgerald also went through the anguish of the husband of a mental patient: the soul-searching and self-reproach, the loss of his wife and difficulty of bringing up his daughter on his own, the financial strain, loneliness, alcoholism and creative sterility. Gradually, he lost all confidence in the future and left his "capacity for hoping on the little roads that led to Zelda's sanitarium."[1]

Zelda's first breakdown was so sudden (the warning signs only became clear retrospectively), the need for restraint and rest so urgent, that there was no time to make careful inquiries about the best psychiatric care. On April 23, 1930, she entered the ominously named Malmaison Hospital, just west of Paris, still desperately concerned about losing time in her ballet career. She was slightly intoxicated when she arrived at the hospital, confessed that she had recently drunk a great deal and explained that she needed alcohol to stimulate her work. Professor Claude—the doctor whom she tried to seduce—gave a vivid report of her mental condition:

> [She entered] in a state of acute anxiety, unable to stay put, repeating continually, "It's frightful, it's horrible, what's going to become of me, I must work and I no longer can, I must die and yet I have to work. I'll never be cured, let me go, I have to see 'Madame' (the dancing teacher), she has given me the greatest joy in the world." . . .
>
> In sum, it is a question of a *petite anxieuse* worn out by her work in a milieu of professional dancers. Violent reactions, several suicidal attempts never pushed to the limit.

Professor Claude also reported that Zelda had an obsessional "fear of becoming a homosexual. She thinks she is in love with her dance teacher (Madame X) as she had already thought in the past of being in love with another woman." Zelda's breakdown forced her to admit, for the first time, her own homosexual desires. It seems clear from this confession that she had projected her own homosexual impulses onto Fitzgerald, and blamed him for her sexual frigidity.

On May 2, after only ten days in Malmaison, Zelda left the hospital, against the doctor's advice, in order to resume the dancing lessons that had precipitated her breakdown. Alluding to Malmaison in *Tender is the Night,* Fitzgerald wrote of her "unsatisfactory interlude at one of the whoopee cures that fringed the city, dedicated largely to tourist victims of drug and drink."[2]

Zelda tried to go back to dancing in Paris. But she became dazed and incoherent, had fainting fits, heard frightening voices and was tormented by nightmares. She had (as Professor Claude noted) previously attempted suicide by taking an overdose of sleeping pills after her affair with Jozan ended in 1925, by throwing herself down the stone staircase in Vence in 1926 and by trying to drive a car off the steep cliffs above Cannes in 1929. Three weeks after leaving Malmaison, she became terrified by her hallucinations and again tried to kill herself. On May 22 she entered the Valmont Clinic in Glion, above Montreux, on the eastern end of Lake Geneva in Switzerland.

In early June Dr. H. A. Trutman wrote his report on Zelda. Though she was now more seriously ill than when she entered Malmaison, she denied her illness and still wanted to return to dancing. Ballet, she said, was a way to independence and a compensation for her unhappy marriage:

At the beginning of her stay Mrs. F. said she hadn't been sick and had been brought to the sanatorium under duress. Every day she repeated that she wanted to return to Paris to resume the ballet in which she thinks she finds the sole satisfaction of her life.

From the organic point of view nothing to report, no signs of neurological illness. It became clearer and clearer that a simple rest cure was absolutely insufficient, and that psychiatric treatment by a specialist in a sanatorium was indicated. It was evident that the relations between the patient and her husband had been shaky for some time and that for this reason the patient had tried to create a life of her own through the ballet (since family life and obligations were not sufficient to satisfy her ambition and her artistic leanings).

Zelda did not mention her homosexual desires at Valmont. But one of the nurses at the clinic had to repulse her "overly affectionate" gestures, and in her next hospital she developed an infatuation for an attractive red-headed girl.

Since Valmont specialized in gastrointestinal illness and Dr. Trutman thought she needed psychiatric treatment, Zelda was examined by a specialist in nervous disorders from the nearby Prangins Clinic. On June 4 she transferred to her third hospital in six weeks. For the next fifteen months, while she was in Prangins, Scott lived near Zelda in Switzerland and visited Scottie, who remained with her governess in Paris, for four or five days every month.

II

Les Rives des Prangins was situated on the shore of the lake, fourteen miles north of Geneva, in Nyon. The grounds were spacious, the gardens immaculately tended; and it had farms, tennis courts and seven private villas for super-rich patients. "With the addition of a caddy house," as Fitzgerald wrote of Dick Diver's clinic in *Tender is the Night*, "it might very well have been a country club." The clientele was international, and many of the patients came from families of distinguished ancestry and great wealth. The cost of treatment at Prangins, during the first year of the Depression, was an astronomical one thousand dollars a month. Fitzgerald assured Zelda's parents that Dr. Forel's clinic, which had just opened that year, "is as I thought *the best* in Europe, his father having had an extraordinary reputation as a pioneer in the field of psychiatry, and the son being universally regarded as a man of intelligence and character."[3]

Auguste Forel, the head of this eminent scientific family (his face appears on the Swiss thousand-franc note), was Professor of Psychiatry at the University of Zurich and an authority on the treatment of alcoholics. His son Oscar, Zelda's doctor and the director of Prangins, was an exceptionally talented and versatile man. Oscar Forel was born in 1891 at Burghölzli, an insane asylum in Zurich where his father was director, and had five brothers and sisters. He studied at the Sorbonne and at the Faculty of Medicine at Lausanne, and believed that religion was incompatible with science. After marrying a lady from Riga, Latvia, he had a son and two daughters, but separated from his wife in 1932. A faculty member at the University of Geneva for more than twenty-five years, he published a number of books, including *La Psychologie des névroses* (1925) and *La Question sexuelle* (1931). Later in life he became a naturalist and a professional photographer; and he was awarded the Legion of Honor by Charles de Gaulle in 1945. Forel's autobiography, *La Memoir du chêne,* appeared in 1980.

According to his son Armand (who was also a doctor as well as a member of the Swiss parliament), Oscar Forel was a tall, thin, well-dressed and highly cultured gentleman. He was very interested in literature, the theater, the arts and music, especially the violin, and gave concerts in the large hall at the clinic. Careful with money and susceptible to flattery, he surrounded himself with a court of sycophants, tended to impose his will on others and was a social dictator. But he was also very sensitive and persuasive, and had a remarkable organizational gift.

Dr. Forel used physical as well as psychiatric methods to cure mental illness, and introduced electric shock and insulin shock treatments at Prangins. Electroconvulsive therapy applies electricity to the brain in order to induce epileptic seizures that are supposed to unsettle whatever brain patterns have caused psychopathic behavior and allow healthier ones to take their place. During insulin shock treatment, the doctor injects insulin into the patient in order to reduce the blood-sugar level and induce a hypoglycemic coma, which also releases inhibitions and allows her to speak freely.[4] Since Oscar Forel cared for Zelda and employed these treatments, it is quite likely that she was subjected to the effects of electric and insulin shocks.

The Sayres, especially her sister and brother-in-law Rosalind and Newman Smith, deliberately misled Dr. Forel by stating that there was no history of insanity in their family. Dr. Forel, focusing on Zelda rather than on her heredity, believed that her recovery depended on her giving up ballet. With the help of a letter from Lubov Egorova, who said Zelda could never become a prima ballerina, she was eventually persuaded to abandon what she wanted most in life: a professional career in dance.

Like his father, Dr. Forel was a great fighter against alcoholism. He believed that Scott was involved in Zelda's illness and wanted him to have therapy to cure his drinking. But Fitzgerald, who thought his mind was already too analytical and depended on intuition for his creative impulse, felt psychoanalysis would destroy his talent. When Dr. Forel treated James Joyce's schizophrenic daughter, Lucia, at Prangins in 1933, he also unsuccessfully urged Joyce to accept treatment for alcoholism.

Fitzgerald knew that his drinking haunted Zelda in her delirium, but excused himself by stating: "I was alone all the time and I had to get drunk before I could leave you so sick and not care." In the summer of 1930 he sent Dr. Forel a long letter explaining why he could not give up alcohol. He said he was devastated by the effect of Zelda's illness, had to struggle to support his family, experienced listlessness, distraction and dark circles under his eyes when he stopped drinking, and noticed a physical improvement when he took moderate quantities of wine. He also maintained that Zelda did not use her talent and intelligence, that she was interested in nothing but dance and dancers, that drink helped him endure her long, boring monologues on this subject as well as her wild accusations that he was a homosexual. Since they had had sexual problems before her breakdown, and he had not been allowed to see her from April to August 1930, it is not surprising that Fitzgerald now drank more than ever. Samuel Johnson once explained how alcohol compensated for sexual deprivation. When asked what he thought was the greatest pleasure in life, he replied: "Fucking; and the second was drinking. And therefore he wondered why there were not more drunkards, for all could drink tho' not all could fuck."[5]

At the end of June, on a visit to town with her nurse, Zelda tried to run away. Restrained and brought back to Prangins, she was transferred from the main building to the Villa Eglantine and, ill with the other ill, confined with the most disturbed and intractable patients. While she was locked up, Zelda sent Scott some despairing letters that intensified his guilt and misery, and shattered his hopes for her quick recovery: "I never realized before how hideously dependent on you I was. . . . Every day it seems to me that things are more barren and sterile and hopeless. . . . At any rate one thing has been achieved: I am thoroughly and completely humiliated and broken if that was what you wanted." Villa Eglantine and Zelda's last sentence would reappear in *Tender is the Night*.

Zelda's nervous disease now began to have physical manifestations. She lost her old vivacity, seemed to age suddenly and sat like a listless invalid in a long, blank trance. From June until August her face, neck and shoulders were covered with severe eczema, which made her existence a living hell. "For two months she had lain under it," Scott wrote in his novel, comparing the skin disease to a medieval instrument of torture, "as imprisoned as in the Iron Maiden. She was coherent, even brilliant, within the limits of her special hallucinations."

Though Dr. Forel eventually cured Zelda's eczema by hypnosis, her hallucinations, depression and mental anguish continued unabated. She poured out her sorrows in letters to Scott, who was powerless to help her:

> For months I have been living in vaporous places peopled with one-dimensional figures and tremulous buildings. . . .
>
> I wish I could see you: I have forgotten what it's like to be alive with a functioning intelligence. . . .
>
> Dancing has gone and I'm weak and feeble and I can't understand why I should be the one, amongst all the others, to have to bear all this—for what?. . .
>
> I can't read or sleep. Without hope or youth or money I sit constantly wishing I were dead. Mamma does know what's the matter with me. She wrote me she did. You can put that in your story to lend it pathos. Bitched once more. . . .
>
> I wonder why we have never been very happy and why all this has happened. . . .
>
> *Please* help me. Every day more of me dies with this bitter and incessant beating I'm taking.[6]

After Zelda's breakdown Fitzgerald had to remain close to her for consultations and visits as well as protect Scottie from the effects of her mother's illness, support the family by writing stories for the *Post* and try to finish the long-neglected *Tender is the Night*. Fitzgerald inevitably suffered the consequences of Zelda's prolonged psychotherapy.

He found it intensely unpleasant to have her doctors probing and analyzing every aspect of their emotional and sexual life, and to endure frequent recriminations as her therapy uncovered their past. In the late summer of 1930, for example, Zelda reminded him, in vague but suggestive terms, of an occasion when he had deeply wounded her. Referring to the time they had "slept together" at the Hotel Miramare in Genoa in November 1924, she bitterly declared: "I think the most humiliating and bestial thing that ever happened to me in my life is a scene that you probably don't remember even, in Genoa." She also said that the incident had brought on an attack of asthma and that she had "almost died in Genoa." Perhaps Scott did not remember this incident because he was drunk at the time. But he probably wanted to take revenge on Zelda for her recent affair with Jozan. In his drunken state, his sexual inhibitions released, he may have attempted a sexual act— possibly sodomy—that they both considered unnatural. In any case, Zelda associated it with homosexuality and with animals, and found it "humiliating and bestial."

Scott had to defend himself yet accept responsibility, and try to explain "why all this has happened" without accusing her. Old friends like John Peale Bishop, who had often seen the Fitzgeralds during the 1920s and remained loyal to Scott, blamed Zelda for the disaster that had overwhelmed them. Bishop later told Edmund Wilson, who seemed to share his views: "I agree with you as to Zelda's partial responsibility for the earlier debacle. In those years in Paris, I came to detest her. She was really a very evil creature and like all evil people, deficient in the common emotions."

Troubled by his own guilty conscience, Scott was more sympathetic to Zelda. But he also blamed her for not taking responsibility for her own actions—even when she tried to kill others by driving a car over a cliff: "Never in her whole life did she have a sense of guilt, even when she put other lives in danger—it was always people and circumstances that oppressed her." Mentioning another flaw in Zelda's character, he also told Scottie: "the insane are always mere guests on the earth, eternal strangers carrying around broken decalogues that they cannot read." In this cryptic statement, Scott meant that Zelda had rejected the moral laws (her "broken decalogues") that were universally accepted by mankind and had always tried "to solve all ethical and moral problems on her own."[7]

In her more lucid moments Zelda realized that mental illness was always worse for the family of the patient than for the person who was ill. Like Miranda in *The Tempest*, Scott could truly say: "O, I have suffered / With those that I saw suffer!" He even felt in danger of losing his own reason when torn by the agonizing, never-ending oscillation between hope and despair. Paradoxically, however, his participation in Zelda's treatment matured and strengthened Fitzgerald's character. Though he could be irritating and self-indulgent, he now achieved, through emotional isolation and intense self-scrutiny, a sweeter temperament, a deeper understanding of others and a more dignified demeanor.

As she burned out her bitterness and achieved new insight, Zelda gradually accepted rather than resented her inevitable dependence on Scott, and expressed gratitude for his sacrifice and support: "I realize more completely than ever how much I live in you and how sweet and good and kind you are to such a dependent appendage." Many years later, after his death, Zelda finally realized how much he had loved her and had done for her when she was ill, and praised him for "keeping faith" and remaining loyal under the pressure of her inescapable necessities. John Dos Passos, who had perceived Zelda's insanity before her breakdown and criticized Fitzgerald's madcap life at Ellerslie, spoke for most of Scott's friends who discerned his nobility of character when faced with personal tragedy: "Scott was meeting adversity with a consistency of purpose that I found admirable. He was trying to raise Scottie, to do the best possible thing for Zelda, to handle his drinking and to keep a flow of stories into the magazines to raise the enormous sums Zelda's illness cost. At the same time he was determined to continue writing firstrate novels. With age and experience his literary standards were rising. I never admired a man more."

Scott always wanted to give Zelda the very best medical care that was available. In late November 1930 Dr. Forel wished to call in Dr. Eugen Bleuler—a professor at Zurich (and teacher of Carl Jung), who had coined the word "schizophrenia" in a famous paper of 1911—to confirm his diagnosis and treatment. Scott agreed to pay the five-hundred-dollar consultation fee, a staggering sum at that time. Bleuler agreed with the current treatment and said Zelda had borderline insanity. No one knew the cause of her illness or how to cure it. He vaguely suggested rest and re-education, and said Zelda should be allowed to go skiing in the nearby mountains and to visit the shops, theater and opera in Geneva. Bleuler also told Fitzgerald that three out of four patients like Zelda were eventually discharged: one recovered completely and two others remained delicate and slightly eccentric. Zelda, however, eventually joined the unfortunate quarter who never recovered. Though discharged from three mental institutions, she had three more breakdowns and would end her days in an insane asylum.

Bleuler thought Zelda was crazy; she thought he was a "great imbecile." But after the confusion, pain, bitterness, anguish, accusations, she slowly got better and, with zany humor, even began to joke about her illness. She said she had gone to Geneva with a "fellow maniac," signed her letter "Zelda, the dowager duchess of detriment" and said they could give their next child the Latin name for schizophrenia: "Dementia Praecox Fitzgerald—Dear how gruesome!"

But Scott's meetings with Zelda, during which he tried to ease her back into normal social and sexual life, were often much worse than not seeing her at all. In January 1931, after nine months of treatment, he told her doctors that when they spent time together she unnervingly slipped in and out of moods and madness, that seeing him had a bad effect on her and that he was repelled by her appearance and behavior: "Then she went into the other personality and was awful to me at lunch. After lunch she returned to the affectionate tender mood, utterly normal, so that with pressure I could have manoeuvered her into intercourse but the eczema was almost visibly increasing so I left early. Toward the very end she was back in the schizophrenia."

The doctors did not know what caused her illness. But in the summer of 1930, Fitzgerald had an artist's brilliant intuition about the etiology of her disease, which he described in the same terms he had used to explain the genesis of his best stories ("there was one little drop of something, not blood, not a tear, not my seed . . . "): "I can't help clinging to the idea that some essential physical thing like salt or iron or semen or some unguessed at holy water is either missing or is present in too great quantity."[8] Fitzgerald rightly perceived, before the doctors discovered it, that a great deal of mental illness is caused by a chemical imbalance in the body. The drug lithium, for example, which is a salt, corrects this imbalance and is now used to control the cycles of manic depression.

III

"One Trip Abroad" contains one of Fitzgerald's finest, and saddest, aphorisms: "Switzerland is a country where very few things begin, but many things end."[9] Sensitive to the accusations of Zelda and of Robert McAlmon that he was a homosexual, and associating Paris with "swarms of fairies," he now came to loathe that city. As he told Edmund Wilson, he preferred the straightforward clinical air of Switzerland, "where nuts are nuts and coughs are coughs." "One Trip Abroad" also describes the gentle and rather moribund life he tried to share with Zelda on the days when she was well enough to leave the hospital, visit the Casino and read popular novels in English that were printed in Germany. Their life turned "on the daily visits of their two doctors, the arrival of the mail and newspapers from Paris, the little walk into the hillside village or occasionally the descent by funicular to the pale resort on the lake, with its *Kursaal,* its grass beach, its tennis clubs and sight-seeing busses. They read Tauchnitz editions and yellow-jacketed Edgar Wallaces; at a certain hour each day they watched the baby being given its bath; three nights a week there was a tired and patient orchestra in the lounge after dinner, that was all."

Fitzgerald's routine life in Switzerland was frequently interrupted, however, by moves to various hotels around the lake and in the mountain villages, by two encounters with Thomas Wolfe, by a love affair and by an unexpected voyage to America. In June 1930, soon after Zelda entered Prangins, Fitzgerald, on his monthly trip to Paris to see Scottie, ran into Thomas Wolfe—who had published *Look Homeward, Angel* with Scribner's in 1929—in the Ritz Bar. Wolfe, who had been to Harvard, found Fitzgerald's collegiate coterie both snobbish and superficial. "I finally departed from his company," Wolfe wrote, "at ten that night in the Ritz Bar where he was entirely surrounded by Princeton boys, all nineteen years old, all drunk, and all half-raw. . . . I heard one of the lads say 'Joe's a good boy, Scotty, but you know he's a fellow that ain't got much background.'"

In July the two novelists met again in Vevey on Lake Geneva. Fitzgerald was impressed by the six-foot six-inch-tall Wolfe, whom Sinclair Lewis described as "a Gargantuan creature with great gusto of life."

Hemingway had more caustically called him "a glandular giant with the brains and the guts of three mice."[10] While Fitzgerald and Wolfe were arguing about books in a mountain village above the town, Wolfe gesticulated so vigorously that he snapped an electric power line and plunged the whole place into darkness. In September 1930 Fitzgerald wrote Perkins, their "common parent," that he found Wolfe comparable to Hemingway: "You have a great find in him—what he'll do is incalculable. He has a deeper culture than Ernest and more vitality, if he is slightly less of a poet that goes with the immense surface he wants to cover. Also he lacks Ernest's quality of a stick hardened in the fire."

In July 1937 Fitzgerald resumed their literary debate in a letter to Wolfe. Focusing on the issue he had often discussed with Hemingway, Fitzgerald urged Wolfe, whose sloppy works were put into coherent order by Perkins, to become a more conscious artist. Echoing Hemingway's famous theory of omission (in which the seven-eighths of the iceberg hidden below the surface of the water give full strength to the essential tip that shows), Fitzgerald allied himself with Flaubert and Hemingway, as opposed to Zola and Wolfe, and expressed an important aesthetic principle: "The more, the stronger, man's inner tendencies are defined, the more he can be sure they will show, the more necessity to rarefy them, to use them sparingly. The novel of selected incidents has this to be said: that the great writer like Flaubert has consciously left out the stuff that Bill or Joe (in his case, Zola) will come along and say presently. He will only say the things that he alone sees. So *Madame Bovary* becomes eternal while Zola already rocks with age."

Wolfe, unhappy about being relegated with Bill and Joe to antiquated Zolaesque fiction, replied by portraying Fitzgerald as Hunt Conroy in *You Can't Go Home Again* (1941). Speaking to Foxhall Edwards (based on Perkins), Wolfe's hero George Webber clearly dissociates himself from the American expatriate writers of the 1920s. Gertrude Stein had called them the Lost Generation and Hemingway popularized the phrase by adopting it as one of the epigraphs of *The Sun Also Rises*. Webber says: "You have a friend, Fox, named Hunt Conroy. You introduced me to him. He is only a few years my senior, but he is very fixed in his assertion of what he calls 'The Lost Generation'—a generation of which, as you know, he has been quite vociferously a member, and in which he has tried enthusiastically to include me. Hunt and I used to argue about it."[11]

In August 1930, the month after he met Wolfe in Vevey, Fitzgerald saw Zelda for the first time since their long separation. Their meeting convinced him that she was still very ill and would remain so indefinitely. So he was particularly responsive to Bijou O'Conor, a sophisticated and scandalous Englishwoman whom he met at the Grand Hôtel de la Paix in Lausanne that fall. Though their affair was brief, and encouraged Fitzgerald's uncontrolled drinking and wild behavior, it also, during one of the darkest periods of his life, distracted him from his pain. A great character, almost as alcoholic and self-destructive as himself, Bijou was far more reckless, a true bohemian without Fitzgerald's conscience and capacity for remorse. He found her utterly fascinating, and would enshrine her in his fiction.

Bijou, whose real name was Violet Marie, was the granddaughter of the second Earl of Minto and the youngest daughter of the diplomat Sir Francis Elliot, a strait-laced, Calvinistic Scot. She was born in 1896 (the same year as Fitzgerald) in Sofia, Bulgaria, where her father was serving as British consul-general. A French nurse provided her nickname just after she was born, but when she was presented to Sir Francis, he exclaimed that she looked more like a toad than a jewel. Educated privately by governesses and tutors, and extremely intelligent, Bijou became an outstanding linguist. Very different from her three older sisters, she passionately rejected her conventional family background.

During the Great War Bijou entertained her friends, who would have been bored by their very proper elders downstairs, in her bedroom in the Athens legation. Compton Mackenzie (whom Fitzgerald had met on Capri in 1925) was then engaged in espionage in Greece and recalled her arty set in his *First Athenian Memories:* "She was the youngest of Sir Francis' daughters and the only one not yet married. In her room tucked away at the top of the Legation the social observer could have discovered the trend of the postwar generation's decorative taste." She represented, to Mackenzie, "the restless advance of youth in spite of the war."

In 1920 Bijou married Lieutenant Edmund O'Conor, a professional naval officer from Dunleer, County Louth, in Ireland, and accompanied him when he was stationed in China. She acquired an expert knowledge of Chinese and, claiming that she had been given two Pekinese by the former Empress of China, developed a lifelong

passion for the pets, which followed her everywhere. Lieutenant
O'Conor had been infected with tuberculosis during the war and died
of that disease in Australia in 1924. Though widowed at twenty-eight,
Bijou never remarried.

Bijou had abandoned her son, Michael, who was born after her
husband's death. He was brought up in the south of France by her stern
Scottish parents and cared for by a nanny until he was sent to school in
England. During their rare meetings Bijou always spoke French to the
boy. He learned his first spoken word, *merde*, from listening to Bijou
exclaim whenever she made a mistake in typing. Though Bijou felt
sorry for the lonely and unsettled Scottie Fitzgerald, who had been
ignored and rejected by her mother and also brought up by nannies,
she lacked maternal feeling for her own child.

Bijou resembled Edith Sitwell. She was thin, chic and *jolie-laide*,
with fine features and soft brown eyes. Very social, a bit intolerant and
rather snobbish, she had rare charm and an air of mystery. An amusing
raconteuse, who kept her circle of intelligent and often homosexual
friends riveted by her fascinating conversation, she smoked heavily and
enjoyed drinking binges. The publisher Anthony Blond recalled that
"she was quite small, quite sharp and quite drunk."

In the early 1930s Bijou told her cousin Sir Brinsley Ford that
Michael had a bad case of whooping cough and needed to recover in
the mild climate of Penzance. Moved by her story, he gave her fifty
pounds to take the boy on a recuperative holiday. A few days later a
friend, who did not know where Bijou had obtained the sudden wind-
fall, told Sir Brinsley that she had lavishly entertained a group of
friends at the Ritz. Wildly extravagant whenever she had any money,
Bijou always left a trail of debts behind her and may even have served
time in prison for this offense.

Bijou lived on a small naval pension and on whatever cash she
could extract from her unwilling father. She may have caught tuberculosis from her late husband, for she spent some time in a sanatorium in
Davos, and was also treated for alcoholism in Switzerland, where she
met Fitzgerald. The reckless Bijou—whom he had first met in the
south of France and at the Closerie des Lilas in the Latin Quarter in
the mid-1920s—reminded Fitzgerald of Zelda. And like Scott, Bijou
was often irresponsible, lived beyond her means, borrowed money,
drank heavily and did not care what people thought of her. Though she

encouraged his worst characteristics, she also alleviated his tormenting guilt about Zelda, provided affection and gave him sexual reassurance in what she described as their "roaring, screaming affair."

The aristocratic Bijou smoked cigarettes in a long amber holder, carried around a half-paralyzed Pekinese, and frightened all the hotel guests and servants. She remembered Fitzgerald typing away in her hotel room, fueled by bottle after bottle of gin. Bijou later claimed, in a taped interview, that she and Fitzgerald had visited Prangins together (though they could have precipitated another breakdown if Zelda had guessed they were lovers), where she saw all the patients dressed for a formal dinner and seated between the doctors and nurses. Bijou also recalled that Fitzgerald bought a Persian kitten for Zelda, who, in a moment of uncontrolled rage, killed it by bashing its head against a wall.

Fitzgerald portrayed Bijou and her friend Napier Alington—whose birth and death dates (1896–1940) were the same as his own—as the widowed Lady Capps-Karr and Bopes, the Marquis of Kinkallow, in "The Hotel Child" (1931). Alington, a dark, good-looking baron and wealthy landowner, belonged to a fast set and was regarded by some as a wicked man. He was painted by Augustus John in 1938, wearing an elegant smoking jacket and bow tie, with a long face, creased cheeks, full lips and prominent oval chin.

"Practically the whole damn [story] is true, bizarre as it seems," Fitzgerald said. "Lord Alington and the famous Bijou O'Conor were furious at me putting them in."[12] In real life, in about 1918, Bijou, care-less with a cigarette, had burnt the ceiling of the guest room in her uncle's house. She must have told Fitzgerald about this embarrassing incident, for in his story Lady Capps-Karr and the Marquis of Kinkal-low are ejected from the Swiss hotel for starting a fire while attempting to cook some potato chips in alcohol.[13]

In "The Hotel Child" the sympathetic heroine Fifi Schwartz, a wealthy Jewish-American teenage girl, is courted by the bogus Hungar-ian Count Borowki, who wants to elope with her. But when she discov-ers he has slipped into their hotel room and stolen her mother's money, she rejects him. (A bogus East European count who lies and steals money from the heroine's room had also appeared in "The Swim-mers.") So Borowki elopes instead with a snobbish English girl, Miss Howard, who has been extremely rude to the young American. When they are caught by the Swiss police, the count is arrested and Miss Howard's reputation is ruined. Fifi then moves on to Paris and America to find a suitable husband.

The young Fifi, whose flashy style has been created by her mother, is repeatedly wounded by the bitchiness of Lady Capps-Karr and the other English guests. They audibly whisper about her "ghastly" and "rotten" taste, about the "gratuitous outrage" (a phrase borrowed from Conrad's "Author's Note" to *The Secret Agent*) of her noisy parties and about the undesirable acquaintances who, they fear, will "contaminate" the public rooms of the hotel.

When the Marquis Kinkallow, a tall, stooped Englishman familiarly known as Bopes, appears in the hotel bar, Lady Capps-Karr, the widow of a baronet, pathetically begs him to "Stay here and save me!" But he abandons her, pursues the much-younger Fifi and, like the count, tries to persuade her to run away with him. After a hasty courtship by Kinkallow, who is fired by "smoldering resentment" because "the whole world had slid into your power," Fifi fights off his crude advances by scoring his face with her nails. At the end of the story Fifi is triumphant, and Lady Capps-Karr and the Marquis Kinkallow are ejected from the hotel. "The whole thing's an outrage and Bopes is furious," she indignantly exclaims. "He says he'll never come here again. I went to the consulate and they agreed that the whole affair was perfectly disgraceful, and they've wired the Foreign Office."[14] The satiric caricatures of Lord Alington and Bijou O'Conor seem to have been inspired by Fitzgerald's powerful reaction against Bijou after their stormy affair had ended.

IV

Soon after he left Bijou, Fitzgerald heard that his seventy-seven-year-old father had died of a heart attack in Washington. In January 1931 he sailed home to attend the funeral in Rockville, Maryland. Arthur Miller has perceptively observed that most modern American male authors— from Fitzgerald and Hemingway to Lowell and Berryman—have tried to compensate for their own weak fathers: "One rarely hears of an American writer . . . whose father was to be regarded as, in any way, adequate or successful. The writer in America is supplanting some-body, correcting him, making up for his errors or failures, and in the process he is creating a new world. He is the power that the father had lost." In *Tender is the Night* Fitzgerald describes Dick Diver's shock when he receives a telegram, forwarded through Zurich—"Your father died peacefully tonight"—as well as Dick's fond memories of his child-hood and of his gentle father, who taught his son to believe in "honor, courtesy, and courage."

Sailing on the *New York*, Fitzgerald noticed a small, dark, attractive and vivacious young woman, who played bridge all day and night with the entourage of a Texas oil man. When they all stood on the deck to see the new liner *Bremen* pass in the night, Fitzgerald overheard her say: "Papa, buy me that!" He was even more intrigued when she con-vinced him, for a time, that she earned her living as a professional card sharp. Fitzgerald thought she would have many good stories to tell and, impressed by her dramatic impersonation of a gambler, urged her to collaborate with him. The woman, who called herself Bert Barr, was born Bertha Weinberg in a Brooklyn slum in 1896. She was the sister of Sidney Weinberg, who became a powerful Wall Street investment banker and adviser to several presidents. Bert later married Louis Goldstein, a prominent Brooklyn judge.

In his story "On Your Own" (1931) Fitzgerald portrayed the attrac-tive Bert as Evelyn and described her as a "girl of twenty-six, burning with a vitality that could only be described as 'professional.'. . . She had enormous, dark brown eyes. She was not beautiful but it took her only about ten seconds to persuade people that she was. Her body was lovely with little concealed muscles of iron. She was in black now and overdressed—but she was always very *chic* and a little overdressed." It seems, from Fitzgerald's letters to Bert, that they were attracted to each other, but that their clash of temperaments and egos precluded a shipboard romance: "It was too bad about us this time—we met like two crazy people, both cross & worried & exhausted & as we're both somewhat spoiled we took to rows & solved nothing. . . . All of which doesn't mean that my tenderness toward you is diminished in the slightest *but only that I want it to go on,* & one more siege like those three days would finish us both & spoil everything for ever."[15]

After his father's funeral in St. Mary's Church, Fitzgerald traveled south to Montgomery to try to reassure the Sayres about Zelda.

Despite his bereavement, he received more hostility than sympathy from her family. They could not conceive how much he had suffered, and secretly thought that *Scott* was the crazy one. Ignoring the pervasive history of mental illness in their family, the Sayres blamed him for Zelda's insanity and accused him of putting her in an asylum in order to get rid of her. In December 1930, a month before Edward Fitzgerald's death, Scott had defended himself in a letter to the Sayres by alluding to one of his father's moral touchstones: "I know you despise certain weaknesses in my character and I do not want during this tragedy that fact to blur or confuse your belief in me as a man of integrity."

Scottie later idealized Fitzgerald's uneasy relations with Zelda's mother (the judge had always disapproved of him). In a letter to Mizener, she said that Grandmother Sayre *"always* trusted and loved Daddy. She liked his writing and she *never* blamed him for anything that happened to Mamma." But Fitzgerald, contradicting this view, told Zelda's doctor that the sweet old lady had quite a ruthless streak: "Mrs. Sayre, when it comes to Zelda, is an entirely irrational and conscienceless woman with the best intentions in the world." When questioned about Fitzgerald late in life, after both Scott and Zelda had died, Mrs. Sayre praised his good looks. But she criticized his character and ignored all the sacrifices he had made for Zelda after her breakdown: "He was a handsome thing, I'll say that for him. But he was not good for my daughter and he gave her things she shouldn't have. He was a selfish man. What he wanted always came first."[16]

Fitzgerald's relations with Zelda's older sister Rosalind—who had witnessed their drunken quarrel at Ellerslie when Scott slapped Zelda and gave her a bloody nose—were infinitely worse. While the Sayres merely hinted at Fitzgerald's guilt, the strait-laced, moralistic Rosalind exacerbated the tragedy by condemning Scott's past behavior and forcing him to justify himself. On June 8, 1930, four days after Zelda entered Prangins, Fitzgerald told Rosalind that the breakdown had taken him by surprise and destroyed his life:

> After three agonizing months in which I've given all my waking & most of my sleeping time to pull Zelda out of this mess, which itself arrived like a thunderclap, I feel that your letter which arrived today was scarcely necessary. The matter is terrible enough without your writing me that you wish "she

would die now rather than go back to the mad world you and
she have created for yourselves." I know you dislike me, I
know your ineradicable impression of the life that Zelda and I
led, and your evident dismissal of any of the effort and
struggle, success or happiness in it.

He also wrote (but did not send) a much harsher response that distinguished between Rosalind's and her husband's view of the matter,
counterattacked more vigorously and threatened to satirize her in a
story: "Your sanctimonious advice was well received. I think without
doubt Newman's instincts were to do the decent thing, but knowing the
very minor quantity of humanity that you pack under that suave exterior of yours I do not doubt that you dissuaded him. Do me a single
favor. Never communicate with me again in any form and I will try to
resist the temptation to pass you down to posterity for what you are."[17]

Fitzgerald was willing to accept his share of responsibility for
Zelda's breakdown. But when attacked by her family, he quoted the
eminent Professor Bleuler, who had wanted to keep Scott as stable as
possible and had truthfully declared: "Stop blaming yourself. You might
have retarded [your wife's illness] but you couldn't have prevented it."
As Scottie later explained to Mizener, though Fitzgerald had contributed to Zelda's tragedy, his guilt was excessive: "Daddy knew he
hadn't *caused* it, and that no events after the age of twelve could possibly have *caused* it, but he felt a sense of guilt at having led exactly the
wrong kind of life for a person with such a tendency." In one of his
most lucid letters Fitzgerald, trying to come to terms with the problem
of her recrimination and his remorse, told one of Zelda's doctors that
he was being torn apart by her illness and wondered how long they
would have to go on paying for their mutual destruction: "Perhaps 50%
of our friends and relatives would tell you in all honest conviction that
my drinking drove Zelda insane—the other half would assure you that
her insanity drove me to drink. . . . Liquor on my mouth is sweet to
her; I cherish her most extravagant hallucinations."[18]

While turning out a string of tales that he called "absolute junk,"
amidst family strife and conflicting accusations, Fitzgerald wrote his
greatest story. The deeply moving and perfectly realized "Babylon
Revisited" appeared in the *Saturday Evening Post* in February 1931.
The immediate inspiration for this story—which concerns his own

responsibility, guilt and retribution—was Scottie's visit, during Zelda's illness, to her Aunt Rosalind and Uncle Newman Smith, who worked for the Guaranty Trust bank in Brussels. Rosalind and Newman Smith were the models for Marion and Lincoln Peters, just as Scottie was for Honoria Wales, who is given the unusual first name of the Murphys' daughter. Fitzgerald could not resist the temptation to satirize Rosalind in a story that expresses his fears that she might try to take Scottie away from him.

The title of the story is complex and allusive. Babylon is not only modern Paris. It is also the decadent and corrupt city in ancient Iraq where the exiled Jews, longing to return to the Promised Land, have been enslaved. The surname of the hero, Charlie Wales, puns on "wails" and suggests the lamentation in Psalm 137 of the Jews in Babylonian captivity. Wales is not only captured and enslaved by his past. He also, by adopting "the chastened attitude of the reformed sinner," recalls Saint Luke's description of the return of the Prodigal Son. In this story, however, he is punished rather than rewarded for his virtuous change of character.

The opening pages vividly evoke the mood of Paris. But they are shot through with nostalgia for the happier times before the Wall Street Crash and the Depression destroyed American expatriate life. Yet Wales, like Fitzgerald, also thinks: "I spoiled this city for myself. I didn't realize it, but the days came along one after another, and then two years were gone, and everything was gone, and I was gone." After leaving the Ritz Bar, Wales goes to his sister-in-law's flat on the rue Palatine (where Scott and Zelda had lived unhappily in the spring of 1929) to see his daughter. But his happiness is ruined when he encounters the "unalterable distrust" and "instinctive antipathy" of Marion Peters. At the end of section I, as Wales rejects the offer of a prostitute but treats her to supper, we learn that Honoria had been taken away from him after his wife's death and during his treatment for alcoholism in a sanatorium.

Wales' lunch with Honoria (who, like Scottie in 1930, is nine years old and speaks excellent French) recalls the tenderness and insight of "Outside the Cabinet-Maker's." Their affectionate conversation is defined, as in the earlier story, by a series of adverbs—expectantly, resignedly, politely, vaguely, tranquilly—that suggest they have inevitably grown apart during their year-and-a-half separation. Their brief idyll is interrupted by the unwelcome appearance of the drunken and parasitic Duncan Shaeffer and Lorraine Quarrles, who (like the characters who feed on the vitality of Dick Diver in *Tender is the Night*) are attracted to Wales "because he was functioning, because he was serious; they wanted to see him because he was stronger than they were now, because they wanted to draw a certain sustenance from his strength." These intrusive friends ultimately prevent Wales from putting a little of his own character and values into his daughter "before she crystallized utterly."

Wales' second visit to the rue Palatine, to discuss the custody of his daughter, provides a striking contrast to the happy lunch and visit to the theater with Honoria. It also reveals the difference between Marion's hostile and Lincoln's sympathetic attitude. Wales insists that he has radically changed. Marion still holds him responsible for his wife's pneumonia and death, which occurred after he had worked himself into a jealous rage and locked her out of the house during a snowstorm. Marion also resents the fact that she and Lincoln had been pinched for money while Charlie and Helen Wales were living a wildly extravagant life. Echoing Rosalind's bitter letter to Fitzgerald, Marion exclaims: "I think if it were my child I'd rather see her [dead]." Despite her anger, Wales eventually persuades Marion that he has expiated his sins. He has become a successful businessman, has invited his sister to live with him, will hire a governess and be a responsible father. After some discussion, Marion finally agrees to let Honoria live with him.

When Wales returns to Marion's flat for the third time, they are interrupted by the unexpected arrival of Duncan and Lorraine, who have found the address he had left at the Ritz Bar. Wales desperately tries to dissociate himself from his disreputable friends and persuade them to leave the flat. But Marion—a nervous wreck who dominates her weak husband—is convinced that he has returned to his dissipated way of life. She suddenly changes her mind and refuses to surrender custody of his daughter. Her distrust has indeed been "unalterable," and their bitter family quarrel has been, in Fitzgerald's striking simile, "like splits in the skin that won't heal because there's not enough material."

The emotionally compressed and extremely effective story ends, as it began, at the Ritz Bar. Its circular structure suggests that Wales is irrevocably trapped by his own past. Without the hope of reunion with his daughter to sustain him, he well may revert (as Marion suspects) to his self-destructive existence. His present life in Paris now seems as unreal as his past life had been: "The men locked their wives out in the snow because the snow of twenty-nine wasn't real snow. If you didn't want it to be snow, you just paid some money."[19] But the snow was real enough to kill Wales' wife, who, like Michael Furey in Joyce's "The Dead," died after standing outside in the snow. Repeating what Fitzgerald had said to Zelda's doctor, Wales, who has lost more in the boom than in the bust, thinks "they couldn't make him pay forever." But Wales has ironically caused his own destruction by leaving his address at the bar, and the story ends in a mood of bitterness, desolation and loss. Though Charlie Wales brought himself back from bankruptcy, alcoholism and broken health, Fitzgerald was never able to achieve this kind of regeneration. Zelda remained permanently ill, and he *did* have to pay forever.

V

In the midst of bitter disputes between her husband and her family, and after more than fifteen months of treatment, Zelda seemed to recover sufficiently to be discharged from Prangins on September 15, 1931. By this time, Zelda's breakdown had affected her appearance as well as her mind and she was no longer the great beauty she had been when she entered the clinic. Her expression, once romantic and inno-cent, was now cynical and embittered. Her face, having lost its softness and gentleness, was now tense, coarse and severe. Her hair was roughly cut, her clothes plain; and she now looked institutional rather than chic. Though Fitzgerald had not followed Dr. Forel's advice about dealing with his own problems, he trusted and respected the doctor, and sought his counsel about Zelda's treatment long after she had left his clinic.

In *Save Me the Waltz* Zelda described their return to Montgomery in late September and suggested that the sluggishness, even entropy of the place might soon overwhelm the new arrivals: "The Southern town slept soundless on the wide palette of the cotton fields. Alabama's ears were muffled by the intense stillness as if she had entered a vacuum. Negroes, lethargic and immobile, draped themselves on the depot steps like effigies to some exhausted god of creation. The wide square, masked in velvet shadows, drowned in the lull of the South, spread like soft blotting paper under man and his heritage." They rented a large, comfortable house at 819 Felder Avenue, near her parents' home, and tried to settle down to a quiet, recuperative life of golf and tennis with a few old friends. Fitzgerald, suffering the steely glances of the Sayres, hoped they would relieve him of some of the anxious burden of caring for Zelda.

In November 1931 Fitzgerald, bored with Montgomery, accepted an offer from Metro-Goldwyn-Mayer to adapt *Red-Headed Woman,* a light sexual comedy, for $1,200 a week. He was particularly eager to work under the producer Irving Thalberg, who had a genius for developing stars and scripts. Thalberg had been put in charge of production at Universal Studios when he was only twenty and had created MGM with Louis Mayer in 1923. Three years younger than Fitzgerald, he was a small, sickly, middle-class Jewish boy from Brooklyn who had received very little education beyond high school. But he had rare taste, self-assurance, decisiveness, respect for excellence and a shrewd commercial sense; and was responsible for the actors, screenplays, shooting and editing of fifty films a year.

Budd Schulberg, who called Thalberg "the intellectual high priest of Hollywood," thought he *was* superior to the other studio heads, but had more ability to use literary works than to understand them. Ring Lardner, Jr., agreed that Thalberg, though brighter and more intellectual than the other producers, was just as interested in achieving box office success and just as ruthless in getting his own way. Thalberg believed the more writers who worked on a script the better, and felt that *he,* as producer of the film, would provide the necessary unity. Fitzgerald was moved by the knowledge that Thalberg had a damaged heart and would probably die young.

In mid-December 1931, about a month after he arrived in Hollywood for the second time, Fitzgerald was invited to join a group of distinguished guests at the house of Thalberg and his actress wife, Norma Shearer. Fitzgerald's awareness of what was at stake made him nervous. Bolstered by drink and reverting to behavior that had once endeared him to others (he had been forced to sing for company as a child), he rashly tried to upstage a roomful of movie stars with one of his old party turns: a ludicrous song called "Dog! Dog! Dog!" which he had written in the early 1920s. Buttoning up his jacket, posing as a dog

lover and gesticulating wildly, he sang it with "imbecile earnestness."
The second stanza suggests the sophomoric flavor of the song:

> Dog, dog—I like a good dog—
> Towser or Bowser or Star—
> Clean sort of pleasure—
> A four-footed treasure—
> And faithful as few humans are!
> Here, Pup: put your paw up—
> Roll over dead like a log!
> Larger than a rat!
> More faithful than a cat!
> Dog! Dog! Dog!

Dwight Taylor, the son of the stage actress Laurette Taylor, has left
a lively account of Fitzgerald's humiliating performance. Fitzgerald first
insulted the actor Robert Montgomery, who appeared at the party in
riding breeches and high boots, by asking: "why didn't you bring your
horse in?" After several drinks, Fitzgerald drew attention to himself by
announcing that he wanted to sing a song about a dog, and Norma
Shearer's pet was brought downstairs as a live stage prop. The other
guests, surprised by his strange offer, gathered round the piano like
people "at the scene of an accident" and watched him plunge into an
awkward situation from which he was unable to escape:

> The song was so inadequate to the occasion, or, indeed, to any
> occasion that I could think of, that the company stood frozen in
> their places, wondering how to extricate themselves from an
> unbearable situation. Scott seemed to sense by this time that
> he was not a success and small beads of perspiration appeared
> on his forehead. But he was no more able to break the tension
> than the others and he plunged into the fourth verse of this
> interminable song like a desperate man plunging into the
> rapids. . . .
> I could see the little figure of Thalberg standing in a
> doorway at the far end of the room, with his hands plunged
> deep into his trouser pockets, his shoulders hunched slightly in
> that characteristic posture of his which seemed to be both a

withdrawal and a rejection at the same time. There was a slight, not unkind smile on his lips as he looked down toward the group at the piano.[20]

After the party Norma Shearer graciously tried to soften the pain by sending him a telegram that said: I THOUGHT YOU WERE ONE OF THE MOST AGREEABLE PERSONS AT OUR TEA. But as soon as Fitzgerald sobered up, he realized he had made a fool of himself in front of a group of influential people and had irrevocably damaged his film career.

Thalberg thought Fitzgerald had tried "to turn the silly book [*Red-Headed Woman*] into a tone poem" instead of "making fun of its sex element." So he rejected Fitzgerald's screenplay, which was eventually rewritten by Anita Loos and made into a mediocre film. To assuage Scott's feelings, everyone at the studio pretended that his script was a great success. But when he came to MGM to say goodbye, the Rumanian-born director Marcel de Sano—with whom Fitzgerald had quarreled, as he had quarreled with Constance Talmadge in 1927—told him he had been deceived and brutally declared: "Anita Loos is starting over from the beginning."

A week after Thalberg's party and five weeks after he arrived in Hollywood, Fitzgerald was suddenly fired. But he had earned six thousand dollars, and was back in Montgomery in time for Christmas. He later summarized this experience in a letter to Scottie. Putting on a brave face, he pretended he had done a good job, been betrayed by the director and been asked to remain in Hollywood instead of being sent home:

I was jittery underneath and beginning to drink more than I ought to. Far from approaching it too confidently [as he had done in 1927] I was far too humble. I ran afoul of a bastard named de Sano, since a suicide, and let myself be gypped out of command. I wrote the picture and he changed as I wrote. I tried to get at Thalberg but was erroneously warned against it as "bad taste." Result—a bad script. I left with the money, for this was a contract for weekly payments, but disillusioned and disgusted, vowing never to go back, tho they said it wasn't my fault and asked me to stay. I wanted to get East when the contract expired to see how your mother was. This was later interpreted as "running out on them" and held against me.[21]

Personal humiliations seemed to inspire Fitzgerald's greatest art, and he managed to salvage a story as well as a check from his unhappy experiences in Hollywood. He had completed *The Great Gatsby* while Zelda was cuckolding him with Jozan. He had transformed the accusations of the Sayre family and his guilt about Zelda into "Babylon Revisited." Now he used his degrading experience at Thalberg's party as the central episode in "Crazy Sunday" (1932). These two stories of the early 1930s represent Fitzgerald's greatest work in this genre. A few years later, he would transfigure his alcoholism and decline into *Tender is the Night* and his own nervous breakdown into "The Crack-Up" essays.

The first two sections of "Crazy Sunday" accurately portray Fitzgerald's behavior at Thalberg's party. The hero, Joel Coles, has a few drinks despite his resolution to stay sober. But instead of singing about dogs, he burlesques the cultural limitations of his bosses, Sam Goldwyn and Louis Mayer. Coles is hissed by a "Great Lover" as Fitzgerald had been by the romantic idol John Gilbert: "It was the resentment of the professional toward the amateur, of the community toward the stranger, the thumbs-down of the clan." Stella Calman (whose name Fitzgerald borrowed from his friend Oscar Kalman) sends a consoling telegram just as Norma Shearer did.

The three scenes in the story take place, mainly in the Calmans' house, on three successive Sundays. At the second party on the second Sunday, Miles and Stella Calman arrive in riding clothes like those worn by Robert Montgomery at the Thalbergs' party. Miles Calman (based on Thalberg) is "nervous, with a desperate humor and the unhappiest eyes Joel ever saw. . . . One could not be with him long without realizing that he was not a well man." Fitzgerald reveals his scepticism about Zelda's treatment when Stella mentions that Miles is being psychoanalyzed. He is devoted to his mother, who lives with him and attends his parties. He has a "mother complex" and, since his father seems to be dead, hires as a substitute father an actor with a long beard who drinks tea with him all afternoon. Having transferred his mother complex to his wife, Miles has now turned his libido toward another woman, and Stella is shocked to discover that he is having an affair with one of her best friends. The revelation of Miles' adultery and Stella's jealousy makes Coles realize that he is in love with her. Since Miles will be out of town the following Saturday, Stella asks Coles to escort her to a party. When he brings her home that night, they become lovers.

The next day (and third Sunday), while Joel is in bed with Stella, with whom he has had unsatisfactory sexual relations ("He had made love to Stella as he might attack some matter to be cleaned up hurriedly before the day's end"), a phone message announces that Miles has died in a plane crash on his way back to Hollywood. Joel expresses his admiration by calling Miles "the only American-born director with both an interesting temperament and an artistic conscience."[22] He also thinks that he made his role-playing wife come alive and turned her into his dramatic masterpiece. Severely shocked, first by her husband's adultery and then by his sudden death, Stella orders Joel to spend that Sunday night with her. He rather bitterly agrees to submit to her wishes, to become a substitute for Miles and to give up his independence. The heroes of "Babylon Revisited" and "Crazy Sunday" have similar names—Wales and Coles—and the stories have similar themes: betrayal, bad conscience, guilt and retributive judgment.

VI

Montgomery, especially after Hollywood, was restful—even soporific. But Zelda's return to her family and to the scene of her early life brought her back to the source of her illness and awakened the disturbing memories she had often discussed during analysis at Prangins. Judge Sayre had been ill with influenza when the Fitzgeralds first arrived in September. He continued to decline and, while Scott was working in Hollywood, died on November 17 at the age of seventy-three. The effect of his death on Zelda, though not immediately apparent, was devastating. Her novel, written early the following year, begins with a reference to her father, who gave her a sense of security and "was a living fortress," and ends with his death and the heroine's statement: "Without her father the world would be without its last resource."

Idealizing the end of Zelda's stay at Prangins (which had included a pleasant two-week holiday at Lake Annecy in France) and their quiet months in Montgomery (when they had been separated for nearly two months), Fitzgerald told her doctor: "The nine months [mid-May 1931 to mid-February 1932] before her second breakdown were the happiest of my life and I think, save for the agonies of her father's death, the happiest of hers."

While mourning for her father Zelda had noticed the recurrence of ominous symptoms: insomnia, asthma and patches of eczema. In January 1932, traveling back to Montgomery after a holiday in St. Petersburg, Florida, she drank everything in Scott's flask and then woke him up to say that horrible things were being secretly done to her. Fitzgerald, who kept in touch with Forel, told him that in February Zelda experienced two hours of psychotic delusions and hysteria. A passage in *Save Me the Waltz*—in which the concept of madness becomes embodied in menacing crows, disemboweled pigs and gouged eyeballs—gives a vivid sense of Zelda's hallucinations: "Crows cawed from one deep mist to another. The word 'sick' effaced itself against the poisonous air and jittered lamely about between the tips of the island and halted on the white road that ran straight through the middle. 'Sick' turned and twisted about the narrow ribbon of the highway like a roasting pig on a spit, and woke Alabama gouging at her eyeballs with the prongs of its letters." Zelda knew she had lost her reason and asked to be admitted to a mental asylum. On February 12, 1932, the day she entered the Henry Phipps Psychiatric Clinic of Johns Hopkins University Hospital in Baltimore, she hopelessly asked Scott: "Isn't it terrible when you have one little corner of your brain that needs fixing?"[23]

In America, as in Europe, Fitzgerald provided the finest medical care for Zelda, who was treated in Phipps by the eminent psychiatrist and director of the clinic, Dr. Adolf Meyer. Like Professor Bleuler, Meyer was considered a leading authority in the diagnosis and treatment of schizophrenia. Born near Zurich of Protestant stock in 1866, he came to the United States at the beginning of his career in 1892 and became president of the American Psychiatric Association in 1928. An elderly, distinguished-looking man with a high forehead, dark eyes, heavy mustache and white goatee, Meyer was praised by a colleague for his energy, insight and originality: "From the first moment you met him you felt you were in touch with a great man, a man of mark, a man whose honesty of purpose and determination to get things done could not be questioned. . . . It is no exaggeration to say that in the space of a few years, Adolf Meyer transformed American psychiatry from a dull, drab, stereotyped routine to a live, vital organization which has set a standard of care for the mentally disordered which has never been surpassed."

Like Dr. Forel, Adolf Meyer wanted to treat both Zelda's insanity and Scott's alcoholism. Fitzgerald once again refused psychotherapy on the grounds that it would interfere with his creative work. But he was unable to give up drinking without psychiatric help. Dr. Meyer, despite his great reputation, had no more success with Zelda than he did with Scott. He was too heavy, ponderous and Germanic to establish an intimate rapport with her, and lacked the wit and humor that would have encouraged her sympathetic response. In a letter to yet another doctor, Fitzgerald unfavorably compared Meyer to Forel, criticizing the former's vague, ineffective theories, and maintaining that he had not been able to help Zelda: "Dr. Forel's treatment of this problem was very different from Dr. Meyer's and all my sympathies were with the former. During the entire time with Dr. Meyer, I could never get from him, save in one letter, an idea of his point of view. . . . In Zelda's case the first [treatment] worked because it gave her hope and refuge at the same time, while Dr. Meyer's theoretical plan was, in her case, a failure. He gave back to me both times a woman not one whit better than when she went in."

Fitzgerald's view of Dr. Meyer's failure was confirmed in a characteristically disturbed letter from Zelda, written a month after she had entered the clinic. She recognized her own illness, and hinted that Scott was also in danger of cracking up. The oddities in her character that had once been attractive were now tragic, and her expressions of love were as painful as her bitter accusations: "I adore you and worship you and I am very miserable that you be made even temporarily unhappy by those divergencies of direction in myself which I cannot satisfactorily explain and which leave me eternally alone except for you and baffled."

After Dr. Meyer had failed to reach Zelda, she was also treated by two other doctors at Phipps—though he remained in charge of the case. She felt close to Dr. Mildred Taylor Squires, a woman thirty years younger than Dr. Meyer, who had been trained at the University of Pennsylvania Medical School. Dr. Squires, who did not specialize in psychiatry and left Phipps after a few years, practiced in New York until the early 1940s. Zelda was grateful for her help and dedicated *Save Me the Waltz* to her in 1932.

Zelda's third doctor at Phipps was Thomas Rennie. He was born in Scotland in 1904, came to America as a child in 1911 and earned a medical degree at Harvard in 1928. He wrote several books on mental illness and became professor of psychiatry at Cornell Medical School. Zelda, who had not had sexual relations with Scott since their unfortunate holiday in St. Petersburg, soon established emotional rapport with the warm, handsome, Nordic-looking young bachelor.

Fitzgerald, who also considered Rennie a kindly friend during his own struggles, needed all the help he could get. During their joint interview with Dr. Rennie in May 1933, Zelda was in a very different mood than when she wrote her tender, grateful letters to Scott. She now bitterly accused him of hating her and prolonging her illness: "You sat down and cried and cried. You were drunk, I will admit, and you said I had ruined your life and you did not love me and you were sick of me and wished you could get away, and I was strained and burdened. . . . It is impossible to live with you. I would rather be in an insane asylum where you would like to put me."[24] While Zelda was still in Phipps, Fitzgerald traveled between Baltimore and Montgomery, where Scottie stayed until the end of the school year. At the end of March he left Alabama, moved into the Hotel Rennert, near Phipps and in the center of town, and began to look for a house on the outskirts of Baltimore.

The prohibition of ballet, the death of her father, the separation from Fitzgerald, the renewal of psychotherapy, the boredom and isolation in the clinic, the mental turmoil, the rivalry with Scott and the desire for self-expression suddenly awakened Zelda's creative impulse while she was being treated at Phipps in the spring of 1932. In Prangins in 1930 she had completed three stories (now lost) "in the dark middle of her nervous breakdown." Fitzgerald told Perkins that they were beautifully written and had "a strange, haunting and evocative quality that is absolutely new." Though her stories were too strange for *Scribner's Magazine,* she began a novel in Phipps—to control her feelings as much as to express them.

Save Me the Waltz, which was aptly abbreviated to *Save Me,* faithfully relates the story of Zelda's girlhood, marriage, husband's youthful success, childbirth, travels in Europe, brief affair with a French aviator and husband's retaliatory affair as well as her passion for dancing and invitation to the San Carlo Theater in Naples, where (in the novel) she gets blood poisoning from an infected foot and is forced to give up her ballet career. She returns to her home in the South and, after the death of her father, must begin her life again.

Alabama's physical illness obviously represents Zelda's insanity, and estranges her both from her husband and from other people. For David "felt of a different world to Alabama; his tempo was different from the sterile, attenuated rhythms of the hospital." The novel is not a personal attack on Fitzgerald, though it expressed considerable resentment, but a tragedy of stagnation and frustration. Its most remarkable feature is perhaps Zelda's ingenuous portrayal of her own extravagance, domestic incompetence, recklessness, jealousy, infidelity, ambition and responsibility for the dissolution of their marriage. *Save Me the Waltz,* which suffered from over-writing and under-editing (Perkins' weakest point), had mixed reviews when it appeared in October 1932, did not sell well and earned only $120 in royalties.

Zelda herself was highly critical of the novel. Though it had an extremely idiosyncratic and sometimes brilliant style, it imitated both Fitzgerald and Hemingway. "It is distinctly École Fitzgerald," she told Scott, "though more ecstatic than yours. Perhaps too much so. Being unable to invent a device to avoid the reiterant 'said' I have emphasized it à la Ernest much to my sorrow." Hemingway wrote of Brett Ashley, for example, "She was built with curves like the hull of a racing yacht"; Zelda elaborated his simple but effective simile into her own baroque cadenza: "[Alabama] was gladly, savagely proud of the strength of her Negroid hips, convex as boats in a wood carving."[25]

Scott was deeply wounded by Zelda's novel. He felt she had not only stolen the clinical material and European locales of the novel he had been working on for seven years but also, during the illness that had delayed the completion of *Tender is the Night,* had completed her own work, in the spring of 1932, in only six weeks. She had sent it to Perkins without showing it to Scott, and had it accepted for publication by his own faithful editor at Scribner's. Fitzgerald later told Ober that *Save Me the Waltz* was "a bad book" because the potentially promising material lacked artistic focus, structure and control: "By glancing over it yourself you will see that it contains all the material that a tragedy should have, though she was incapable as a writer of realizing where tragedy lay as she was incapable of facing it as a person."[26]

Scott's just criticism of Zelda's uneven but always lively and perceptive novel raises the question of the comparative merit of their work. Fitzgerald undoubtedly used Zelda's speech, diaries, letters, personal experience and mental illness in his fiction, and published her lively but derivative stories and essays under his own name. Though Zelda had ideas, style and wit, she did not have the professional knowledge and discipline to perfect her stories and novel. Her stories would not have appeared in print if she had not been married to Fitzgerald and if he had not revised them for publication. Zelda's best stories may have been equal to Scott's mediocre tales, but she was utterly incapable of equaling his finest work. There is a vast qualitative difference between the deeply flawed *Save Me the Waltz* and the high art of *Tender is the Night*.

On June 26, 1932, after four and a half months in Phipps, Zelda was discharged from the clinic. Though Scott retrospectively felt she was "not one whit better than when she went in," her doctors thought she was well enough to go home. After her treatment in Prangins, Zelda had managed to survive in Montgomery for only five months before suffering her second breakdown. After a much shorter and less successful treatment at Phipps, she remained relatively well for twenty more months before experiencing her third mental breakdown. Zelda's phases of remission aroused Scott's hope that she would recover. But she spent eight out of the last ten years of Fitzgerald's life in mental hospitals.

Chapter Ten

LA PAIX AND *TENDER IS THE NIGHT*, 1932–1934

I

In May 1932, a month before Zelda was discharged from Phipps, Fitzgerald found La Paix, a fifteen-room Victorian house on a large estate in Rodgers Forge, near Towson, just north of Baltimore. The dim, cavernous, rather run-down old place had gables, an open front porch and reddish brown paint fading on the gingerbread trimming. It also had a small swimming pond, a tennis court and a patch of grass, circled by a gravel driveway, that doubled as a boxing ring. Zelda captured the mournful mood of the house in an idiosyncratic letter to Max Perkins: "We have a soft shady place here that's like a paintless playhouse abandoned when the family grew up. It's surrounded by apologetic trees and warning meadows and creaking insects and is gutted of its aura by many comfortable bedrooms which do not have to be floated up to on alcoholic inflation past cupolas and cornices as did the ones at Ellerslie."

The Fitzgeralds' retreat to the quiet, isolated La Paix was, as Zelda remarked, a notable contrast to the wild weekend parties at Ellerslie. In the fall of 1933 Fitzgerald said they had dined out only four times in the last two years. Zelda remained near Phipps for frequent consultations with her doctors, and the Turnbull family, who owned the property and lived in the main house on the estate, provided another stabilizing influence. Bayard Turnbull, a wealthy architect and graduate of Johns Hopkins, was (according to his younger daughter) a rather distant Victorian gentleman who did not drink and was careful about money. He disapproved of Fitzgerald. But his wife, Margaret, a proper but cultured woman, shared Scott's interest in literature and became a good friend. The Turnbulls had three children—Eleanor, Frances and the eleven-year-old Andrew, who was the same age as Scottie.

Frances liked Fitzgerald, found him charming and felt he had the rare ability, when he spoke to her, of conveying the impression that she was the most important person in the world. But young Andrew—who became a surrogate son and later wrote a fine biography of Fitzgerald—was closest to Scott. They tossed around a football, went to Princeton football games and lunched at the Cottage Club, played erratic tennis, boxed with squashy gloves on the front lawn, shot a hairtrigger rifle, practiced card tricks, arranged battles with French lead soldiers, read and discussed books, and performed original plays. Fitzgerald even showed Andrew, after an unusually heavy snowstorm, how to make a little igloo—a Baltimore "ice palace" cut by a Minnesota pro. "He was the inventor, the creator, the tireless impresario," Andrew wrote, "who brightened our days and made other adult company seem dull and profitless."[1]

When Fitzgerald moved to Baltimore he visited his old friend H. L. Mencken on several occasions, and asked him to recommend a bootlegger and a doctor (in that logical order). But Mencken, late in life, had married Sara Haardt, a girlhood friend of Zelda from Montgomery. Since Sara was an invalid and the Menckens had to live a quiet life, he disapproved of Fitzgerald's drunken binges and eventually stopped seeing him. Though Fitzgerald continued to drink heavily, he also hired an efficient secretary, Isabel Owens, worked steadily on *Tender is the Night* and finally completed the book at La Paix.

In February 1933, when T. S. Eliot was lecturing on the Metaphysical poets at Johns Hopkins University, the Turnbulls invited Fitzgerald to dine with him at their house. *The Waste Land* had influenced *The Great Gatsby*, and Eliot had warmly praised the novel. Fitzgerald behaved himself on this august occasion and their meeting was a success. As he told Edmund Wilson, "T. S. Eliot and I had an afternoon and evening together last week. I read him some of his poems and he seemed to think they were pretty good. I liked him fine." But he was also somewhat disappointed, as he had been with John Galsworthy and Compton Mackenzie, when encountering the great man in person, and added that the forty-four-year-old Eliot was "very broken and sad & shrunk inside."

Eliot inscribed a copy of *Ash-Wednesday* "with the author's homage," and later provided a statement that was used on the dust jacket of *Tender is the Night:* "I have been waiting impatiently for another book by Mr. Scott Fitzgerald with more eagerness and curiosity than I should feel towards the work of any of his contemporaries except that of Mr. Ernest Hemingway." Eliot, a director of Faber & Faber, was interested in publishing the English edition of the novel but wary of poaching on his rival. So he wrote Fitzgerald a sly letter that left the initiative to him: "Chatto and Windus is a good firm, and it would in any case be contrary to publishing ethics to attempt to seduce you away from them, but of course you are quite free in this matter, it is up to you to send the manuscript first to whatever firm you elect."[2] In the end Scribner's decided to stay with Chatto & Windus, which had published *The Great Gatsby* in England.

Margaret Turnbull not only introduced Fitzgerald to Eliot, but also advised him about how to bring up the adolescent Scottie, who was then a day student at a local prep school. Zelda's frequent hospitalizations and absorption in her own illness made it difficult for her to express interest in Scottie. Her withdrawal from her husband and daughter placed the burden of caring for Scottie entirely on Fitzgerald, who had always felt that Scottie was more his daughter than Zelda's. In any case, she had always neglected her domestic duties (a constant source of contention), and revealed her very limited conception of maternal responsibility by telling Scott: "All you *really* have to do for Scottie is see that she does not go to Bryn Mawr [School] in dirty blouses. Also, she will not voluntarily wash her ears." When his younger sister Annabel was fourteen, Scott had written her a long letter instructing her about how to attract boys. But Fitzgerald, who felt he had been spoiled and weakened by his mother, was usually strict and puritanical with Scottie—though he would also neglect her when he was drinking. He tried to make up to Scottie for Zelda's lack of affec-

tion and to compensate for his own lack of self-discipline by directing
Scottie's behavior, social life and education.

Fitzgerald encouraged Scottie to invite her friends to the house
and then became irritated when their noise interfered with his work.
He also got annoyed when the bored and exhausted Scottie kept falling
asleep during his "background briefings" on Walter Scott's medieval
novel, *Ivanhoe*. "Very little of my extra-curricular education took," Scottie later wrote, "some of it backfired, in fact, for I was made to recite so
much Keats and Shelley that I came to look up on them as personal
enemies."

Margaret "Peaches" Finney, the daughter of Fitzgerald's Princeton
friend Eben, was Scottie's closest friend at Bryn Mawr School. She first
saw Fitzgerald in his "office," which consisted solely of a desk in the
corner and a chair in the middle of a large, bare room. He made her
feel awkward by asking her to sit in the chair, telling Scottie to leave the
room and then questioning Peaches about what she was going to do
when she grew up. In contrast to Andrew Turnbull, who idolized
Fitzgerald, Peaches felt that he never should have had children, that he
did not understand them or know how to reach them. Fitzgerald's
intense love for Scottie and anxiety about her future often quelled his
sense of fun and zest for play where his own child was concerned. His
rigid attitudes and harsh judgments on her behavior and academic performance were to cause her unhappiness later on.

When Honoria Murphy and then Peaches Finney asked Scottie if
she was embarrassed by her parents' violent quarrels and bizarre conduct, she ingenuously replied: "Oh, no! That's mommy and daddy. All
parents are like that." Scottie would pretend that Zelda's insanity and
Fitzgerald's drunkenness were simply not there, and this protective
veneer allowed her to distance herself from their dreadful problems.
When things became intolerable at home, Scottie would move in with
the Finneys. Fitzgerald's secretary, Isabel Owens, the Turnbulls and
later on the Obers also helped in times of crisis and provided an element of domestic tranquillity in Scottie's life. Despite all this, Scottie
loved her parents very much. She once told Peaches that she seemed
immune to their malign influence and remarked on how strange it was
that such a mundane child could be the product of two fanciful Peter
Pans.[3]

In *Tender is the Night* Fitzgerald ignored his neglect of his daughter and defended his strictness with Scottie, whom he portrayed as Topsy Diver: "She was nine and very fair and exquisitely made like Nicole, and in the past Dick had worried about that. . . . [She was] not let off breaches of good conduct—'Either one learns politeness at home,' Dick said, 'or the world teaches it to you with a whip and you get hurt in the process. What do I care whether Topsy "adores" me or not? I'm not bringing her up to be my wife.'"

Despite his good intentions, Fitzgerald sometimes behaved as badly with Scottie as he did with Zelda. Like Sara Murphy, Scottie complained that he made her feel uneasy by constantly nagging, probing and criticizing; by trying to control every aspect of her life and refusing to give her the freedom to make her own mistakes. When the twelve-year-old Scottie wore a dress that Fitzgerald disliked, he got into a drunken rage and tore it right off her body. Scottie discreetly told Sheilah Graham, who knew her well in the late 1930s, that Fitzgerald was "a father I didn't get along with." And Sheilah, who knew how much he loved Scottie, more bluntly declared: "as the father of an adolescent girl, Scott Fitzgerald was a bust."[4]

Zelda left Phipps and moved into La Paix in late June 1932. She followed a strict regimen of exercise and rest, and occupied herself with swimming, tennis, horseback riding, ballet dancing and painting. Fitzgerald had told Margaret Turnbull about Zelda's beauty, brilliance, courage and attractiveness to men. But all that was gone, and she now played the mad Ophelia to his tortured Hamlet. They still had bitter quarrels about their insoluble problems: financial, alcoholic, sexual and medical. They fought about their competitive careers, about Zelda's desire to write of her illness while he was still working on *Tender is the Night* and about his attempt to control her life. They also discussed the possibility of a divorce.

Zelda seemed, to Peaches Finney, cold, indifferent and withdrawn. She often wore a tutu and picked at the bits of eczema on her ravaged face. Andrew Turnbull remembered her "as a boyish wraith of a woman in sleeveless summer dresses and ballet slippers, with not much expression on her hawk-like face and not very much to say." While at La Paix, Zelda told John Peale Bishop of the torments she had suffered and suggested, in her strange way, the profound confusion of their lives: "Don't *ever* fall into the hands of brain and nerve specialists unless you are feeling very Faustian. Scott reads Marx—I read the cosmological [mystical?] philosophers. The brightest moments of our day are when we get them mixed up."

Zelda could say, as Shelley did in "The Witch of Atlas," "Men scarcely know how beautiful fire is." She had impulsively summoned the fire department during her childhood in Montgomery and during the early years of her marriage in Westport, and in 1927 had expressed her resentment of Lois Moran by burning her new clothes in the bathtub of their cottage at the Ambassador Hotel. In mid-June 1933, Zelda set fire to the roof and second story of La Paix while trying to burn things in a fireplace that was no longer used. The newspapers, following Scott's attempt to cover up the real cause, tactfully reported that a short circuit in the wiring had started the fire. Scott rescued his manuscripts but lost his collection of books about ghoulish injuries in World War I. He and Zelda were photographed on the front lawn amidst her paintings and the books, cushions, lamps, mattresses and wicker furniture they had managed to salvage from the fire. Standing up and wearing an old overcoat, Scott looks wearily at the camera; the seated Zelda looks up at Scott with a glazed and guilty stare.

Their smoky, scattered possessions formed the core of the wasteful and expensive junk that Zelda catalogued in her autobiographical essay, "Auction—Model 1934." The Fitzgeralds never owned a house, constantly packed and unpacked as they shifted their chaotic lives from place to place and, apart from jewelry and clothes, had very little to show for all the money Scott had once earned. "We have five phonographs, including the pocket one, and no radio," Zelda wrote, with a characteristically *je m'en fiche* attitude, "eleven beds and no bureau. We shall keep it all, the tangible remnant of the four hundred thousand we made from hard words and spent with easy ones these fifteen years. And the collection, after all, is just about as valuable now as the Polish and Peruvian bonds of our thriftier friends."

La Paix was damaged by fire, smoke and water, but did not burn down. Bayard Turnbull was not at all pleased by Zelda's carelessness but, since he was covered by insurance, did not become angry about it. Fitzgerald, making the final push on *Tender is the Night*, asked that repairs on the house be postponed so he would not be disturbed by the workmen. And so, Andrew Turnbull wrote, Scott labored on for the next six months "amid the waterstained walls and woodwork in that hulk of a house, whose bleakness matched the color of his soul."

During the summer and fall of 1932 Zelda had written an unreadable and unactable "farce-fantasy" called *Scandalabra*. Her play reversed the plot of *The Beautiful and Damned*—in which millions are withheld by a puritanical grandfather because of his heir's unconscionable waste and extravagance—and dealt with a pleasant young farmboy who is suddenly willed millions if he agrees to follow a life of wickedness and dissipation. The play was to be performed by the Junior Vagabonds, an amateur theater group in Baltimore, and run for six performances—one week after the fire—from June 26 to July 1, 1933.

The dress rehearsal of *Scandalabra* lasted nearly five hours, and the play had to be radically cut by Fitzgerald, with the aid of the cast, in an all-night session just before the opening. Despite his efficient surgery—and a character delightfully called Anaconda Consequential—the first performance, though fairly well attended (Fitzgerald stood out on the sidewalk like a circus barker and tried to draw innocent pedestrians into the theater), was an embarrassing failure. Subsequent audiences, after harsh and baffled reviews, dwindled to a few curious spectators. Scottie later defended her father (who felt Zelda had stolen "his material" in *Save Me the Waltz*, but allowed the novel to be published when he could easily have suppressed it at Scribner's) against the charge that he was hostile to Zelda's artistic careers. In her foreword to an exhibition catalogue of Zelda's paintings, published in 1974, Scottie substantiated her belief that Fitzgerald "greatly appreciated and encouraged his wife's unusual talents and ebullient imagination. Not only did he arrange for the first showing of her paintings in New York in 1934, he sat through long hours of rehearsals of her one play, *Scandalabra*, staged by a Little Theater group in Baltimore; he spent many hours editing the short stories she sold to *College Humor* and to *Scribner's* magazine; and though I was too young to remember clearly, I feel quite sure that he was even in favor of her ballet lessons."[5]

Fitzgerald's failures in the early 1930s matched Zelda's. The fees for his *Post* stories began to fall as rapidly as they had once ascended. After reaching a peak of $4,000 in 1929, they had dropped in increments of $500 to $2,500; and his income of $16,000 in 1932 was half what it had been the previous year. Not only was the quality of his stories falling (partly because he gave less attention to them as he got absorbed in the completion of his novel), but he was also, for the first time in his professional career, writing work he could not publish. In 1933 he made five false starts on stories, had another story rejected by the *Post*, wrote a long, unsold radio script for the comedienne Gracie Allen and completed a film treatment of *Tender is the Night* that was rejected. Making the best of adversity, Fitzgerald composed an interesting essay about his difficulties, "One Hundred False Starts" (1933), which described his search for a meaningful emotion—"one that's close to me and that I can understand"—that would spark his creative impulse.

II

In December 1933, after completing *Tender is the Night*, Fitzgerald moved from the fire-damaged and rather spooky La Paix to a smaller and cheaper home in the center of Baltimore. The narrow, three-story house at 1307 Park Avenue, at the corner of Lanvale, had white steps, shuttered windows and a high front door, and was in a slightly run-down neighborhood. Fitzgerald thought the change of scene would help Zelda, but the move actually made things worse.

She had been relatively stable for the past twenty months, since leaving Phipps. But in August 1933, just after the performance of *Scandalabra*, Zelda's brother Anthony—depressed about losing his job and worried about his lack of income—suffered a mental breakdown. He entered a hospital in Mobile, Alabama, and committed suicide by jumping out of a window in his room. (After Fitzgerald's death, his brother-in-law Newman Smith also killed himself.) Troubled by Anthony's suicide, Zelda began to lose weight and again became suicidal. She had her third breakdown in the Baltimore house and reentered Phipps Clinic on February 12, 1934. Kept under constant observation to prevent suicide, she had to remain in bed and under sedation. In the clinic she began smiling to herself, would not respond to questions and would suddenly burst out laughing for no discernible reason.

Fitzgerald had never liked Dr. Meyer's treatment of Zelda at Phipps. When she made no progress during February, Fitzgerald consulted Dr. Forel. The Swiss doctor suggested that Zelda transfer to a luxurious clinic on a large country estate that resembled Prangins. On

March 8, after less than a month at Phipps, Zelda moved to Craig House Hospital in Beacon, New York, and was cared for by Forel's friend, Dr. Clarence Slocum. Born in Rhode Island in 1873, Dr. Slocum had earned his medical degree at Albany. Craig House, located on 350 acres above the Hudson River near West Point, housed its patients in scattered cottages, each with an individual nurse. The hospital organized bridge and ping-pong tournaments, had indoor and outdoor swimming pools, tennis courts and a golf course with club house and pro, which made it seem even more like a country club than Prangins.

Soon after she arrived Zelda told Scott: "This is a beautiful place; there is everything on earth available and I have a little room to paint in. . . . [Scottie] would love it here with the pool and the beautiful walks." Though not as expensive as Prangins, the cost of $175 a week was considerably more than at Phipps, and both Scott and Zelda worried about the drain on their dwindling resources. The initial report on Zelda's condition was extremely imperceptive and might just as well have been made by the golf pro. Dr. Slocum thought she was suffering from fatigue, and described the bright, talented and suicidal Zelda as "mildly confused and mentally retarded—with a degree of emotional instability." After two and a half months at Craig House Zelda fell into a catatonic state. On May 19, 1934, she moved to her third clinic in three months. Sheppard and Enoch Pratt Hospital in Towson, Maryland, was—ironically—adjacent to the grounds of La Paix.

Zelda's third breakdown, which coincided with the serialization of *Tender is the Night* in *Scribner's Magazine,* devastated Fitzgerald and destroyed his hopes for her recovery. Zelda had now become, for him, a case—not a person. Yet Scott emphasized his Faustian bond to her when he told a friend: "Life ended for me when Zelda and I crashed. If she would get well, I would be happy again and my soul would be released. Otherwise, never." He continued to feel guilty about her illness, which was emotionally connected with his own perception of his drinking, his sexual inadequacy, and his use of Zelda as muse and subject of his fiction.

Most of Scott's friends were married and he believed, despite his personal experience, that marriage was the best arrangement for a writer. But he complained that Zelda, even when well, never understood or helped him, never recognized his stature as an author. In the late 1930s, thinking bitterly of his relations with Zelda, he told an aspiring writer: "I think a great deal of your problem will depend on whether you have a sympathetic wife who will realize calmly and coolly, rather than emotionally, that a talent like yours is worth saving."[6]

After leaving his relatively structured life at La Paix, Fitzgerald felt depressed, isolated and adrift, and began a dangerous slide into uncontrolled alcoholism and his own milder form of mental illness. When asked in 1928 about his greatest interests in life, Fitzgerald had mentioned "scandal touching upon his friends, everything about the late war, discovering new men and books of promise, Princeton, and [thinking of the Murphys] people with extraordinary personal charm." Nine years later, in response to *Contemporary American Authors,* his interests had dwindled (only military history remained from the previous decade) to "swimming, mild fishing, history, especially military, bucolic but civilized travel, food and wine, imaginary problems of organization, if this makes sense." Since he rarely went swimming or fishing, traveled infrequently, cared very little for food or wine, this list was rather fanciful. His main interest, though he expressed it vaguely, was now aesthetic. He was primarily concerned with how to conceive and structure a work of art. In a private letter of September 1934 to Christian Gauss of Princeton, Fitzgerald let his guard down and said more frankly: "Outside interests generally mean for me women, liquor or some form of exhibitionism."[7]

Scott would have agreed with Zelda, who once replied, when asked why she drank: "Because the world is chaos and when I drink I'm chaotic." While living in Baltimore Fitzgerald was treated for alcoholism by Mencken's doctor, Benjamin Baker. Between 1933 and 1937, Scott entered Johns Hopkins Hospital eight different times to recover from alcoholic binges or to seek treatment for mild bouts of tuberculosis. According to Dr. Baker, Fitzgerald did not blame his drinking on Zelda's illness and took responsibility for it himself. He did not deny that he was an alcoholic but, despite frequent medical treatment, was unable to control his drinking—or his behavior. During a dinner in West Chester, Pennsylvania, at the house of the novelist Joseph Hergesheimer, Fitzgerald "caused a sensation" by rising from the dinner table, dropping his pants and exposing his sexual parts.[8]

In April 1934, after Zelda had returned to the mental clinics, Fitzgerald arranged a different sort of exhibition. He organized a show of twenty-eight of her paintings and drawings at the gallery of Cary Ross, whom they had met in Paris, on East 86th Street in New York. After the failure and bad notices of *Save Me the Waltz* in 1932 and of *Scandalabra* the following year, and Scott's unwillingness (for both his sake and her own) to let her write about her illness in her projected novel, *Caesar's Things,* Zelda, still seeking a creative outlet, focused her attention on painting.

The tragic and ironic motto on the gallery's brochure was *Parfois la Folie est la Sagesse* (sometimes madness is wisdom), and the psychopathic element in Zelda's paintings was clearly visible. Gerald Murphy, a knowledgeable artist, observed that "everyone who saw [the paintings] recognized that quality of repellent human life: they were figures out of a nightmare, monstrous and morbid." The art critic of *Time* magazine was also unenthusiastic about her derivative and distorted pictures:

> The work of a brilliant introvert, they were vividly painted, intensely rhythmic. A pinkish reminiscence of her ballet days showed figures with enlarged legs and feet—a trick she may have learned from Picasso. An impression of a Dartmouth football game made the stadium look like portals of a theatre, the players like dancers. *Chinese Theatre* was a gnarled mass of acrobats with an indicated audience for background. There were two impressionistic portraits of her husband, a verdant *Spring in the Country* geometrically laced with telephone wires.[9]

The sales were as disappointing as the reviews, and all the buyers—including Max Perkins' wife, Tommy Hitchcock, the Murphys and Dorothy Parker, who bought a portrait of Scott, with piercing blue eyes, wearing a crown of thorns—were loyal friends of the artist. Zelda also gave away several pictures to her doctors and to Gertrude Stein.

In the spring of 1934, when Zelda was shifting through several mental hospitals and Scott was making frequent trips to New York to deal with the publication of his novel, he had a brief, drunken affair with the troubled and sympathetic Dorothy Parker. They had first met through the Murphys at Juan-les Pins in the summer of 1926. Born in New York three years before Fitzgerald, half-Jewish and half-Catholic,

Parker was an attractive, talented and sardonic satirist. Her most enduring work is her light verse, which wittily confronts loneliness, failure and despair—themes that linked her both artistically and emotionally to Fitzgerald. Parker's many lovers included the playwrights Elmer Rice and George S. Kaufman as well as several of Scott's friends—Deems Taylor, Charles MacArthur and Ring Lardner. Her promiscuity had led to several abortions. She was also an alcoholic, prone to depression, who had attempted suicide by slashing her wrists and taking overdoses of Veronal.

When Scott's tender obituary of Ring Lardner appeared in October 1933, Parker told him: "I think your piece about Ring is the finest and most moving thing I have ever read." The following April, Fitzgerald sent her an inscribed copy of *Tender is the Night*. Parker later told Lillian Hellman that in the spring of 1934, at the time the novel appeared, she had slept with Scott in a casual and quite spontaneous one or two nights' affair. "Since he was an alcoholic like herself," Parker's biographer observed, "she could feel compassion for him, but he made her uncomfortable for the same reason. She despised in him the very qualities she hated in herself—sniveling self-pity, the way they both wasted their talent, their lack of self-discipline."[10] These two exiles from the Eastern intellectual world would later renew their friendship in Hollywood where both, with different degrees of success, were screenwriters.

III

On April 12, 1934, soon after his brief affair with Parker and while Zelda's disturbing paintings were being exhibited in New York, Fitzgerald finally published his long-awaited novel, *Tender is the Night*. A considerable advance on *The Great Gatsby*, both in narrative technique and psychological depth, it has a dense, dazzling texture that reveals the pains he took and the pain it cost him to write. In this ambitious and complex novel, Fitzgerald attempts to understand why Zelda went mad, how this ruined his life and to what extent he was responsible for their tragedy.

Parts of the novel could be called (like Ingmar Bergman's film) *Scenes from a Marriage,* in its bitter episodes of betrayal and regret, its portrait of a couple locked in mortal combat. It is also Fitzgerald's season in hell, his descent into alcoholism, his exploration of the death of his own high hopes. During the long period of the novel's composition, Fitzgerald developed the capacity to write about himself and Zelda with objectivity and insight. This helps to account for the book's extraordinary power: the combination of psychological conflict and intense introspection with style, wit and literary sophistication.

The novel's unusual time scheme—which begins in 1925, loops back to 1917, returns to where the story left off and ends in 1930—shows Fitzgerald's hard struggle with the task of writing about a fictional hero who revealed so much about the author. He realized that he had to control the point of view very carefully to achieve the requisite blend of sympathy and censure for Dick Diver. Though he tinkered with the novel's chronology after it was published, he did not improve upon it.

The novel begins on a French Riviera beach when Dick and Nicole Diver, a wealthy and glamorous couple, are in their twenties. We see them through the eyes of the teenage movie actress, Rosemary Hoyt, who observes and envies their apparently perfect social life, and who instantly falls in love with him. Dick is an ideal figure: a doctor, handsome, charming and kind, an "organizer of private gaiety, curator of a richly incrusted happiness." Dick also falls in love with Rosemary, despite his sense of responsibility and protectiveness about Nicole, and in his desire to save Rosemary from a bizarre scandal, precipitates Nicole's mental breakdown.

At this point, just as we begin to lose sympathy for Dick, Part I of the novel ends and we go back in time to 1917, when Dick is a medical student in Zurich, at the tail end of his "heroic period," and when he can still approve of himself. Nicole's breakdown also signals the beginning of Dick's decline, but Fitzgerald turns our attention away from the harm Dick is doing and takes us back to the beginning of the story to explain how this situation has developed.

From the beginning of Part II Dick's point of view predominates. We learn that Nicole Warren has suffered previous mental illness, that Dick has been her doctor, that he married his beautiful patient and that they live on her money in the South of France. The narrative then continues up to events in Paris and beyond. When Dick becomes a partner in a sanatorium in Switzerland (financed by the Warren family as a way to control Dick and deal with Nicole's increasing madness), Nicole has

a retaliatory affair, and Dick gradually descends into drink and degradation. The novel ends on the same beach on the Riviera as Nicole, now
well, prepares to marry another man and Dick takes his leave of the
luxurious world of the South to bury himself in an obscure town in
upstate New York.

The narrative scheme reveals the harm each does to the other. At
first it seems that Dick is responsible for Nicole's madness. Then we
learn about her incestuous relationship with her father, and how Dick
has been ensnared by her love and money; how they waver between
health and sickness, sobriety and drunkenness, in control and out of it.
Nicole's mental illness forms the emotional core of the novel just as
Dick's responsibility for his wife is its moral center. As in André Gide's
The Immoralist, the narrative traces the recovery of the sick at the
expense of the healthy. In "The Choice" W. B. Yeats had declared: "The
intellect of man is forced to choose / Perfection of the life, or of the
work." Dick tries to have both—ignoring the necessity to choose, trying
to perfect Nicole's life through his work as a doctor—and fails at both.

In 1932 Fitzgerald had drawn up his plan for the final version of
the long-projected novel and suggested some of the reasons for Dick
Diver's descent from a brilliant young doctor to a weak failure: "The
novel should do this: Show a man who is a natural idealist, a spoiled
priest, giving in for various causes to the ideas of the haute Bourgeoisie,
and in his rise to the top of the social world losing his idealism, his talent, and turning to drink and dissipation. Background one in which the
leisure class is at their truly most brilliant & glamorous, such as Murphys." The phrase "spoiled priest," which describes Stephen Dedalus in
Joyce's *Ulysses* (1922), suggests the similarities between the roles of the
psychiatrist and the priest. Toward the end of the novel, when he rescues Lady Caroline and Mary North from the French police and is disgusted by their behavior, "Dick nodded gravely, looking at the stone
floor, like a priest in the confessional."[11] On the last page he repeats the
"apostolic gesture" he had made at the beginning of the book and
"blessed the beach." This beach had originally been compared to the
concentrated brilliance of a "bright tan prayer rug," used by Moslems
for worship of God and by the American hedonists for pagan worship of
the sun. Dick's blessing is a final, ritualistic gesture of renunciation and
farewell that releases Nicole from his Prospero-like spell and at the
same time calls her back to him.

The hero as psychiatrist is also a metaphor for the novelist. As his name suggests, Dick Diver (like Fitzgerald) is an explorer of inner lives who unlocks the secrets of minds and hearts. Fitzgerald saw that the rise of modern psychiatry had made doctors and analysts the successors to priests. His choice of Dick's profession is a sardonic parallel to his own unhappy role in Zelda's treatment.

Dick's confessional mood and sense of a lost religion, his role as the moral center of an elite group of restless and dissipated American expatriates, ruined by drink and money, recall Hemingway's hero Jake Barnes and the themes of *The Sun Also Rises* (1926). Both novels contrast groups of appealing and unattractive people, one of which obeys and the other ignores an unwritten moral code. Both have minor European characters—the hotel owners, Montoya in Spain and Gausse in France—who express traditional values. Both novels portray the destructive force of beautiful, aristocratic women who dominate and wound the weaker heroes. Both are filled with sexual disorder and uncontrollable violence. Both conclude with the collapse of desperately unhappy love affairs that were doomed from the start.

The characters that surround Dick Diver exemplify his temptations and weaknesses: Baby Warren, money; Abe North, liquor; Tommy Barban, anarchy; Albert McKisco, self-betrayal; Rosemary Hoyt, infidelity. The immorality of the class that leads Dick from idealism to corruption is symbolized by sexual perversions: Luis Campion and Royal Dumphrey are homosexuals, Mary North and Lady Caroline pose as lesbians, Baby is onanistic, Dick is mistaken for a rapist and Devereux Warren has committed incest with his daughter, Nicole. Warren's actual incest is symbolically repeated by Dick: first with Nicole, whom he meets when she is sixteen, then with Rosemary—the daughter of a deceased doctor and the star of *Daddy's Girl*—whom he meets when she is seventeen.

The essential unreality of Dick's life is subtly expressed through the theme of illusion that pervades the novel. As the characters lounge endlessly on the beach, which the Divers "invented," "the true world thundered by" up north. All the characters seem to live in a dream world; and as the novel progresses, their infantile search for "fun" (a recurrent theme) becomes increasingly hopeless and meaningless. Dick has a dangerously inflated idea of himself as a doctor, husband, athlete, leader and lover. Abe North is usually in a drunken stupor.

Rosemary can never free herself from her role-playing profession. Nicole is a schizophrenic with a precarious hold on reality. And in the risky and potentially fatal duel, both Barban and McKisco manage to miss their shots and escape without wounds.

In Part I of the novel Fitzgerald shows that the Divers know each other intimately, that they have a great capacity to hurt each other and that, in such a relationship, they must hide their deepest insights about each other. In Paris, after they have put Abe North on the boat train and witnessed a crime of passion at the railroad station, they have lunch in a restaurant. Nicole has been simmering with jealousy of Rosemary. Dick "saw a flash of unhappiness on her mouth, so brief that only he would have noticed, and he could pretend not to have seen." But Nicole is also silently assessing Dick's weaknesses. She acknowledges that "there was a pleasingness about him that simply had to be used," that people with such charm had to "go along attaching people that they had no use to make of." Dick's charm and narcissism inspire his attraction to Rosemary.

When Rosemary (provoked by her ambitious but reckless mother) naively tries to seduce Dick, who has kissed her in a taxi on the way to their hotel, he is both surprised and frightened, and reverts to his safe paternal role with "Daddy's Girl." Eager for sexual experience despite her considerable fears, Rosemary assumes a stagey voice, audaciously emphasizes her innocence and, in her parody of bedroom intimacy, assumes the role of a spoiled nun:

> She came close up against him with a forlorn whisper.
> "Take me."
> "Take you where?"
> Astonishment froze him rigid.
> "Go on," she whispered. "Oh, please go on, whatever they do. I don't care if I don't like it—I never expected to—I've always hated to think about it but now I don't. I want you to."
> She was astonished at herself—she had never imagined she could talk like that. She was calling on things she had read, seen, dreamed through a decade of convent hours. Suddenly she knew too that it was one of her greatest rôles and she flung herself into it more passionately.

Both Dick and Rosemary are more excited by *hearing* about each other's sex life than by experiencing it. When lunching in the Parisian restaurant with the Divers, Rosemary overhears Dick expressing his sexual desire for Nicole and arranging a time to make love to her. Involving herself in their secret intimacy, Rosemary "stood breathless" in response to Nicole's orgasmic "gasping sigh," and feels an unidentified but profound current of emotion pulsing through her virginal body.

A few chapters later Dick also feels a throb of jealousy as his imaginative reconstruction of reality becomes more powerful than reality itself. Rosemary's Southern boyfriend Collis Clay excites Dick's imagination by describing an incident in which Rosemary and another young boyfriend, Bill Hillis, had locked themselves in a train compartment and had "some heavy stuff going on" before they were interrupted by an angry train conductor. Though this love scene is *twice* removed, since both Clay and Hillis stand between Dick and Rosemary, Dick becomes emotionally distraught. He vividly pictures the "hand on Rosemary's cheek, the quicker breath, the white excitement of the event viewed from outside, the inviolable secret warmth within." Dick then invents a scenario in which Hillis uses and Rosemary acquiesces in an old seducer's ruse: "Do you mind if I pull down the curtain?" "Please do. It's too light in here."[12] This motif recurs throughout the rest of the novel.

When Dick finally consummates his affair with Rosemary in Rome, he discovers that his lack of real feeling for her actually increases his desire and his jealousy. This experience also reminds him of his far deeper love for Nicole, "a wild submergence of soul, a dipping of all colors into an obscuring dye. . . . Certain thoughts about Nicole, that she should die, sink into mental darkness, love another man, made him physically sick." When Rosemary no longer loves him, his vanity is hurt and he characteristically expresses his disappointment in narcissistic terms: "'I guess I'm the Black Death,' he said slowly. 'I don't seem to bring people happiness any more.'" Dick has taken pride in his vitality and sexual prowess, but now gradually declines into emotional vacuity, physical deterioration and self-hatred, while Nicole becomes increasingly stronger and self-assured.

Dick and Rosemary's first attempt to make love is interrupted by the arrival of Abe North, and leads to the climax of Part I, the greatest crisis of the novel. When Rosemary discovers that a Negro has been

15. FITZGERALD, NICE, C. 1924:
Handsome, confident and poised, Fitzgerald was at the height of his powers while writing *The Great Gatsby*. *(Courtney Vaughan)*

24. IRVING THALBERG AND NORMA SHEARER THALBERG, MID-1930S: "The intellectual high priest of Hollywood" had rare taste, self-assurance, decisiveness and respect for excellence.

25. SHEILAH GRAHAM, C. 1930: "So much innocence and so much predatory toughness [went] side by side behind this gentle English voice."

murdered and dumped in her bedroom, Dick carries the bloody sheets into the room he shares with Nicole, who then breaks down completely. In his *Notebooks* Fitzgerald recorded: "Went into the bathroom and sat on the seat crying because it was more private than anywhere she knew." In the novel Nicole retreats into a traditionally inviolable sanctuary, cracks up and—like the fool in *King Lear*—screams out the truth in her madness. Realizing that Dick has sacrificed her to save Rosemary from scandal, Nicole exclaims: "I never expected you to love me—it was too late—only don't come in the bathroom, the only place I can go for privacy, dragging spreads with red blood on them and asking me to fix them."[13] Dick's three desperately rational repetitions of "Control yourself!" reveal at last his true relationship with Nicole: that he is her doctor, she his only patient. His guilty impulse to protect Rosemary has sacrificed Nicole's sanity.

Dick has forced Nicole to associate what she imagines to be the bedsheets bloodied by Dick's defloration of Rosemary with the even more horrible bloody sheets she had lain on when seduced by her own father. And, like her father, Dick is more concerned with covering up the problem than acknowledging his guilt. Nicole's mental breakdown, like the earlier one witnessed by Violet McKisco at the Villa Diana, has been caused by her sexual jealousy of Rosemary. Dick has therefore been fully aware of the consequences of continuing the affair.

Nicole's third breakdown, in another unbearably intense scene, is again caused by sexual jealousy. The mother of a mental patient writes a wounding letter to Nicole explaining that she has withdrawn her fifteen-year-old daughter from the clinic because Dick has kissed and tried to seduce her. This time Nicole cracks up at a Swiss fair while riding on a ferris wheel—a metaphor for both the up and down phases of her madness and for the Catherine-wheel torture of her existence. As they drive home with their two children on the steep curving road that leads to the clinic, "the car swerved violently left, swerved right, tipped on two wheels and, as Dick, with Nicole's voice screaming in his ear, crushed down the mad hand clutching the steering wheel, righted itself, swerved once more and shot off the road. . . . She was laughing hilariously, unashamed, unafraid, unconcerned. No one coming on the scene would have imagined that she had caused it; she laughed as after some mild escape of childhood. 'You were scared, weren't you?' she accused him. 'You wanted to live!'"

This incident is described from Dick's point of view, with all the confusion of violence and screams. The steering wheel, which recalls the ferris wheel, becomes the symbol of their marriage as Dick tries to wrest control from Nicole and she—who had once been disfigured by eczema—tries "to tear at Dick's face." When Dick recognizes that Nicole truly wanted to kill him at that moment, even if it meant killing herself and her children, he decides to separate from her temporarily.

Leaving Nicole in the care of his partner at the clinic, he goes away to ski for a few days by himself. He tries to think tenderly of Nicole, to love "her best self." But, attempting to preserve his own sanity, Dick realizes that "he had lost himself—he could not tell the hour when, or the day or the week, the month or the year. Once he had cut through things, solving the most complicated equations as the simplest problems of his simplest patients. Between the time he found Nicole flowering under a stone on the Zürichsee and the moment of his meeting with Rosemary the spear had been blunted." He reflects that "he had been swallowed up like a gigolo, and somehow permitted his arsenal to be locked up in the Warren safety-deposit vaults." This passage suggests the almost therapeutic drive in the novel: the search to determine when things had gone wrong, where Fitzgerald had "lost himself" and, most poignantly, how he could continue to see Zelda as the person he had once loved and had wanted to impress with his worldly success.

The drunken brawl with the police in Rome, which takes place at the end of Part II, parallels Nicole's breakdown at the end of Part I. In the winter of 1924 Fitzgerald had actually been beaten by the police in Rome after he had punched a plainclothes policeman. The brawl in the novel starts when Dick slaps a policeman's face (which recalls Barban slapping McKisco's face to provoke the duel) and echoes the sad fate of Abe North, who has been beaten to death in a speakeasy. When Baby Warren rescues Dick from jail, she firmly establishes her moral superiority and uses it to control and to "own" him.

Dick's infidelity with Rosemary and degradation in Rome persuade Nicole to have a retaliatory affair with the tough and heroic Tommy Barban. Before offering herself to Tommy (who is wearing Dick's borrowed clothes) Nicole opposes Dick's will, for the first time, by giving Tommy some rare camphor rub for his sore throat. At this symbolic moment, she transfers her emotions from Dick to Tommy and takes over Dick's role as physician and dispenser of medicine. When she drives away with Tommy a little later, Nicole echoes the expression of sexual desire that Rosemary had overheard at the beginning of the novel by begging Tommy to stop the car so they can immediately have sex. Though Nicole, on the previous occasion, had to wait several hours to sleep with Dick, she cannot wait a minute longer to sleep with Tommy. Nicole's recovery becomes complete, after she sleeps with Tommy, when *she* feels sorry for Dick. As he tries to save himself from despair, she finally expresses the crucial truth about their disastrous marriage: "You're a coward! You've made a failure of your life, and you want to blame it on me."

Tender is the Night has a melodramatic plot (a duel, two murders, incest and three mental breakdowns) and an excess of coincidence. Violet McKisco overhears the Divers at the Villa Diana and Rosemary overhears them in a Paris restaurant. Dick accidentally meets Nicole on a Swiss funicular, meets Tommy in Munich, meets Rosemary and then Baby Warren in Rome, and meets Tommy once again at a party on a yacht. Despite its faults in structure and plot, which Fitzgerald later hoped to remedy by changing the original chronology of the novel, it remains a carefully constructed work of art.

Dick's decline from promising idealist to hopeless failure is precisely calibrated. He begins to drink heavily, kisses his patients, sleeps with Rosemary, is beaten up, betrays his son at Mary North's house, loses interest in his career, his book and his clinic, breaks with his partner Franz Gregorovius, quarrels with Mary North, fights with his French cook, fails at water sports while trying to impress Rosemary, and adopts an increasingly passive and pathetic role with Franz, Rosemary, Tommy, Nicole and his children.

Fitzgerald used the details of his own life and Zelda's illness as material for the novel. Nicole's letters to Dick contain extracts of actual letters Zelda wrote. Many of the bitter conversations in the novel have the ring of real exchanges, and give the book a hard, Wildean brilliance. In Nicole's dispute with Abe North at the station we hear the wife reproaching the husband for his drinking:

> "I am a woman and my business is to hold things together."
> "My business is to tear them apart."
> "When you get drunk you don't tear anything apart except yourself."

Abe's sardonic epigram: "Trouble is when you're sober you don't want to see anybody, and when you're tight nobody wants to see you," could have been written by Dorothy Parker.

Fitzgerald also peoples his novel with characters drawn from life. It was dedicated to Gerald and Sara Murphy, who were the models for the positive side of Dick and Nicole Diver, before their tragic descent. Gerald's Irish good looks, jockey cap and ritual of raking the sand, Sara's skill in cooking and gardening, her habit of sunning her pearls on the beach, were portrayed in the novel along with their daughter Honoria, a partial model (with Scottie) for Topsy, and their luxurious house, the Villa America, which Fitzgerald calls the Villa Diana.

Abe North, the alcoholic composer, was based on Fitzgerald's drinking companion Ring Lardner, and Tommy Hitchcock inspired the soldier of fortune, Tommy Barban, as he had inspired Tom Buchanan in *The Great Gatsby*. Nicole's sister Baby Warren—whose callousness, unrequited sexuality and crass materialism provide a powerful contrast to Rosemary's elegant innocence—was partly based on Zelda's older sister and Fitzgerald's bête noire, Rosalind Smith, who (like Baby in the novel) unfairly blamed Fitzgerald for Zelda's mental breakdown. Rosemary Hoyt was modeled on Lois Moran, whom Fitzgerald had an affair with in 1927. It is significant that in the novel Dick's affair with Rosemary occurs *before*—and directly provokes—Nicole's retaliatory adultery with Tommy Barban. Fitzgerald had apparently tried to apportion blame more equally for their unhappy marriage.

Fitzgerald took some revenge, in his minor characters, on people he had known. The pretentious, corrupt and successful writer, Albert McKisco, was partly based on the alternately hard-boiled and sentimental novelist Robert McAlmon. An American expatriate and minor *littérateur* on the fringe of Fitzgerald's Parisian circle of friends, McAlmon was notorious for his caustic tongue and malicious gossip. He spread the rumor that Fitzgerald and Hemingway were homosexuals.

The satiric caricature of Bijou O'Conor, begun in "The Hotel Child," took more serious and substantial form in *Tender is the Night*. In this novel she reappears as the fragile, tubercular, decadent Lady Caroline Sibley-Biers, who is doing a dance of death as the Sepoys assault the ruined fort. This phrase, and Lady Capps-Karr's favorite expression, "After all a chep's a chep and a chum's a chum"—Fitzgerald's bizarre notion of quintessential upper-class English speech, which

Bijou would never have actually said—occur both in "The Hotel Child" and in *Tender is the Night*, linking Lady Capps-Karr and Lady Caroline Sibley-Biers to their common model, Bijou O'Conor.

Tommy Barban thinks Lady Caroline is the wickedest woman in London and Nicole cattily remarks: "it was incredible that such narrow shoulders, such puny arms, could bear aloft the pennon of decadence, last ensign of the fading empire."[14] At the end of the novel Lady Caroline and Mary North dress up as sailors and are arrested—as Dick had been after a drunken brawl in Rome—after picking up two French girls. Though Dick had been insulted by Lady Caroline, he rescues them from an Antibes jail—as Baby Warren had rescued him from a Rome jail. As the French police express their disgust and Dick observes Lady Caroline's lack of any sense of evil, he bitterly concludes that she represents the "concentrated essence of the anti-social."

Though *Tender is the Night* is intensely autobiographical, it also transcends the personal by placing the characters against a detailed contemporary background. The tragic episodes of the novel take place in the context of violent political events, suggested by the allusions to Ulysses Grant, the victorious general in the American Civil War, who "invented mass butchery." Dick and Abe take Rosemary on a tour of the World War I battlefields, which had left "the dead like a million bloody rugs." There is an implicit comparison between Dick—who spent most of the war as a medical student in neutral Switzerland and who feels a corresponding guilt for not having risked his life in the war—and Tommy Barban, a volatile mercenary who will fight for any side that pays him. Fitzgerald refers to the Russian Revolution and the fighting between the Communists and Nazis in Munich, to the Spanish-Moroccan war in the Riff near the western edge of Europe and the Greco-Turkish war near the eastern.

Most importantly, the novel criticizes the capitalistic system that provoked and paid for these wars, and emphasizes the fissure between great wealth and moral values. The vast fortune of the Warren family— which includes trains, factories, stores and plantations—has engendered Devereux's incest, Nicole's madness and Baby's masturbatory self-absorption, and brings about Dick's corruption. Fitzgerald is once again writing about money and the power of the rich. But here the ducal class represented by the Warrens—and by Mary North's second husband, a Moslem potentate whose money flows from manganese deposits in southwestern Asia—are viewed from the disillusioning perspective of the 1929 Wall Street Crash, the hardships of the Depression and Fitzgerald's own financial difficulties. *Tender is the Night* is a representative between-the-wars novel. It expresses guilt about surviving the Great War, portrays anxiety about the present and senses the menace of the future. When Dick bids farewell to the beach, he also says goodbye to the twenties, to youth and to hope.

The outcome of the novel for Dick is tragic. He is sacrificed so that Nicole can be well, and she is now free to remain in the sun while he is condemned to live as a failure in obscure country towns. This conclusion must have afforded Fitzgerald some private gratification. Dick, at the end of the novel, is no longer tormented by Nicole's madness. But Scott could never actually escape from Zelda.

IV

Fitzgerald's friends, well aware of the intensely personal nature of the novel, responded enthusiastically. John Peale Bishop, who had often been condescending to Fitzgerald, was deeply moved by its tragic content: "I come fresh from reading *Tender is the Night* and overcome with the magnificence of it. It surpasses *The Great Gatsby*. You have shown us, what we have wanted so long and impatiently to see, that you are a true, a beautiful and a tragic novelist. I have only praise for its understanding, its characterization, and its deep tenderness." James Branch Cabell, Carl Van Vechten and Robert Benchley also admired the novel. Dos Passos, an early witness of Zelda's madness, found the structure "enormously impressive" and declared: "the whole conception of the book is enormous—and so carefully understated that—so far as I know—not a single reviewer discovered it."

Gilbert Seldes, who had visited Fitzgerald on the Riviera and had acclaimed *The Great Gatsby*, concluded, in the first important review, that Fitzgerald "has stepped again to his natural place at the head of the American writers of our time." In the *New York Times* the critic John Chamberlain praised Fitzgerald's technique and style: "his craftsmanship, his marvelous sense of what might be called social climate, his sheer writing ability. Judged purely as prose, *Tender is the Night* is a continually pleasurable performance."[15] Mary Colum, a perceptive Irish critic, felt the novel was flawed but lauded Fitzgerald's "distinctive gifts—a romantic imagination, a style that is often brilliant, a swiftness of movement, and a sense of enchantment in people and places." But Philip Rahv, writing in the Communist *Daily Worker*, obtusely condemned the novel for deviating from the Party line. And William Troy, in the Left-wing *Nation*, found Dick Diver's character unconvincing and depressing.

D. W. Harding, a professor of psychology at the University of London, felt that Fitzgerald (despite all he had been through) lacked insight into the "pathetic" and "harrowing" subject of the novel. But he thought that Fitzgerald managed to convey the idea that "people who disintegrate in the adult world don't at all win our respect and can hardly retain even our pity." Fitzgerald was especially pleased, therefore, by a psychiatrist's anonymous review in a professional magazine, the *Journal of Nervous and Mental Disease*, which extolled his "fascinating" and "valuable" clinical account. "As one grasps fully the scope of the author's aim," the doctor wrote, "and his discernment in face of the balance of psychotic cause and effect, the rich endowment of the book in regard to conscious mastery of authentic experience and exceptional descriptive powers becomes increasingly evident."[16]

The man Fitzgerald most wanted to please remained silent. On May 10, a month after publication, Fitzgerald desperately wrote Hemingway: "Did you like the book? For God's sake drop me a line and tell me one way or another. You can't hurt my feelings. I just want to get a few intelligent slants at it to get some of the reviewers' jargon out of my head." Two weeks later Hemingway—influenced by personal knowledge of the Murphys and perhaps by jealousy of Fitzgerald's achievement—bluntly replied that Scott had ruined the novel by conflating his own and Zelda's characteristics with those of the Murphys, creating an unconvincing composite and wrecking the logical consistency of their behavior:

> I liked it and I didn't like it. It started off with that marvelous description of Sara and Gerald. . . . Then you started fooling with them, making them come from things they didn't come from, changing them into other people and you can't do that. . . .

Invention is the finest thing but you cannot invent anything that
would not actually happen. . . .

You took liberties with peoples' pasts and futures that
produced not people but damned marvelously faked case
histories. . . . For God's sake write and write truly no matter
who or what it hurts but do not make these silly compromises.

Fitzgerald defended himself in a letter to Sara Murphy by stating
that his theory of fiction, antithetically opposed to Hemingway's, was
that "it takes half a dozen people to make a synthesis strong enough to
create a fiction[al] character." Gerald agreed with Fitzgerald and wrote,
a year after the novel appeared, that his imaginative reconstruction of
their lives was truer than reality: "I know now that what you said in
Tender is the Night is true. Only the invented part of our life—the
unreal part—has had any scheme, any beauty." Four years later Hemingway reread the novel, saw its merits more clearly and revised his
opinion. Recognizing Fitzgerald's deep insight and ability to objectify
his own tragic experience, he told Max Perkins: "It's amazing how
excellent much of it is. If he had integrated it better it would have been
a fine novel (as it is) much of it is better than anything else he ever
wrote. . . . Reading that novel much of it was so good it was frightening."[17]

Fitzgerald had very high hopes for the novel that had evolved from
so much suffering. He felt it was his last chance to restore his reputation, his self-confidence and his wealth. *This Side of Paradise* had sold
more than 49,000 copies by the end of 1921. But *Tender is the Night*,
partly because of the economic depression and because his subject
matter was unfashionable during those politically conscious years, sold
only 13,000 copies. It earned just five thousand dollars, which was not
even enough to repay his debts to Scribner's and to Ober. Zelda's third
breakdown in February 1934 and the relative failure of *Tender is the
Night* in April propelled Fitzgerald into his own crack-up, from which
he never completely recovered.

Chapter Eleven

Asheville and "The Crack-Up," 1935–1937

I

When Zelda came out of her catatonic state at Sheppard-Pratt she tried to commit suicide by strangling herself. Despite constant surveillance she made frequent attempts on her life. Once, while walking with Scott on the grounds of the clinic, she tried to throw herself beneath a passing train and he caught her just before she reached the tracks. Gradually she calmed down and became accustomed to institutional living, one of three hundred patients in the huge towered and turreted red-brick Victorian buildings.

Dr. William Elgin—who was born in Cincinnati in 1905, graduated from Washington and Lee University in Virginia and earned his medical degree at Johns Hopkins—found Zelda confused, withdrawn and expressionless. The once active and vibrant woman now seemed to him a colorless "blob" who moved in slow motion and felt threatened by hallucinatory voices. Yet her tender and poignant letter of June 1935 showed that Zelda was all too aware of the devastation her illness had caused. She showed considerable insight into her emotional hollowness and expressed great sadness about all they had sacrificed. She also returned to the themes of lost identity and negation of the self which Scott considered in his "Crack-Up" essays:

Dearest and always Dearest Scott:
I am sorry too that there should be nothing to greet you but an empty shell. The thought of the effort you have made over me, the suffering this *nothing* has cost would be unendurable to any save a completely vacuous mechanism. Had I any feelings they would all be bent in gratitude to you and in sorrow that all of my life there should not even be the smallest relic of the love and beauty that we started with to offer you at the end. . . .

Now that there isn't any more happiness and home is gone and there isn't even any past and no emotions but those that were yours where there could be my comfort—it is a shame that we should have met in harshness and coldness where there was once so much tenderness and so many dreams. . . . I love you anyway— even if there isn't any me or any love or even any life.

Three months later, after one of his heart-wrenching visits to the hospital, Fitzgerald told a friend that they still had, despite Zelda's insanity, a powerful bond that could never be broken: "she was fine, almost herself, has only one nurse now and has no more intention of doing away with herself. It was wonderful to sit with her head on my shoulder for hours and feel as I always have even now, closer to her than to any other human being." Friends who saw Scott with Zelda during her visits outside the hospital confirmed the intensity of feeling that both destroyed and sustained him:

He was so dreadfully unhappy [said his Asheville friend Nora Flynn]. Zelda was then in the sanatorium. Once, after she got out, he brought her over to visit. She wore such odd clothes, and looked so ill—and walked about just touching things. Finally she started to dance for us. And Scott sat over there. I shall never forget the tragic, frightful look on his face as he watched her. He had loved her so much—they both had loved each other. Now it was dead. But he still loved that love and hated to give it up— that was what he continued to nurse and cherish, that love which had been, and which he could not forget.

Margaret Banning—a Minnesota novelist and graduate of Vassar, who also saw them in Asheville—noted that Zelda had completely lost her elegance and displayed a greedy urge for alcohol. "She came in looking like Ophelia, with water lilies she had brought, and in a sagging and not very stylish bright-colored dress. Wine was served and she drank it in an eager gulp and right away it set her off. Then Fitzgerald sat down and played a game with her, pretending she was a princess in a tower and he was her prince—so tragic it was heartbreaking to watch. He still loved her."[1] Scott's reckless princess was, at last, safely locked away in a tower.

Their love was now undermined by a tragic and increasingly clear-sighted despair. Zelda, who would remark, "Well, I guess it's time to go back to my incarceration," realized that all Scott's brave efforts to find the best doctors, hospitals and treatments were hopeless. To someone as sick as she was, one place was much the same as another. Writing to his confidants Margaret Turnbull and Harold Ober in the summer of 1935, Scott confessed that Zelda now seemed more pitiful than ever, that he could scarcely endure "the awful strangling heart-rending quality of this tragedy that has gone on now more than six years, with two brief intervals of hope."

In February 1935, depressed about Zelda and by a flare-up of tuberculosis, Fitzgerald left the house on Park Avenue in Baltimore. He went down to Tryon, a tiny health resort thirty-five miles south of Asheville in the Blue Ridge mountains of western North Carolina (where the Georgia-born poet Sidney Lanier had died of tuberculosis in 1881). He spent a month in a top-floor room of the Oak Hall Hotel, on a bluff above the main street.

He chose Tryon because his wealthy friends Maurice and Nora Flynn held court there. The tall, handsome Maurice, who was always called Lefty, had many of the qualities Fitzgerald admired in Tommy Hitchcock. He had been an All-American football star at Yale, a cowboy actor in silent films and (like Scott's brother-in-law) a naval aviator during the war. Lefty, once an alcoholic, had been cured by Nora, a Christian Scientist, after she left her first husband to marry him in 1931. (Nora's daughter by her first marriage became the British actress Joyce Grenfell.) Fitzgerald's story "The Intimate Strangers" (1935) is a fictionalized account of their romantic courtship.

The glamorous and vivacious Nora, the youngest of the five beautiful Langhorne sisters of Virginia, was born in about 1890. Her father was a wealthy tobacco auctioneer and railroad builder. Her older sister, Nancy, who married Viscount Astor, succeeded her husband as Conservative M.P. for Plymouth in 1919 and became the first woman in Parliament. Nancy's biographer, Christopher Sykes, writes that Nora was (like Bijou O'Conor) the disreputable bohemian of the family: "During her life she became involved in many scandals and ran up many debts, from both of which she was rescued regularly by the Astors, on conditions which were regularly broken. She shared three principal things with Nancy, comic acting ability, an extraordinary power to attract affection so that everyone who knew her, including her numerous and often infuriated critics, loved her, and an ardent faith in Christian Science." Unlike Fitzgerald, the bold and exciting Nora "never looked behind" and would raise his flagging spirits by announcing: "tighten up your belt, baby, let's get going. To any pole."[2]

Nora also attracted Fitzgerald's affection, and Edmund Wilson told Mizener that they apparently had an affair. Zelda, who met Nora in Asheville, may have instinctively sensed Fitzgerald's attachment, realizing that Nora provided an antidote to her own deep depressions: "Nora Flynn—he loved her I think—not clandestinely, but she was one of several women he always needed around him to turn to when he got low and needed a lift." The well-born and elegant Nora noticed Scott's sense of social inferiority and found "a certain streak of something queer in him—gaudy, blatant, almost vulgar." But it seemed to friends in Tryon that Nora—who loved to rehabilitate alcoholics—was also attracted to Scott and led him on.

Nora herself, when questioned about her friendship with Scott, agreed that he loved her but was ambiguous about their sexual relations: "He always said he was terribly in love with me. And it was so foolish. I cared so much for Lefty [who later left her], and he did too. And it was such an obvious relief to Scott when I finally told him off, and we could forget the sex and just be friends. He was so charming and such fun to talk with. He could describe things with such feeling." Nora also confirmed Oscar Kalman's belief that Fitzgerald's deep-rooted puritanism and guilty scruples about Zelda severely limited the possibilities of sexual pleasure: "His conscience was so powerfully developed," she observed, "and it kept him from completely enjoying his efforts at dissipation and from experiencing sensations.

For he was fundamentally a moralist, and a very religious person."

Though Fitzgerald was grateful for the Flynns' generous hospitality and friendship, and frequently visited them throughout 1935, he also resented their wealth and social position. Tony Buttitta, another Asheville friend, said Fitzgerald considered them socialites and would tear them apart when drunk. Yet Fitzgerald paid tribute to Nora, whom he saw as a cross between a Florence Nightingale and a Job's comforter, in a letter of 1936 to his childhood friend Marie Hersey: "During the mood of depression that I seem to have fallen into about a year ago she was a saint to me, took care of Scottie for a month one time under the most peculiar circumstances, and is altogether, in my opinion, one of the world's most delightful women."[3]

II

After a month in Tryon, Fitzgerald returned to Baltimore for March and April in order to be near Zelda, who was still confined in Sheppard-Pratt. On March 20 he published *Taps at Reveille*, his fourth collection of stories and the last book to appear in his lifetime. The title of the book, dedicated to the faithful Harold Ober, suggested sadness and premature death. Like *All the Sad Young Men*, this volume had outstanding and mediocre stories indiscriminately mixed together. Some of his best recent work—"Outside the Cabinet-Maker's," "The Swimmers," "One Trip Abroad" and "The Hotel Child"—was excluded, partly because he had extracted the best bits from the last three for use in *Tender is the Night*.

The nostalgic and retrogressive Basil and Josephine stories, based on his childhood and on the character of Ginevra King, reflected the superficial values—founded on looks, wealth and status—that had characterized his tales of the early 1920s. These eight stories incongruously appeared in the same volume as "Babylon Revisited" and "Crazy Sunday," which, like Hemingway's two African stories of the late 1930s, were mature masterpieces in this genre.

Taps at Reveille received generally lukewarm reviews from mainly undistinguished critics who noted the triviality of most of the stories. There were, however, a few insights. Gilbert Seldes called "Babylon

Revisited" Fitzgerald's "saddest and truest story"; T. S. Matthews in the *New Republic* noted the contrast between the serious and superficial stories; and William Troy in the *Nation* noted the disparity between their acute moral interest and the immature moral vision. This collection—which sold only a few thousand copies, was never reprinted and never appeared in England—did little to sustain Fitzgerald's reputation as a serious writer.

The month after his stories were published an X-ray examination revealed that Fitzgerald's lungs had, as he feared, deteriorated during the past two years. He had a tubercular cavity in his left lung and large areas of infiltration in the right one. Benjamin Baker, his Baltimore physician, immediately sent him to a specialist in Asheville, the home town of Thomas Wolfe and a center for the treatment of pulmonary disease.

Instead of entering a sanatorium, Fitzgerald stayed at the Grove Park Inn, a luxurious, fortress-like hotel, near the Vanderbilt estate, on the outskirts of town. It was built of massive blocks of stone, had opened in 1913 and called itself "The Finest Resort Hotel in the World." Fitzgerald occupied two of the more modest adjoining rooms, at number 441, which faced the front courtyard and did not have the magnificent rear view of the extensive grounds and the Blue Ridge mountains.

He soon met Tony Buttitta, a small, lively and cultured man, who was eleven years younger than Scott. Buttitta was born in Chicago, had earned his degree from the University of Texas and had taken a graduate workshop in playwriting at the University of North Carolina. In the summer of 1935 he was doing publicity for the North Carolina Symphony Orchestra and running the Intimate Book Shop in the arcade of the George Vanderbilt Hotel in downtown Asheville. He was a great admirer of Fitzgerald's work, but could not sell a single copy of *Tender is the Night*.

Buttitta, who came to know Fitzgerald quite well and later published a memoir about him, was disillusioned by his sometime hero. "That summer in Asheville everything had crashed about him," Buttitta wrote. "He was a physical, emotional, and financial bankrupt. He smoked and drank steadily, but ate very little; he took pills to sleep a few hours. . . . Often when I saw him he cried, suddenly, as if he were an overwrought, indulged child." He added that people in Asheville were completely unaware that Fitzgerald was an important writer. Some thought he was a strange person; others saw him as just another fussy and unreliable "pain in the neck" who messed up his hotel room and was always pressed for money.[4]

Apart from his friendship with Tony, during his time in Asheville Fitzgerald relied heavily on several women who served as secretary, nurse, decoy, mistress and whore. In early June he met the attractive Laura Guthrie. A few years older than Scott and waiting for a divorce, she supported herself, dressed as a gypsy, by reading palms in the lobby of the Grove Park Inn. Like Tony, Laura had literary ambitions and admired Fitzgerald's work. But, unwilling to become involved with a married alcoholic, she had to fend off his ardent attempts at seduction. "I was nearly crazy some of the time with thoughts of him," she confessed to her diary. "He reaches women through their minds and yet he wants their bodies. He makes a woman who must keep her body to herself a wreck, either mental or physical—whichever part is weakest goes."

When Laura rejected his advances, Fitzgerald raised the siege and hired her as secretary and companion. According to Laura, who also kept an elaborate record of his behavior and conversation, he was extremely dictatorial and expected to be instantly obeyed. He smoked heavily, never ate a decent meal, was ashamed of his drinking but could not control it, consumed (beginning at breakfast) as many as thirty-seven beers a day and took pills in order to sleep. He trembled, was desperately lonely and tried to acquire a suntan to hide the effects of his dissipation.

Despite his wretched condition, Fitzgerald turned on the charm and conducted affairs with several lady friends during the summer of 1935. Unlike Laura Guthrie, Beatrice Stribling Dance actually pursued him and became his mistress in mid-June. She came from a wealthy family in Memphis, was six years younger than Fitzgerald, and had blond hair and a strangely attractive stutter. Faithfully married for eleven years to Du Pre Rainey "Hop" Dance, a rich San Antonio businessman and sports enthusiast, Beatrice had a young daughter, who was called "Tulah."

Beatrice, staying at the Grove Park Inn on a recuperative holiday with her physically sick and mentally unstable sister Eleanor, attracted Fitzgerald's attention by reading The Great Gatsby in the hotel lobby.

After dinners, dancing and drinks with both Mrs. Dance and her sister, Scott became Beatrice's lover. The excitement of the adulterous affair was intensified by the vicarious participation of Laura Guthrie who (after cautiously rejecting Scott) now became his confidante and go-between, by the awareness of the hotel staff who served as audience to their bedroom farce and by the strong sexual emotions he aroused in Beatrice. He told Laura she was "terribly passionate, almost a nympho-maniac." Though he said he would never leave Zelda, Beatrice declared, "I am rich. I will pay for everything," and suggested they run away to some exotic place. But he also found Beatrice arrogant, spoiled, selfish and not terribly bright.[5]

Hop Dance visited Asheville for two weeks in mid-July, and the Dances, to avoid awkward confrontations with Scott, stayed at the nearby Highlands resort. Scott and Beatrice, using Laura to deceive her sister, arranged a secret meeting at the Vanderbilt Hotel. But Hop's suspicions were aroused. After leaving Asheville, he kept phoning his wife late at night and discovered she was not in her room. On August 7 Hop suddenly returned to Asheville with his family physician, Dr. Cade. That night Scott, armed with a beer can opener, went to the Dances' hotel room with Laura. They all had an amiable chat and Scott instinctively liked Hop—as he had liked Lefty Flynn. As they got up to leave Scott boldly asked Beatrice if he could kiss her goodnight and, when she eagerly agreed, took that liberty in front of her husband. Hop became enraged, pushed Scott out of the room and slammed the door.

The next morning Dr. Cade warned Scott about the potentially tragic consequences of the affair and persuaded him to stop seeing Beatrice. That day she wrote Laura, who now served as confidante for both of them: "It has been decided that it is better for me to go to-day.—Take care of Scott for me—there was nothing I could do for him anyway—except to love him." Ten days later Laura, still playing the go-between, fatalistically told Beatrice that Scott "remembers and suffers over everything just as you do. But how else could it end?" And Bea-trice, using the language of a ladies' romance, sadly replied: "I had never loved anyone before as I loved Scott and shall love him till I die."[6]

The affair had serious consequences—apart from the effect on Beatrice's marriage and her daughter. The unstable Eleanor had become dangerously depressed. And Beatrice, who desperately tried to

keep in touch with Scott after she returned to San Antonio, also suffered greatly. Like Nicole during Dick's affair with Rosemary in *Tender
is the Night*, she had a nervous breakdown, entered a hospital and took
a long time to recover.

Beatrice sent Scott many presents during the next few years and he
wrote intimate letters to her for the rest of his life. At first he tried to
ease her pain by saying how much he had loved her and by expressing
contrition for the way things had ended:

> There is still no image of you emerging—only a memory of
> beauty and love and pain. . . . I had been looking for you [for] a
> long time I think here & there about the world and when I
> found you there occurs this tragedy or this mess. . . . All I know
> is I'd like to sit for a thousand years and look at you and hear
> your voice with the lovely pathetic little *"peep"* at the
> crescendo of the stutter. I think the word lovely comes into my
> mind oftenest when I think of you. . . .
>
> You are the loveliest human being I have ever known. . . . I
> love you—you are crystal clear, blown glass with the sun
> cutting always very suddenly across it. . . .
>
> With all my heart I am sorry to have brought so much
> sorrow into your life.

But by September he took a sterner tone and tried to buck her up
by reminding the broken Beatrice of *her* moral responsibility: "There
are emotions just as important as ours running concurrently with
them—and there is literally no standard in life other than a sense
of duty. . . . We can't just let our worlds crash around us like a lot of
dropped trays. *You have got to be good.*" Two weeks later, in a letter to
Laura about Beatrice, Fitzgerald (who must have been struck by the
irony of their Dantesque and Petrarchan names) still seemed surprised
by her tragic response to the end of the affair. Her wealth, social position, husband and child could not compensate for the loss of Fitzgerald:
"I never saw a girl who *had so much* take it all so hard. She knew from
the beginning there would be nothing more, so it could scarcely be
classed even as a *disappointment*—merely one of these semi-tragic
facts that must be faced." Despite the ephemeral, farcical and hysterical aspects of this hotel drama, Scott did seem to be genuinely fond of

her. In the late 1930s he told Sheilah Graham he had been in love with Beatrice. And in November 1940, he was still pondering the effects of the affair and wrote Beatrice: "That wild last week in Asheville has a nightmare quality in retrospect—that curious legal phantom [Dr. Cade?] who reminded me of something out of my most sinister imaginings—those hotels with their dead monotony and the dead people in them."[7]

In his *Notebooks* Fitzgerald linked the personalities of Zelda, Nora and Beatrice—all of whom came from prominent families, had adulterous affairs and were emotionally involved with him in 1935—and considered himself conservative and relatively balanced when compared to them: "I am astonished sometimes by the fearlessness of women, the recklessness—like Nora, Zelda, Beatrice—in each case it's partly because they are all three spoiled babies who never felt the economic struggle on their shoulders. But it's heartening when it stays this side of recklessness. . . . Except for the sexual recklessness, Zelda was cagey about throwing in her lot with me before I was a money-maker, and I think by temperament she was the most reckless [and the most unbalanced] of all." But Fitzgerald himself, usually so responsible about Zelda, had been swept into recklessness by Beatrice. Though he emerged unscathed from their liaison, he left several casualties: Beatrice, Eleanor, Hop, Tulah and even Laura. Like Tom and Daisy at the end of *The Great Gatsby*, he "retreated back into . . . [his] vast carelessness . . . and let other people clean up the mess [he] had made."[8]

Fitzgerald almost became yet another casualty when he discovered an ominous rash on his skin. Full of guilty anxiety, he thought it was a sign of syphilis, believed he had contracted it from an Asheville prostitute, Lottie, and feared he had passed it on to Beatrice. Lottie, who walked the streets with two black poodles and a book under her arm, had reassured Fitzgerald about the size of his sexual equipment but confided to Buttitta that he was prone to premature ejaculation. (Beatrice had no complaints about this and seemed fully satisfied by their sexual relations.) Fitzgerald had a Wassermann test for syphilis in a different town and called from a pay phone for the reassuring result. Later he learned that the rash was caused by the drugs he was taking to calm his nerves and prevent insomnia.

III

In September 1935 Fitzgerald fled his emotional entanglements in Asheville, returned to Baltimore and moved into the Cambridge Arms Apartments, a red-brick building across from the Johns Hopkins campus, at the corner of Charles and 34th Street. He felt guilty not only about his betrayal of Zelda (whom he visited), but also about the pain Beatrice had suffered. In early September he gloomily wrote Ober: "If only I would die at least [Scottie] and Zelda would have the life insurance and it would be a general good riddance, but it seems as if life has been playing some long joke with me for the past eight months and can't decide when to leave off."

After two lonely and despairing months in Baltimore, Fitzgerald impulsively packed his bag and traveled south to Hendersonville, a drab little town eighteen miles south of Asheville. He took a penitential dollar-a-day room in the Skylands Hotel at the corner of 6th and Main Street in the center of town. A *Notebook* entry for November 1935 described his ascetic existence—a great contrast to the luxury of the Grove Park Inn. It recorded that he could no longer eat much food, and mentioned that he was deeply in debt (to Scribner's and Ober as well as to Perkins and his mother) and very close to destitution:

> I am living very cheaply. Today I am in comparative affluence, but Monday and Tuesday I had two tins of potted meat, three oranges and a box of Uneedas [biscuits] and two cans of beer. The food totaled 18 cents a day—and I think of the thousand meals I've sent back untasted in the last two years. It was fun to be poor—especially [if] you haven't enough liver power for an appetite. But the air is fine here and I liked what I had—and there was nothing to do about it anyhow because I was afraid to cash any checks and I had to save enough postage for the story. But it was funny coming into the hotel and the very deferential clerk not knowing I was not only thousands, nay tens of thousands in debt, but had less than 40 cents cash in the world and probably a $13 deficit at my bank.

In mid-November he explained that he had become severely depressed and had suffered a mild nervous breakdown. He also said he was living as cheaply as possible while trying to recover: "Suffice to say I cracked entirely after the strain of doing too many things at once and simply fled down here which I had no economic right to do. But since it was that or break up again and that would be an even more expensive business to dependents and creditors, here I am."

Nora Flynn, who had an expensive and elegant house, painted a grim picture of Fitzgerald absorbed in his misery at Skylands: "He went off to that frightful hotel in Hendersonville, drunk and ill. And he lay there thinking about himself, as usual. He never was interested in any one or anything but himself. It was such a horrid place. I can still see it—with collar buttons on the bureau, and neckties hanging from the light chair, and dirty pajamas strewn all over." After a month in Hendersonville Fitzgerald still claimed to enjoy, after long years of dissipation, washing his own clothes and eating two cheap meals a day. But, back in Baltimore for Christmas, he realized that he needed decent surroundings to produce his stories and firmly declared: "Have tried life on subsistence level and it doesn't work."[9]

Fitzgerald was, as Nora observed, drinking more than ever. His wife was crazy, his health was poor, he could not write and he was deeply in debt. He felt he could not survive without liquor, which put him into a stupor and made him forget his overwhelming problems. He had once asked a friend: "Can you name a single American artist except James and Whistler (who lived in England) who didn't die of drink?" and now saw himself in the destructive yet romantic tradition that began with his much-admired Poe.

In Asheville during the previous summer he had tried to drink sufficient quantities of beer to give him as much alcohol as he used to get from gin. One visitor, stumbling over the hidden bottles in his rooms, was astonished at how he was nearly buried beneath them: "I have never, before or since, seen such quantities of beer displayed in such a place in such a fashion. Rows of unopened bottles lined the tops of bureaus and chests of drawers in each room. As many cases as possible were jammed under each of the four beds. Each trash basket was full of empties. So was the tub in one of the baths. Stacks of cases served as tables for manuscripts, books, supplies of paper."

In Hendersonville he had abandoned the pretense of controlling his alcoholism by drinking only beer and gone back to his habitual gin. His doctors had warned him to confine himself to only one shot a day, so he carefully measured out one shot at a time until he had emptied the whole bottle. This heavy drinking inevitably took its toll. His damaged liver no longer allowed him to eat solid food, his skin was raw and ashen, and he had a rasping tubercular cough. Constant dizziness and blurred vision forced him to hold on to the furniture when he crossed the room. He also suffered episodes of *delirium tremens* and once told Sheilah Graham—"in full skin-crawling detail—how in 1935 he saw beetles and pink mice scurrying all over him and elephants dancing on the ceiling."[10]

Thomas Mann, who emigrated to the United States in 1938, observed that "America is a cruel land, whether in success or in failure." But Fitzgerald—both a failure as a success and a failure as a failure—suffered much more than he deserved. Reflecting on his crack-up years, he wrote of the difficulty of recovery and regeneration: "When you once get to the point where you don't care whether you live or die—as I did—it's hard to come back to life. . . . It's hard to believe in yourself again—you have slain a part of yourself." But he also felt pathological satisfaction in hitting the bottom and knowing he had reached the extreme level of degradation. Having reached this depth Fitzgerald, as Eliot said of Coleridge, transformed his ruin into a vocation.

While subsisting in the Skylands Hotel in November 1935 Fitzgerald began to write his three "Crack-Up" essays—one of the seminal documents in modern American literature. In "Sleeping and Waking," another essay about insomnia, he described his compulsive ritual before going to bed and mentioned the hope that his semi-conscious mind would throw off a creative spark: "All is prepared, the books, the glass of water, the extra pajamas lest I awake in rivulets of sweat, the luminal [sedative] pills in the little round tube, the note book and pencil in case of a night thought worth recording."[11] But most of the time his hopes were futile, and he finally decided to write about his creative sterility. In "The Crack-Up," a distraction from and substitute for his fictional efforts, he could write about not writing instead of actually writing about what he wanted to write.

George Orwell once remarked that "autobiography is only to be trusted when it reveals something disgraceful." "The Crack-Up"—a fascinating mixture of public therapy, confession, apologia and self-punishment—substantiates this observation and explores Fitzgerald's worst characteristics. As in *Tender is the Night,* he achieves an astonishing objectivity about his own suffering and expresses an intensity of feeling reminiscent of Dostoyevsky and Strindberg.

"The Crack-Up" begins with two rather abstract premises, one previously held and now rejected by Fitzgerald, the other retained. During the early 1920s, his years of success and fame, he had believed that "life was something you dominated if you were any good." Sara Murphy, then going through a tragic period in her own life, strongly objected to the naive belief that one could conquer malign fate and angrily asked Scott: "Do you *really* mean to say you honestly thought [this]? . . . Even if you meant your *own* life it is arrogant enough—but life!"

The second premise, which he still believed, was that "the test of a first-rate intelligence is the ability to hold two opposed ideas in the mind at the same time, and still retain the ability to function." Though this crucial statement has been quoted scores of times, no one has ever mentioned where it comes from and how it applies to the theme of "The Crack-Up." The source is Keats' letter to his brothers, of December 22, 1817, which defines his concept of *"Negative Capability,* that is, when a man is capable of being in uncertainties, Mysteries, doubts, without any irritable reaching after fact and reason."[12] Fact and reason, the bases of logical thought, deny the Mysteries at the same time that the "first-rate intelligence" tries to grasp them. Fitzgerald implies that the two simultaneous but antithetical ideas in his own mind are that Zelda is permanently insane but will recover, and that he is a hopeless failure but will eventually succeed.

After mentioning several crucial events of his early life, Fitzgerald reveals that for the past two years "my life had been drawing on resources that I did not possess, that I had been mortgaging myself physically and spiritually," and that "my vitality had been steadily and prematurely trickling away." In short, he has been overcome by emotional exhaustion. The symptoms of his condition are a desire to be alone, a rejection of people, listlessness, apathy and lack of feeling as well as a purely mechanical response to experience, hypersensitivity to both noise and silence, irritation, irrational prejudice and a sense of being emotionally undernourished. "In a real dark night of the soul," writes the insomniac Fitzgerald, alluding to the Spanish mystic St. John of the Cross, "it is always three o'clock in the morning, day after day."

As Fitzgerald holds out "the tin cup of self-pity" and becomes the unwilling witness of the disintegration of his own personality, he tries to explain what has brought him to this desperate state. He had, it seems, weakly surrendered vital aspects of his moral being to his closest friends. Edmund Wilson had warned him, as early as 1919, to "brace up your artistic conscience, which was always the weakest part of your talent!" Fitzgerald claimed, in his Introduction to the Modern Library reprint of *The Great Gatsby* (1934), that he had kept his artistic conscience pure while writing his most flawless book. But in "The Crack-Up" he admits that having foolishly depended on Wilson to be his intellectual conscience, on his Princeton friend Sap Donahoe to be his moral conscience, on Hemingway to be his artistic conscience and on Gerald Murphy to be his social conscience, there was, not surprisingly, "not an 'I' any more—not a basis on which I could organize my self-respect."

Like *Tender is the Night*, "The Crack-Up" is an attempt to account for his personal decay. But in the essays Fitzgerald circles around the events of his life and announces that he has cracked up without actually explaining why he did so. Like Rudolph Miller in "Absolution," Fitzgerald confessed, but could not confess everything. There are many flashes of revelation and insight, but no honest reference to his drinking, the breakdown of his marriage or his guilt about the insanity of his wife. In 1922 he had asked Wilson to delete all references to Fitzgerald's drinking in his review of *The Beautiful and Damned*. In 1936 he again conceals his alcoholism and vaguely states that at the time of his crack-up he had "not tasted so much as a glass of beer for six months—it was [my] nervous reflexes that were giving way—too much anger and too many tears." Though "The Crack-Up" was praised by reviewers for its honesty and candor, it was more a complex work of art than a frank revelation. Just as Fitzgerald had once carefully created the image of the golden boy of the 1920s, so he now offered a cunningly constructed negative image to complement the earlier one. He later told Scottie he was "too much a moralist at heart and really want[ed] to preach at people in some acceptable form."[13] In "The Crack-Up" he preached at himself.

Critics have been intrigued by what Glenway Wescott called Fitzgerald's "self-autopsy and funeral sermon." Scottie, who picked up this clinical metaphor, compared her father to "a surgeon performing an operation upon himself, hurting terribly but watching the process with a fascinated detachment." In 1945 Joseph Wood Krutch praised the work's intelligence, sophistication and artistic sincerity. And Mark Schorer, one of Fitzgerald's most perceptive readers, called it "a beautiful and moving confession; without a hint of self-pity, it is one of the most extraordinary self-revelations in literature."[14]

Fitzgerald acknowledged in "The Crack-Up" that "there are always those to whom all self-revelation is contemptible." And he explained to Beatrice Dance that many friends—from Hemingway and Dos Passos to Perkins and Ober—thought he had done himself great harm, when the articles were published in *Esquire* in the spring of 1936, by announcing to the world that he was morally and artistically bankrupt. Amid all this criticism of Fitzgerald, Arnold Gingrich, the editor of *Esquire,* was a persuasive dissenting voice. He felt that Fitzgerald had indeed hit rock bottom, but that *any* publicity—good or bad—was helpful and that "The Crack-Up" actually had a beneficial effect on Scott's career:

> Can't feel that it did any damage. So it got him a brutal letter from Ernest Hemingway and a rather hoity-toity one from Dos Passos. And an interviewer from the New York *Post,* stimulated by it to look him up, did a nasty piece about him that Marjorie Kinnan Rawlings deplored. But don't forget, at this point, sixteen years after his first fame, a lot of people thought he was dead. So the publicity occasioned by the publication of the "Crack-Up" series undoubtedly reminded Hollywood that he was still around, and led either directly or indirectly to his getting his second chance out there, with his contract that took him out there in July of '37. At the "Crack-Up" stage nothing could harm his career—it could only help.

The personal revelations in "The Crack-Up" blasted open the reticence that had characterized American literature before World War II and had a liberating influence on the writers who followed Fitzgerald's innovative path. Like Fitzgerald, Truman Capote, Tennessee Williams and Norman Mailer deliberately provoked bad publicity in order to gain attention and revealed their pathetic or violent alcoholism. More significantly, "The Crack-Up" had a powerful impact on confessional poets like W. D. Snodgrass, Robert Lowell, John Berryman, Anne Sexton and Sylvia Plath, who wrote openly about their personal anguish and mental breakdowns, as well as on literary accounts of alcoholism, drugs and depression in works like William Styron's *Darkness Visible* (1990).

Fitzgerald makes a connection between insomnia, frequent changes of drenched pajamas and the torment of writing that Lowell adopts and elaborates in "Night Sweat":

> for ten nights now I've felt the creeping damp
> float over my pajamas' wilted white . . .
> Sweet salt embalms me and my head is wet,
> everything streams and tells me this is right;
> my life's fever is soaking in night sweat—
> one life, one writing![15]

Fitzgerald's "dark night of the soul" also foreshadowed the mood of Lowell's "Skunk Hour." And, following Fitzgerald's example of sacrificing human feelings on the altar of art by using Zelda's diaries and letters in *Tender is the Night*, William Carlos Williams wove his mistresses' love letters into *Paterson* (1946–51) and Lowell quoted the anguished correspondence of his former wife in *The Dolphin* (1973).

IV

On April 8, 1936, when Fitzgerald was publishing his third "Crack-Up" essay in *Esquire* and had decided to leave Baltimore for North Carolina, he transferred Zelda to Highland Hospital in Asheville. This move made his visits to Zelda and her short trips outside the hospital much easier, and brought her much closer to her mother in Montgomery. Located at an altitude of 2,500 feet in the healthy mountain country in the western part of the state, Highland—with swimming pool, tennis courts and buildings scattered throughout the spacious grounds—resembled a small college campus. The hospital had been opened in 1904 when Asheville had a number of tuberculosis clinics and many wealthy people spent their holidays at the Grove Park Inn, about four miles away. An advertisement in a contemporary brochure on mental clinics described Highland as "an institution employing all rational methods for the treatment of Nervous, Habit and Mild mental cases; especially emphasizing the natural curative agents—Rest, Climate, Water, Diet and Work."

The director of the hospital, Dr. Robert Carroll, was a friend of Adolf Meyer (head of Zelda's alma mater, Phipps Clinic) who referred many difficult patients to Highland. Born in Cooperstown, in western Pennsylvania, in 1869, the son of a minister, Carroll began his career as a pharmacist in Cleveland. After graduating from Marion Sims College of Medicine (later St. Louis University Medical School) in 1893, he started a general practice in medicine and surgery in Calvert, a small town in central Texas. He took psychiatric training at Rush Medical College in Chicago (where Hemingway's father had studied) and practiced in a small sanatorium near Columbus, Ohio, before coming to Highland.

The forceful and aggressive Dr. Carroll—a bald man with wire spectacles, large nose and ears, and a long, thin mouth—was a strong believer in a strict diet that would eliminate "toxic conditions of the blood"; in outdoor exercise and physical work; in hiking, camping, sports, crafts and music. He offered dancing classes to all patients and employees, held a religious service in the hospital every Sunday, and took patients on trips to the World's Fair and around the world. He also invited successfully cured patients to join his staff.

Dr. Carroll also wrote *The Grille Gate* (1922), an autobiographical novel of hospital life, as well as a number of popular books on medical subjects whose spiritually uplifting subtitles suggest his heartening and commonsensical approach to mental illness: *The Mastery of Nervousness: Based Upon Self Reeducation* (1917), *Our Nervous Friends: Illustrating the Mastery of Nervousness* (1919), *The Soul in Suffering: A Practical Application of Spiritual Truths* (1919), *Old at Forty or Young at Sixty: Simplifying the Science of Growing Old* (1920) and—imitating the title of Anderson and Stallings' *What Price Glory?* (1924)—*What Price Alcohol?* (1941). In his Preface to the latter, Adolf Meyer praised Carroll's success with patients and said he had "proved his hospital one of the most effective systematic agencies in the treatment of the victims of alcohol." Like Forel and Meyer, Carroll also scrutinized Fitzgerald and saw that he was desperately in need of treatment.

Reminiscing in the hospital magazine, a former nurse described the vigorous routine of the clinic and the formidable personality of Dr. Carroll:

> [The patients] started with calisthenics; volley ball in the morning, then gardening for two hours. Then they came in and had lunch around a quarter to one. The patients were always served meals on trays with nice linen tray covers and linen napkins. Each one had a napkin ring and flowers on every tray. . . .
>
> I didn't always like [Dr. Carroll] in every way, but I admired him. To tell you the truth, our class was a little frightened of him. He was always kind, considerate and very generous, but all of us were in awe of *Doctor*.[16]

Fitzgerald hoped that the sensitive and athletic Zelda would respond to Highland's attractive setting and to Dr. Carroll's emphasis on achieving physical well-being through diet, exercise and manual work. But, as Zelda herself realized after her third breakdown in February 1934, it was now harder than ever to escape the ravages of mental disease. She got no better during her two years in Sheppard-Pratt than she had in any of the other hospitals. When she entered Highland in the spring of 1936 she weighed only eighty-nine pounds and, instead of improving, had been going downhill fast.

In his first report to Fitzgerald, Dr. Carroll said that Zelda "was entirely irresponsible, highly excitable, and had just emerged from a three-month period of intense suicidal mania." After two weeks at Highland, Fitzgerald told Beatrice Dance, Zelda had made some improvement but still had a dismal prognosis: "Zelda seems comparatively happy there. She is no longer in a suicidal state but has an equally difficult hallucination which I won't go into. It seems pretty certain she will never be able to function in the world again."

The once-beautiful Zelda, now dull-eyed and frazzle-haired, was a humiliated and broken figure. She had entered a phase of religious mania and become obsessed with the Bible; she believed she was in direct contact with God, imagined her friends were doomed to hell and was zealous in her efforts to save them. Her painting of a Deposition from the Cross (*Zelda* catalogue, no. 36), which she completed during this phase, portrayed herself as a tortured Christ figure and bore an uncanny resemblance to Stanley Spencer's great *The Resurrection: Cookham* (1927).

One of Zelda's nurses at Highland emphasized the conservative and "rational methods" that kept her from suicide and gradually diminished her hallucinations, but did not eliminate her mania nor enable her to regain her sanity: "We were careful with Zelda; we never stirred her up. She could be helped, but we never gave her deep psychotherapy. One doesn't do that with patients if they are too schizophrenic. We tried to get Zelda to see reality; tried to get her to distinguish between her fantasies, illusion and reality."

But during her stay at Highland Zelda was given (as she had probably been given at Prangins) a much more extreme form of therapy: thirty to ninety insulin shock treatments. These shocks produced convulsions or coma that lasted from twenty minutes to an hour and were supposed to jolt her out of psychopathic behavior. Her last doctor, Irving Pine, noted an "improvement" in Zelda after these shocks and felt she was "reborn."[17] But she remained in Highland until April 1940 and, with periods of remission, for the rest of her life.

During the next few years Fitzgerald wrote to many of his friends about Zelda. He felt she was, more than Scottie, his child and that he "was her great reality, often the only liaison agent who could make the world tangible to her." For this reason, and as long as she was helpless, he would never leave her or allow her to feel she had been deserted. He praised the paternal Dr. Carroll for bringing Zelda, during a very difficult phase of her illness, to a certain level of stability. But when Scott faced reality, he knew her case was hopeless. "With each collapse she moves perceptibly backward," he told Beatrice Dance in early 1937, "there is no good end in sight. She is very sweet and tragic. For the majority of creative people life is a pretty mean trick."[18]

V

After settling Zelda in Highland and moving back into the Grove Park Inn in July 1936, Fitzgerald once again came into conflict with Hemingway. Their relations had soured since the great days of their friendship in 1925–26, and he had seen Hemingway only twice since the ill-fated boxing match with Callaghan in 1929. In October 1931 they spent a congenial afternoon at a Princeton football game. But in January 1933, during dinner in New York with Hemingway and Edmund Wilson, Fitzgerald got drunk and humiliated himself. In April 1935, a year after his harsh letter about *Tender is the Night,* Hemingway asked their intermediary Max Perkins to tell Fitzgerald that the novel, in retrospect, got better and better. Delighted by Hemingway's approval, Fitzgerald repeated to Perkins what he had told Hemingway a decade earlier, when leaving Europe in December 1926: "I always think of my friendship with him as being one of the high spots of life."

In the spring of 1935 Perkins had urged Fitzgerald to accompany him on a visit to Hemingway in Key West. But Fitzgerald—drinking heavily and in poor health—was unwilling to compete with Hemingway on his own sporting turf and refused to see him except under the "most favorable circumstances." Despite Hemingway's attacks, Fitzgerald—who craved Hemingway's good opinion and had been crushed by his criticism—praised him that summer to Tony Buttitta. Though Hemingway had mistreated him, Fitzgerald felt he deserved it. He believed that his own character and art, when measured against Hemingway's, were not much good.

As Fitzgerald dropped into despair and Hemingway's reputation continued to rise, Ernest's criticism seemed to increase Scott's admiration for his rival. He thought Ernest exemplified the highest standard of personal courage and would always be read for his great studies of fear. He urged the teenage Scottie to read *A Farewell to Arms* and then quizzed her on the poem ("Blow, blow, ye western wind") that haunted Frederic Henry during the retreat from Caporetto. He considered Hemingway the "final reference" as an artist and called him, after the death of Kipling in 1936, the greatest living writer in English. But this generous praise had a discouraging effect on his own work. He believed that Hemingway had surpassed him and would last longer than Fitzgerald himself. "I don't write any more," he confessed to Thornton Wilder in 1937. "Ernest has made all my writing unnecessary."[19]

Just as Anthony Patch, the hero of *The Beautiful and Damned,* planned to devote his life to writing a history of the Middle Ages, so Fitzgerald—who was fascinated by Hemingway's Byronic intensity—chose to glorify him in the Count of Darkness stories, which he forced himself to write in 1935. Yet, as Edmund Wilson observed, Fitzgerald also had a sharp eye for Hemingway's weaknesses. Noting Hemingway's tendency to attack rivals, especially those who had once helped him, Fitzgerald wrote that "Ernest would always give a helping hand to a man on a ledge a little higher up." Recalling how their fortunes had become reversed since their first meeting, and perhaps forgetting that he had crawled under the table during their last, embarrassing dinner, Fitzgerald also stated: "I talk with the authority of failure—Ernest with the authority of success. We could never sit across the table again." In September 1936—when Hemingway appeared to be at the height of his powers and had displayed his overweening ego in works like *Death in the Afternoon* (1932) and *Green Hills of Africa* (1935)—Fitzgerald made an astonishingly prescient remark about his friend's psychological vulnerability: "He is quite as nervously broken down as I am but it manifests itself in different ways. His inclination is toward megalomania and mine toward melancholy."

Few writers were more accident-prone than Hemingway. But his injuries—from football and boxing, bulls, boats and bullets, car and plane crashes—always seemed testaments to his stoic heroism. In late July 1936, just before his conflict with Hemingway flared up in public, Fitzgerald had his own, distinctly unheroic accident, which made him more dispirited and vulnerable than ever. In "Winter Dreams" (1922), Dexter Green imagined himself "surrounded by an admiring crowd, [giving] an exhibition of fancy diving from the spring-board of the club raft." At Juan-les Pins in the summer of 1926 Fitzgerald had accepted—and somehow survived—Zelda's challenge to make dangerous dives from the high cliffs into the sparkling sea. At the end of *Tender is the Night* (1934) Dick Diver avoids high diving, tries to show off for Rosemary by lifting a man on his shoulders while riding an aquaplane, but reveals his physical deterioration (and suggests his loss of sexual potency) by failing to perform the stunt he had once done with ease.

Two years later in Asheville, Fitzgerald tried to repeat his past performance. But alcoholism and tuberculosis undermined his attempt to show off for Zelda. He fractured his right shoulder while diving and woke up in a massive plaster cast that began below his navel, left his stomach bare, rose up to his neck and kept his right arm extended in a half-hearted salute. In September he told Beatrice Dance how the injury had been compounded by what seems to have been a drunken accident: "I got the broken shoulder from diving from a fifteen-foot board, which would have seemed modest enough in the old days, and the shoulder broke before I hit the water—a phenomenon which has diverted the medicos hereabout to some extent; and when it was almost well, I tripped over the raised platform of the bathroom at four o'clock one morning when I was still surrounded by an extraordinary plaster cast and I lay on the floor for forty-five minutes before I could crawl to the telephone and get rescued."[20]

Fitzgerald's injury and weakness made him long, more than ever, to absorb into himself some of the qualities that made Hemingway so attractive, to lean on him in times of physical and psychological distress. But Hemingway despised Fitzgerald's weakness and self-pity, and tended to bully him. In one of his own megalomaniacal moments, Fitzgerald told Laura Guthrie: "I never knew any person but one . . . who is as strong as I am. That is Ernest Hemingway." And, writing of their friendship in his *Notebooks,* he said: "Ernest—until we began trying to walk over each other with cleats." But these statements were absurd. He still hero-worshiped Hemingway and was destined to be trampled upon in their unequal combat.

Hemingway (as we have seen) took pot-shots at Fitzgerald in "Homage to Switzerland" (1933) and *Green Hills of Africa* (1935). In 1935 he sent Fitzgerald a poem with the grandiose and demeaning title: "Lines to Be Read at the Casting of Scott Fitzgerald's Balls into the Sea from Eden Roc (Antibes, Alpes Maritimes)." And his disturbing letter about the falsity of *Tender is the Night* repeated Sara Murphy's serious charge about Scott's naive approach to understanding others: "You think if you just ask enough questions you'll get to know what people are like, but you won't. You don't really know anything at all about people." Hemingway also attacked Fitzgerald with some well meant but painful truths about his personal limitations which, Ernest felt, explained the defects of his work: "A long time ago you stopped listening except to the answers to your own questions. . . . That is where it all comes from. Seeing, listening. You see well enough. But you stop listening."[21] Fitzgerald implicitly accepted this criticism when he told Laura Guthrie, an aspiring writer: "In the first place, listen. Just listen to how people talk," and when in 1937 he told Hemingway: "I wish we could meet more often. I don't feel I know you at all."

In "The Crack-Up" Fitzgerald had called Hemingway his "artistic conscience"; and Hemingway chose to exercise that prerogative when he wrote Fitzgerald "a furious letter" and told him that he "was stupid to write that gloomy personal stuff." Like Sara Murphy, Hemingway also disapproved of Fitzgerald's fatuous former belief that "Life was something you dominated if you were any good." A key passage in *A Farewell to Arms*, which Fitzgerald greatly admired, exalted, by contrast, the stoic acceptance of tragic defeat: "If people bring so much courage to this world the world has to kill them to break them, so of course it kills them. . . . It kills the very good and the very gentle and the very brave impartially." Hemingway's "furious letter" to Fitzgerald seems to be lost; but he expressed his strong views about "The Crack-Up" in a letter to Max Perkins that condemned Scott's self-exposure and accused him of self-pity: "He seems to almost take a pride in his shamelessness of defeat. The *Esquire* pieces seem to me to be so miserable. There is another one coming too. I always knew he couldn't think—he never could—but he had a marvellous talent and the thing is to use it—not whine in public. Good God, people go through that emptiness many times in life and come out and do work."

Hemingway's angry advice to Fitzgerald—"you especially have to be hurt like hell before you can write seriously. But when you get the damned hurt use it—don't cheat with it"[22] —helps to explain the personal attack on him in "The Snows of Kilimanjaro." For Hemingway, Fitzgerald was a frightening example of a good writer who had—like the hero of his story—betrayed his talent and been destroyed by literary fame. "The Snows of Kilimanjaro" appeared with Fitzgerald's "Afternoon of an Author" in the August 1936 issue of *Esquire*, four months after the publication in that magazine of his third "Crack-Up" essay and one month after his diving accident. This story, though written at the height of Hemingway's worldly success, reveals his anxiety about his incipient moral corruption (symbolized by the hero's gangrene) and predicts his failure as a writer and his spiritual death. One of Hemingway's greatest works, it is in fact a more subtle, covert and artistically sophisticated version of "The Crack-Up": an incisive confrontation of failure and analysis of what had caused it. Fitzgerald's essays hit Hemingway at a vulnerable point and provoked him to violate fictional norms by cruelly attacking Fitzgerald in the *Esquire* version of the story.

The hostile reference to Fitzgerald originated in a sharp exchange between Hemingway and the quick-witted Irish writer Mary Colum when they were dining in New York in 1936. After Hemingway declared: "I am getting to know the rich," Mary Colum replied: "The only difference between the rich and other people is that the rich have more money." Hemingway avenged himself by appropriating the remark and victimizing Fitzgerald when he was particularly vulnerable: "He remembered poor Scott Fitzgerald and his romantic awe of [the rich] and how he had started a story once that began, 'The very rich are different from you and me.' And how some one had said to Scott, Yes, they have more money. But that was not humorous to Scott. He thought they were a special glamorous race and when he found they weren't it wrecked him just as much as any other thing that wrecked him." (Scott's name was changed to "Julian" when "The Snows of Kilimanjaro" appeared in *The Fifth Column and The First Forty-Nine Stories* in 1938.)

Hemingway's luxurious house, boat and African safari had been paid for by his wife's wealthy uncle, Gus Pfeiffer, and he had also befriended the rich while hunting big game in Kenya and fishing for marlin in Key West. But he felt he could define himself in opposition to the rich, who lived on unearned income, because he wrote for a living and made enough money to support himself. He justified the passage in the story by stating that Fitzgerald's revelation of his personal failure in "The Crack-Up" left him open to the kind of public castigation that Hemingway had previously given—with Fitzgerald's encouragement—to the declining Sherwood Anderson. Though Hemingway had made his own personal confession in "The Snows of Kilimanjaro," he convinced himself that the brutal truth in the story would give Fitzgerald a salutary jolt and shake him out of his self-pity.

A passage mercifully deleted from *To Have and Have Not* (1937), which also deals with the corruption of the rich, summarizes Hemingway's view of Fitzgerald's weaknesses and anticipates the more extensive critique of Scott's character in *A Moveable Feast*. Hemingway said that Scott wrote too much when he was very young, lacked good sense and had a great deal of bad luck that was not his fault. He had charm and talent, but no brains, was romantic about money and youth, and went directly from youth to senility without passing through manhood. He thought old age came right after youth—and for him it did. If he gave up self-pity, he still might pull himself together.

Fitzgerald, deeply humiliated by Hemingway's criticism, admired the art of his story but expressed anger about the personal attack. He justified his own work by alluding to Oscar Wilde's apologia and told Hemingway: "If I choose to write *de profundis* sometimes it doesn't mean I want friends praying aloud over my corpse.... It's a fine story—one of your best—even though the 'Poor Scott Fitzgerald, etc.' rather spoiled it for me.... Riches have *never* fascinated me, unless combined with the greatest charm or distinction." Fitzgerald told Max Perkins (who later persuaded Hemingway to delete the reference to Fitzgerald) that he still loved Ernest, no matter what he said or did, but admitted that he had been wounded by Hemingway's statement that he was "wrecked": "It was a damned rotten thing to do, and with anybody but Ernest my tendency would be to crack back. Why did he think it would add to the strength of his story if I had become such a negligible figure? This is quite indefensible on any grounds."[23] If Fitzgerald had answered his own question, he might have realized that Hemingway had attacked him so that Scott would share his own guilt about selling out to the rich.

Hemingway's charge continued to rankle, especially when another old friend, John Peale Bishop, repeated it in a critical essay, "The Missing All" (1938). When responding to the essay, Fitzgerald ignored his own past friendships with the millionaires in Gatsby-like Great Neck and with the heiress Emily Vanderbilt (whom he had met in Paris in 1928), as well as his lifelong fascination with the luxurious life of Hollywood film stars. Instead, he expressed his sense of betrayal by another rich friend whom he had also helped at the beginning of his literary career. And he defended himself, when down and out in Hollywood, in a letter to Edmund Wilson:

[Bishop] reproached me with being a suck around the rich. I always thought my progress was in the other direction.— Tommy Hitchcock and the two Murphys are not a long list of rich friends for one who, unlike John, grew up among nothing else but. I don't even *know* any of the people in "café society." It seems strange from John. I did more than anyone in Paris to help him finish his Civil War book [*Many Thousands Gone,* 1931] and get it published. It can't be jealousy for there isn't much to be jealous of any more.

Though Hemingway was extremely critical of Fitzgerald, he owned most of Scott's books, studied them carefully and learned a great deal from them. He had accepted many of Scott's editorial suggestions about *The Sun Also Rises* and "Fifty Grand," and (as we have seen) took the concluding sentence of *A Farewell to Arms* from chapter five of *The Great Gatsby*. Zelda may have contributed to the creation of Margot Macomber; and Albert McKisco's reaction to his duel with Tommy Barban in *Tender is the Night* influenced the character of the similarly named Francis Macomber. When McKisco is challenged by Barban after his wife gossips about Nicole Diver's mental breakdown, Rosemary sensibly urges him not to fight. He replies that his wife would force him to take part in the duel:

> Of course even now I can just leave, or sit back and laugh at the whole thing—but I don't think Violet would ever respect me again. . . . She's very hard when she gets an advantage over you. . . . She called me a coward out there tonight.

When the equally predatory Margot Macomber witnesses her husband's flight from the charging lion, she loses respect for him, seizes the psychological advantage and sleeps with the white hunter Wilson to punish Francis for his cowardice. As Wilson observes of Margot:

> They are, he thought, the hardest in the world; the hardest, the cruelest, the most predatory and the most attractive and their men have softened or gone to pieces nervously as they have hardened.

After McKisco, provoked by his wife, proves his courage, confronts Barban and fights the duel, he regains confidence, feels exultant and struts "toward the car through the now rosy morning." Macomber is emotionally transformed in the same way. After he regains his courage and redeems his honor by killing the charging buffalo, he tells Wilson: "You know I don't think I'd ever be afraid of anything again. . . . Something happened in me after we first saw the buff and started after him. Like a dam bursting. It was pure excitement." The influence on Hemingway continued after Fitzgerald's death, for the title of the last novel published in Ernest's lifetime, *Across the River and into the Trees*

(1950), came from Scott's quotation of General Stonewall Jackson's last words in "Afternoon of an Author": "Let us cross over the river and rest under the shade of the trees."[24]

VI

The summer of 1936 was the saddest period of Fitzgerald's life. In addition to the chronic problems of Zelda's insanity, his heavy drinking, poor health and crippling debts, he had broken his shoulder in July and been attacked by Hemingway in August. But worse was to come. On September 2 his mother died of a cerebral hemorrhage, and on September 25 he was publicly humiliated by a cruel interview in the New York *Post*.

In mid-September, after his mother's death, he told friends how deeply moved he was by the loss of a woman he had never liked or been close to, but who seemed to stand protectively between him and death. "A most surprising thing in the death of a parent," he told Oscar Kalman, "is not how little it affects you, but how much. When your Father or Mother has been morbidly perched on the edge of life, when they are gone, even though you have long ceased to have any dependence on them, there is a sense of being deserted." And in a letter to Beatrice Dance, he praised his mother's character, mentioned his own lack of filial feeling and illogically concluded that she had died for his sake: "She was a defiant old woman, defiant in her love for me in spite of my neglect of her, and it would have been quite within her character to have died that I might live."

Scott was more dependent on Mollie Fitzgerald than he admitted to Kalman, for he had borrowed five or six thousand dollars from her. He now felt her death would enable him to "live" by providing some desperately needed funds. In 1934 he had sold the Count of Darkness stories to *Redbook* for $1,250 to $1,500 each, sold three other stories to the *Post* and earned the substantial income of $20,000. In 1935 he could still earn $3,000 for a story, but his productivity fell and his income dropped to $17,000. In 1936—when Zelda's annual fees at Highland were about $3,000 and Scottie's fees at the Ethel Walker School in Connecticut (recommended by Gerald Murphy as one of the best in the country) were reduced from the normal rate of $2,200 a year—his income fell by nearly half to $10,000. Fitzgerald made matters more difficult by giving Harold Ober substandard work, by making foolish phone calls and sending damaging letters to magazine editors and movie executives instead of letting his agent conduct his affairs.

The settlement of his mother's estate led to a quarrel with his sister Annabel, who was five years younger than Scott. Since he was away at prep school and college when she was growing up, they had not been close in childhood and rarely saw each other in adult life. The pious and conventional Annabel was dismayed by her brother's scandalous, alcoholic life. And she was baffled by his marriage to an insane woman, with whom she had nothing in common and could not possibly understand. As Annabel's daughters explained in their privately published life of their father:

> The estrangement that existed between Mother and her brother [Scott] was undoubtedly caused, in part, by the different lifestyles each had chosen and had not ended at the time of their mother's death. . . . We remember Mother telling us that the dispute and hard feelings brought on at the time of our grandmother's death stemmed from F. Scott Fitzgerald's desire that the money he had earlier borrowed periodically from Grandmother not be deducted from his inheritance. Daddy felt that this was unfair to Mother.[25]

Annabel, quite reasonably, prevailed. And Fitzgerald, after his considerable debts were settled, got only $5,000 from his share of his mother's $42,000 estate.

Three weeks after Mollie's death, on his fortieth birthday (September 24), Fitzgerald was interviewed in his room at the Grove Park Inn by Michel Mok of the New York *Post*. In "The Crack-Up" Fitzgerald had neither explained the real reasons—his weak father, his alcoholism, Zelda's suicidal insanity—for his nervous breakdown nor described the physical effects of his drinking. Mok's hostile and damaging, yet extremely revealing interview gives a much more precise account of his crack-up.

Michel Mok, a shadowy but significant figure in Fitzgerald's life, was born in Amsterdam in 1888, graduated from the university in that city, knew several European languages, spoke English with a faint

accent and became the translator of several works by Anne Frank. Tall
and thin, with dark hair and a Roman nose, intense eyes and drawn
face, Mok was a star journalist on the *Post* from 1933 to 1940. He was
married, had three children and lived in Greenwich Village. He later
taught journalism at Temple University in Philadelphia and worked as a
theatrical press agent for Rodgers and Hammerstein. One newspaper
colleague described him as "a courtly, continental type who never quite
lost many traces of his European origins." His continental charm
helped persuade Fitzgerald to grant him an interview.

Mok's son believed that his father admired Fitzgerald as a novelist,
but "saw it as a tragedy that Fitzgerald was an alcoholic who at times
'squandered his talent.'" Using the same reasoning as Hemingway to
justify his sharp attack, Mok told his son that "he hoped his piece
would have the effect of holding a mirror up to the author" and would
exert "a constructive, sobering influence." But just as Hemingway's true
motive was to denigrate a rival, so Mok's real aim, when moving in for
the kill after "The Crack-Up," was to pursue the story and achieve a
startling journalistic success.

Tony Buttitta, who was loyal to Fitzgerald and subsequently met
Mok through the publicity business in New York, called him a
pompous man and frustrated writer who liked to tear into people and
specialized in harsh interviews with literary and theatrical figures.
Buttitta felt that Mok—"a self-important bastard"—took advantage of
Fitzgerald, who had been kind and hospitable, and was deeply
wounded by Mok's betrayal.[26]

On September 25, 1936, Mok portrayed Fitzgerald, as Hemingway
would later do in *A Moveable Feast*, as a weak, childish, lonely and
despairing drunkard. Like Zelda, Fitzgerald seemed broken and hopeless.

> The poet-prophet of the post-war neurotics observed his
> fortieth birthday yesterday. . . . He spent the day as he spends
> all his days—trying to come back from the other side of
> Paradise, the hell of despondency in which he has agonized for
> the last couple of years. He had no company except his
> nurse—a soft spoken, Southern, maternal young woman—and
> this reporter. . . .
>   There was obviously little hope in his heart. . . . [His
> fractured shoulder] did not account for his jittery jumping off

and onto his bed, his restless pacing, his trembling hands, his twitching face with its pitiful expression of a cruelly beaten child.

Nor could it be held responsible for his frequent trips to the highboy, in a drawer of which lay a bottle. Each time he poured a drink into the measuring glass on his bedside table, he would look appealingly at the nurse and ask, "Just one ounce?"

When Mok asked how he had got into such a desperate state, Fitzgerald (using Hemingway's favorite name for himself) became vague and evasive: "'A series of things happened to papa,' he said with mock brightness. 'So papa got depressed and started drinking a little.' What the 'things' were he refused to explain. 'One blow after another,' he said, 'and finally something snapped.'" Yet in his "long, rambling, disjointed" talk, Fitzgerald made some fascinating revelations about his family background, father, childhood, army years, advertising job and early literary career. Despite Hemingway's recent attack, Fitzgerald praised him twice during the interview. When Mok asked Fitzgerald about "the jazz-mad, gin-mad generation" he had characterized and helped to create, Fitzgerald gave a grim account of what the Depression had done to all the sad young men: "'Some became brokers and threw themselves out of windows. Others became bankers and shot themselves. Still others became newspaper reporters. And a few became successful authors.' His face twitched. 'Successful authors!' he cried. 'Oh, my God, successful authors!' He stumbled over to the highboy and poured himself another drink."[27]

Mok's interview inspired a series of strange events. Three days after it appeared, Fitzgerald appealed for help from Hemingway, who had started the demolition job that Mok had completed. But Scott did not specify what he expected his "best friend" to do. When he learned that Hemingway was not in New York but hunting in Montana, Scott cooled down and realized that nothing could be done.

According to Ober, Scott was so shocked by his terrible photograph in the *Post* that he briefly stopped drinking. The interview was given much wider circulation when *Time* magazine reprinted it on October 5, 1936. Terrified that Scottie would see it, Fitzgerald phoned her headmistress at Ethel Walker and asked her to destroy the copy in the school library. Soon afterward, the Scribner's novelist Marjorie Rawlings told Perkins that Fitzgerald's nurse Dorothy Richardson "had left because they had become intimate and she was terrified of becoming pregnant."

Rawlings also explained that Mok had secured the interview by lying about his own emotional problems. Scott "was terribly hurt," she told Perkins, "for he had listened to a sob story from him, to let him in at all, and had responded to a lot of things the man told him—possibly spurious—about his own maladjusted wife, by talking more freely than he should have done." Fitzgerald was so ashamed at his own credulity and so disturbed by Mok's interview that he attempted to kill himself. But he vomited from an overdose of morphine. He later told a friend that he was even a failure at committing suicide.

Fitzgerald explained the circumstances of the interview in a long letter of October 5th to Harold Ober. He invented a high fever to rationalize his deception, minimized his extraordinary indiscretion by saying he had spoken rather freely, unconvincingly claimed he had never sought publicity and revealed that the tragedy had ended in farce:

About the article about Michael Muck. I was in bed with temp about 102 when the phone rang and a voice said that this party had come all the way from New York to interview me. I fell for this like a damn fool, got him up, gave him a drink and accepted his exterior good manners. He had some relative with mental trouble (wife or mother) so I talked to him freely about treatments, symptoms, etc., about being depressed at advancing age and a little desperate about the wasted summer with this shoulder and arm—perhaps more freely than if I had been well. I hadn't the faintest suspicion what would happen and I've never been a publicity seeker and never gotten a rotten deal before. When that thing came it seemed about the end and I got hold of a morphine phial and swallowed four grains, enough to kill a horse. It happened to be an overdose and almost before I could get to the bed I vomited the whole thing and the nurse came in and saw the empty phial and there was hell to pay for a while and afterwards I felt like a fool.[28]

The final disaster of 1936 involved his daughter Scottie in another sad farce. In the spring of that year, while Fitzgerald was settling Zelda in Highland and traveling back and forth between Maryland and North Carolina, Scottie, in her last year at Bryn Mawr School, often lived in Baltimore with his secretary, Isabel Owens. Scott wrote many letters to Mrs. Owens with strict and elaborate instructions about how Scottie should behave. Fitzgerald had maintained his over-protective and over-critical attitude toward his exceptionally beautiful fifteen-year-old daughter. When she was visiting relatives in Norfolk in June 1935, he told his cousin Cecilia Taylor not to let "any unreliable Virginia boys take my pet around. . . . Scottie hasn't got three sisters—she has only got me. Watch her, *please!*" When she entered prep school he frequently reminded Scottie about how poor they were.

Grateful for the sacrifices he had made, Scottie later praised his "heroic struggle to maintain the family during the Baltimore days, which he did, and not too badly at all." She also told Mizener that she had always tried to please her parents, never judged them and never blamed Fitzgerald for anything until the fall of 1935, when he reached a low point in life and began to write "The Crack-Up" in Hendersonville: "I *never* was [impudent] in those days, and I never evaluated my parents at all, just accepted them. . . . I never thought evil of Daddy in any way . . . until I was fourteen years old." But she also expressed quite justified rage and resentment about his criticism of her ingratitude and his refusal to acknowledge his alcoholism: "Didn't know I could *still* get mad," she wrote in 1948, "but I still can, particularly [his remarks] about what an angelic parent he had been in Baltimore against the most terrific odds & what a *rotten* child I was not to appreciate it, when he was drunk roughly 75% of the time."[29]

Scottie was especially angry about the afternoon tea dance at the Belvedere Hotel in Baltimore. Fitzgerald organized the dance to celebrate her homecoming from her school in Connecticut for the Christmas holidays in 1936. He tried to limit the guests to sixty (though eighty eventually turned up) and hinted at trouble to come by alarming Scottie, who hoped for an elegant event, and joking about the musical arrangements: "I am determined to have a hurdy-gurdy for the orchestra—you know, an Italian with a monkey, and I think the children will be very content with that. . . . However, in the next room I will have some of the older people with a swing orchestra that I have engaged, and from time to time you may bring some of your choice friends in there to dance.—But remember that I expect you and your crowd to dance by the hurdy-gurdy during the whole afternoon, quietly and slowly and without swing music, just doing simple waltz dancing." Though Fitzgerald considered himself an extremely good dancer, Scottie more accurately described his performance as "dashing but inaccurate dancing—he could not carry a tune and he had a very uncertain sense of rhythm."

At the tea dance Fitzgerald inevitably got drunk and made a fool of himself before a crowd of people, just as he had done at Irving Thalberg's party in Hollywood. He tottered around the room with bleary eyes and insisted on dancing with Scottie's friends, who were both embarrassed and frightened. Scottie resorted to self-protective measures and later recalled: "I knew that there was only one way for me to survive his tragedy, and that was to ignore it." When her father became pitiful, Scottie acted as if he were not there, and explained: "if I'd allowed myself to care I couldn't have stood it. . . . After the ghastly tea-dance . . . Peaches Finney and I went back to her house in a state of semi-hysteria."

Peaches remembered that Fitzgerald went to a lot of trouble to make the arrangements and hire the orchestra. About seventy-five to one hundred people, including Peaches' parents, were there, just before Christmas. Scottie said: "Daddy's behaving dreadfully." But most of the guests were unaware of his sad state. At the end of the party he hired the orchestra for another hour and sat in the middle of the room, surrounded by the musicians and drinking his bottle of gin.[30] Fitzgerald spent Christmas drying out at Johns Hopkins Hospital and was glad to see the end of the most calamitous year of his life.

Gerald and Sara Murphy, meanwhile, to whom Fitzgerald had often turned during his own personal crisis, had been suffering, with an astonishing nobility of spirit, even greater tragedies than the Fitzgeralds'. The Murphys had always been fanatical about the health and cleanliness of their three children. They had always instructed the children to use two washcloths, one for the face, the other for the rest of the body; and whenever they traveled, they hung sterile sheets in their train compartments. In March 1935 their older son Baoth died of spinal meningitis. After his funeral, Sara raised her clenched fists to the sky and cursed God. Hemingway showed the gentle, compassionate side of his character in a moving letter of condolence: "I can't be brave about it and in all my heart I am sick for you both. . . . Very few people ever really are alive and those that are never die, no matter if they are gone. No one you love is ever dead."

At the end of that year Gerald wrote Scott that his suffering enabled him to understand their feelings better than anyone else: "Of all our friends, it seems to me that you alone knew how we felt these days—still feel. You are the only person to whom I can ever tell the bleak truth of what I feel. . . . When you come North let me talk to you." Less than two years after Baoth's death, the Murphys' younger son Patrick died of tuberculosis after an eight-year struggle with the disease. Fitzgerald's letter of condolence in January 1937 (the month after the disastrous tea dance) expressed the depth of feeling for his closest friends, suggested the possibility of hope, and (as he had done in *Tender is the Night*) alluded to the golden bowl and to the natural cycle of birth and death in the twelfth chapter of Ecclesiastes: "Then shall the dust return to the earth as it was: and the spirit shall return unto God who gave it." He also uncannily echoed the conclusion of Hemingway's letter:

> Another link binding you to life is broken and with such insensate cruelty that it is hard to say which of the two blows [Baoth's and Patrick's deaths] was conceived with more malice. . . . But I can see another generation growing up around Honoria and an eventual peace somewhere, an occasional port of call as we all sail deathward. Fate can't have any more arrows in its quiver for you that will wound like these. Who was it said that it was astounding how the deepest griefs can change in time to a sort of joy? The golden bowl is broken indeed but it *was* golden; nothing can ever take those boys away from you now.[31]

Chapter Twelve

THE GARDEN OF ALLAH AND
SHEILAH GRAHAM, 1937–1938

I

In January 1937, the month he consoled Gerald Murphy about the death of his son Patrick, Fitzgerald moved back to the Oak Hall Hotel in Tryon, North Carolina, where he had lived in February 1935. In that remote and tranquil setting he waited with mixed feelings for the call from Hollywood. Speaking of the hero of *The Vegetable* (1923), who has temporarily disappeared, one of the characters remarks: "Maybe he's gone to Hollywood to go in the movies. They say a lot of lost men turn up there." Twelve years later, when Fitzgerald was considering the possibility of a film offer, he had told Ober: "I hate the place like poison with a sincere hatred. It will be inconvenient in every way and I should consider it only as an emergency measure." Now it was his last hope.

Fitzgerald knew that his previous trips to Hollywood in 1927 and 1931 had been, despite the enormous salary, bitter failures. But he now owed $40,000, had written no significant fiction since the publication of *Tender is the Night* in 1934 and was desperately eager to be offered a screenwriting job. He refused to put Zelda in a public insane asylum or place Scottie in a public school, and had to find some way to pay their enormous bills. The publication of "The Crack-Up" essays, as all his friends realized, made it difficult for him to get work in the movie business. As the director Fred Zinnemann observed: "alcoholics or people regarded as troublemakers found it very hard to get a job in any studio. Warnings traveled fast on the bush telegraph."[1] Despite his past failures and battered reputation, Fitzgerald's fiction was still respected in Hollywood. In July 1937, after he had spent an idle six months in Tryon, Metro-Goldwyn-Mayer offered him a six-month contract at the extremely high salary of $1,000 a week.

Fitzgerald believed "there are no second acts in American lives." But he also thought he could find a way to beat the studio system and exert control over his own work. Though his former patron Irving Thalberg had died of pneumonia at the age of thirty-seven in September 1936, Fitzgerald rather naively told Scottie that he intended to "find out the key man among the bosses and the most malleable among the collaborators—then fight the rest tooth and nail until, in fact or in effect, I'm alone on the picture. That's the only way I can do my best work." In fact, he was crushed by the system and it was never possible for him to do his best work. He had no influence with the studio executives, got stuck with a series of unsympathetic co-authors and collaborated with as many as fifteen writers on *Gone with the Wind.*

During his last trip to Hollywood—a life sentence—he failed as a screenwriter. He worked on sixteen films between 1927 and 1940 as one of the highest-paid writers in the business, but received only one credit. He polished two scripts, worked on three for less than a week, labored on ten that were either rejected or not produced, and was dismissed from three of them. It was a dismal record.

Despite this failure, Fitzgerald was rescued, not ruined, by going to Hollywood. Though he did not publish anything while working on six scripts for MGM during 1937–38, he earned $88,500 in eighteen months and achieved most of his aims. He revived his career, supported his family, paid off his debts and saved enough money to buy time for his next novel, which was based on his experience in Hollywood.

Fitzgerald arrived in early July and moved into the Garden of Allah, a hotel and writers' hangout at 8152 Sunset Boulevard, where he lived for the next nine months. (Thomas Wolfe, when writing to Scott, refused to believe there really was such a place.) Originally built as the residence of the silent film star Alla Nazimova, it had two-story Spanish stucco bungalows surrounding the main house, the patio and the swimming pool, which was shaped like the Black Sea to remind the actress of her birthplace in Yalta. Fitzgerald paid $300 a month for half a bungalow with a small but pleasant parlor, bedroom and bath. He believed the sun was bad for his tuberculosis, and never sat outdoors or swam in the pool.

As restless as he had always been, Fitzgerald moved frequently during his three and a half years in Los Angeles. In April 1938 he rented for $200 a month a cheaper and healthier green-shuttered, clapboard cottage—with four bedrooms, a sunroom, a dining room, a captain's walk and a small garden—at 114 Malibu Beach. Six months later, when Malibu became too cold and damp in the winter, he moved to a small house on "Belly Acres," the estate of the actor Edward Everett Horton, at 5521 Amestoy Avenue, Encino, in the San Fernando Valley, northwest of Hollywood. He found the Valley too hot in summer, and when his lease expired in May 1940 made his final move to a modest $110-a-month flat at 1403 North Laurel Avenue, around the corner from Schwab's drugstore in Hollywood.

Fitzgerald was enthusiastic at first and wrote Anne Ober, who acted as surrogate mother to Scottie, announcing that he had soberly rejected the glamorous life to devote himself to hard labor:

I have seen Hollywood—talked with [Robert] Taylor, dined with [Fredric] March, danced with Ginger Rogers . . . been in Rosalind Russell's dressing room, wise-cracked with [Robert] Montgomery [whom he had insulted at Thalberg's party], drunk (ginger ale) with [the studio executives] Zukor and Lasky, lunched alone with Maureen O'Sullivan, watched [Joan] Crawford act. . . .

    This is to say I'm through. From now on I go nowhere and see no one because the work is hard as hell, at least for me and I've lost ten pounds. So farewell Miriam Hopkins, who leans *so* close when she talks, so long Claudette Colbert as yet unencountered, mysterious Garbo, glamorous Dietrich, exotic Shirley Temple—you will never know me. . . . There is nothing left, girls, but to believe in reincarnation.

By the end of his stay, degraded and thoroughly disillusioned by the film stars and the movie business, he asked another friend: "Isn't Hollywood a dump—in the human sense of the word? A hideous town, pointed up by the insulting gardens of its rich, full of the human spirit at a new low of debasement."[2]

In the beginning, however, he seemed content and saw many old friends. On June 4 Fitzgerald had heard Hemingway give a stirring anti-Fascist speech to an audience of 3,500 at a writers' congress in New York. Five weeks later Hemingway flew to Los Angeles to show his idealistic film, *The Spanish Earth*, at the house of Fredric March. The evening was a great success and Hemingway's speech inspired the small number of guests, including Fitzgerald, to contribute $17,000 to buy ambulances for Spain. "Ernest came like a whirlwind," Scott told Perkins. "I felt he was in a state of nervous tensity, that there was something almost religious about it."

Hemingway's impressive appearance once again emphasized the striking contrast between them. Ernest was one of the few writers to resist the temptation of the film industry (*Faulkner* wrote the screenplay of *To Have and Have Not*). Unlike Scott, he had been a journalist and had war experience. His robust health and high energy now allowed him to report the war in Spain and support the Loyalist cause with *The Spanish Earth*, while Scott had come to Hollywood to collaborate on mediocre movies. Hemingway now enjoyed the independence and prestige that Fitzgerald had sacrificed. Aware of the disparity between them, Scott shied away from Hemingway during this visit and was reluctant to speak to him until he had achieved success with his next novel.

Though they never met again, Fitzgerald kept close watch on Hemingway's triumphant career and occasional mishaps. In August 1937, after Hemingway's physical fight with Max Eastman in Scribner's offices had provoked some bad publicity, Fitzgerald (recalling his own recent humiliation by Michel Mok) emphasized Ernest's megalomania but expressed sympathy for him in a letter to Perkins. "He is living at the present in a world so entirely his own that it is impossible to help him even if I felt close to him at the moment, which I don't. I like him so much, though, that I wince when anything happens to him, and I feel rather personally ashamed that it has been possible for imbeciles [in the press] to dig at him and hurt him."

Fitzgerald's relations with eminent authors in Hollywood—Donald Ogden Stewart, the "precious lazybones" Dorothy Parker, Robert Benchley, Ogden Nash, S. J. Perelman and his brother-in-law Nathanael West, as well as the English novelists Anthony Powell and Aldous Huxley—were much more cordial. They welcomed him to parties in private homes and at the Garden of Allah and to the writers' lunch table at the MGM studio. Still sensitive about Hemingway's and Bishop's criticism that he was "a suck around the rich," Fitzgerald had condemned Stewart (whom he had first met in St. Paul) for taking "a long pull at the mammalia of the [millionaire] Whitneys." But Stewart had changed dramatically. After marrying Lincoln Steffens' widow, he became a leftist and helped organize the screenwriters' union. Before being blacklisted and forced into exile by the Hollywood witch-hunts that took place during the Cold War, Stewart had an extremely successful career as a screenwriter and would win an Academy Award for the film version of Philip Barry's *The Philadelphia Story* in 1940.

In July 1937 Fitzgerald lunched with Anthony Powell at the canteen in the Metro studio. Powell, who admired his work, later wrote that in those days Fitzgerald, "as a novelist, was scarcely at all known in the United Kingdom. *The Great Gatsby* had appeared in England in 1926, making no stir at all. Indeed, when *Tender is the Night* followed in 1934, the London publisher [Chatto & Windus] did not even bother to list *Gatsby* opposite the title-page." Powell has also described Fitzgerald's variable moods and surprising lack of awareness about the subtle gradations of English society: "I thought he was obviously extremely bright, and not in the least broken down, as generally described at that period, but no doubt I struck a good day, as he could be very tiresome if you met him on a bad one. He said, and obviously thought, he would never go over in England. He was very obsessed with England, and inclined to lay down the law about life there, of which he had not the faintest grasp: social life, who was grand, and so on."[3]

In 1934 Fitzgerald had written a film treatment of *Tender is the Night* with a young Baltimore protégé, Charles Warren. He then provided Warren with letters of introduction and sent him to Hollywood to sell the project. Though Warren was unsuccessful in this mission, his enthusiastic letter of October 1934, which reported that Fitzgerald still had a great reputation in Hollywood, undoubtedly encouraged him to make a final assault on that citadel: "your name is big and hellishly well known in all the studios. You rate out here as a high-brow writer but you [also] rate as a thoroughbred novelist and not a talkie hack, and therefore people look up to you." Powell gave a more realistic assessment of Fitzgerald's status when, confirming Arnold Gingrich's view, he observed: "one could not fail to notice the way people in Hollywood spoke of Fitzgerald. It was almost as if he were already dead."

All Fitzgerald's writer friends noticed a radical alteration in his character, after his misfortunes and nervous breakdown, which manifested itself in shyness with Hemingway, awkwardness with Powell (he apologized for wisecracks about English aristocrats after learning that Powell's wife was the daughter of an earl) and extreme insecurity—intensified by temporarily going on the wagon—with everyone else. Ring Lardner, Jr., who as a child had known Fitzgerald in Great Neck, saw him with Dorothy Parker and her new husband, Alan Campbell, at the opening of A Star is Born in 1937. He recalled that Scott had asked, with a strange combination of sophistication and naïveté: "are there going to be any movie stars here?" Lardner had "never seen quite such a change of personality, from a brash, cheerful, optimistic, ambitious, driving young man to this withdrawn, very quiet, shy man that he had become."[4]

John O'Hara, who had first met Fitzgerald in Baltimore in 1935 and saw him again in Hollywood, agreed that he "was completely alone, had lost confidence, was wounded, insecure and uncertain." Anita Loos attributed his change of personality to the difficult process of drying out after years of hard drinking and said he "had taken on that apologetic humility which is often characteristic of reformed drunks." Though most friends felt Scott was now sweeter and more sympathetic than he had been during his wild years, Loos pointed out that he had lost the ability to excite and entertain. She remarked that "between being dangerous when drunk and eating humble pie when sober, I preferred Scott dangerous."

Fitzgerald's ambiguous status in Hollywood—as the author of The Great Gatsby and a self-proclaimed failure, respected by his fellow writers and treated callously by the bosses—led him to question (as Zelda had done) the very nature of his being. In 1932 he had told Perkins: "Five years have rolled away from me and I can't decide exactly who I am, if anyone." In "The Crack-Up" (1936) he proclaimed: "there was not an 'I' any more." And in the summer of 1937, soon after he arrived in Hollywood, he emphasized his loneliness and the Poe-like split in his personality by writing a strange and disturbing postcard to himself: "Dear Scott—How are you? Have been meaning to come in and see you. I have [been] living at the Garden of Allah. Yours. Scott Fitzgerald."[5]

II

Fitzgerald's profound confusion about himself and his lack of self-confidence undermined his prospects for success in the studio, which paid writers well but did not respect their work. The intelligent, Austrian-born Fred Zinnemann, who witnessed the hypocrisy and power struggles at MGM for seven years, said the studio "was earnest and sanctimonious; there was an aura of people being wary and suspicious." Anthony Powell, who hated Hollywood and left very quickly, roundly condemned the inefficient but omnipotent studio bosses as "grasping, stupid, wasteful, procrastinating collectively in their business; the fact that their own morals were rarely to be held up as an ideal standard did not prevent them from being hypocritical, unctuous, Pecksniffian in the highest degree."

Nathanael West, who brilliantly satirized Hollywood in *The Day of the Locust* (1939), also attacked the system that forced a writer to come to the studio every day and work like a drudge in an office from nine to five: "There's no fooling here. All the writers sit in cells in a row and the minute a typewriter stops someone pokes his head in the door to see if you are thinking." Like Fitzgerald, Raymond Chandler at first thought he could beat the collaborative system, which produced an endless series of revisions and completely destroyed the integrity of the original work. But he too was forced to concede defeat:

> I was convinced in the beginning that there must be some discoverable method of working in pictures which would not be completely stultifying to whatever creative talent one might happen to possess. But like others before me, I discovered that this was a dream. Too many people have too much to say about a writer's work. It ceases to be his own. And after a while he ceases to care about it. He has brief enthusiasms, but they are destroyed before they can flower.[6]

Fitzgerald was extremely conscientious in his duties. Just as he had once turned himself into a professional writer by studying the techniques and audience of the slick magazine market, so he now (rather belatedly) took the same mechanical approach to screenwriting. He saw scores of old movies, summarized the plots and diagrammed the structure. He even, in a rather misguided attempt to learn the craft, bought from a nearby bookstore three copies of Georges Polti's 36 *Dramatic Situations* (1921). His laborious efforts led the director Billy Wilder to compare him to "a great sculptor who is hired to do a plumbing job. He did not know how to connect the pipes so the water would flow."

The most convincing explanation of Fitzgerald's failure was made by Nunnally Johnson, who wrote the highly successful scripts for *The Grapes of Wrath* (1940) and *Tobacco Road* (1941). He felt Fitzgerald had abandoned fiction, which he had mastered, to grope around in a medium for which he had no instinct or training. His transformation from professional novelist to amateur screenwriter, even when adapting his own fiction, led Fitzgerald, who had no belief in films as an art form, to debase his talent and offer the kind of work he thought was required:

> This amateurism of Fitzgerald's led him into all kinds of naive enthusiasm about his own work in pictures, which so far as I could see was never very good. He was immensely proud of a script that he did [in 1940] from his short story "Babylon Revisited," one of the very best he or any other American short story writer ever wrote, but I read it a few years ago and to me it is unusable. To me he managed to destroy every vestige of all the fineness in his own story. He padded it out with junk and nonsense and corn to an unbelievable extent. . . .
>
> He floundered badly as a screen writer and his failure here was no miscarriage of justice. . . . He was next to useless. He had wit in his conversation and he had wit in narration but what he set down for wit in his dialogue always seemed to me rather trifling wisecracks.

Johnson also believed that Fitzgerald—like James and Conrad before him—could not master dramatic dialogue and failed to justify his high salary:

The explanation for his continual failure as a screen writer is that he was simply unable to understand or turn out dramatic work. . . . He wasn't the first novelist who was unable to master the technique of dramatic writing. . . .

His biggest misfortune, which I doubt he ever realized, was that they paid him fat money at the very beginning. And even though he blew his chances with inadequate work he believed that he should continue to draw such salaries or even larger ones.[7]

Fitzgerald was clearly unsuited—by experience, knowledge and talent—for many of the films to which he was assigned. He spent the first eight days on *A Yank at Oxford,* presumably because Jay Gatsby had been briefly educated at that institution; and later worked on *Marie Antoinette,* though his understanding of eighteenth-century France was confined to his portrayal of the "scenes of ladies swinging in the gardens of Versailles" in Myrtle Wilson's tasteless New York apartment.

His most substantial and significant work, from August 1937 to February 1938, was on the film script for Erich Remarque's anti-Nazi novel, *Three Comrades* (1937). The producer of the film, who hired Fitzgerald after getting the approval of the head of MGM, Louis Mayer, was the magisterial and well-respected Joseph Mankiewicz. He began his career as a screenwriter at Paramount in the late 1920s, produced *Fury* and *The Philadelphia Story* at MGM in the 1930s, and went on to win four Academy Awards in two years as both writer and director of *Letter to Three Wives* (1949) and *All About Eve* (1950).

Mankiewicz explained, shortly before his death in 1993, that in 1937 Fitzgerald was *not* a washed-up has-been, but an attractive symbol of the vanished 1920s. Though everyone in Hollywood knew about his alcoholism and crack-up, his name still brought considerable prestige to the studio. Insecure, unkempt and a little frayed, Fitzgerald would appear at MGM with patches of stubble on his badly shaved cheeks. But he was still handsome and had considerable style.

Though the political element in Remarque's novel was alien to Fitzgerald and his film dialogue was weak, Mankiewicz employed Scott to create the continental atmosphere and enhance the romantic aspects of the story:

I hired Scott for *Three Comrades* because I admired his work. More than any other writer, I thought he could capture the European flavor and the flavor of the twenties and early thirties that *Three Comrades* required. I also thought that he would know and understand the girl.

I didn't count on Scott for dialogue. There could be no greater disservice done him than to have actors read his novels aloud as if they were plays. Mr. Hemingway, Mr. Steinbeck, Mr. Fitzgerald, Mr. Sinclair Lewis—all of them wanted to write plays and none of them could write one to save [his] soul. After all, there is a great difference between the dialogue in a novel and in a play. In a novel, the dialogue enters through the mind. The reader endows it with a certain quality. Dialogue spoken from the stage enters through the ear rather than the mind. It has an emotional impact. Scott's dialogue lacked bite, color, rhythm.

On September 9 Fitzgerald completed the first draft and returned to the east coast to take Zelda on a trip to Charleston. Although Mankiewicz disliked the script, he sent a telegram complimenting Scott on it and assuring him that he would not have to work with a collaborator. Later on, he defended his duplicity by saying he *had* to reassure Fitzgerald to prevent him from going on an alcoholic binge.

When Fitzgerald returned from his trip, Mankiewicz, following the common practice, provided Edward Paramore, an old acquaintance, as his collaborator. Handsome, hard drinking and a great ladies' man, Paramore came from Santa Barbara, had attended the Hill School with Edmund Wilson and had graduated from Yale. After the war, while sharing a New York apartment with Wilson, Paramore had an affair with Margaret Canby, who later became Wilson's second wife. In *The Beautiful and Damned* Fitzgerald had satirized him as the rather pompous Frederick E. Paramore, who had been to Harvard with the hero Anthony Patch. When the fictional Paramore, a social worker at a settlement house in Stamford, Connecticut, is asked what he has been doing since college, he replies: "'Oh, many things. I've led a very active life. Knocked about here and there.' (His tone implies anything from lion-stalking to organized crime)."[8]

Mankiewicz thought Paramore was a solid, run-of-the-mill writer— good on the first draft. According to Wilson, Fitzgerald had requested

Paramore as a collaborator when he first came to Hollywood; according to Budd Schulberg, Paramore resented working with a tyro like Fitzgerald. Scott was soon discouraged by the extreme banality of Paramore's ideas and appalled when he had an angry German sergeant say: "Consarn it!" Their draft lacked both Fitzgerald's imagination and Paramore's technical expertise.

In "A Flash-Back in Paradise," which concludes the first chapter of *The Beautiful and Damned,* Fitzgerald disrupts the realistic tone of the novel by having Beauty (or Gloria) sent to earth by The Voice. A similarly fanciful failure occurs in his script of *Three Comrades.* He again violates reality and invents an absurd scene in which Robert Taylor calls Margaret Sullavan for a date and the switchboard is operated by an Angel and Saint Peter:

Angel (sweetly)
One moment, please—I'll connect you with heaven.

CUT TO:
THE PEARLY GATES
St. Peter, the caretaker, sitting beside another switchboard.

St. Peter (cackling)
I think she's in.

On January 20, 1938, after Mankiewicz had rewritten the script Fitzgerald had collaborated on with Paramore, Fitzgerald pleaded with him to restore the original version. He began by referring to his (now-tarnished) literary reputation: "For nineteen years, with two years out for sickness, I've written best-selling entertainment, and my dialogue is supposedly right up at the top." But this argument, weakened by "supposedly," carried no weight with his boss, who knew the difference between fictional and cinematic dialogue. "I am utterly miserable," Fitzgerald continued, "at seeing months of work and thought negated in one hasty week. I hope you're big enough to take this letter as it's meant—a desperate plea to restore the dialogue to its former quality—to put back . . . all those touches that were both natural and new. Oh, Joe, can't producers ever be wrong? I'm a good writer—honest. I thought you were going to play fair." Fitzgerald's pathos and premises—based perhaps on his relations with Perkins—were both misconceived. Producers were never wrong, he was not an effective screenwriter and it was naive to expect "fair play" in Hollywood, where time, money and commercial interests were paramount.

Mankiewicz claimed he never received this letter. But Gore Vidal, in one of the best essays on Fitzgerald, has shown that Mankiewicz did in fact follow Fitzgerald's suggestions when revising and improving the screenplay. Vidal does not mention one significant detail: that Mankiewicz also improved Fitzgerald's version by lifting a line from *The Great Gatsby* ("'What'll we do with ourselves this afternoon?' cried Daisy, 'and the day after that, and the next thirty years?'") and having Robert Taylor ask: "What on earth are we going to talk about for the rest of our lives?"[9]

Fitzgerald was in the extremely awkward position of being, at the same time, an experienced novelist and an apprentice screenwriter. Instead of accepting his own limitations, the collaborative system and the power of the bosses, he rebelled, pleaded and was defeated. After breaking with Beatrice Dance he had told Laura Guthrie: "I never saw a girl who *had so much* take it all so hard." But in his *Notebooks*, he admitted that he also took "things hard—from Ginevra [King] to Joe Mank." His quarrel with Mankiewicz and failure with *Three Comrades* transformed his initially positive attitude into a bitter hatred of Hollywood. It also drove home a fundamental truth about the business. Like every serious writer who had ever gone there, he finally realized that "conditions in the industry somehow propose the paradox: 'We brought you here for your individuality but while you're here we insist that you do everything to conceal it.'"

Fitzgerald's anger and bitterness prevented him from seeing the defects in his own work and admitting that Mankiewicz was more skillful and experienced than he was. Mankiewicz later declared that Fitzgerald's work was not sacred and that revisions had to be made: "I personally have been attacked as if I had spat on the American flag because it happened once that I rewrote some dialogue by F. Scott Fitzgerald. But indeed it needed it! The actors, among them Margaret Sullavan, absolutely could not read the lines. It was very literary dialogue, novelistic dialogue that lacked all the qualities required for screen dialogue. The latter must be 'spoken.' Scott Fitzgerald really wrote very bad spoken dialogue." Mankiewicz also explained that in his first major film project Fitzgerald was both inflexible and rather desperate. He stood on his past reputation, imitated himself, was blind to his own faults and could not make the necessary changes.[10]

When the troublesome film was finally completed, it ran into political problems. Remarque's novel condemned the ideology and militarism of the Nazis. Though the Hollywood establishment was almost entirely Jewish, the studio executives, ignorant of politics and worried about their commercial interests in Germany, were unwilling to criticize the Nazis. Budd Schulberg reported that when Louis Mayer heard that a friend was going to interview Hitler, he innocently urged him "to put in a good word for the Jews." Before releasing the film, the studio showed it as a courtesy to the German consul in Los Angeles, who strongly objected to the anti-Nazi theme. Mayer and Joseph Breen, the movie censor, wanted to solve the problem by changing the Nazis to Communists. Mankiewicz refused to do this, but the anti-Nazi theme was finally deleted. Instead of remaining in Germany to fight the Fascists, the two surviving comrades withdraw to a non-political life in South America.

Two-thirds of the final screenplay was by Mankiewicz, the rest by Fitzgerald, who thought the whole thing was awful. Despite its fake studio sets and the wooden performance by Robert Taylor, it received wonderful reviews, became a commercial success and was considered one of the ten best films of 1938. The mawkish Margaret Sullavan was nominated for an Academy Award and won the New York Film Critics Award for the best actress of the year. Most important of all Fitzgerald, through Mankiewicz's efforts, got his first and only screen credit, which in December 1937 led to the vitally important renewal of his MGM contract for another year at $1,250 a week. Fitzgerald stressed the irony of the situation in a letter of March 1938 to Beatrice Dance: "I am now considered a success in Hollywood because something which I did not write is going on [the screen] under my name, and something which I did write has been quietly buried."

Fitzgerald's film work for the rest of 1938 was comparatively trivial. From February to May he was assigned to *Infidelity*, which was to star Joan Crawford. When she heard he had been put on her film, she urged him to "write hard, Mr. Fitzgerald, write hard!" "Of course, infidelity," Fitzgerald told Beatrice Dance, who was experienced in this matter, "in the movies is somewhat different from infidelity in life, being always forestalled in time and having beautiful consequences." But the script, though bland, still encountered censorship problems. Despite an expedient change of title to *Fidelity*, the film was never made.

From May to October Fitzgerald was engaged on the script of Clare Boothe Luce's play *The Women* (1936), a satire on wealthy Americans. It was, he cynically said, "a rather God-awful hodgepodge of bitter wit and half-digested information which titillated New York audiences for over a year. Most of the work has been 'cleaning it up' for [Thalberg's widow] Norma Shearer."[11] She had sent the kindly telegram, after he made a fool of himself at her party, to soften the blow of his humiliation and imminent dismissal by her husband.

In late 1938 Fitzgerald, who had failed his science courses at Princeton, worked on a screenplay about Madame Curie, who had discovered radium. The script had originally been written by Aldous Huxley, another resident of the Garden of Allah. Reviewing *Crome Yellow* in 1922, Fitzgerald had called Huxley, after Max Beerbohm, "the wittiest man now writing in English." Ten years later the English novelist achieved international acclaim with *Brave New World*. In *The Last Tycoon* Huxley appears as Boxley, an eminent author, "looking very angry in a British way." He vehemently objects to being teamed with two hack writers who spoil his fine work and is given a useful lesson in screenwriting by the head of the studio, Monroe Stahr. But Huxley's wit and eminence did him little good in Hollywood. When the talented Salka Viertel took over from Fitzgerald in the relay writing, she asked the MGM executive Bernie Hyman what had happened to Huxley's work: "Embarrassed, he admitted that he had had no time to read it but had given it to Goldie, his secretary, who told him 'it stinks.'"[12]

Fitzgerald fared no better than Huxley. The producer Sidney Franklin felt there was only one good speech in his version of *Madame Curie*. After receiving a renewal and a raise in December 1937, Fitzgerald was shocked and horrified when MGM did not renew his all-too-lucrative contract in December 1938. He was cut adrift without a salary and now had to scramble for free-lance work in Hollywood.

III

While struggling to make his way in pictures, Fitzgerald had to support three different households—in California, North Carolina and New York—just as he had done in France and Switzerland after Zelda's breakdown in 1930. During this time he made extraordinary—though often unsuccessful—efforts to be a good father to Scottie and a good husband to Zelda, and to stimulate and direct the lives of his wife and daughter. He persuaded Scottie during her last years at Ethel Walker to take difficult courses like chemistry and physics, which he had hated, though she preferred (like him) to write stories for the school magazine and plays for the dramatic society.

In June 1937 Scottie got into serious trouble at school. While studying for her college entrance exams, Scottie and a friend broke the strict rules, went to New Haven, had dinner with two Yale students and were caught coming back at nine o'clock that night. Scottie was suspended, and Fitzgerald felt she had ruined her chances of getting into Vassar. He wrote her an angry letter but also pleaded on her behalf with the dean at Vassar, and did not entirely forgive his daughter until she was finally admitted to Vassar the following spring.

In August 1937 the actress Helen Hayes, who was married to Fitzgerald's old drinking companion Charles MacArthur, took Scottie to visit her father in Hollywood. To avoid friction with him, Scottie stayed with Helen Hayes at the Beverly Hills Hotel. Fitzgerald introduced Scottie to many movie stars and tried to give her a good time, but was tense and on edge with her. He embarrassed his friends by his overbearing attitude and unfair criticism of his daughter.

The following summer, after Scottie had graduated from prep school and traveled to war-threatened Europe with Fitzgerald's old Paris friend, Alice Lee Myers, she made a second trip to Hollywood with Peaches Finney. While they were all living in Malibu, he got into a great fight with Scottie about her college roommate, whom he hated and called "a bitch." When Peaches, shocked by his behavior, boldly told him that it was awful to talk to his daughter like that, he became contrite and seemed to accept her criticism.

Fitzgerald probably chose Vassar for Scottie because he knew and respected four graduates: the romantic poet Edna St. Vincent Millay, who had been Edmund Wilson's mistress; Fitzgerald's childhood companion Marie Hersey; his St. Paul friend Katherine Tighe, who had given him excellent editorial advice and shared with Wilson the dedication of *The Vegetable;* and Margaret Banning, whom he had met in Tryon in 1935. Having failed out of college himself, he vicariously participated in Scottie's experiences at Vassar, and his hectoring letters emphasized that she was now in the same precarious financial position that he had been in at Princeton.

He tried to compensate for Zelda's absence by playing the roles of both father and mother, but was unnecessarily strict and domineering. Scottie told Mizener that Fitzgerald "didn't want me to have the fun of making my own mistakes—he wanted to make them for me." She also mentioned that he "gave up in despair trying to nag & bully me into [becoming] a worthwhile character." When his criticism became intolerable, Scottie sought the help of her adviser at college, who defended her (as Peaches had done) and told him: "I was horrified by your letter . . . because I can't see how a [seventeen]-year-old girl could have behaved badly enough to merit so much parental misgiving and despair—such dark bodings for the future." Scottie finally stopped reading his intensely irritating letters (though she thought enough of him to save them) and merely extracted the checks—if any—from the envelopes. Fitzgerald unintentionally hurt Scottie because he loved her so much.

He also tried to help Zelda, but his relations with her were no more successful than those with Scottie. He wanted more freedom for Zelda and urged Dr. Carroll to let her use Highland as a base and remain outside the hospital for as much as half the time. Dr. Carroll disagreed and felt she should be confined for all but six weeks a year. After many arguments, Fitzgerald followed his advice. The Sayres, however, who had first blamed him for her breakdown, now insisted that *he* was responsible for keeping Zelda in the hospital against her will.

Since Fitzgerald believed he was Zelda's lifeline to reality, he made frequent flights across the country to take her away from the clinic on brief holidays—during which time he did not receive any salary. They went to Charleston and Myrtle Beach, South Carolina, two months after he arrived in Hollywood, in September 1937; to Miami and Palm Beach, Florida, in January 1938; with Scottie to Virginia Beach, Virginia, and to see his cousins in Norfolk, in March 1938; and to Cuba in April 1939. These expensive trips disrupted his work, were physically exhausting and emotionally devastating, and upset him for several weeks afterward.

These holidays did not help Zelda and seemed to make things worse for both of them. His feeling for her diminished and confirmed the impossibility of an equitable reunion. He felt that making love to Zelda was like "sleeping with a ghost." On the disastrous trip to Norfolk, she quarreled with Scottie, he got completely drunk, and Zelda ran up and down the corridor of their hotel telling everyone that he was a dangerous madman who had to be carefully watched. The following month he told Dr. Carroll that Zelda merely reminded him, in the most painful way, of the past happiness they had forever lost: "each time that I see her something happens to me that makes me the worst person for her rather than the best, but a part of me will always pity her with a sort of deep ache that is never absent from my mind for more than a few hours: an ache for the beautiful child that I loved and with whom I was happy as I shall never be again."[13]

IV

Scott had sought to escape his difficulties with Zelda—before their marriage, after her infidelity with Jozan and during her mental illness—in affairs with a surprising number of beautiful and talented women. Though he was puritanical and repressed, sexually insecure and even sexually inept, his good looks, charm, wit, sympathetic character, literary reputation and sometimes pathetic condition made him attractive to Rosalinde Fuller in 1919, Lois Moran in 1927, Bijou O'Conor in 1930, Dorothy Parker in 1934, Nora Flynn, Beatrice Dance and Lottie of Asheville in 1935, his nurse Dorothy Richardson in 1936 and his last love, Sheilah Graham, in 1937. Though often hostile to both the English and the Jews, he soon forgot his prejudice with good-looking women. Rosalinde Fuller and Bijou O'Conor were English, Dorothy Parker was Jewish, and Sheilah Graham was both.[14]

Sheilah had been working as a gossip writer in Hollywood for over a year when Fitzgerald first met her. On July 14, 1937, a few days after Hemingway showed *The Spanish Earth,* Fitzgerald saw her for the first time at Robert Benchley's party at the Garden of Allah. A week later Scott danced with her at the Writers' Guild dinner at the Ambassador Hotel. After a brief courtship, they became lovers. He had been attracted to Nora and Beatrice because they shared Zelda's recklessness. He said he was attracted to Sheilah because of her physical resemblance to Zelda. Their attachment developed because they both were eager to put the past behind them, to establish a new identity in the alien and rather ruthless society of Hollywood, and to gain financial security. In addition to romance, Sheilah offered him warmth, companionship and devotion.

KING'S COLLEGE CAMBRIDGE CB2 1ST

Telephone 01223 331100   Fax 01223 331315

with compliments

Like Jay Gatsby, Sheilah sprang from a platonic conception of herself and invented a glamorous past and a new identity to disguise her humble origins. When Fitzgerald met her, she had established herself as an upper-class Englishwoman and consistently maintained this role in her professional life. During her three and a half years with Fitzgerald, and for many years afterward, she kept up this carefully constructed public persona. But Fitzgerald soon sensed that the image she presented was false. Like Joel Coles with the actress Stella Calman in "Crazy Sunday," he "couldn't decide whether she was an imitation of an English lady or an English lady was an imitation of her. She hovered somewhere between the realest of realities and the most blatant of impersonations." Under his persistent interrogation, she gradually confessed the truth about her background to him, but she revealed nothing about her past in public until she published *Beloved Infidel* in 1958. Ostensibly a memoir of her relationship with Fitzgerald, this book was also her first attempt at autobiography. She was to repeat or recycle this account in seven books and in numerous articles and interviews that were partly or entirely about Fitzgerald.[15]

According to her own, often false accounts, she was born Lily Sheil (in 1904, though she never gave her real age) in a poverty-stricken tenement in the East End of London. Her father died of tuberculosis when she was an infant, her sickly mother was a cook in an institution. Unable to support Lily, the youngest of a large family, Mrs. Sheil placed her at the age of six in the East London Home for Orphans, where she spent a miserable eight years. After working in a factory and as an under-housemaid in Brighton, she began her career by demonstrating toothbrushes at Gamage's department store in Holborn, London, where she met her first husband, Major John Graham Gillam, and by selling fancy goods in his small import company.

After rejecting the proposal of an elderly millionaire, and while still in her teens, she married Gillam. This paternal businessman, twenty-five years her senior, was impotent. He came from a comfortable middle-class family but lacked commercial skill, and his company eventually failed. He supported Sheilah's ambition to go on the stage and paid for her brief training at the Royal Academy of Dramatic Art. She invented a new past and changed her name by adapting her own last name and taking her husband's middle name.

The attractive Sheilah then became one of C. B. Cochran's "Young

Ladies," a chorus girl in popular musical comedies of the Noel Coward era. She substituted for the sick leading lady and wrote her first newspaper article about breaking out of the chorus line. With her husband's acquiescence, she was entertained by aristocratic admirers after the musicals and eventually taken up by English society. She played tennis at a smart club, went riding and skiing, and was, with her husband, "presented at Buckingham Palace."

· In June 1933 she emigrated to America—where she could more easily convince people of her new identity—in order to escape the burden of her past, make a better living and get away from a failing marriage. For the next two years she worked as a journalist and wrote a gossip column, "Sheilah Graham Says," for the *New York Evening Journal.* In late 1935 she was hired to write a Hollywood gossip column by the North American Newspaper Alliance (which sent Hemingway to report the Spanish Civil War) and flew to Los Angeles on Christmas Eve. She divorced the elderly Gillam in early 1937, and became "engaged" to the playboy Marquess of Donegall, who was also a gossip writer, in July. When Fitzgerald first met her, she was making $160 a week as a journalist and he was earning $1,000 a week as a screenwriter.

Sheilah's journalistic ambitions were powered by two concerns: a deep shame about her background and an equally profound fear of poverty. She wanted to be a success in order to have complete financial security. In Hollywood, social class, good breeding and education had little to do with success; beauty, energy and a ruthless vulgarity were much more important. Sheilah had all these—and, like Louella Parsons and Hedda Hopper, the best-known gossip writers of the day—she understood the mentality of those who, like herself, had risen from obscurity to create for the eager public a new and glamorous version of themselves.

Sheilah is virtually the only source of information about the events of her life before she came to America. Though she claimed to reveal the truth about herself, her series of gossipy autobiographies tell a number of deliberate lies. This is scarcely surprising in a woman who described herself as a "purveyor of glamour" and who distorted the facts of her life to achieve the most effective public image. When some of the crucial facts are checked, Sheilah's version of her personal history starts to crumble. She said, for example, that she had been "pre-

sented at Buckingham Palace," and to substantiate this story reproduced in *Beloved Infidel* a studio photograph of herself and Major
Gillam in court dress. However, the Lord Chamberlain's Office in
Buckingham Palace has disproved this claim by reporting that "a thorough search of our records has been made and sadly no reference to
the Gillams has been found."

Sheilah also claimed, in the BBC documentary about Fitzgerald,
that before meeting Scott she had already bought notepaper bearing
the Donegall coronet. But her "engagement" to the sixth Marquess of
Donegall is equally fraudulent. A year older than Sheilah, graduate of
Eton and Christ Church, Oxford, and later on, war correspondent and
lieutenant colonel during World War II, Donegall would have been a
formidable rival to Fitzgerald. But he must have looked into Sheilah's
background at least as carefully as Scott did, and his widow categori-
cally states: "Sheilah Graham was never engaged to 'Don' officially. He
didn't marry his first wife until he was forty [in 1943] and got himself
'engaged' to quite a lot of women before—in fact he had [already] been
'engaged' to his first wife fifteen years before then! When it was taken
too seriously—he always managed to get out of it. Miss Graham—being
a great self-publicist—made a meal of it!"[16]

Sheilah's darkest secret was the fact that she was Jewish. In the
London of the 1920s, as in the Hollywood of the 1930s, it seemed expedient to disguise the Jewish background that would impede her career.
Though the rich and powerful studio heads were largely Jewish, country clubs, schools and many hotels were still restricted, and film actors
consistently cultivated a gentile and genteel image. Sheilah, who had
very little religious or family loyalty, consigned both her poverty and
her Jewishness to the same black hole of denial. But Fitzgerald was
capable of using this information against her. During one of their many
drunken quarrels (*he* was the drunkard; she rarely drank) he betrayed
her confidence by screaming out all her secrets and telling his nurse
that Sheilah was really a Jew.

Ring Lardner, Jr., who worked with Sheilah on the *New York Daily
Mirror* in the early 1930s and was not favorably impressed by her genteel pretensions, thought "she sometimes exaggerated her posh accent
and overdid her greatest role, but usually concealed her lack of background quite well and seemed terribly upper-class British." Sheilah's
affected manner and liaison with Donegall intensified Fitzgerald's

antipathy to the British. Mocking her origins, he would say, "Amedican.
. . . You Amedicans," and "used to put on a horrible Cockney accent
until [Sheilah] exclaimed: 'Oh, my God, that's awful, you mustn't do
that.'" While living with Sheilah in the summer of 1940, however, he
was strongly impressed by the gallant English spirit at Dunkirk—
inspired by Winston Churchill, with whom he had dined in 1921—and,
adopting English slang, told Perkins: "The only cheerful thing is the
game scrap the British are putting up."[17]

Most of Fitzgerald's friends thought Sheilah—though deceitful,
ambitious and calculating—was genuinely in love with him. She took
care of him, encouraged him to stop drinking and finally enabled him
to complete a significant portion of *The Last Tycoon*. Frances Kroll—a
gentle, intelligent nineteen-year-old brunette, who became Fitzgerald's
secretary in November 1938—saw a great deal of Sheilah and came to
know her well. Frances said she had big dark eyes, beautiful skin and a
bright smile. She was not a natural blonde, but always tinted her hair
tastefully and looked attractive. She had good legs, was athletic and
played tennis on the Horton estate in Encino. Though Sheilah's liveli-
hood depended on being assertive and aggressive, she could also seem
breathless, fey, even quite helpless in order to manipulate men in a
socially acceptable way.

After clawing her way toward the top of her profession, Sheilah
accepted a quiet life with Fitzgerald. They rented modest houses and
flats, and lived simply among the rich of Hollywood. They were fairly
reclusive, saw few friends and did not entertain. But they went to a few
parties, and to many movies and restaurants. Sheilah recalled that they
used to eat in "a Jewish delicatessen, and he would ask the names of
things. I think *knish* just floored him. He would ask again and again for
it just to hear it pronounced."

Sheilah had English charm, was quick-witted and good at dissimu-
lation, but Frances Kroll disliked the fake and superficial side of her
character. She never believed in Sheilah, whose entire career was
based on gossip, who exploited people and who was ignorant about
everything but the ability to survive. Sheilah took a lot of abuse from
Fitzgerald, who even tried to destroy her career, but she put up with
his drunken rages because he was the first man who had ever really
loved her. He knew that she was ignorant, shallow and rather vulgar.
But she gave him a sense of peace and well-being.

Other friends who knew Sheilah were also ambivalent about her. Budd Schulberg thought she was clever and sharp-minded, created an effective public image and wrote a good bitchy column. Attractive and seductive, she was also materialistic, grasping and self-serving. Though helping Fitzgerald was out of character, she seemed to love him sincerely. Joseph Mankiewicz took a more cynical view. He called Sheilah "a chorus girl who missed the bus" and thought Fitzgerald showed poor taste when he took her as his girl. She was rather bright, had a wonderful laugh and was good fun. She also had a masochistic need to care for a great (or once-great) man and was proud to be with Fitzgerald when they walked into a room—though he often had to be carried out.[18]

Sheilah described the handsome but rather sad and weary Fitzgerald, who was forty when they met, as having "hair pale blond, a wide attractive forehead, grey-blue eyes set far apart, set beautifully in his head, a straight, sharply chiseled nose and an expressive mouth that seemed to sag a little at the corners, giving the face a gently melancholy expression." His hair was thinning on top and he carefully combed it over his bald patch. Aware that tuberculosis (which had killed her father) was infectious, he warned her not to use the same cutlery and dishes as he did. But he did not, paradoxically, think it dangerous for Sheilah to become his lover. His craving for sweets, when he gave up alcohol, was insatiable; he drank endless Coca-Colas and gorged himself on fudge. He also went in for exotic dishes like turtle soup and chocolate soufflé. Insomniac and addicted to barbiturates, he took a heavy dose of chloral and two or more Nembutals to put himself to sleep, and needed several benzedrine pills to wake up.

Fitzgerald frankly told Sheilah he would never abandon Zelda. He felt he had no right to monopolize Sheilah and thought he was unworthy of her. He feared people would pity him as a has-been author, and once told an airline stewardess: "I'm F. Scott Fitzgerald, the very well-known writer." An incident that took place late in 1938 reveals Fitzgerald's difficulty in accepting his status as a once-famous and now forgotten writer, who was both respected and scorned in Hollywood.

After seeing a notice in the Los Angeles Times announcing that the Pasadena Playhouse was to present a dramatic version of "The Diamond as Big as the Ritz," Fitzgerald, eager for recognition and considering it a prelude to a Broadway production, told Sheilah they would attend the opening and make it a festive occasion. They would "dress in evening clothes, dine at the Trocadero, and go on to Pasadena—not in his bouncy little [second-hand] Ford but in a sleek, chauffeur-driven limousine." As their automobile pulled up to the theater, they were surprised to find no other people or cars arriving for the grand event. Fitzgerald made inquiries and explained to Sheilah: "'It's the students—they're giving the play in the upstairs hall [rather than in the theater itself],' he said, trying to be casual. I said nothing as we climbed the stairs and found ourselves in a small hall with a little stage and perhaps fifteen rows of wooden benches. No one else had arrived. . . . About ten minutes before curtain time a few students appeared, women and girls wearing mostly slacks and skirts—perhaps a dozen in all. They looked curiously at us sitting alone on a bench in full evening clothes."[19]

Though Sheilah always hid her age and Jewish origins, and gave extremely distorted versions of her early life, she was in her later books remarkably frank about her sexual relations with Fitzgerald. Soon after they met, the ever-inquisitive Scott asked Sheilah how many lovers she had had, and when she responded with an extremely conservative estimate of "eight" (including the director King Vidor), the worldly puritan was visibly shocked. They were both rather shy, despite their extensive sexual experience, and never saw each other completely naked. Embarrassed about her large breasts at a time when many glamorous women were extremely thin, she made things rather difficult for Scott by always keeping her bra on in bed.

Sheilah did not believe that he had ever asked Hemingway to check out the size of his member. "He could say and do outrageous things when he was drunk," she declared, "but never about his own person." Well informed about all shapes and sizes of male sexual organs, she found the tubercular, drug-addicted and often alcoholic Fitzgerald a creditable performer—"very satisfactory . . . in terms of giving physical pleasure." After lovemaking, they would lie happily in each other's arms for a long time.

Scott's hostile portrait of Sheilah in "Last Kiss," written in 1940 when they were quarreling, captures the contradictory aspects of her character, in which "so much innocence and so much predatory toughness could go side by side behind this gentle English voice."[20] In The

Last Tycoon Kathleen Moore (who was based on Sheilah) is a beautiful young English girl who reminds Monroe Stahr of his dead wife—just as Sheilah reminded Scott of Zelda. Stahr falls in love with Kathleen and becomes her lover, but she marries another man—as Sheilah claimed she would marry Donegall.

Fitzgerald's fictional tribute to Sheilah could scarcely compensate for the violent and vituperative quarrels—much fiercer than those he had with Zelda—that took place when he became depressed and turned to alcohol. As Sheilah remarked: "The two things I feared most were drunkenness and insanity. With Scott, I had both." The gentle Helen Hayes thought Sheilah was good to Scott, but that he treated her badly because (as Mankiewicz had implied) "she represented to Scott's fevered mind the second-rate he had fallen into." He abused Sheilah's kindness and tested her love as he had previously done with the Murphys.

Fitzgerald was not drinking when they met, and she did not notice at first that his hand trembled when he lit a cigarette. But, as his *Esquire* editor Arnold Gingrich pointed out, "being his friend was almost a full-time career. He had amazing charm and personality. But you never could tell when he would turn on you—and for no reason. . . . [He was] a vicious drunk, one of the worst I have ever known."[21] Sheilah, like many others, vividly evoked the image of a demonically buffoonish or aggressive Fitzgerald, "his face flushed, a filthy handkerchief in his breast pocket, smiling devilishly, organizing everyone, and being completely compelling, until he fell flat on his face or started a fight."

When he became depressed, could not sleep and got drunk, Fitzgerald fought bitterly with Sheilah. He screamed abuse, threw a bowl of soup against the wall, kicked his nurse, slapped Sheilah, threatened to kill her with a gun and sent her a melodramatic telegram that said: "Get out of town, Lily Sheil, or you will be dead in 24 hours." He also behaved badly in front of strangers. During a weekend at Cottage Club just after his wedding in April 1920, he had told all his friends that Zelda was his mistress. At Ellerslie in November 1928, he had told Hemingway that the black maid serving dinner was the best piece of tail he ever had. And during a drunken flight to Chicago in the fall of 1937, accompanying Sheilah, who was to make a national radio broadcast, he told all the passengers what "a great lay" she was. After calling

Sheilah "a silly bitch" and punching her sponsor at the radio studio, Fitzgerald summoned Gingrich to his room in the Drake Hotel. As the editor sobered him up by shoveling steak into his mouth, the food dribbled onto his bib and he tried to bite Gingrich's hand. Though completely incapacitated, he kept saying of Sheilah: "I just got to have this cunt." Sheilah screamed: "You have ruined me! I hate you, I never want to see you again!" (On another occasion, when he threatened to kill himself, she said: "Shoot yourself, you son of a bitch. I didn't raise myself from the gutter to waste my life on a drunk like you.")[22] After Sheilah left, he tried, for the second time in two years, to commit suicide by taking an overdose of sleeping pills.

Fitzgerald always managed to win her back when he had sobered up. Filled with contrition, he made sincere and abject apologies. In a characteristic conclusion to a particularly venomous fight, he got the tactful Frances Kroll to intercede with Sheilah and offer, on his behalf, to make any restitution that would satisfy her. "Everything he did seems perfectly abominable to him," Frances said. "He wants to know if it will be any help if he leaves Hollywood for good. He has . . . no intention of trying to see you. He merely wants to remove as much of the unhappiness as is possible." Fitzgerald's own letter to Sheilah blamed himself for all their difficulties. He condemned his character and was so pitiful that she forgave him and resumed their affair. "I'm glad you can no longer think of me with either respect or affection," Scott wrote. "People are either good for each other or not, and obviously I am *horrible* for you. I loved you with everything I had, but something was terribly wrong. You don't have to look far for the reason—I was it. Not fit for any human relation. . . . I want to die, Sheilah, and in my own way. I used to have my daughter and my poor lost Zelda. Now for over two years your image is everywhere. . . . You are too much for a tubercular neurotic who can only be jealous and mean and perverse."

Sheilah later rejected Helen Hayes' statement that Fitzgerald had treated her badly. Sheilah could have left him whenever she wished, but felt she would rather be Scott's mistress than someone else's wife. He once gave her a copy of *This Side of Paradise* with the tender inscription: "For my darling Sheilah—after *such* a bad time, from Scott."[23] But just after his death she received a great shock. When she examined a photograph she had given to him, she discovered his hidden scorn for her in the bitter words scrawled on the back: "Portrait of a Prostitute."

Fitzgerald's complex relations with Sheilah had one other significant aspect. Anthony Powell had noticed the didactic element in Fitzgerald: "He loved instructing. There was a schoolmasterish streak, if at the same time an attractive one; an enthusiasm, simplicity of exposition, that might have offered a career as a teacher or a university don." Just as Isak Dinesen's lover, Denys Finch-Hatton, "taught her Greek, acquainted her with the Symbolists, played Stravinsky for her, tried to inform her taste for modern art," so Scott found in Sheilah a much more eager and docile pupil than Scottie had been. He formed their "College of One," drew up extensive reading lists (she had never read any of his books when they met), and compensated for his own lack of education, as well as for hers, by patiently teaching her to understand the books that he loved.

In the fall of 1938 Fitzgerald took Sheilah to visit his old friends on the East Coast—the Murphys, Perkins, Ober and Wilson. Like Fitzgerald's Hollywood friends, Wilson was struck by the great change in his character. He attributed Scott's new normality and tameness to Sheilah, who had urged him to give up alcohol. At the same time (and retrospectively) Wilson held Zelda responsible for Scott's crazy behavior. But, as he told Christian Gauss, Fitzgerald, though now calm, had also lost a good deal of his old vitality: "He doesn't drink, works hard in Hollywood, and has a new girl, who, though less interesting, tends to keep him in better order than Zelda. . . . He seems mild, rather unsure of himself, and at moments almost banal."[24] Gerald Murphy was also surprised to see Scott wearing a homely pair of overshoes, which he took off and miraculously *remembered* to put on again when he left.

Wilson's brilliant wife, Mary McCarthy, was astonished by Fitzgerald's colossal ignorance, found him boring and was struck by Wilson's arrogant condescension toward his old friend. Fitzgerald seemed to find this quite normal and, after this meeting, resumed his youthful role as Wilson's disciple. "Believe me, Bunny," he wrote, stressing as always Wilson's superior intellect, "it meant more to me than it could possibly have meant to you to see you that evening. It seemed to renew old times learning about Franz Kafka and latter things that are going on in the world of poetry, because I am still the ignoramus that you and John Bishop wrote about at Princeton."

Wilson's intellectual influence continued until the end of Fitzgerald's life. When working with Budd Schulberg on the screenplay for *Winter Carnival,* he frequently and respectfully referred to Wilson in their conversations. Trying to develop his political awareness in the troubled 1930s, Fitzgerald would sit in the California sunshine reading Marx's *The Eighteenth Brumaire* "like an eager sociology student bucking for an A in Bunny Wilson's class in social consciousness." Despite his apparent political naïveté, Fitzgerald resisted the *Zeitgeist.* He never swallowed, as did the more sophisticated Wilson, the illusory bait of Communism. As he shrewdly told Perkins, while attempting to explain Wilson's gloom: "A decision to adopt Communism definitely, no matter how good for the soul, must of necessity be a saddening process for anyone who has ever tasted the intellectual pleasures of the world we live in."[25]

The unusual calm that Wilson noticed in Fitzgerald had been achieved only after a desperate struggle to give up drink. Fitzgerald was disciplined and could work whenever he needed the money; but he could not work and drink at the same time, and would shift to Coca-Cola when he had to write. As Frances Kroll, whose duties included disposing of Scott's gin bottles, told Mizener: "Drink, in small quantities, acted as a stimulus and did not affect the quality of his writing. Although he continued to write when he was roaring drunk, as well, most of the effort had, in the long run, to be discarded, though it had a kind of humor that would be hard to duplicate under normal conditions."

Fitzgerald gradually realized that alcohol hurt his work, damaged his reputation, ruined his health and almost destroyed his relations with Sheilah. Remembering the sad fate of the original Edgar Poe, he told his Princeton classmate and Baltimore lawyer, Edgar Allan Poe, Jr.: "It seems to be the fate of all drunks that in the end they have to give up not only liquor but a whole lot of other good things." Refusing at first to admit that he was an alcoholic, Fitzgerald drank secretly or switched to beer. He had also tried every conceivable method to cure his disease—stopping suddenly or gradually, smoking or eating candy when he got the urge—but nothing had worked. Finally, he hired a doctor and nurses, forced himself to endure an agonizing three-day cure, was fed intravenously, could not sleep and retched miserably throughout the night. At last, he was able to report that even a single drink made him deathly sick. In May 1937 he proudly (if prematurely) told Ober: "since stopping drinking I've gained from just over 140 to over 160. I sleep at last and tho my hair's grey I feel younger than for four years."[26] Despite all these efforts, he was not able to give up drink completely until the last year of his life, when he raced against time to complete *The Last Tycoon*.

Chapter Thirteen

HOLLYWOOD HACK AND
THE LAST TYCOON, 1939–1940

I

Despite the stigma of failure at MGM Fitzgerald's name had a lingering aura in Hollywood and producers still wanted him to work on romantic subjects. Unlike Dorothy Parker and other cynical writers, he was hardworking, eager to learn and respectful to the studio executives. In January 1939 he was hired to polish the dialogue of *Gone with the Wind*. His efforts were absurdly impeded, however, when he was forbidden to use any words that had not already been written by Margaret Mitchell. When lines had to be invented, Fitzgerald would diligently thumb through her novel as if it were Scripture and find familiar words to fit the new scene.

The film's producer, David Selznick, subjected Fitzgerald to the duplicity and humiliation that all but the most successful writers had to suffer in Hollywood. Selznick's biographer wrote that George Cukor, soon to be replaced as director of the film,

> was present at the story conferences with Fitzgerald. At the close of one of them, David told the writer, "Scott, I want to

thank you for all you've done on the picture. Now, we've talked about these pages. Go away and write them—and we'll meet tomorrow." But as soon as Fitzgerald had left, Selznick picked up the phone and dictated a cable firing him, telling him not to report the next day. As Cukor observed it, David had needed to act out his superiority to the once great writer. Yet he had not managed to do it face-to-face.

This assignment ended after two weeks.

Fitzgerald's most sordid and calamitous experience as a film writer took place in February when he was hired by the producer Walter Wanger. He was to collaborate with Budd Schulberg on an apparently congenial script about the Dartmouth Winter Carnival and be paid at his MGM salary of $1,250 a week. Mankiewicz respected Wanger, who also produced *Stagecoach* in 1939, and considered him well educated and well read. But he admitted that Wanger had lost control of *Winter Carnival*. Schulberg, much more severe about his former boss, called him "a Dartmouth dropout with intellectual pretensions." Later on, he elaborated his original judgment. Wanger, he said, was a poseur. Though he smoked a pipe, talked about books and liked to seem more cultivated than most producers, he was crass and tactless with writers. Both Fitzgerald and Schulberg looked down on him.[1]

The twenty-four-year-old Budd—son of B. P. Schulberg, the former head of production at Paramount—had recently graduated from Dartmouth and was trying to break into movies. Sheilah Graham described him as a gangling and seemingly shy young man who "stuttered rather painfully. He was always knocking things over and apologizing in a mumble of words." When Wanger told Schulberg he had hired Fitzgerald to work with him on the script, Budd (confirming Anthony Powell's statement) exclaimed: "'My God, isn't Scott Fitzgerald dead?' 'On the contrary,' said Wanger, 'he's in the next office reading your script.'" Budd, honored to be working with his literary hero, was shocked at how sad and anxious he looked. His skin was pallid and unhealthy, and he seemed much older than forty-two.

The two men spent many hours together, supposedly working on the script, but actually engaged in long literary discussions. Budd's youthful admiration for his work encouraged Scott to reminisce about his past success and talk about his future novels. According to Schulberg, Fitzgerald spoke of himself as a has-been, but felt his creative powers had not been entirely extinguished: "You know, I used to have a beautiful talent once, Baby. It used to be a wonderful feeling to know it was there, and it isn't all gone yet. I think I have enough left to stretch out over two more novels. I may have to stretch it a little thin, so maybe they won't be as good as the best things I've done. But they won't be completely bad either, because nothing I ever write can ever be completely bad."[2]

Wanger wanted Fitzgerald to pick up the local color and to advise the film crew by attending the Dartmouth Winter Carnival. Fitzgerald, all too familiar with college celebrations, thought the long and tiring journey was unnecessary. Remembering his alcoholic trip to Chicago with Sheilah in 1938, he feared the festivities would upset the calm routine he had established with her and tempt him with drink. The studio executives were well aware of his alcoholism. But his film agent, H. N. Swanson, had assured them, since Scott *had* been on the wagon, that drink was no longer a problem. Schulberg believed that Wanger's real motive was to show off Fitzgerald, his tame bear and captive writer, to the appreciative English professors at Dartmouth.

Sheilah, worried about Scott, took the same flight across the country. But since their affair had to be kept secret in moralistic Hollywood, she sat apart from him in the plane and waited in New York while he and Budd took the train up to Hanover, New Hampshire. Her fears were well founded. Budd's father gave them two bottles of champagne to divert them on the flight, and this set Fitzgerald off on a week-long, non-stop binge.

On arrival they discovered that no one had made reservations for them at the Hanover Inn. The only place available on that busy weekend was a bare servants' room in the attic, with a double bunk bed. This makeshift arrangement symbolized their menial status and intensified their resentment. The Dartmouth English professors, disappointed by Fitzgerald's drunken and rambling conversation at the faculty reception, treated him rudely and scarcely bothered to conceal their derision. One of them remarked, with considerable hostility: "He really is a washed up old drunk."

But even when Fitzgerald was a falling-down drunk, he never lost his heightened perception of what was happening around him and continued to mutter shrewd observations under his breath. "Wanger will never forgive me for this," he told Schulberg, "because he sees himself as the intellectual producer and above all wanted to impress Dartmouth with the fact that he used real writers, not vulgar hacks, and here I, his real writer, have disgraced him before all these people."

On February 12, after Fitzgerald had spent three idle and miserable days in Hanover, Wanger, who was there with the film crew, discovered that he had been drinking heavily and that very little of the screenplay had been written. He angrily declared: "That son-of-a-bitch gave me his word that he wouldn't go off the wagon," and instantly fired both writers. Eager to get them out of town as quickly as possible, Wanger put them on the next train, without giving them time to pack their bags, and said the luggage would be sent after them. Angry and mortified at having lost the job, Fitzgerald went completely out of control on the train. When they got to New York—without luggage, unshaven, unkempt and completely drunk—no hotel would admit them. With Sheilah's help Fitzgerald finally entered Doctors Hospital and took three days to dry out.[3]

During the next half century Schulberg repeated the sad story of Fitzgerald at Dartmouth in a series of articles, books, interviews and lectures. He always portrayed Wanger as the intolerant villain and himself as the exasperated but loyal keeper of his unruly charge. But he was partly responsible for what happened to Fitzgerald. Schulberg's youthful lark with a great writer was Fitzgerald's unmitigated disaster. Because Budd did not try to restrain Scott and write the screenplay with him as he was hired to do, Fitzgerald got horribly drunk, was fired, became seriously ill and never got another job with a film studio. Schulberg, protected by his powerful father, was rehired by Wanger to complete the embarrassingly bad script. And he went on to have a successful film career.

After this episode his relations with Fitzgerald were predictably strained. When Fitzgerald dropped by Schulberg's house, eager to discuss the historical theories of Oswald Spengler, Budd abandoned him for a trivial dinner invitation. Though he later felt guilty about his rudeness, the incident shows that he felt Scott could be as tedious when sober as he was when drunk, and that he had much less respect for Fitzgerald than he later claimed to have had.

When Fitzgerald read the typescript of Schulberg's first Hollywood novel, *What Makes Sammy Run?* (1941), he recorded the harsh judgment: "Budd, the untalented." Budd was hurt by Fitzgerald's appropriation in *The Last Tycoon* of his early life in Hollywood and by the negative portrayal of his personality in the character of the young narrator, Cecilia Brady. This resentment provoked the hostile portrait of Fitzgerald in his best-selling novel, *The Disenchanted* (1950), which described Scott's appalling behavior at Dartmouth. Though most of Fitzgerald's friends disliked the novel, which tarnished his reputation, Scottie said: "I really felt I was in the room with Daddy the entire time during the drunken scenes—that was *exactly* the way he talked and acted during those bouts."[4] Though Mankiewicz has been the villain and Schulberg the hero in biographies of Fitzgerald, Scott received a screen credit and had his contract renewed after working with Joe, but had his film career destroyed when working with Budd.

The experience at Dartmouth also destroyed whatever remained of Fitzgerald's confidence and reputation. His principal handicap in the picture business, he told Ober in July 1939, was "a neurosis about anyone's uncertainty about my ability." But he now lived with his own uncertainty principle. Though he worked sporadically on a few more films until July 1940, the rest of his screen work was trivial. His health continued to deteriorate under the assault of alcohol, and when drunk he quarreled again with Sheilah. Despite his attempts to comply with their wishes, he ended up on bad terms with most of the producers who had hired him, and all the film projects he proposed—including a Marx Brothers version of *The Wizard of Oz*—were rejected.

In September 1939 David Niven, who saw him on the set of *Raffles*, condescendingly noted his physical decline, his addiction to sweets and his singularly depressing conversation: "he looked so frail that he seemed to be floating: mid-forties, Valentino profile, rather weak mouth, and haunted eyes. He carried a large writing pad and a cardboard container of Coca-Cola bottles when I first saw him and made a little nest for himself in a corner of the sound stage.... Actually, I found him rather heavy going, with his long silences and tales of bad luck at the hands of the movie moguls."

In April 1940, still anxious about money and eager to buy time to write his novel, Fitzgerald sold the screen rights of his best story, "Babylon Revisited," to the producer Lester Cowan for one thousand dollars. He received another five thousand dollars for completing a screenplay of the story (called *Cosmopolitan*), which Nunnally Johnson had thought was so poor. Fitzgerald tried to interest Shirley Temple in playing the daughter, Honoria, but she refused the role and that film was not made. Like David Niven, Shirley Temple noted Fitzgerald's sickly appearance, craving for sweet drinks and ludicrous six-pack of Cokes: "I remember Fitzgerald as a kindly, thin and pale man, who was recovering from an illness. The thing that impressed me the most as an eleven or twelve-year-old was that he drank six or eight Coca-Colas during his visit. As a young girl, I thought this to be a stunning accomplishment—in fact, I *still* do." In 1954 Cowan resold the rights of "Babylon Revisited" to MGM for forty thousand dollars and the film, which had little to do with the story, was made with Elizabeth Taylor and Van Johnson as *The Last Time I Saw Paris*.

Fitzgerald was well suited for his final job, which lasted from August to October 1940: a film script based on Emlyn Williams' stage play, *The Light of Heart*, about an alcoholic actor. But Fitzgerald's screenplay was rejected and he was replaced by Nunnally Johnson, whom he had tried to warn about the dangers of writing for Hollywood. In May 1940 Fitzgerald had truthfully told Perkins: "I just couldn't make the grade as a hack—that, like everything else, requires a certain practiced excellence."[5]

Fitzgerald also tried to help another promising writer, Nathanael West, whom he had met through S. J. Perelman in early 1939. Unlike Hemingway, who felt threatened by younger rivals, especially when they invaded his territory, Fitzgerald, even when his own career was in decline, was always kind and helpful to his colleagues. In 1934 he had included West's *Miss Lonelyhearts* (along with Wilson's *I Thought of Daisy*) in a list of "Good Books That Almost Nobody Has Read." In his Introduction to the Modern Library edition of *The Great Gatsby* (1934) he pleaded for more generous book reviewing, made a favorable reference to West and said: "it has been saddening recently to see young talents in fiction expire from sheer lack of a stage to act on: West, [Vincent] McHugh and many others." He also recommended West for a Guggenheim Fellowship that year, recognizing his talents and calling him "a potential leader in the field of prose fiction." And in 1939 he wrote a blurb for the dust wrapper of West's great novel, *The Day of the Locust*. Emphasizing the most effective scenes and the weird mood of the book, Fitzgerald said: "I was impressed by the pathological crowd at the premiere, the character and handling of the aspirant actress and the

uncanny almost medieval feeling of some of the Hollywood background set off by those vividly drawn grotesques."[6] The day after
Fitzgerald died, West was killed in a car crash near the Mexican border.

II

While struggling to survive in distant Hollywood, Fitzgerald tried as
always to be a good father and husband. As Scottie grew more mature
and independent, and Fitzgerald continued to criticize her during their
infrequent meetings, she drew even closer to the kindly Obers. They
lived fairly near Vassar and Scottie usually stayed with them during her
school holidays. Fitzgerald had to play the strict parent while the Obers
spoiled her. As he tried to stiffen Scottie's backbone and get her to
work hard in college, Anne Ober irritated him by buying her party
dresses. He willingly gave the Obers parental authority and was grateful for their kindness, but also resented their usurpation of his role and
criticized their efforts on his behalf.

He admitted that he was often too nervous and too dogmatic with
Scottie. In August 1939, just before her summer visit to Hollywood, he
apologized (in a letter to Zelda) for apparently rejecting his daughter
and for harshly telling her "that she had no home except Vassar." But
he defended himself by explaining that Scottie had actually rejected
him: "When I tried to make a home for her she didn't want it, and I
have a sick-man's feeling that she will arrive in a manner to break up
such tranquility as I have managed to establish after this illness." In late
September 1939, when the college term was about to begin, he sent
Scottie a pitiful telegram that was meant to make her feel guilty about
what he had done for her: YOU CAN REGISTER AT VASSAR STOP IT COST A
HEMORRHAGE BUT I RAISED SOME MONEY FROM ESQUIRE.

When Fitzgerald confessed that he and Zelda had been bad parents and urged Scottie to reject their negative example, she seized the
initiative, defended herself and spoke out publicly for her own generation in *Mademoiselle* of July 1939. "We feel we know what's right and
wrong for us better than our parents," Scottie insisted. "The fact that
we've turned out as well as we have is more to our credit than that of
our parents."[7]

Scottie, not surprisingly, was deeply ambivalent about her parents: saddened about her mother's emotional withdrawal and exasperated by her father's misguided attempts to direct her life. She later spoke bitterly to scholars and friends, and published several essays about her unhappy relations with her father. "We never got along at all well," she told Mizener, "except in letters (which have given everyone the impression we were a most devoted father and daughter)." Late in life she told an Alabama confidante that her childhood and youth had been extremely difficult, and that it had been hard to have a writer as a father: "I can remember nothing except the troubles of the 30s which were reflected in our relations: my mother's hopeless illness, Daddy's own bad health and lack of money and, hardest of all, I think, his literary eclipse. . . . In my next incarnation, I may not choose again to be the daughter of a famous author. People who live entirely by the fertility of their imagination are fascinating, brilliant and often charming but they should be sat next to at dinner parties, not lived with."

Yet Fitzgerald's deeply moving *Letters to His Daughter*—edited by Andrew Turnbull and introduced by Scottie in 1965—*did* show his devotion to her. Though Scott and Zelda were unstable and unreliable, the very antithesis of conventionally good parents, they nevertheless gave Scottie—with the help of governesses and generous friends—the love and happiness that was necessary to develop and strengthen her character. As Scottie herself observed: "Daddy never let me feel the tragedy of mother's illness and I never had a sense of being unloved."[8]

In his fiction Fitzgerald paid tribute to Scottie, who (like Zelda) inspired a number of charming characters: Daisy's daughter Pammy in *The Great Gatsby*, the wise little girl in "Outside the Cabinet-Maker's," Honoria in "Babylon Revisited," Topsy in *Tender is the Night*, Gwen in the four stories of 1935–36 and Cecilia, the Hollywood child and Bennington student who is hopelessly in love with Monroe Stahr, in *The Last Tycoon*.

Zelda also tried, in her rare lucid moments, to be a good mother to Scottie. But their relations remained troubled during her daughter's adolescence and teenage years. So Fitzgerald could not count on Scottie's help when caring for Zelda. Despite—or perhaps because of—his guilt-ridden liaison with Sheilah, he continued to fly east to take the intensely disturbing but only vaguely therapeutic holidays with Zelda. In April 1939, after a particularly unpleasant fight with Sheilah, he impulsively flew across the country and took Zelda on a trip to Cuba. He had been beaten up while drunk and aggressive at Cottage Club in Princeton in 1920, in the Jungle Club in New York in 1921 and, worst of all, by the police in Rome in 1924. Though now forty-two, he was still remarkably combative. In Havana Scott fought with a cab driver, incensed that he could not speak English. In a sudden access of humanitarianism or confused heroism, he also tried to stop a local cockfight, which involved heavy betting, and was badly beaten up for his pains. After he returned to New York, he rounded off his horrible holiday by quarreling, on the way to Ober's house in Scarsdale, with another cab driver who gave him a black and swollen eye. This trip was the last time he saw Zelda.

The debate about the terms of her confinement continued to disturb Fitzgerald's relations with the Sayres. In January 1939, three months before the trip to Cuba, he told his mother-in-law that it would be dangerous to let Zelda out of Highland: "Carroll says that if I take her away he will not take her back—he feels that I will weakly destroy his entire work of bringing her from a state of horror, shame, suicide and despair to the level of a bored and often grouchy but by no means miserable invalid." Scott was afraid that he would be morally and legally responsible if Zelda killed herself or hurt someone else when she was out of the hospital. Nevertheless, Dr. Carroll finally changed his mind. In April 1940, after four years in Highland, Zelda was allowed to return to the rather run-down family house at 322 Sayre Street in Montgomery and to live with her eighty-year-old mother.

Even before Mrs. Sayre assumed immediate responsibility, Scott began to find the strain intolerable and to withdraw from the woman who called herself a "middle-aged, untrained, graduate of half-a-dozen mental Institutes." During a bout of tuberculosis in October 1939, he begged Zelda to "leave me in peace with my hemorrhages and my hopes." And he bitterly told Dr. Carroll: "She has cost me everything a woman can cost a man—his health, his work, his money."[9]

Scottie confirmed Fitzgerald's remark by telling Mizener, in an important letter, that Zelda had destroyed Scott: "She was extravagant, yes, but that was part of her disease, and God knows she was an overwhelming egotist and probably a terribly tough person to live with on a day-to-day basis—and she probably ruined Daddy." Even Zelda seemed to recognize the truth about their marriage when in 1939 she thanked Scott for all the sacrifices he had made during her mental illness: "I am always grateful for all the loyalties you gave me. . . . I love, always, your fine writing talent, your tolerance and generosity; and all your happy endowments. Nothing could have survived our life."[10]

III

While his relations with Scottie and Zelda were deteriorating, Fitzgerald also quarreled irrevocably in July 1939 with Harold Ober, who had been his agent, adviser, banker and faithful friend since 1919. He had managed to pay off his huge debt to Ober during his first eighteen months in Hollywood. But when MGM failed to renew his contract, he began once again to slide into debt. In his Christmas card of 1937 Fitzgerald—who said he had paid his "bill collector" more than fifty thousand dollars in commissions for magazine stories—emphasized the difference in financial status between the wealthy agent, comfortably housed in Scarsdale, and the impoverished author, enslaved in the salt mines of Hollywood: "I recognized the dogs individually in your Christmas card. I'm going to have my suite photographed with the mice in the hall for next Xmas."

During the Depression Fitzgerald had depended on Ober to advance money (contrary to normal practice) for stories he had conceived and promised, but not yet written. By 1939, however, Fitzgerald had either failed to complete many of the promised stories or sent inferior work that Ober was unable to sell. Having paid off his debt, Fitzgerald thought his credit was still good. Well aware of Fitzgerald's declining reputation and failure in Hollywood, Ober believed he would never recover his debt if he allowed it to pile up again. So he gave up on Fitzgerald and decided to cut his losses. On June 21, 1939, Ober wrote but—to spare Scott's feelings—*did not mail* a carefully considered letter that stated his new financial policy: "I think, however, it would be a great mistake for us to get back into the position we were in. I think it is bad for you and difficult for me. The margin of profit in the agency business is very narrow. The expenses are many and high and I reckon the net profit is only about three per cent. I hope, therefore, we can keep things on a 'Pay as we go' basis."

Scottie later defended Ober, saying that he had discussed this matter with both Perkins and Scribner, who agreed with him, and then telephoned Sheilah to explain his decision and ask her to convey it to Scott. Despite Ober's attempts to warn his client, on July 14 Fitzgerald asked for his usual advance on an undelivered story. And Ober was forced to telegraph a polite refusal: SORRY COLLECTIONS SLOW AND IMPOSSIBLE MAKE ADVANCE. Scott was shocked and furious about Harold's disloyalty. He wrote on the telegram: "The insult to my intelligence in the phrase 'collections slow' makes me laugh,"[11] returned it to Ober and decided to break with him.

Fitzgerald, at first, accepted responsibility for this incident in a surprisingly clear-minded letter of July 18 to Kenneth Littauer, his editor at *Collier's:* "Harold is a fine man and has been a fine agent and the fault is mine. Through one illness he backed me with a substantial amount of money (all paid back to him now with Hollywood gold) but he is not prepared to do that again with growing boys to educate." But as time passed his resentment increased. He then reversed his position and began to blame Ober for what had happened. Writing to him on August 2, he portrayed himself as a drowning victim, whom Ober had been morally obliged to rescue: "I don't have to explain that even though a man has once saved another from drowning, when he refuses to stretch out his arm a second time the victim has to act quickly and desperately to save himself. For change you did, Harold, and without warning." It is unlikely, however, that Ober's warning, if sent, would have discouraged Fitzgerald's demands.

Scott also complained to Perkins, who had urged him to remain with his agent, that Ober's original interest in his works and forgiveness of his sins had now changed to a lack of confidence in his literary prospects and a general disapproval of his behavior. He also said that he had never been emotionally or intellectually close to Ober. Though Ober had witnessed his drunkenness and decline throughout the 1930s, in October 1939 Fitzgerald called him "a stupid hard-headed man [who] has a highly erroneous idea of how I live; moreover he has made it a noble duty to piously depress me at every possible opportunity." Though Fitzgerald maintained his friendship with Perkins and Murphy, he had by mid-1939 drifted away from Edmund Wilson, become estranged from Zelda and Scottie, and quarreled with three of his closest friends: first Hemingway and Bishop, and then Ober—an essential ally.

Fitzgerald earned $21,500 in 1939 but owed money for federal taxes, life insurance, Zelda's hospital and Scottie's college. After Ober dried up as a source of money, Scott was forced to borrow from Perkins, Murphy and his St. Paul friend Oscar Kalman. Trying to bolster the pathetic sales of his books, Scott bought all the copies he could find in Los Angeles and gave them away to friends. Almost everyone who writes about Fitzgerald mentions that during the last year of his life he sold only forty copies of his books and received a princely royalty of $13.13. But no one has noticed that his book sales were virtually the *same* at the end of the 1920s as they were at the end of the 1930s. In 1927, two years after he published *The Great Gatsby*, his books earned only $153; in 1929 they earned $32. Most of his income, throughout his career, came from magazine stories and screenwriting rather than from books.

Fitzgerald found it extremely difficult to accept this painful fact. Toward the end of his life, when *The Great Gatsby* was dropped from the Modern Library because it failed to sell, he told Perkins that he felt rather neglected. He also asked his editor to salvage the remnants of his reputation by reprinting some of his earlier works. Speaking of himself in the past tense, he lamented his moribund career: "But to die, so completely and unjustly after having given so much. Even now there is little published in American fiction that doesn't slightly bear my stamp—in a *small* way I was an original."[12]

Fitzgerald's failure and obscurity were driven home once again when Scribner's published in October 1940 Hemingway's long-awaited, highly acclaimed and immensely successful novel about the Spanish Civil War, *For Whom the Bell Tolls*. The novel was a Book-of-the-Month Club selection, sold more than half a million copies in the first five months and was bought by the movies for one hundred thousand dollars. Fitzgerald was deeply moved when he received a copy inscribed, "To Scott with affection and esteem Ernest." He carefully studied the technical aspects of the book and praised the battle scenes in a rather insincere letter to the author: "It's a fine novel, better than anybody else writing could do. Thanks for thinking of me and for your dedication. I read it with intense interest, participating in a lot of the writing problems as they came along and often quite unable to discover how you brought off some of the effects, but you always did. The massacre was magnificent and also the fight on the mountain and the actual dynamiting scene. . . . The scene in which the father says goodbye to his son is very powerful."

But, envious of Hemingway's success, Scott failed to recognize the greatness of the novel. When speaking and writing to friends, he condemned the love scenes—his own strong point. In his *Notebooks* he called it "a thoroughly superficial book that has all the profundity of [Daphne du Maurier's] *Rebecca*"—which Selznick and Hitchcock had just made into an extremely popular film. And he told Schulberg, at great length, how the romantic encounters between Robert Jordan and Maria were "dreadful." In *The Last Tycoon* he slyly mocked the most famous love scene in *For Whom the Bell Tolls* ("Did thee feel the earth move?") when Kathleen says to Stahr: "When you do that, you can feel the earth turn, can't you?" Scott told Sheilah: "It's not up to his standard. He wrote it for the movies," and complained that his former hero, in his public pronouncements, "has become a pompous bore." He also sent Zelda a more seriously considered judgment: "It is not as good as *A Farewell to Arms*. It doesn't seem to have the tensity or the freshness, nor has it the inspired poetic moments. . . . It is full of a lot of rounded adventures on the *Huckleberry Finn* order and of course it is highly intelligent and literate like everything he does."[13]

Hemingway had come a long way from the humble flat near the sawmill in Paris, and their original positions were now exactly reversed. When they first met in May 1925 Fitzgerald was the well established author and Hemingway was virtually unknown. By 1940 Fitzgerald's reputation had disappeared while Hemingway had become the preeminent American novelist. After Scott's death Ernest took steps to maintain his considerable advantage. He was conspicuously absent from the friends who paid tribute to Fitzgerald in *The Crack-Up* volume. In a series of fascinating letters to Mizener, he consistently denigrated his former and ever-more-threatening rival, and wittily remarked: "He had a very steep trajectory and was almost like a guided missile with no one guiding him."

When Mizener published an innocuous article on Fitzgerald in *Life* magazine of January 1951, just before the appearance of *The Far Side of Paradise*, Hemingway, fearing what might one day happen to him, poured a torrent of abuse on the head of the innocent biographer: "I would rather clean sewers for a living, every day, or bounce in a bad whorehouse or pimp for a living than to sign such an article." He also felt that Schulberg's novel, *The Disenchanted*, was "grave robbing." But Hemingway did more damage to Fitzgerald's reputation than Mizener and Schulberg ever did and tried to "destroy" him in *A Moveable Feast* just as he claimed Zelda had done in real life. Hemingway's most sincere but ambivalent judgment of his old friend, recorded by his son Gregory, distinguished between the early and the mature novels, and recognized that Scott had overcome formidable obstacles to achieve a strong finish. In the end, the guided missile hit the target:

> Papa rarely forgot Scott Fitzgerald when we had these [literary] talks. "*Gatsby* was a great book. I've read it twice in the last five years. It gets better with each reading. *Tender is the Night* is a fine book, too. Flawed in the middle. But so is my *To Have and Have Not*. *This Side of Paradise* is a joke, though. And *The Beautiful and Damned* is so damned unbeautiful I couldn't finish it! Scott's writing got better and better, but no one realized it, not even Scott. Despite his rummyhood and perhaps *because* of Zelda, who really made him the box with the handles, he got better and better. The stuff he was writing at the end was the best of all. Poor bastard."[14]

Fitzgerald and Hemingway, who were obsessed with each other throughout their lives, seemed completely different. But, as Fitzgerald had predicted ("he is quite as nervously broken down as I am"), they actually had many of the same weaknesses. Though Ernest had consistently scorned Scott's flawed character, he became tragically like Fitzgerald at the end of his life. He too had become a Catholic, been dazzled by the rich, turned into a celebrity, created a legend that made his life better known than his works; he too had been blocked as a writer, failed in marriage, escaped into alcoholism and become suicidal.

IV

As Fitzgerald's film work petered out after the *Winter Carnival* fiasco, he returned to short fiction and to the Hollywood novel he hoped would restore his reputation and place him on the same level as Hemingway. In the fall of 1939 the emotionally battered writer (who owed money to Highland Hospital) told Dr. Carroll that he was no longer capable of producing the slick, formulaic tales that had earned high fees from the *Saturday Evening Post:* "I seem to have completely lost the gift for the commercial short story, which depends on the 'boy-meets-girl' motif. I can't write them convincingly any more which takes me completely out of the big money in that regard."

Fitzgerald published no fiction during his first two years in Hollywood (July 1937 to July 1939), but wrote twenty-four stories during the last eighteen months of his life. All but two of these stories were sold to Arnold Gingrich at *Esquire.* But Fitzgerald's fee had dropped to $250; and it now took sixteen stories to earn the $4,000 the *Post* used to pay for each one. The best late story was "The Lost Decade" (December 1939), an effective description of a man trying to get back in touch with the real world after ten years in an alcoholic stupor.

Seventeen of Fitzgerald's late, rather thin stories, published between January 1940 and May 1941, concerned the Hollywood hack Pat Hobby. They caught the desperation of a washed-up writer who was still trying to sell himself and portrayed, in an extreme form, what might happen to Fitzgerald himself if he could no longer earn any money in films. Pat Hobby is an impoverished alcoholic, hanger-on and con man, homeless and sleeping at the studio; a parasitic, thrice-divorced, intellectual thief. His old car is owned by the finance company, he has no real friends and he must live by his wits. But he somehow manages to survive.

While living in role-playing Hollywood, spending most of his time with the self-created Sheilah and portraying the worst aspects of his own character in the Pat Hobby stories, Fitzgerald had another unsettling identity crisis. As early as 1924 he had told Perkins that he wished to discard his old image and establish a new literary identity with *The Great Gatsby:* "I'm tired of being the author of *This Side of Paradise* and I want to start over." He had said there was no "I" any more in "The Crack-Up," and written himself the strange, dissociated postcard while living at the Garden of Allah. In February 1940 he sent Arnold Gingrich (who took *everything* he wrote) another Pat Hobby story and, remembering Father Darcy in his first novel, urged him to "publish it under a pseudonym—say, John Darcy? I'm awfully tired of being Scott

Fitzgerald anyhow, as there doesn't seem to be so much money in it."
Though he did not want to be himself, it was extremely difficult to shed
his own identity and adopt another one.

In September 1939 Fitzgerald had sent Kenneth Littauer of *Collier's* magazine his plan for *The Last Tycoon,* and the editor had agreed
to pay up to thirty thousand dollars for serial rights if he approved the
first 15,000 words. Though he was sometimes interrupted by short
spells of film work, Fitzgerald now devoted most of his time to the
novel. Fiction allowed him to do what he could not do as a screenwriter: use his Hollywood experience, work without a supervisor or collaborator, retain complete control and do the kind of writing that best
suited his talents. But during the last year of his life he could work for
only a few hours at a time before becoming completely exhausted. His
secretary Frances Kroll recalled that "he wrote in bed, in longhand. . . .
Once the plan for a story or idea was clear in his mind, he wrote
rapidly. Although it took him several years to accumulate and coordinate notes for *The Last Tycoon,* the actual writing time of the unfinished novel was only four months."[15]

Monroe Stahr, the hero of *The Last Tycoon,* is closely modeled on
the gifted producer Irving Thalberg, whose successful films of the
1930s included *Grand Hotel, Mutiny on the Bounty* and *Camille.* Thalberg's charm, good looks, bountiful achievements and imminent
tragedy had fascinated Fitzgerald ever since their first meeting in 1927.
Like Thalberg, Stahr is Jewish, fairly short, attractive and of limited
education. He lives in a rented house, comes to the studio at 11 A.M.
and has a habit of tossing a coin in the air. Hard-working and loyal to
subordinates, he is also reserved and dignified; he never puts his name
on a film and is willing to take a loss on an experimental picture. Good
at establishing high morale among his employees, he also uses teams of
different writers working separately—and unknowingly—on the same
script. Stahr also has a damaged heart from a childhood bout of
rheumatic fever and does not have long to live.

Stahr's struggle for control of the studio with Pat Brady, an executive who is interested only in money, was based on Thalberg's dispute
with Louis Mayer, the most powerful man in Hollywood, about taking
protracted medical leave. While the sickly Thalberg was traveling in
Europe in 1933, Mayer suddenly relieved him of his duties as head of
production at MGM. Stahr's violent quarrel with the union leader

Brimmer was based on Thalberg's vehement and ultimately effective opposition to the Screen Writers Guild, which (like Brady) threatened his preeminence in the studio. "I never thought that I had more brains than a writer has," Stahr arrogantly tells Brimmer in the novel. "But I always thought that his brains *belonged* to me—because I knew how to use them."

When Thalberg died in 1936, leaving Fitzgerald free to write about him, Scott expressed his complex feelings about the man in a letter to Oscar Kalman. Fitzgerald had portrayed Thalberg's suspicion of his wife's infidelity in the love affair of Joel Coles and Stella Calman in "Crazy Sunday"; but he too had suspected Thalberg of ruining the prospects of a film based on his most recent novel: "Thalberg's final collapse is the death of an enemy for me, though I liked the guy enormously. He had an idea that his wife and I were playing around, which was absolute nonsense, but I think even so that he killed the idea of either [Miriam] Hopkins or Fredric March doing *Tender is the Night*."[16]

Stahr demonstrates his personal and intellectual superiority throughout *The Last Tycoon*. The airline pilot in the opening scene says he could teach him to fly in ten minutes. He shows qualities of heroism and leadership, and courageously cancels four inferior films. He teaches Boxley about screenwriting and relieves Roderiguez's fears of impotence; exhibits decisiveness and good taste when removing a director, Red Ridingwood, who has lost artistic control of a film, and shows compassionate interest in the health of Zavras, a Greek cameraman. Despite his potentially fatal heart disease, he drives himself mercilessly and sacrifices himself for the good of the studio. He is always in control of the situation, revealing a complete mastery of all the technical and artistic aspects of his films. Violently opposed to a screenwriters' union, Stahr confronts Brimmer. When their negotiations break down, he tries to punch him (Fitzgerald's method of settling disputes in real life) and is beaten up by Brimmer. Unlike the brutal film producer Joseph Bloeckman, who thrashes the drunken Anthony Patch in *The Beautiful and Damned*, Stahr is the kind of Jew who is "butchered" because he is "too wise."

Though Brady was based on Mayer (whom Fitzgerald disliked) and Brimmer was a Communist organizer (with whom he had little sympathy), neither of them was, as one might expect, portrayed as a Jew. Fitzgerald told Kenneth Littauer that he had also minimized Thalberg's

Jewishness and that "the racial angle shall scarcely be touched on at all." But he provides crucial information about the religious background of the stubborn and single-minded Stahr: "He was a rationalist who did his own reasoning without benefit of books—and had just managed to climb out of a thousand years of Jewry into the late eighteenth century." Intelligent and thoughtful, "he had an intense respect for learning, a racial memory of the old *schules*." An admiring director, noting the grandeur of Stahr's vision, deliberately rejects a deep-rooted stereotype and thinks: "He had worked with Jews too long to believe legends that they were small with money."

After forming friendships with many sympathetic and generous Jews in New York, Europe and Hollywood, Fitzgerald had rejected the anti-Semitism, endemic among middle-class white Americans, which he had learned during his youth in St. Paul.[17] The radical transformation in his personal attitude was clearly reflected in his novels, which moved from the extremely negative portraits of Joseph Bloeckman and the gangster Meyer Wolfsheim to an unbounded respect for Monroe Stahr, his most impressive and appealing fictional character. Fitzgerald strongly identified with Thalberg, who was torn between his emotional life and his professional career, and was also a sickly artist doomed to destruction by the materialistic power of Hollywood.

In *The Last Tycoon,* as in *Tender is the Night,* most of the characters were based, like Stahr and Brady, on real people. We have seen that the English screenwriter Boxley was modeled on Aldous Huxley, Stahr's English lover, Kathleen, on Sheilah Graham. Kathleen reminds Stahr of his dead wife, Minna, just as Sheilah reminded Scott of his insane wife, Zelda. Brady's daughter, Cecilia, who is hopelessly in love with Stahr, was a composite of Scottie (a Catholic student at Vassar, rather than at Bennington) and Budd Schulberg (who had grown up in Hollywood and had movie stars come to his birthday parties). The lovable Jane Meloney, who earns three thousand dollars a week and is married to an alcoholic husband who beats her, seems based on the highly paid and heavy-drinking Dorothy Parker, who had a tumultuous marriage to her much-younger co-author, Alan Campbell. Red Ridingwood, the incompetent director who is deftly fired by Stahr, seemed to be a retaliatory portrait of Joseph Mankiewicz. And Brimmer was probably a mixture of both Donald Ogden Stewart and Max Eastman, who were actively involved in Communist politics.

The novel opens as Cecilia Brady meets Monroe Stahr, along with the screenwriters Manny Schwartz and Wylie White, on a westward cross-country flight. During a forced stop in Nashville, Cecilia, White and Schwartz make a visit at dawn to Andrew Jackson's house, the Hermitage. Their inability to enter the locked house, or even to see it clearly, symbolizes the lamentable failure of the film industry to embody and represent the ideals and traditions of America.

Their strange visit to the Hermitage is a reprise of the disillusioning scene in *The Beautiful and Damned* in which Anthony and Gloria Patch visit, while on their honeymoon, Robert E. Lee's mansion in Arlington, Virginia. Fitzgerald probably chose the home of Jackson because he was a hero in the War of 1812, which had inspired Francis Scott Key's "The Star-Spangled Banner." Fitzgerald himself once made an unscheduled stop in Nashville during a stormy transcontinental flight. As he told Ober in February 1938: "We had a terrible trip back and the plane flew all over the South before it could buck through the winds up to Memphis, then it flew back and forth for three hours between Memphis and Nashville, trying to land."

This dangerous flight undoubtedly gave Fitzgerald premonitions of disaster. In "Crazy Sunday" Joel Coles sleeps with Stella Calman on the night that her husband Miles (a character also based on Thalberg) is killed in a plane crash on the way back to Hollywood. According to Fitzgerald's plan for the end of the novel, Stahr, on the way to New York to call off the murder of Brady, who had planned to murder *him*, is also killed in a plane crash. His personal possessions—his symbolic heritage—are salvaged from a mountain by a group of schoolchildren, who gradually learn to admire his achievements.

Stahr's tragic defeat in the projected plane crash at the end of *The Last Tycoon* was influenced by the plane crash at the end of André Malraux's *Man's Hope* (1938) and by its idealistic culminating scene, in which a procession of peasants expresses solidarity with the Loyalists by carrying the dead and wounded down the side of a mountain. Malraux, like Hemingway, spoke in Hollywood, while Fitzgerald was there, to raise money for the Spanish Loyalists. Fitzgerald owned a copy of *Man's Hope* and wrote notes about the sources of *The Great Gatsby* on the endpaper of Malraux's book.

In *Tender is the Night* Fitzgerald had made some shrewd comments about the movies, based on his observation of the careers of

Carmel Myers and Lois Moran. In *The Last Tycoon* he anatomizes the film industry more thoroughly and offers an oblique explanation of his own failure. Fitzgerald's Hollywood is dominated by the meretricious beauty of the film stars, by status and power, by crude toadyism and sexual corruption. In that rotten yet illusory atmosphere—which consistently destroys artistic integrity and moral identity—writers, struggling for a screen credit, are soon driven to alcohol. Self-betrayal is a dominant theme in both novels. The later book portrays the conflict between Stahr's self-consuming career in film and his courtship of Kathleen. During their romance she describes her "College of One" education with a previous lover and they make love in the half-finished movie set of a house he is building at Malibu. In the end Stahr cannot fully commit himself to her. He chooses to remain an artist, an enlightened despot and a tycoon, and she leaves him to marry another man.

The Last Tycoon has a strong love story and many dramatic incidents: Manny Schwartz's suicide, an earthquake and flood in the studio when Stahr first sees Kathleen floating on the head of the Goddess Shiva, Cecilia's discovery of a naked secretary hiding in her father's office, Stahr's fist fight with Brimmer and his fatal plane crash. Fitzgerald was therefore confident that *Collier's* would buy the serial rights and finance the completion of the novel. In November 1939, after planning the entire book and writing the first chapter, he sent 6,000 words instead of the promised 15,000 to *Collier's* and asked for an immediate decision. Littauer quite reasonably wired back: FIRST SIX THOUSAND PRETTY CRYPTIC THERFORE DISAPPOINTING. . . . CAN WE DEFER VERDICT UNTIL FURTHER DEVELOPMENT OF STORY?

Ober had warned the volatile Fitzgerald not to deal directly with editors. As shattered by this rejection as he had been by Ober's in July, Fitzgerald impulsively broke off negotiations instead of allowing Littauer to see more of his work. After throwing away the chance of substantial payment from *Collier's*, he could not sell serial rights to another magazine. He then went on a compensatory and self-punishing alcoholic binge, and had his most violent quarrel with Sheilah. *Collier's* rejection forced him back into occasional film work and once again delayed completion of *The Last Tycoon*. While struggling to finish the novel in October 1940, Fitzgerald, who had once thought "life was something you dominated," bitterly told Scottie: "life is essentially a cheat and its conditions are those of defeat."[18]

Fitzgerald wrote the first half of the novel before he died and left an outline for the rest. His notes show how the book came into being and comment on the part that was completed. Had he lived to finish it, the novel would have been much more polished and densely textured. But, like Hemingway's A *Moveable Feast*, Fitzgerald's last work proved that he retained his full creative powers and wrote some of his best fiction at the very end of his life. When *The Last Tycoon* appeared posthumously in October 1941, critics tried to atone for their neglect of Fitzgerald. J. Donald Adams in the *New York Times Book Review*, Fanny Butcher in the *Chicago Tribune*, Clifton Fadiman in the *New Yorker*, Margaret Marshall in the *Nation* and James Thurber in the *New Republic* all praised it as a major work, equal to *The Great Gatsby*, and called it the finest novel about Hollywood. Four years later the novelist J. F. Powers, in a perceptive essay, agreed that it "contained more of his best writing than anything he had ever done and Fitzgerald's best had always been the best there was."[19]

V

Fitzgerald's work on the novel was also delayed by bad health. After the trip to Cuba in April 1939 a lesion was discovered in one of his lungs and he had to spend the next two months in bed. In July he told Scottie that he not only had had a flare-up of tuberculosis, but he had also suffered another nervous breakdown that threatened to paralyze both arms. In fact, his arms got twisted in the bedclothes when he was drunk and his doctors, to scare him away from alcohol, threatened him with paralysis.

He was overcome by another imaginary illness in March 1940 when he was again flying across the country. He suddenly felt terribly sick, panicked and rather grandly asked the airline stewardess to wire for a doctor, nurse and ambulance to meet him at Tucson airport. By the time they landed, Fitzgerald had miraculously recovered and decided to remain on the plane. When pressed for payment by the Lusk Detective and Collection Agency, B. A. Budd, attorney-at-law, and Bring's Funeral Home, he candidly replied: "You can't get blood out of a stone." But he took the precaution of telling Perkins not to disclose his private address. "The claimant is, of all things, an undertaker," Scott explained, rather enjoying the ghoulish joke. "Not that I owe him for a corpse, but for an ambulance which he claims that I ordered. In any case he now writes me threatening to serve me with a summons and a complaint." Perkins was also instructed to say that he did not know if his wayward author was in New Orleans or at the North Pole.

But Fitzgerald's illness was not entirely fanciful. Like Monroe Stahr, he was perilously close to ambulances and funeral homes. When the playwright Clifford Odets saw him at Dorothy Parker's cocktail party in September 1940, he apprehensively noted: "Fitzgerald, pale, unhealthy, as if the tension of life had been wrenched out of him." Scott was taking potentially lethal doses of barbiturates and forty-eight drops of digitalis to keep his heart working overnight. But his medicine did not do much good. In late November 1940 he had his first heart attack in Schwab's drugstore. He almost fainted, and said that "everything started to fade."

After this attack he could no longer climb the stairs to his third-floor apartment on Laurel Avenue and moved into Sheilah's first-floor flat at 1443 North Hayworth Avenue, on the next street. He was glad to leave his place, which had an unnerving surrealistic element: a woman tenant, who performed professionally on radio, regularly practiced laughing and screaming. Fitzgerald settled into a sickbed routine, writing whenever he could; and told the California tax commissioner, who also failed to extract money from him: "life is one cardiogram after another, which is a pleasant change from X-rays."[20] In October 1940—remembering his father's heart disease and wondering if he was near the finish line—Scott had bravely told Zelda: "the constitution is an amazing thing and nothing quite kills it until the heart has run its entire race."

On December 20, after seeing a film with Sheilah, he had a second heart attack and just managed with her help to stagger out of the Pantages Theater. The following day, Saturday, December 21, at three o'clock in the afternoon, Fitzgerald suffered his third—and this time fatal—heart attack. He was in Sheilah's apartment, sitting in a green armchair, finishing a chocolate bar and making notes on an article in the *Princeton Alumni Weekly:* "An Analytical Long Range View of the 1940 Football Team." Suddenly, he started out of his chair as if jerked by a wire, clutched at the mantelpiece and fell silently to the floor. He lay on his back, breathing heavily. Sheilah summoned medical help, which arrived too late to save him.[21] Like Robert Louis Stevenson and D. H. Lawrence, Fitzgerald died at the age of forty-four.

His body was taken to the Wordsworth Room of Pierce Brothers Mortuary at 720 West Washington Boulevard, in a seedy part of downtown Los Angeles. Defaced by a cosmetic mortician, he had highly rouged cheeks and looked like a badly painted portrait. One of the few visitors recalled:

> Except for one bouquet of flowers and a few empty chairs, there was nothing to keep him company except his casket. . . . I never saw a sadder [scene] than the end of the father of all the sad young men. He was laid out to look like a cross between a floor-walker and a wax dummy. . . . But in technicolor. . . . His hands were horribly wrinkled and thin, the only proof left after death that for all the props of youth, he actually had suffered and died an old man.

When Fitzgerald heard of the death of his literary master, he had stood on a balcony overlooking the Mediterranean and mournfully repeated: "Conrad is dead!"[22] When Dorothy Parker saw Fitzgerald in the Los Angeles funeral home, she ironically quoted Owl-eyes' comment on Jay Gatsby and said: "The poor son-of-a-bitch."

Fanny Myers was shocked to hear that her friend Scottie had gone to the opera—probably to distract her from the tragedy—on the day her father died. Gerald Murphy reported, the day before the funeral, that the nineteen-year-old Scottie was distraught, that Zelda was devastated and that Sheilah would be tactfully excluded from the ceremony:

> Little Scottie is tragic and bewildered tho' she says that she has thought for so long that *every* day he would die for some reason. . . . Zelda seized upon his death as the only reality that had pierced the membrane since they separated . . . gave weird orders for the disposition of the body . . . then collapsed. She is not allowed to come to the funeral. . . . Sheilah Graham had wired that she wants to see us and she arrives by plane Saturday.

Fitzgerald's original will had requested a rather grand funeral in "accordance with my station." Later on, realizing he had no station, he crossed this phrase out and substituted "the cheapest possible funeral." Because he had not been a practicing Catholic, the authorities in Maryland—where Father Fay once had great pull with Cardinal Gibbons—would not permit, despite the urgent pleas of family and friends, a Catholic funeral service in St. Mary's Church in Rockville or burial next to his parents in his ancestral cemetery. Instead, an Episcopal service was conducted on December 27 by the Reverend Raymond Black in the Pumphrey Funeral Home in Bethesda. It was attended by about twenty people, including Scottie, cousin Cecilia Taylor and her four daughters from Norfolk, Scott's brother-in-law Newman Smith, Gerald and Sara Murphy, Max and Louise Perkins, Harold and Anne Ober, John and Anna Biggs, Ludlow Fowler (the best man at Scott's wedding) and the Turnbulls. Judge Biggs, a Princeton friend and sometime Scribner's novelist, resented Scott's success and said he had "the estate of a pauper and the will of a millionaire."[23] But his estate, mainly derived from his life insurance policy (since he had no assets and his royalties were then worth very little), came to $44,000 gross and about $32,000 after his debts had been paid.

In late December 1940 Zelda seemed to recover her lucidity, once again expressed her gratitude to Scott and paid tribute to his magnanimous character in two moving letters to Harold Ober and the Murphys:

He was as spiritually generous a soul as ever was. . . . In retrospect it seems as if he was always planning happinesses for Scottie, and for me. Books to read—places to go. Life seemed so promisory always when he was around: and I always believed that he could take care of anything.

I grieve for his brilliant talent, his faithful effort to keep me under the best of very expensive care and Scottie in school; his devotion to those that he felt were contributing to the aesthetic and spiritual purposes of life—and for his generous and vibrant soul that never spared itself, and never found anything too much trouble save the fundamentals of life itself.[24]

Fitzgerald could never decide where he wanted to live and had never bought a house. He seemed permanently torn between America

and Europe, St. Paul and Montgomery, city life in Manhattan and suburban life in Westport and Great Neck; between Wilmington and New
York, Baltimore and Asheville. Even in Los Angeles he drifted between
hotels, flats and houses in Hollywood, the Valley and the beach at Malibu. And, like Poe's heroines, he continued to move about after death.
In 1975 the Catholic authorities changed their minds. The bodies of
Scott and Zelda were then disinterred, and moved from Rockville
Union Cemetery to St. Mary's Church in the busy center of town. The
last line of *The Great Gatsby*—"So we beat on, boats against the current, borne back ceaselessly into the past"—was cut on their gravestone.

VI

Strongly influenced by "The Crack-Up," by Mok's damaging interview
and by Fitzgerald's alcoholism and declining reputation, the brief obitu-
aries ignored his achievements. They suggested that he had not fulfilled
his early promise, had faded out and been forgotten during the last
decade of his life. The rabidly Right-wing journalist Westbrook Pegler
was the nastiest of the lot. He declared that Fitzgerald had a malign
influence on the "queer brand of undisciplined and self-indulgent brats"
of the 1920s, and that this "cult of juvenile crying-drunks . . . seized
upon Fitzgerald's writing as an excuse to . . . flout every ordinance of
morality, responsibility, respectability and manhood."

Edmund Wilson, who had often scorned Scott during his lifetime,
was primarily responsible for reviving his reputation after he died. Just
after hearing about Scott's death, Wilson stressed, in a letter to Zelda,
his closeness to Fitzgerald, who seemed to represent an aspect of his
own character that had somehow failed to develop: "I feel myself as if I
had been suddenly robbed of some part of my own personality."
Deeply moved by Scott's death and perhaps remorseful that he had not
fully reciprocated his friendship and appreciated his genius, Wilson
attempted to make amends for his blindness and occasional cruelty by
becoming the guardian of Fitzgerald's posthumous reputation. In
February and March 1941 Wilson commissioned for the *New Republic*
critical essays on Fitzgerald by Dos Passos, Glenway Wescott, John
O'Hara and Budd Schulberg, and "The Hours," an elegy by John

Bishop. Wilson edited and supplied the title for *The Last Tycoon,* and compiled Fitzgerald's uncollected essays, notebooks and letters (more than half of them to Wilson) in *The Crack-Up* (1945).

Writing to Perkins in February 1941, Wilson ignored the portrayal of psychiatry in *Tender is the Night* and rather grudgingly conceded that *The Last Tycoon* was "the only one of Scott's books that shows any knowledge of any field of human activity outside of dissipation." His two-page Foreword called it "Fitzgerald's most mature piece of work" and "the best novel we have had about Hollywood." For Wilson, the unfinished work had almost the look of a classic. He thought Fitzgerald would "stand out as one of the first-rate figures in the American writing of the period." In a letter to Christian Gauss, who had known Scott as an undergraduate, Wilson praised the seriousness and technical skill of his last novel: "I think it would have been in some ways his best book—certainly his most mature. He had made some sort of new adjustment to life, and was working very hard at the time of his death. He had written the last pages the day before he died of a heart attack. In going through his MSS and notes, I was very much impressed to see what a conscientious artist he had become."[25] Wilson's reconstruction of Fitzgerald's notes, which suggested how the fragmentary novel would develop and conclude, was absolutely brilliant.

Wilson's editorial work on *The Crack-Up* was also extensive and important. He told Perkins that he had hated Fitzgerald's confessional essays (as he had originally disliked *The Beautiful and Damned*) when they first appeared in *Esquire* in 1936. They must have reminded him, in a menacing way, of his own alcoholism and nervous breakdown in 1929. But he admitted, after Fitzgerald's death, that "there was more truth and sincerity in it, I suppose, than we realized at the time." Perkins did not agree with this assessment, and the valuable and influential book was eventually brought out by New Directions. This volume included, in addition to Fitzgerald's work, admiring letters to him from Gertrude Stein, Edith Wharton, T. S. Eliot, Thomas Wolfe and John Dos Passos; essays by Dos Passos, Paul Rosenfeld and Glenway Wescott; and elegiac poems by Bishop and Wilson.

In his play *The Crime in the Whistler Room* (produced in 1924), Wilson had portrayed Fitzgerald as the brilliant but brash and unstable writer, Simon Delacy, who likes to speed in roadsters, impregnates a young lady and elopes with her. Wilson's elegy is a very different sort of work. Written in heroic couplets in Wellfleet on Cape Cod in February 1942, it was influenced by the description of the Atlantic gale in Yeats' "A Prayer for My Daughter." At the start of the poem Wilson mentions that he had edited his friend's work from the very beginning until the very end of Fitzgerald's literary career. His life's work, it seemed, was to correct that errant genius. Even in this memorial poem, however, Wilson portrays him in a narcissistic and degrading moment. At Princeton Wilson had once found him with

> Pale skin, hard green eyes, and yellow hair—
> Intently pinching out before a glass
> Some pimples left by parties at the Nass;
> Nor did [he] stop abashed, thus pocked and blotched,
> But kept on peering while I stood and watched.

The poem concludes more sympathetically by returning to the once-emerald and now-dead eyes of his lost friend:

> Those eyes struck dark, dissolving in a wrecked
> And darkened world, that gleam of intellect
> That spilled into the spectrum of tune, taste,
> Scent, color, living speech, is gone, is lost.

While preparing *The Crack-Up* Wilson, referring to Fitzgerald and Bishop, honestly told Christian Gauss: "I was more fortunate than either of them, not in gifts, but in the opportunity to survive."[26] But Wilson, who outlived Fitzgerald by thirty-two years, survived as a critic. Fitzgerald, with Wilson's ambivalent help, survived as an artist.

Fitzgerald would have taken melancholy pleasure in seeing his final—though posthumous—triumph as readers belatedly recognized the delicacy and depth in his work. Reviewing Wilson's edition of *The Last Tycoon* in 1941, Stephen Vincent Benét (a Yale friend of Gerald Murphy) had prophetically announced: "You can take your hats off now, gentlemen, and I think perhaps you had better. This is not a legend, this is a reputation—and, seen in perspective, it may well be one of the most secure reputations of our time." This judgment was fortified in John O'Hara's Introduction to *The Portable Fitzgerald*, edited by Dorothy Parker and published, a month after *The Crack-Up*, in September 1945.

In 1950 Budd Schulberg published *The Disenchanted*, his fictionalized version of the drunken Fitzgerald at Dartmouth. The novel
became a Broadway play and aroused considerable interest in Scott's
chaotic life. A crucial but little-noticed factor in the Fitzgerald revival
was the accidental death of Zelda in 1948, which allowed Arthur
Mizener to discuss her insanity in his biography, *The Far Side of Paradise* (1951). Edmund Wilson (like Hemingway) carried on an extensive correspondence with Mizener, correcting errors and putting forth
his own view of Fitzgerald. Though Wilson himself liked to draw attention to the discreditable aspects of Scott's life, he too was shocked by
Mizener's truthful revelations and delivered an unduly harsh judgment
to Gauss: "[Mizener] has assembled in a spirit absolutely ghoulish
everything discreditable or humiliating that ever happened to Scott."

Two other books appeared in 1951 to strengthen Fitzgerald's reputation: Malcolm Cowley's edition of twenty-eight of Scott's best stories and
Alfred Kazin's collection, *F. Scott Fitzgerald: The Man and His Work*,
which included thirty appreciative reviews and essays by the leading critics of the time. In 1958 Sheilah Graham brought out *Beloved Infidel*, the
first of her gossipy autobiographies, to satisfy the intense curiosity that
had been aroused by Schulberg and Mizener. The following year her
book was made into a tear-jerking film with Gregory Peck as the too-
classy Scott and Deborah Kerr as the far-too-refined Sheilah. Between
Afternoon of an Author in 1957 and *Poems* in 1981, nineteen other
posthumous collections were published by industrious if undiscriminat-
ing editors to meet the increasing demand for Fitzgerald's books.

We have noted the significant impact of "The Crack-Up" on Robert
Lowell and the American confessional poets. Fitzgerald's ability to create and exploit a negative public image influenced writers like Dylan
Thomas and Jack Kerouac. His influence has also been felt in the more
genteel novelistic tradition of manners and morals represented in the
novels of John O'Hara, John Marquand, John Cheever and John
Updike, who praised the "brilliant ease in [Fitzgerald's] prose, the
poignant grace glimmering off every page."[27] Fitzgerald's "The Swimmers," for example, had a clear impact on one of Cheever's best stories,
"The Swimmer" (1964). Cole Porter, who met Fitzgerald on the French
Riviera, lifted a phrase from the first sentence of "Absolution"—"in the
still of the night"—and in 1937 turned it into one of his best songs. The
persistent snow that fell in "The Dead" and drifted through "Babylon

Revisited" finally settled in J. F. Powers' superb story "Lions, Harts, Leaping Does" (1943). And Fitzgerald's negative portrayal of a Germanic priest from the Upper Midwest in "Absolution," and of Judy Jones' wild golf ball that strikes another player in "Winter Dreams," reappear in Powers' novel *Morte d'Urban,* which won the National Book Award in 1963. In 1989 the German playwright Peter Handke echoed Scott's title and dedicated *The Afternoon of a Writer* "To F. Scott Fitzgerald."

Fitzgerald inspired not only the rather limp elegies by Wilson and Bishop, but also (beginning early in his career) many sympathetic portraits in novels, plays and poems.[28] After his death five films (in addition to *Beloved Infidel*) were made from his works: *The Great Gatsby* with Alan Ladd and Betty Field in 1949; *The Last Time I Saw Paris,* loosely adapted from "Babylon Revisited," in 1954; *Tender is the Night* with Jason Robards and Jennifer Jones in 1962; *The Great Gatsby,* directed by Jack Clayton, with Robert Redford, Mia Farrow and Bruce Dern, in 1974; and—most disappointing—*The Last Tycoon,* directed by Elia Kazan from a leaden script by Harold Pinter, with Robert De Niro and Ingrid Boulting, in 1976. Scottie sold rights to the second *Great Gatsby* to Paramount for $350,000 and a percentage of the profits; and the Bantam paperback brought out in conjunction with the film was published in an edition of 1,450,000 copies. By 1980 *The Great Gatsby* (which had been dropped from the Modern Library for lack of interest during the 1930s) was selling at the rate of 300,000 copies a year and total sales of Fitzgerald's books had reached eight million. At the San Francisco Book Fair in February 1993, Fitzgerald's letters to his Baltimore secretary Isabel Owens, with detailed instructions about how to bring up Scottie, were being offered for $25,000—two and a half times his annual salary when he employed her.

Zelda received very little benefit from Scott's astonishing posthumous success. From the mid-1930s she was possessed by religious mania. She carried a Bible around with her and would suddenly kneel in public places to repeat her prayers. The once-dazzling beauty, who had conquered New York in 1920, returned to Montgomery in a broken and pitiful state, and would wander the streets (as Scott's mother had once done) in a long black dress and a tattered floppy hat. In 1947 she sadly told her sister: "I have tried so hard and prayed so earnestly and faithfully asking God to help me, I cannot understand why He leaves me in suffering."

Zelda continued to wander in the borderlands between hysteria and insanity. When she felt the onset of madness—in August 1943, early 1946 and again in November 1947—she retreated to Highland for half a year at a time and endured yet another series of insulin shock treatments. She had always been obsessed by fire. After predicting the damnation of many of her sinful friends during her phases of religious mania, she herself met an apocalyptic ending.

On March 10, 1948, two years after Dr. Carroll had retired as director of Highland, a fire flared up at midnight in the kitchen of the Central Building. It quickly spread through the dumbwaiter shaft and down the corridors of the top floor, where Zelda was sleeping. The hospital had no fire alarm or sprinkler system, and the external wooden fire escapes soon burned up.

Dr. Irving Pine, who had been treating her, stated that "had she not been asleep, Zelda ought to have been well enough to have escaped and walked away from the top floor where she was trapped in the fatal fire." But the *New York Herald Tribune* of March 12, 1948, reported that she could not escape because she was locked in: "six patients were trapped on the fourth floor. Chains and padlocks prevented the windows from being opened far enough for patients to escape."[29] Zelda died with eight other women (out of twenty-nine patients in the hospital) and was identified only by a charred slipper lying beneath her equally charred body. Her mother, who lived until the age of ninety-eight, died ten years later. The house at 819 Felder Avenue in Montgomery, where Scott and Zelda lived in 1931–32, is now the Fitzgerald Museum.

Despite her unstable childhood and the tragic deaths of her parents, Scottie turned out to be surprisingly well adjusted. In February 1943 she married a handsome young naval officer, Samuel Jackson Lanahan, who came from a wealthy Baltimore family. Zelda (though not in Highland) did not attend the wedding, which was organized by Anne Ober, and Harold gave away the bride. Scottie had her first story, "A Wonderful Time," accepted by the *New Yorker* when she was only eighteen and published on October 19, 1940. After graduating from Vassar, she worked for the *New Yorker* from 1944 to 1948, and made her career as a professional journalist. She was a researcher for *Time*, a publicist for the Radio City Music Hall, a journalist in New York and Washington for the *Reporter*, the *Democratic Digest* and the *Northern*

Virginia Sun, and in the 1960s wrote for the society page of the *Washington Post* and *New York Times.*

Brendan Gill, who knew her when she was a reporter for the *New Yorker,* suggested that Fitzgerald had done a fine job in bringing up Scottie. She had none of her parents' faults and a great deal of their charm: "She was a small, fine-boned, good-looking young woman, exceptional in energy and in her sunny good nature—none of the series of misfortunes that dogged her parents appeared to have cast the least shadow over her."

The biographer Meryle Secrest knew Scottie twenty years later when they both worked for the *Washington Post.* She described Scottie as a petite woman with a trim figure and small, regular features. An entirely conventional woman, she was not interested in journalists or artists. She wanted to be part of Georgetown culture, was passionately involved with fund-raising for the Democratic party and was acquainted with leading political figures like Adlai Stevenson and the Kennedys. Lanahan, Secrest said, was a large, square-jawed man with heavy, rough-cut features. He and Scottie seemed friendly, relaxed and happy with each other at their fashionable parties.

The Lanahans had four children in rapid succession. Their eldest son, Timothy, born in 1946, went to Princeton and died, apparently a suicide, in Hawaii. Eleanor, born in 1948, is divorced and lives in Vermont. Cecilia is married and lives in Pennsylvania. And Jack junior has a computer firm in Oregon. Scottie later divorced Lanahan, was disappointed by a man she loved and had another affair with a well-known cartoonist. She then married Grove Smith, "a sweet, supportive man, also very interested in politics."[30] But she left Grove Smith and moved from Washington to Montgomery in 1973—mainly to care for her aunt (and Fitzgerald's great enemy) Rosalind Sayre Smith—and divorced her second husband in 1980. Six years later the generous and much-loved Scottie died in Montgomery of cancer of the esophagus and was buried next to her parents.

Sheilah had the most extraordinary career of all. In 1941 she married a rather dull Englishman, Trevor Westbrook, who was head of aviation production in Churchill's wartime government. She had a daughter, Wendy, a teacher at Brooklyn College, and a son, Robert, a writer. After divorcing Westbrook, Sheilah had an equally unsuccessful third marriage in the 1950s to W. S. Wojkiewicz, a much younger man who was a boys' football coach. She exploited her affair with Fitzgerald to the fullest possible extent, and eventually had a syndicated gossip column, a radio program and a television show. She outlived Scottie by two years, and died rich and famous in Florida in 1988. Four years later her daughter published a soppy autobiography, *One of the Family*, which corrected some of the mythologizing of *Beloved Infidel* and revealed that Wendy was the illegitimate daughter of the Oxford philosopher A. J. Ayer, with whom Sheilah had an unlikely affair a few months after Scott's death.

Fitzgerald's short life was in many ways a tragic one. He was a legend in his own time, famous for his youth and talent. His early novels, with their sad young men and beautiful young women eager to risk ruin in order to live intensely, were enormously popular. He and Zelda epitomized and publicized a particular era, and were the first literary couple to be glamorous in an egoistic way.

His greatest work shows what happens to people who pursue illusory American dreams, and how society (which they have rejected) fails to sustain them in their desperate hour. *The Great Gatsby* embodies the failure of romantic idealism, while *Tender is the Night* intimately reveals how this apparently perfect American couple plunged into estrangement, mental illness and alcoholism. In both these novels the hero achieves a great deal. But he also loses the individual qualities that defined him at the beginning of the book and ends, as he lived, essentially alone. In "Babylon Revisited," "Crazy Sunday" and "The Crack-Up" Fitzgerald courageously explored and revealed his own character. He has left us, not a glamorous legend, but a vivid record of self-examination.

He deserved greater recognition than he received in his last years, but he did not become bitter about his fate. He remained loyal to Zelda, writing her weekly letters until his death. He did everything he could to care for his wife and daughter, while he led a modest existence, and died doing what he knew how to do best—writing a novel. *The Last Tycoon*, even in its unfinished state, examines the essential problem of his life: the struggle to achieve artistic integrity.

Fitzgerald had, as Raymond Chandler observed, "one of the rarest qualities in all literature . . . charm as Keats would have used it. . . . It's a kind of subdued magic, controlled and exquisite." The magic of his prose surely derived from the magic of his personality, which so many of his friends described and admired. This image of Fitzgerald's charm—and of his heroic struggle against adversity—outlasts the catalogue of ills and frustrations that marked the last decade of his life. His old friend Alice Toklas, summarizing his life in one perceptive sentence, called him "the most sensitive . . . the most distinguished—the most gifted and intelligent of all his contemporaries. And the most lovable—he is one of those great tragic American figures."[31]

Appendix I

POE AND FITZGERALD

Fitzgerald was influenced not only by Poe's literary works, but also by a keen awareness of the parallels between Poe's life and his own. Both men were the same height and weight: five feet eight inches and 140 pounds. Both had eminent ancestors: Poe's grandfather was a quartermaster in the Revolutionary Army, Fitzgerald was descended from Francis Scott Key. But since Poe's father was an alcoholic actor and Fitzgerald's father a pathetic failure, the writers, uneasy about their dubious social status, were attracted to old families and envied solid wealth. Both emphasized the dark side of their character by falsely claiming to be descended from the Revolutionary War traitor, Benedict Arnold. Though Poe was born in Boston and Fitzgerald in St. Paul, they associated themselves with the Southern gentility and courtly manners of Virginia (where Poe grew up) and of Maryland (where Fitzgerald's father was raised). Poe left the University of Virginia, as Fitzgerald left Princeton, without graduating. After serving as an enlisted man, Poe was expelled from West Point; Fitzgerald had an undistinguished career in American military camps and never crossed the ocean to fight in the European war.

Fitzgerald strongly identified with the histrionic personality of Poe, whose tragic life initiated the pattern of the self-destructive American writer that Fitzgerald was to follow. In *This Side of Paradise*, Amory Blaine reads "The Fall of the House of Usher" and "used to go for far walks by himself—and wander along reciting 'Ulalume' to the cornfields, and congratulating Poe for drinking himself to death in that atmosphere of smiling complacency." Both men were alcoholics who became drunk after only one or two glasses, often lost control of themselves, and acted in an abject and humiliating manner. Like Poe, Fitzgerald sometimes drank for a week at a time, was jailed for drunkenness and sobered up in towns like Brussels without any idea of how he had got there. Francis Melarky, the hero of *Our Type*, an early version of *Tender is the Night*, suggests a modern counterpart of the myth of Edgar Poe. A Southerner who had been dismissed from West Point, Melarky later gets into a drunken brawl and falls into habits of waste and dissipation.

Though the pattern of Poe's life was tragic, Fitzgerald was proud of their similarities. When he visited Baltimore in September 1935, he found the decadent city warm and pleasant, and nostalgically wrote: "I love it more than I thought—it is so rich with memories—it is nice to look up the street and see the statue of my great uncle and to know Poe is buried here and that many ancestors of mine have walked in the old town by the bay. I belong here, where everything is civilized and gay and rotted and polite."

Both men proposed to their beloved in a cemetery and had tragic marriages. Virginia Poe died of tuberculosis at the age of twenty-four; Zelda Fitzgerald became insane when she was twenty-nine. Fitzgerald tutored his mistress Sheilah Graham just as Poe had tutored Virginia. Both men wasted their artistic talent as hack writers for popular magazines, yet were desperately short of money and frequently had to borrow from their friends. Poe ruined his chances by offending influential literary editors just as Fitzgerald did with powerful film producers. Both attempted suicide, and pleaded with women to save them from their self-destructive impulses. Both authors suffered from hypoglycemia, which made it difficult to metabolize alcohol, died from the effects of drink and were buried in the state of Maryland. Their reckless personal life damaged their literary reputations, and their work was not revived until many years after their deaths.

Fitzgerald's identification with Poe was strengthened during his own decline in the 1930s by his friendship with the lawyer Edgar Allan Poe, Jr., who was a collateral descendant of the writer and had been at Princeton with Fitzgerald. Early in 1937 Fitzgerald mentioned the lawyer's name to a friend and then exclaimed: "Conceive of that—Edgar Allan Poe and Francis Scott Key, the two Baltimore poets a hundred years after!"

Appendix II

Zelda's Illness

First breakdown:

April 23–May 2, 1930 (ten days). Malmaison Hospital, west of Paris. Treated by Professor Claude. Discharged herself against the doctor's wishes.

May 22–June 4, 1930 (two weeks). Valmont Clinic, Glion, above Montreux, in Switzerland. Dr. H. A. Trutman. Transferred from a hospital that treated physical disease to a psychiatric clinic.

June 4, 1930–September 15, 1931 (15½ months). Les Rives des Prangins Clinic, Nyon, fourteen miles north of Geneva, in Switzerland. Dr. Oscar Forel. Apparently well enough to be discharged by the hospital.

Second breakdown:

February 12–June 26, 1932 (4½ months). Henry Phipps Psychiatric Clinic of Johns Hopkins University Hospital, Baltimore. Dr. Adolf

Meyer, Dr. Mildred Squires and Dr. Thomas Rennie. Apparently recovered and discharged.

Third breakdown:

February 12–March 8, 1934 (one month). Phipps Clinic. Dr. Thomas Rennie. Made no progress and transferred to a rural clinic (like Prangins) on the recommendation of Dr. Forel.

March 8–May 19, 1934 (2½ months). Craig House Hospital, Beacon, New York, on the Hudson River above West Point. Dr. Clarence Slocum. Became catatonic and transferred to another clinic for a different kind of treatment.

May 19, 1934–April 7, 1936 (two years). Sheppard and Enoch Pratt Hospital, Towson, Maryland, outside Baltimore. Dr. William Elgin. Transferred to Highland after making no progress, when Fitzgerald moved to Asheville.

April 8, 1936–April 13, 1940 (four years). Highland Hospital, Asheville, North Carolina. Dr. Robert Carroll. Apparently recovered and discharged to live with her mother in Montgomery.

Readmissions to Highland Hospital:

August 1943–February 1944 (six months). Apparently recovered and discharged to mother.

Early 1946–late summer 1946 (eight months). Apparently recovered and discharged to mother.

November 2, 1947–March 10, 1948 (four months). Died, while locked in her room, in a hospital fire.

Appendix III

THE QUEST FOR BIJOU O'CONOR

In 1975 an eccentric old lady who lived near Brighton with a Pekinese gave a taped interview about her affair in 1930 with Scott Fitzgerald. Recent Fitzgerald biographers have mentioned the evocatively named Bijou O'Conor and quoted bits from her tape, but no one had discovered anything significant about her background, appearance or character. The husky, upperclass voice intrigued me, and I wondered what had brought them together and how Fitzgerald fitted into *Bijou's* life. Happening to be in London during the summer of 1992, I tried to find out more about her. As I have often discovered, someone who seems utterly obscure, dead and forgotten can be brought to life once you tap into the institutions that survive her: in this case, her family, an Oxford college, the Foreign Office.

I began with the *Who's Who* entry of Bijou's father, Sir Francis Elliot (1851–1940). A grandson of the second Earl of Minto, he rowed for Balliol College, entered the diplomatic service, and served as consul general in Sofia from 1895 to 1903 and as Minister in Athens from 1903 to 1917. I thought I would try telephoning the present Earl of

Minto, whom I imagined pacing the armor-lined corridors of his crum-
bling castle in the Highlands. Instead of the servant I had expected, the
Earl himself answered the telephone. Though he had not heard of
Bijou, his curiosity was aroused by my questions about his family. He
spoke to me for a leisurely twenty minutes and shrewdly suggested various lines of inquiry.

Following the Earl's advice, I wrote to the records department of
the British Foreign Office, which sent me the address of Bijou's niece
in Exeter. *Debrett's Peerage* provided the address of the Honourable
Mary Alington Marten, O.B.E., the daughter of Bijou's friend Napier
Alington. But Mary Alington was only eleven years old when her father
died and knew nothing about Bijou. William Furlong, who conducted
the taped interview with Bijou, had heard about her by chance through
a mutual friend in Hove, near Brighton. He characterized her as a mysterious and rather ruthless woman, who responded to male attention
and seemed genuinely concerned about the welfare of Scottie Fitzgerald. Furlong promised to look through the original transcripts and to
send me any new material he could find.

My first breakthrough came from Claire Eaglestone of Balliol College, who was intrigued by my query about Sir Francis and, putting my
letter on the top of her correspondence, rang me up at once. Though
Sir Francis had no sons, his grandson had (as I suspected) gone to his
old college. Captain William Elliot-Young (1910–42) had been killed in
the war, but his son, the tenth baronet, Sir William Neil Young, now
lived in London. When he did not answer my letter (which had been
forwarded to his new home in Edinburgh), I rang him up at the Saudi
International Bank. They told me he had moved to Coutts Bank, which
put me right through to him.

Sir William was in the midst of his work but, like the Earl of Minto,
was fascinated by his great-aunt and disposed to chat about her. He
described her extravagance, her alcoholism, her mythomania—and her
wooden leg. Most importantly, he put me in touch with Gillian Plazzota, the former wife of Bijou's son. Mrs. Plazzota told me more about
Bijou's striking appearance and bohemian character, and about Bijou's
son, Michael O'Conor. She gave me his phone number, but suggested I
"be gentle with him, and ask about photographs and letters before
requesting information about Bijou."

Though slightly suspicious at first, Michael O'Conor—curious about why I was so interested in Bijou, amused by the circuitous trail I had followed to find him, and eager to hear what I knew about Bijou and Fitzgerald—agreed to see me the following morning in Surrey. He had been educated at Radley and Oxford, become a petroleum engineer and worked for the Kuwait Oil Company and for Shell in Venezuela. Many of the oil wells he had built and supervised had recently been destroyed in the Gulf War. He showed me a photograph of Bijou's Pekinese, a pet he had inherited on her death, but, significantly enough, he did not have one of his mother. Michael said that the most serious of Bijou's numerous lovers was a Russian photographer, Vladimir Molokhovets (the spelling is uncertain), who had a studio on Wilton Street in Belgravia. Hoping his family might have letters from or a photograph of Bijou, I searched for him in reference books and rang up the photographic department of the National Portrait Gallery, but was unable to find any trace of him.

When I rang Sir William the following day to thank him for his help and ask whether he had a photo of Bijou, he promised to send me one and also suggested I see her first cousin, the elderly Edwardian gentleman Sir Brinsley Ford, a distinguished art historian and trustee of the National Gallery. Sir Brinsley told me family stories and personal memories of Bijou. At one point in our interview his attractive granddaughter made a dramatic appearance and kissed his bald dome in greeting. She was delighted to learn that her distant cousin had been Fitzgerald's mistress and that her highly respectable family included an eccentric rebel.

The conversations with Michael O'Conor, Sir Brinsley Ford and Sir William Young enabled me to reconstruct Bijou's life before she met Fitzgerald as well as to follow her strange career after their affair had ended. Sir Francis Elliot, Napier Alington and Fitzgerald all died in 1940. Most of Bijou's possessions—including her Picasso drawings and the letters Fitzgerald wrote to her in the early 1930s—had been stored in Druce's furniture warehouse when her father returned from France in 1936 and were destroyed during the London Blitz in 1940. After transport routes had suddenly been changed during the Blitz, Bijou was knocked down one dark night by a bus. Her leg had to be amputated and she was fitted with a wooden one. When she sued London Transport for reckless driving, their lawyer enraged the judge (who later became Lord Denning) by claiming she had suffered "a trifling injury," and she was awarded substantial damages, which supported her for many years. One of her *louche* friends once persuaded her to smuggle contraceptives into Ireland in the hollow of her artificial leg.

During the war Bijou—a notoriously indiscreet but highly gifted linguist in French, Russian, Polish, Greek and Chinese—worked for the Russian Department of military intelligence at the War Office in Northumberland Street, off Trafalgar Square. She became a great friend of Major-General Sir Guy Glover and of Major-General Edward Spears (whose wife, the novelist Mary Borden, had been Wyndham Lewis' mistress before her marriage).

Bijou resumed her luxurious but parasitic life in Monaco in the late 1940s and early 1950s. At the end of that decade she spent several uneasy months with Michael, who had scarcely known his mother, at his home in Nottinghamshire. She planned but never wrote her autobiography, to be called *Interlude in Attica*. After living alone at 88 Eccleston Square near Victoria Station, she finally settled into a near-penniless existence with a circle of old-age pensioners in Hove, where she died, shortly after the taped interview was made, in the fall of 1975.

Christopher Clairmonte, who painted two portraits of the elderly Bijou, recalled the squalid end of her adventurous life in the *Sunday Times Magazine* of July 3, 1983: "She was nearly blind, and had an artificial leg as a result of an accident, so there was not a lot she could do for herself. We turned back a rug, and found it was a heaving mass of insects, so we took it straight out and dumped it in a skip. The place was a mass of dog messes because her Peke—she always had Pekes and adored them—hadn't been able to get out regularly."

Despite her brief appearance in Fitzgerald's life, Bijou was more important to Scott than he was to her. Though he reacted against her arrogant attitude and reckless way of life, and satirized her in his fiction, he desperately needed her companionship and enjoyed her wit and charm. Fitzgerald was one of Bijou's more interesting lovers. She recognized herself in his works, made him the subject of her own amusing stories and survived to have the last word about their affair.

Notes

Chapter One: St. Paul and the Newman School

1. F. Scott Fitzgerald, *Notebooks,* ed. Matthew Bruccoli (New York, 1978), pp. 267–268; Grace Flandrau, "The Untamable Twin," *The Taming of the Frontier,* ed. Duncan Aikman (New York, 1925), p. 149; Matthew Josephson, *The Robber Barons: The Great American Capitalists, 1861–1901* (New York, 1934), p. 236.

2. F. Scott Fitzgerald, *This Side of Paradise* (1920; New York, 1948), pp. 219, 273; F. Scott Fitzgerald, "Absolution," *Short Stories,* ed. Matthew Bruccoli (New York, 1989), p. 264; F. Scott Fitzgerald, *The Great Gatsby* (1925; New York, 1953), p. 169. For works on Hill, see William Cunningham, "Hill, James Jerome," *Dictionary of American Biography,* ed. Dumas Malone (New York, 1932), 9:36–41, and Albro Martin, *James J. Hill and the Opening of the Northwest* (Oxford, 1976).

3. F. Scott Fitzgerald, *Letters,* ed. Andrew Turnbull (1963; London, 1968), p. 522; Sheilah Graham, *The Real Scott Fitzgerald* (New York, 1976), p. 34; Andrew Turnbull, *Scott Fitzgerald* (1962; London, 1970), p. 34.

4. F. Scott Fitzgerald, *Tender is the Night* (1934; New York,

1962), p. 203; F. Scott Fitzgerald, "Author's House," *Afternoon of an Author,* Introduction and notes by Arthur Mizener (New York, 1957), p. 184; Letter from Dr. M. R. Ramsey to James Hill of Boston, February 11, 1964, Firestone Library, Princeton University.

5. F. Scott Fitzgerald, *Ledger: A Facsimile,* Introduction by Matthew Bruccoli (Washington, D.C., 1972), p. 157; F. Scott Fitzgerald, *Correspondence,* ed. Matthew Bruccoli and Margaret Duggan (New York, 1980), p. 4; Fitzgerald, *Letters,* p. 469.

6. Fitzgerald, *Letters,* p. 554; F. Scott Fitzgerald, "An Author's Mother" (1936), *The Price Was High: The Last Uncollected Stories,* ed. Matthew Bruccoli (London, 1979), pp. 736–737; *Dear Scott/Dear Max: The Fitzgerald-Perkins Correspondence,* ed. John Kuehl and Jackson Bryer (London, 1971), p. 135; F. Scott Fitzgerald, "The Death of My Father," *Princeton University Library Chronicle,* 12 (Summer 1951), 187–188. An earlier draft of this important essay was published in *The Apprentice Fiction of F. Scott Fitzgerald,* ed. John Kuehl (New York, 1965), pp. 177–182, and a later version was fictionalized in *Tender is the Night,* pp. 203–204.

7. Fitzgerald, *Correspondence,* p. 5; F. Scott Fitzgerald, *In His Own Time,* ed. Matthew Bruccoli and Jackson Bryer (1971; New York, 1974), p. 296; Arthur Miller, *Death of a Salesman* (New York, 1949), p. 56.

Robert Lowell's father, who was fired from Lever Brothers as Edward had been sacked from Procter & Gamble, was also plagued by failure but managed to live well on his navy pension and wife's money. See Robert Lowell, "Commander Lowell," *Life Studies* (New York, 1959), p. 71:

> With seamanlike celerity
> Father left the Navy,
> and deeded Mother his property.
>
> He was soon fired. Year after year,
> he still hummed "Anchors aweigh" in the tub—
> whenever he left a job,
> he bought a smarter car.
> Father's last employer
> was Scudder, Stevens & Clark, Investment Advisors,
> himself his only client.

8. F. Scott Fitzgerald, "That Kind of Party," *The Basil and Josephine Stories*, ed. with an introduction by Jackson Bryer and John Kuehl (New York, 1973), p. 1; Fitzgerald, *Letters*, p. 19; Fitzgerald, *Correspondence*, p. 398; Quoted in Matthew Bruccoli, *Some Sort of Epic Grandeur: The Life of F. Scott Fitzgerald* (New York, 1981), p. 375.

9. F. Scott Fitzgerald, "The Scandal Detectives," *Taps at Reveille* (1935; New York, 1988), p. 7; Fitzgerald, *This Side of Paradise*, p. 14.

10. Shane Leslie, "Some Memories of Scott Fitzgerald," *Times Literary Supplement*, October 31, 1958, p. 632; Graham, *Real Scott Fitzgerald*, p. 36; Fitzgerald, "Who's Who—and Why," *Afternoon of an Author*, p. 83.

11. Quoted in Turnbull, *Scott Fitzgerald*, p. 50; Fitzgerald, *In His Own Time*, p. 234.

12. Fitzgerald, "One Hundred False Starts," *Afternoon of an Author*, p. 134; Fitzgerald, *Ledger*, pp. 155, 157, 158; B. F. Wilson, "Notes on Personalities IV—F. Scott Fitzgerald," *Smart Set*, 73 (April 1924), 31.

13. Interview with Frances Kroll Ring, Beverly Hills, California, December 21, 1991; Tony Buttitta, *The Lost Summer: A Personal Memoir of F. Scott Fitzgerald* (1972; New York, 1987), pp. 41, 112–113.

14. Fitzgerald, *This Side of Paradise*, pp. 113–114; Fitzgerald, *Correspondence*, p. 41. In "Crazy Sunday," Fitzgerald describes Miles Calman as "artist from the top of his curiously shaped head to his niggerish feet" (Fitzgerald, *Short Stories*, p. 704).

15. Fitzgerald, "The Freshest Boy," *Taps at Reveille*, p. 25; Fitzgerald, *The Romantic Egoist* (an early version of *This Side of Paradise*), quoted in Turnbull, *Scott Fitzgerald*, p. 41; Quoted in Arthur Mizener, *The Far Side of Paradise: A Biography of F. Scott Fitzgerald*, revised edition (Boston, 1965), pp. 23–24.

16. Letter from Charles "Sap" Donahoe to Arthur Mizener, January 10, 1948, Princeton; Fitzgerald, "The Freshest Boy," *Taps at Reveille*, pp. 26, 30, 46; Fitzgerald, *The Great Gatsby*, pp. 176–177.

17. Joseph G. H. Barry, *Impressions and Opinions* (New York, 1931), p. 245; Margaret Chanler, *Autumn in the Valley* (Boston, 1936), p. 80; Henry Dan Piper, *F. Scott Fitzgerald: A Critical Portrait* (New York, 1965), p. 47.

18. Fitzgerald, *This Side of Paradise*, p. 24. In *The Great Gatsby*,

Jordan Baker's aunt is named Mrs. *Sigourney* Howard and Daisy's maiden name is Fay.

Three years after Fay's death, five of his sermons and fifteen of his conventional religious poems, which explain his conversion to Catholicism, were published, with an anonymous biographical Foreword and an Introduction by Cardinal Gibbons, as *The Bride of the Lamb and Other Essays* (New York, 1922). For more on Fay, see Rev. R. C. Nevius, "A Note on F. Scott Fitzgerald's Monsignor Sigourney Fay and His Early Career as an Episcopalian," *Fitzgerald–Hemingway Annual,* 3 (1971), 105–113.

19. Letters from Shane Leslie to Fitzgerald, September 8, 1918 and January 23, 1919, Princeton; Fitzgerald, *In Our Own Time,* p. 134. For more on Leslie, see his lively autobiography, *Long Shadows* (London, 1966).

Chapter Two: Princeton

1. Quoted in Scott Donaldson, *Archibald MacLeish: An American Life* (Boston, 1992), p. 52; Fitzgerald, *This Side of Paradise,* p. 36; Fitzgerald, "Who's Who—and Why," *Afternoon of an Author,* p. 84.

2. Fitzgerald, "Princeton," *Afternoon of an Author,* p. 72; F. Scott Fitzgerald, *As Ever, Scott Fitz: Letters Between F. Scott Fitzgerald and His Literary Agent, Harold Ober, 1919–1940,* ed. Matthew Bruccoli and Jennifer Atkinson (Philadelphia, 1972), p. 357.

3. Fitzgerald, "Princeton," *Afternoon of an Author,* p. 75; Fitzgerald, *Letters,* p. 104. See also Alfred Noyes, "Princeton Days," *Two Worlds for Memory* (Philadelphia, 1953), pp. 98–103.

4. Quoted in Bruccoli, *Some Sort of Epic Grandeur,* p. 68; Letter from an unidentified English professor to Arthur Mizener, January 28, 1951, Princeton; Christian Gauss, "Edmund Wilson: The Campus and the *Nassau Lit.*," *Princeton University Library Chronicle,* 5 (February 1944), 49.

5. Gauss, *Princeton University Library Chronicle,* p. 50; Fitzgerald, *This Side of Paradise,* p. 50; Quoted in Robert White, *John Peale Bishop* (New York, 1966), p. 25.

6. Fitzgerald, *In His Own Time,* p. 269; Letter from Cornelius

Van Ness to Henry Dan Piper, May 25, 1947, Morris Library, Southern Illinois University, Carbondale; Letter from Whitney Landon to Jeffrey Meyers, January 12, 1992.

7. Fitzgerald, *Letters*, p. 85; Mizener, *The Far Side of Paradise*, p. 34; Fitzgerald, *This Side of Paradise*, p. 44.

8. Fitzgerald, *Notebooks*, p. 205; Fitzgerald, *This Side of Paradise*, p. 63; Fitzgerald, *Correspondence*, pp. 15–17.

9. Quoted in Elizabeth Friskey, "Visiting the Golden Girl," *Princeton Alumni Weekly*, 75 (October 8, 1974), 10–11; Letter from Ginevra King Pirie to Arthur Mizener, December 4, 1947, Princeton.

10. Letter from Ginevra King Pirie to Henry Dan Piper, May 12, 1946, Southern Illinois University; Letters from Ginevra King Pirie to Arthur Mizener, November 7, 1947 and January 14, 1958, Princeton; Telephone conversation with Richard Lehan, February 19, 1992, based on his interviews with Ginevra King Pirie and her sister Marjorie Beldon.

11. Fitzgerald, *Letters*, p. 34; William Butler Yeats, "The Tower," *Collected Poems*, Definitive Edition (New York, 1956), p. 195.

12. Fitzgerald, *This Side of Paradise*, p. 184; Fitzgerald, "Basil and Cleopatra," *Afternoon of an Author*, p. 59; Letter from Ginevra King Pirie to Henry Dan Piper, May 12, 1946, Southern Illinois University; Fitzgerald, *The Great Gatsby*, pp. 120, 9.

13. Fitzgerald, *In His Own Time*, p. 171; Fitzgerald, *Letters*, p. 482; *The Romantic Egoists: Scott and Zelda Fitzgerald*, ed. Matthew Bruccoli, Scottie Fitzgerald Smith and Joan Kerr (New York, 1974), p. 29.

14. F. Scott Fitzgerald, "Handle With Care," *The Crack-Up*, ed. Edmund Wilson (New York, 1945), p. 76; Edmund Wilson, *A Prelude* (New York, 1967), p. 148.

15. Mizener, *The Far Side of Paradise*; Fitzgerald, *Ledger*, p. 170; Glenway Wescott, in Fitzgerald, *The Crack-Up*, p. 329.

Chapter Three: The Army and Zelda

1. Fitzgerald, *This Side of Paradise*, p. 55; Fitzgerald, *Letters*, pp. 434, 471; Stephen Ambrose, *Eisenhower* (New York, 1983), p. 61.

2. Fitzgerald, "Who's Who—and Why," *Afternoon of an Author*,

p. 84; Quoted in *Living Authors*, ed. Stanley Kunitz (New York, 1931), p. 128.

3. Quoted in Roger Burlingame, *Of Making Many Books* (New York, 1946), p. 48; Fitzgerald, *Correspondence*, p. 31.

4. Letter from Devereux Josephs to Henry Dan Piper, May 1, 1947, Southern Illinois University; Quoted in Mizener, *The Far Side of Paradise*, p. 84; Alonzo Myers, "Lieutenant F. Scott Fitzgerald, United States Army," *Papers on Language and Literature*, 1 (Spring 1965), 174, 171.

5. Fitzgerald, *The Crack-Up*, pp. 85, 70; Quoted in James Drawbell, *An Autobiography* (New York, 1963), p. 176.

6. Fitzgerald, *Correspondence*, p. 24 and Letter from Father Sigourney Fay to Fitzgerald, June 13, 1918, Princeton; Fitzgerald, *Correspondence*, p. 20.

7. Letter from Father Sigourney Fay to Fitzgerald, June 6, 1918, Princeton; Fitzgerald, *Correspondence*, pp. 29–30, 33.

8. Fitzgerald, *Letters*, pp. 394–395. For other sources on Fay, see *The Catholic Encyclopedia and Its Makers* (New York, 1917), pp. 56–57; the obituary in the *Baltimore Catholic Review,* January 18, 1919; "Monsignor Fay: In Memoriam," *Catholic University Bulletin* (Washington, D.C., 1919), pp. 177–178; Barry, *Impressions and Opinions,* pp. 219, 245; Monsignor Edward Hawks, *William McGarvey and the Open Pulpit* (Philadelphia, 1935), pp. 101–102, 110, 117, 128–129, 132, 135, 138, 153, 161–163, 178; William Hayward, *The C.S.S.S.* [Companions of the Holy Savior]: *The Quest and Goal of the Founder, the Right Reverend William McGarvey* (Philadelphia, 1940), p. 327; *New Catholic Encyclopedia* (New York, 1967), 5:862; *Dictionary of American Catholic Biography* (Garden City, New York, 1984), pp. 178–179.

9. Fitzgerald, "The Ice Palace," *Flappers and Philosophers* (New York, 1920), pp. 48–49; Robert Edward Francillon, *Zelda's Fortune* (Boston, 1874), p. 30; Zelda Fitzgerald, *Save Me the Waltz*, in *The Collected Writings,* ed. Matthew Bruccoli, Introduction by Mary Gordon (New York, 1991), p. 9.

10. Fitzgerald, *This Side of Paradise*, pp. 170–172; Virginia Foster Durr, *Outside the Magic Circle* (Tuscaloosa, Alabama, 1985), p. 64; Interview with Virginia Foster Durr, Montgomery, Alabama, January 15, 1992; Fitzgerald, *Letters*, pp. 94–95.

11. Quoted in Laura Hearne, "A Summer with F. Scott Fitzgerald," *Esquire*, 62 (December 1964), 258; Quoted in Nancy Milford, *Zelda* (1970; New York, 1974), p. 64.

12. Quoted in Scott Donaldson, *Fool for Love: A Biography of Scott Fitzgerald* (1983; New York, 1989), pp. 71, 66.

13. Fitzgerald, "My Lost City," *The Crack-Up*, pp. 24–25.

14. Fitzgerald, *Correspondence*, p. 44; Fitzgerald, *This Side of Paradise*, p. 196; Quoted in Turnbull, *Scott Fitzgerald*, p. 210.

15. Quoted in Donaldson, *Fool for Love*, p. 65; Fitzgerald, "My Lost City," *Crack-Up*, p. 26.

16. Donald Ogden Stewart, *By a Stroke of Luck!: An Autobiography* (New York, 1975), pp. 86–87; Fitzgerald, *Notebooks*, p. 153; *Dear Scott/Dear Max*, p. 21.

17. Edmund Wilson, "Thoughts on Being Bibliographed" (1944), *Classics and Commercials* (1950; New York, 1962), p. 110; Fitzgerald, *Letters*, p. 345.

18. Edmund Wilson, *Letters on Literature and Politics, 1912–1972*, ed. Elena Wilson (New York, 1977), pp. 45–46.

19. Quoted in James Mellow, *Invented Lives: F. Scott and Zelda Fitzgerald* (Boston, 1984), p. 82.

20. Quoted in Turnbull, *Scott Fitzgerald*, p. 108; Fitzgerald, *Correspondence*, pp. 50, 53.

21. Quoted in Turnbull, *Scott Fitzgerald*, p. 111; Fitzgerald, *Correspondence*, p. 559; Fitzgerald, *Letters*, p. 47.

Chapter Four: *This Side of Paradise* and Marriage

1. Fitzgerald, *This Side of Paradise*, pp. 282, 104; Fitzgerald, *Correspondence*, p. 30; Fitzgerald, *Letters*, p. 396.

2. Fitzgerald, *This Side of Paradise*, p. 138; Letter from Sally Taylor Abeles to Jeffrey Meyers, June 3, 1992.

3. Fitzgerald, *This Side of Paradise*, pp. 58, 175; Fitzgerald, *In His Own Time*, pp. 244–245.

4. Fitzgerald, *Correspondence*, p. 79; Franklin P. Adams, "The Conning Tower," *New York Tribune*, July 14, 1920, p. 8; Fitzgerald, *In His Own Time*, pp. 310, 305, 311.

5. Fitzgerald, *Correspondence*, p. 49; John Peale Bishop, "The Missing All" (1937), *Collected Essays*, ed. Edmund Wilson (New York, 1948), p. 76.

6. Edmund Wilson, "The Literary Spotlight: F. Scott Fitzgerald," *Bookman* (New York), 55 (March 1922), 21–22; Quoted in Mizener, *Far Side of Paradise*, p. 132.

7. *Dear Scott/Dear Max*, p. 245; Fitzgerald, "Early Success," *Crack-Up*, p. 88.

8. H. L. Mencken, "Taking Stock," *Smart Set*, 67 (March 1922), 139; Fitzgerald, *Correspondence*, p. 58; Fitzgerald, *Letters*, p. 482.

9. Quoted in Henry Bragdon, *Woodrow Wilson: The Academic Years* (Cambridge, Mass., 1967), p. 272; John Davies, "Scott Fitzgerald & Princeton," *Princeton Alumni Weekly*, 66 (February 8, 1966), 8.

10. Morley Callaghan, *That Summer in Paris* (1963; London, 1979), p. 251; *Dear Scott/Dear Max*, p. 42.

11. Catherine Drinker Bowen, "Harold Ober, Literary Agent," *Atlantic Monthly*, 206 (July 1960), 35, 38; *As Ever, Scott Fitz*, p. xvi.

12. Fitzgerald, "Early Success," *Crack-Up*, p. 89; Fitzgerald, *Letters*, p. 515.

13. F. Scott Fitzgerald, *The Beautiful and Damned* (1922; New York, 1950), p. 19; James Branch Cabell, *Between Friends: Letters of James Branch Cabell and Others*, ed. Padraic Colum and Margaret Freeman Cabell (New York, 1972), p. 254.

14. Fitzgerald, *This Side of Paradise*, p. 88; Fitzgerald, "Princeton," *Afternoon of an Author*, p. 79; Fitzgerald, "My Lost City," *Crack-Up*, pp. 28–29.

15. Fitzgerald, *Letters*, p. 479 (her behavior inspired the "Zelda Fitzgerald Emotional Maturity Award" in Woody Allen's *Manhattan*); Zelda Fitzgerald, *Save Me the Waltz*, p. 94; Quoted in *Ingenue Among the Lions: Letters of Emily Clark to Joseph Hergesheimer*, ed. Gerald Langford (Austin, 1965), p. 120; Carl Van Vechten, *Letters*, ed. Bruce Kellner (New Haven, 1987), p. 96.

16. Carmel Myers, "Scott and Zelda," *Park East* (New York), 2 (May 1951), 18; Fitzgerald, *Tender is the Night*, p. 274; Letter from Zelda Fitzgerald to Henry Dan Piper, n.d., Southern Illinois University.

17. Quoted in Malcolm Cowley, *A Second Flowering* (New York, 1973), p. 30.

18. Drawbell, *Autobiography*, p. 173; Quoted in Mizener, *Far Side of Paradise*, p. 93.

19. Ernest Hemingway, "Cat in the Rain," *Short Stories* (New York, 1938), p. 170; Fitzgerald, *In His Own Time*, p. 262; Zelda Fitzgerald, "Eulogy on the Flapper," *Collected Writings*, p. 391.

20. Quoted in Milford, *Zelda*, p. 103; Turnbull, *Scott Fitzgerald*, pp. 119–120; Milford, *Zelda*, p. 107; Turnbull, *Scott Fitzgerald*, p. 122; Fitzgerald, *Letters*, p. 351.

McKaig, with all his perception, ended up as tragically as Zelda. On January 7, 1936, Bishop wrote Wilson that McKaig had become "hopelessly and completely insane. It sounds like paresis. He is unable to receive any communication and only sporadically and uncertainly recognizes visitors" (quoted in Mellow, *Invented Lives*, p. 443).

21. William Rothenstein, *Men and Memories* (1913; New York, 1934), 2:164; Quoted in Mizener, *Far Side of Paradise*, p. 145; Fitzgerald, *Letters*, p. 399; Fitzgerald, *In His Own Time*, pp. 125–126.

22. Wilson, *Letters on Literature and Politics*, p. 63; Letter from John Dowling to the Vatican, June 3, 1921, Princeton; Fitzgerald, *Ledger*, p. 175.

23. Fitzgerald, *Letters*, p. 346; Quoted in Piper, *F. Scott Fitzgerald*, p. vii.

24. Zelda Fitzgerald, "The Girl the Prince Liked," *Collected Writings*, p. 311; Fitzgerald, *Ledger*, p. 176 (see also *The Great Gatsby*, p. 17); Scott and Zelda Fitzgerald, *The Romantic Egoists*, p. 87; Fitzgerald, *The Great Gatsby*, p. 10.

25. Fitzgerald, *Notebooks*, p. 244; Fitzgerald, *Correspondence*, p. 247.

26. Frances Fitzgerald Lanahan, "Introduction" to *Six Tales of the Jazz Age* (New York, 1960), p. 5; Scott and Zelda Fitzgerald, *Romantic Egoists*, p. 96; Cyril Connolly, *Previous Convictions* (London, 1963), p. 302; Fitzgerald, *In His Own Time*, p. 253.

27. Buttitta, *The Lost Summer*, p. 31; Quoted in Laura Hearne, "A Summer with Scott Fitzgerald," p. 258; Fitzgerald, "One Hundred False Starts," *Afternoon of an Author*, p. 132.

28. Letter from Burton Rascoe to George Jean Nathan, April 3, 1920, Princeton; Letter from Charles Norris to Fitzgerald, c. 1921, Princeton.

29. Fitzgerald's best stories, in addition to these two, are "The Dia-

mond as Big as the Ritz," "Winter Dreams," "Absolution," "The Rich Boy," "The Swimmers," "One Trip Abroad" and especially "Babylon Revisited" and "Crazy Sunday."

30. Fitzgerald, "The Ice Palace," *Flappers and Philosophers*, p. 47; Fitzgerald, *Correspondence*, pp. 44–45; Fitzgerald, "The Ice Palace," *Flappers and Philosophers*, pp. 58, 65, 60, 68.

31. Fitzgerald, "May Day," *Short Stories*, p. 126; Fitzgerald, "Echoes of the Jazz Age," *Crack-Up*, p. 13.

32. Jackson Bryer, *F. Scott Fitzgerald: The Critical Reception* (New York, 1978), pp. 40, 39, 43.

Chapter Five: *The Beautiful and Damned* and Great Neck

1. Fitzgerald, *The Beautiful and Damned*, pp. 423, 296, 62.

2. *Ibid.*, pp. 212, 204; Fitzgerald, *Correspondence*, p. 600. Scott took Zelda's advice about concluding the novel with Anthony's last speech on the ship, which echoes the title of D. H. Lawrence's volume of poems *Look! We Have Come Through!* (1917) and unconvincingly affirms: "It was a hard fight, but I didn't give up and I came through!"

3. Zelda Fitzgerald, "Friend Husband's Latest," *Collected Writings*, p. 388; Fitzgerald, *In His Own Time*, p. 419; Bryer, *Critical Reception*, pp. 92, 107, 74.

4. Fitzgerald, *The Beautiful and Damned*, p. 285; Wilson, *Letters on Literature and Politics*, pp. 56, 78–79.

5. Fitzgerald, *Letters*, p. 350; Wilson, "The Literary Spotlight," p. 22; Fitzgerald, *Correspondence*, p. 119.

6. Fitzgerald, *Correspondence*, p. 111; Fitzgerald, *Tales of the Jazz Age*, pp. ix, vii.

7. Fitzgerald, "Early Success," *Crack-Up*, p. 87; Fitzgerald, *Notebooks*, p. 131.

8. Edgar Allan Poe, *Selected Writings*, ed. Edward Davidson (Boston, 1956), p. 95; Fitzgerald, *Short Stories*, pp. 185–186, 188, 212, 204, 209; Fitzgerald, *Crack-Up*, p. 82. For more on Poe and Fitzgerald, see Appendix I.

9. John Dos Passos, *The Best Times* (New York, 1966), p. 129;

Interview with Ring Lardner, Jr., New York, March 14, 1992; Lane Yorke, "Zelda: A Worksheet," *Paris Review*, 89 (Fall 1983), 219; Fitzgerald, "Ring," *Crack-Up*, p. 35.

10. Ring Lardner, *What Of It?* (New York, 1925), pp. 18, 59, 118.

11. Scott and Zelda Fitzgerald, *Romantic Egoists*, pp. 157, 115.

12. Ring Lardner, Jr., *The Lardners* (New York, 1976), pp. 164–165; Ernest Hemingway, *Selected Letters, 1917–1961*, ed. Carlos Baker (New York, 1981), p. 200; Fitzgerald, "Ring," *Crack-Up*, pp. 38, 34, 39, 36.

13. Fitzgerald, *Tender is the Night*, pp. 9, 82–83.

14. Dos Passos, *Best Times*, pp. 129–130; P. G. Wodehouse, *Yours Plum: The Letters of P. G. Wodehouse*, ed. Frances Donaldson (London, 1990), pp. 28–29.

15. Van Wyck Brooks, *Days of the Phoenix* (New York, 1957), p. 109; Edmund Wilson, "Imaginary Conversations: Mr. Van Wyck Brooks and Mr. Scott Fitzgerald," *New Republic*, 38 (April 30, 1924), 249; Carl Van Vechten, *Parties* (New York, 1930), p. 78.

16. W. A. Swanberg, *Dreiser* (New York, 1965), p. 272; Fitzgerald, *Correspondence*, p. 138; Quoted in Mellow, *Invented Lives*, p. 272.

17. Nelson Aldrich, Jr., *Old Money* (New York, 1988), p. 182. See also Nelson Aldrich, Jr., *Tommy Hitchcock: An American Hero* (privately printed, 1984). In World War II Tommy became a lieutenant colonel in the Air Force and air attaché at the American Embassy in London. He was head of a fighter squadron in Texas, helped develop the Mustang plane and died in a test flight in April 1944. He was posthumously decorated with the Legion of Merit, the Bronze Star and the Distinguished Flying Cross.

18. Fitzgerald, *Notebooks*, p. 327; Fitzgerald, *Letters*, p. 64; Fitzgerald, *Great Gatsby*, pp. 6–7; Fitzgerald, *Tender is the Night*, p. 18.

19. *Dear Scott/Dear Max*, p. 57; Quoted in William Goldhurst, *F. Scott Fitzgerald and His Contemporaries* (New York, 1963), p. 88; F. Scott Fitzgerald, *The Vegetable* (1923; New York, 1976), p. 143.

20. Wilson, *Letters on Literature and Politics*, p. 84; Wilson, "A Selection of Bric-à-Brac," *Vanity Fair*, 20 (June 1923), 18; Quoted in Bruccoli, *Some Sort of Epic Grandeur*, pp. 187, 189; Fitzgerald, "How to Live on $36,000 a Year," *Afternoon of an Author*, pp. 93–94.

21. Fitzgerald, *Correspondence*, p. 456; Martin Esslin, *The Theatre of the Absurd* (New York, 1961), p. 288.

22. *Dear Scott/Dear Max,* pp. 69–70; Quoted in Mizener, *Far Side of Paradise,* p. 134; Fitzgerald, "How to Live on $36,000 a Year," *Afternoon of an Author,* p. 95.

Chapter Six: Europe and *The Great Gatsby*

1. Quoted in Mellow, *Invented Lives,* p. 203; Fitzgerald, *Letters,* p. 317; Fitzgerald, "How to Live on Practically Nothing a Year," *Afternoon of an Author,* p. 111.

2. Frances Fitzgerald Smith, "Où Sont Les Soleils d'Antan? Françoise 'Fijeralde'?" *F. Scott Fitzgerald and Ernest M. Hemingway in Paris,* ed. Matthew Bruccoli and C. E. Frazer Clark (Bloomfield Hills, Michigan, 1972), n.p.; Fitzgerald, "How to Live on Practically Nothing a Year," *Afternoon of an Author,* p. 105.

3. Quoted in Honoria Murphy Donnelly with Richard Billings, *Sara & Gerald: Villa America and After* (New York, 1982), p. 14; Dos Passos, *Best Times,* p. 152; Interview with Fanny Myers Brennan, Kew Gardens, New York, March 14, 1992.

4. Quoted in Milford, *Zelda,* pp. 430–431; Interview with Honoria Murphy Donnelly, Palm Beach, Florida, February 7, 1992.

5. Quoted in Turnbull, *Scott Fitzgerald,* p. 172; Interview with Ellen Barry, Hobe Sound, Florida, February 7, 1992; Calvin Tomkins, *Living Well is the Best Revenge* (New York, 1972), pp. 125–126.

While living in Havana in 1939, Hemingway behaved in a remarkably similar fashion: "During his high-spirited fortieth birthday party at Sánchez's house, Hemingway got completely drunk, threw Thorwald's clothes out the window and began to break the Baccarat crystal glasses while Tina Sánchez screamed for her butler to lock them up" (Jeffrey Meyers, *Hemingway: A Biography,* New York, 1985, p. 332).

6. Quoted in Mellow, *Invented Lives,* p. 269; Fitzgerald, *Correspondence,* pp. 196–197, 398; Quoted in Laura Hearne, "A Summer with Scott Fitzgerald," p. 209.

7. Quoted in Tomkins, *Living Well is the Best Revenge,* p. 128; Fitzgerald, "Handle with Care," *Crack-Up,* p. 79; Fitzgerald, *Letters,* p. 447.

8. Quoted in Tomkins, *Living Well is the Best Revenge,* p. 120;

Wanda Corn, "Identity, Modernism and the American Artist After World War I: Gerald Murphy and *Américanisme*," *Nationalism in the Visual Arts* (Washington, D.C.: National Gallery of Art, 1991), p. 169.

9. Fitzgerald, *Letters,* p. 377; Quoted in Milford, *Zelda,* p. 141; Zelda Fitzgerald, *Save Me the Waltz, Collected Writings,* p. 86; Quoted in Milford, *Zelda,* p. 433.

10. Fitzgerald, "Handle with Care," *Crack-Up,* p. 77; Fitzgerald, *Correspondence,* p. 246; Fitzgerald, *Notebooks,* p. 113.

11. Scott and Zelda Fitzgerald, *Romantic Egoists,* p. 120; Zelda Fitzgerald, "Show Mr. and Mrs. F. to Number———," *Crack-Up,* pp. 44–45 (this work is attributed to Zelda in Scott's *Ledger*); Letter from Scott Fitzgerald to Charles Warren, December 6, 1934, Princeton.

12. F. Scott Fitzgerald, "The High Cost of Macaroni," *Interim* (Seattle), 4 (1954), 15; Fitzgerald, *Correspondence,* p. 349; Myers, "Scott and Zelda," p. 32; Fitzgerald, *Correspondence,* p. 160.

13. Joseph Conrad, *Collected Letters. Vol. III, 1903–1907,* ed. Frederick Karl and Laurence Davies (Cambridge, England, 1988), pp. 230, 239, 241; D. H. Lawrence, *Letters. Volume III: 1916–1921,* ed. James Boulton and Andrew Robertson (Cambridge, 1984), p. 469; Fitzgerald, *Letters,* pp. 197, 376.

14. *Dear Scott/Dear Max,* pp. 82–84.

15. Fitzgerald, *Letters,* p. 501; Joseph Conrad, "The Secret Sharer," *The Shadow-Line and Two Other Tales,* ed. Morton Zabel (New York, 1959), p. 123; Fitzgerald, *Great Gatsby,* p. 99.

16. Joseph Conrad, *Lord Jim* (New York, 1931), pp. 81, 215; Fitzgerald, *Great Gatsby,* p. 111; Fitzgerald, *Letters,* pp. 383–384, 329.

17. Fitzgerald, *Letters,* pp. 378, 499.

18. Fitzgerald, *Great Gatsby,* pp. 65, 129–130; Herbert Asbury, "The Noble Experiment of Izzy and Moe," *The Aspirin Age, 1919–1941,* ed. Isabel Leighton (New York, 1949), p. 34.

19. Fitzgerald, *Great Gatsby,* pp. 74, 172; Quoted in Turnbull, *Scott Fitzgerald,* p. 143.

20. Fitzgerald, *Letters,* p. 218; T. S. Eliot, "Gerontion" (1920), *Complete Poems and Plays, 1909–1950* (New York, 1952), p. 22; James Joyce, *Ulysses,* ed. Hans Gabler (New York, 1986), p. 178 (for the names in the execution scene, see p. 252); Fitzgerald, *Great Gatsby,* pp. 93, 97.

The shirt display may have been partly inspired by Zelda. Speaking of Zelda in a letter of January 17, 1950, Sara Murphy told Mizener: "Cleanliness and order were a sort of fetish with her.—Bureau drawers the admiration of all" (Princeton).

21. Fitzgerald, *Great Gatsby*, pp. 131, 133, 134, 180.

22. Wilson, *Letters on Literature and Politics*, pp. 121, 173; Fitzgerald, *Correspondence*, p. 158; Stein, in Fitzgerald, *Crack-Up*, p. 308.

23. Edith Wharton, *Letters*, ed. R. W. B. Lewis and Nancy Lewis (New York, 1988), pp. 481–482; Hemingway, *Selected Letters*, p. 163; Eliot, in Fitzgerald, *Crack-Up*, p. 310.

24. *Dear Scott/Dear Max*, p. 102; Fitzgerald, *Letters*, pp. 375–376; *As Ever, Scott Fitz*, p. 175; Quoted in Henry Dan Piper, *F. Scott Fitzgerald*, p. 126.

Chapter Seven: Paris and Hemingway

1. Quoted in Mizener, *Far Side of Paradise*, p. 193; Zelda Fitzgerald, *Save Me the Waltz*, *Collected Writings*, p. 95; Frances Fitzgerald Smith, *F. Scott Fitzgerald and Ernest M. Hemingway in Paris*, n.p.

2. Hemingway, *Selected Letters*, p. 689; Ernest Hemingway, *The Sun Also Rises* (1926; New York, 1954), p. 44; Ernest Hemingway, *Across the River and into the Trees* (New York, 1950), p. 45.

3. Fitzgerald, *Letters*, p. 322; Hemingway, *Selected Letters*, p. 176; Fitzgerald, "Author's House," *Afternoon of an Author*, p. 186; Janet Flanner, *Paris Was Yesterday, 1925–1939*, ed. Irving Drutman (New York, 1972), p. xix.

4. *Dear Scott/Dear Max*, p. 194; Hemingway, *Selected Letters*, pp. 162–163; Fitzgerald, *Letters*, pp. 503–504; Quoted in James Woodress, *Booth Tarkington, Gentleman from Indiana* (Philadelphia, 1954), p. 265.

5. Meyers, *Hemingway*, p. 159; Glenway Wescott, in Fitzgerald, *Crack-Up*, p. 325; *Dear Scott/Dear Max*, p. 78.

6. Fitzgerald, *In His Own Time*, pp. 148–149; Fitzgerald, *Correspondence*, p. 183; *Dear Scott/Dear Max*, pp. 127, 131.

7. Ernest Hemingway, *The Torrents of Spring* (1926; London,

1966), p. 92; Fitzgerald, *In His Own Time*, p. 275.

8. Fitzgerald, *Notebooks*, p. 319; Hemingway, *Selected Letters*, p. 483; Hemingway, *A Moveable Feast* (1964; New York, 1965), p. 147.

9. Hemingway, *Selected Letters*, p. 438. Clemenceau, whom Hemingway had interviewed in 1922, said: "America is the only nation in history which miraculously has gone directly from barbarism to degeneration without the usual interval of civilization" (John Bartlett, *Familiar Quotations*, 15th ed., Boston, 1980, p. 643). Henry Adams has also been credited with this *mot*: "American society was the first in history to go from barbarism to decadence without passing through an intervening stage of civilization" (quoted in Aldrich, *Old Money*, p. 46). And in his essay on A. E. Housman in *The Triple Thinkers* (1938), Edmund Wilson wrote that the poet "has managed to grow old without in a sense ever knowing maturity" (London, 1962, p. 84). Fitzgerald may actually have said something like this to Hemingway, for in unpublished notes Scott wrote that growing up was "a terribly hard thing to do. It is so much easier to skip it and go from one childhood to another" (quoted in Donaldson, *Fool for Love*, p. 214).

10. James Thurber, "Scott in Thorns," *Reporter,* 4 (April 17, 1951), 36; Letter from Joan Kennedy Taylor to Jeffrey Meyers, April 22, 1992.

11. *Dear Scott/Dear Max*, p. 41; Wilson, "Imaginary Conversations," p. 254; Hemingway, *Selected Letters*, p. 165. Hemingway came close to realizing this fantasy in the early 1930s when he had a house with wife and children in Key West and a beautiful American mistress, Jane Mason, in Havana.

12. Hemingway, *A Moveable Feast*, p. 182; Edmund Wilson, "That Summer in Paris" (1963), *The Bit Between My Teeth* (New York, 1965), p. 522; Fitzgerald, *Letters*, p. 365.

13. Fitzgerald, *Letters*, p. 326; *Dear Scott/Dear Max*, p. 177; Fitzgerald, *Notebooks*, p. 326; Fitzgerald, *Correspondence*, p. 243; Hemingway, *Selected Letters*, p. 877.

14. Quoted in Sotheby Parke Bernet, *Fine Modern First Editions* (New York, October 25, 1977), lot 425, letter of September 16, 1951; Quoted in Turnbull, *Scott Fitzgerald*, p. 41; Hemingway, *A Moveable Feast*, p. 179.

15. William James, *Varieties of Religious Experience* (1902; New York, 1958), p. 297; Fitzgerald, *Tender is the Night*, p. 103; Fitzgerald, "A New Leaf," *Short Stories*, p. 637.

16. Laura Hearne, "A Summer with Scott Fitzgerald," p. 260; William Styron, *Darkness Visible* (New York, 1990), p. 40; Corey Ford, *Time of Laughter* (Boston, 1967), p. 164.

17. Quoted in Donaldson, *Fool for Love*, p. 214; Quoted in Mizener, *Far Side of Paradise*, pp. 84–85; *The Oxford Textbook of Medicine*, ed. D. J. Weatherall *et al.* (Oxford, 1987), 9:95.

18. Hemingway, *A Moveable Feast*, pp. 183–184; Quoted in Esther Murphy Arthur, "A Farewell to Hemingway," 1961, BBC Archives; Quoted in Sara Mayfield, *Exiles from Paradise: Zelda and Scott Fitzgerald* (1971; New York, 1974), pp. 137, 141.

19. Quoted in Milford, *Zelda*, p. 156; Hemingway, *A Moveable Feast*, p. 184; Charles Angoff, *H. L. Mencken: A Portrait from Memory* (New York, 1956), p. 99; Hemingway, *Selected Letters*, p. 408.

20. Quoted in Donaldson, *Fool for Love*, p. 52; Elizabeth Beckwith MacKie, "My Friend, Scott Fitzgerald," *Fitzgerald-Hemingway Annual*, 2 (1970), 20–21.

21. Callaghan, *That Summer in Paris*, p. 207; Fitzgerald, *Notebooks*, p. 17; Quoted in Bruccoli, *Some Sort of Epic Grandeur*, p. 272; Edmund Wilson, *The Thirties* (New York, 1980), p. 303.

22. Hemingway, *A Moveable Feast*, pp. 188–189. See Arnold Gingrich, "Coming to Terms with Scott and Ernest," *Esquire*, 99 (June 1983), 56; Sheilah Graham, *A State of Heat* (New York, 1972), p. 146; and Buttitta, *Lost Summer*, p. 113.

23. Mizener's notes on his conversation with Wilson, Princeton; Quoted in Buttitta, *Lost Summer*, pp. 56, 113, 134; Mizener's notes on his conversation with Oscar Kalman, Princeton.

24. Hemingway, *A Moveable Feast*, p. 182; Fitzgerald, *Notebooks*, p. 158; Hemingway, *Short Stories*, p. 426.

25. Ernest Hemingway, "The Art of the Short Story," *Paris Review*, 79 (1981), 89; Letter from Hemingway to Mizener, February 1, 1951, McKeldin Library, University of Maryland; Fitzgerald, *Great Gatsby*, p. 97.

26. Hemingway, *Selected Letters*, p. 306; *Dear Scott/Dear Max*, p. 102; Fitzgerald, *Letters*, p. 327; Ernest Hemingway, *Green Hills of Africa* (New York, 1935), p. 23.

27. Hemingway, *A Moveable Feast*, p. 14; Ruth Sokoloff, *Hadley: The First Mrs. Hemingway* (New York, 1973), p. 50; Alice B. Toklas, *Staying on Alone: Letters*, ed. Edward Burns (New York, 1973), p. 169;

Gertrude Stein, *The Autobiography of Alice B. Toklas* (New York, 1933), p. 218.

28. Alice B. Toklas, "Between Classics," *New York Times Book Review*, March 4, 1951, p. 4; Yorke, "Zelda: A Worksheet," p. 220; Turnbull, *Scott Fitzgerald*, pp. 258–259.

29. Quoted in Mizener, *Far Side of Paradise*, p. 168; Zelda Fitzgerald, "Show Mr. and Mrs. F. to Number————," *Crack-Up*, p. 43; R. W. B. Lewis, *Edith Wharton* (New York, 1975), p. 468. In an appendix to his biography, Lewis prints "Beatrice Palmato," Wharton's astonishing pornographic fragment. Had Fitzgerald known about her taste for *louche* anecdotes, he would surely have provided the necessary data.

30. Fitzgerald, *Tender is the Night*, p. 3; Fitzgerald, *Ledger*, p. 179; *Dear Scott/Dear Max*, p. 127; Frank Swinnerton, *Figures in the Foreground* (New York, 1964), p. 158.

31. Henry Dan Piper, "Fitzgerald, Mark Twain and Thomas Hardy," *Fitzgerald Newsletter*, ed. Matthew Bruccoli (Washington, D.C., 1969), p. 31; "Power Without Glory," *Times Literary Supplement*, January 20, 1950, p. 40; Fitzgerald, *Correspondence*, p. 84; "Young America?" *Manchester Guardian*, May 27, 1921, p. 5; "New Novels— This Side of Paradise," *Times Literary Supplement*, June 23, 1951, p. 402.

32. *Dear Scott/Dear Max*, p. 121; "New Novels—*The Great Gatsby*," *Times Literary Supplement*, February 18, 1926, p. 116; L. P. Hartley, "New Fiction," *Saturday Review*, February 20, 1926, p. 234; Fitzgerald, *Letters*, p. 237.

33. *As Ever, Scott Fitz*, p. 84; Grace Moore, *You're Only Human Once* (Garden City, New York, 1944), p. 114; Zelda Fitzgerald, "Auction—Model 1934," *Crack-Up*, p. 58 (this work is attributed to Zelda in Scott's *Ledger*).

34. Fitzgerald, *Tender is the Night*, p. 32; Letter from Sara Murphy to Mizener, January 17, 1950, Princeton; Fitzgerald, *Correspondence*, p. 178.

35. Fitzgerald, "Absolution," *Short Stories*, pp. 259, 271; Fitzgerald, "Winter Dreams," *Short Stories*, pp. 235–236; Fitzgerald, "The Rich Boy," *Short Stories*, p. 318.

36. Fitzgerald, "Winter Dreams," *Short Stories*, p. 228; Fitzgerald, *Correspondence*, pp. 152, 182.

37. Thomas Boyd, "Genius and Pains," Minneapolis *Journal*,

March 7, 1926, Editorial section, p. 11; Fitzgerald, *In His Own Time*, p. 365, 368; Fitzgerald, *Letters*, p. 318.

Chapter Eight: Ellerslie and France

1. Letter from John Barrymore to Fitzgerald, n.d. (c. early 1927), Princeton; Letter from Lois Moran Young to Mizener, c. April 1948, Princeton; Quoted in Mizener, *Far Side of Paradise*, p. 348; Fitzgerald, *Tender is the Night*, pp. 3–4.

2. Fitzgerald, *Correspondence*, pp. 247, 240; Fitzgerald, *Great Gatsby*, p. 10; Quoted in Mizener, *Far Side of Paradise*, p. 227; Fitzgerald, *Correspondence*, p. 206.

3. Fitzgerald, *Correspondence*, p. 480; Quoted in Donaldson, *Fool for Love*, p. 54; Quoted in Milford, *Zelda*, pp. 269, 215, 300; Letter from Lois Moran Young to Mizener, February 26, 1951, Princeton. In 1935 Lois married Clarence Young, who became assistant secretary of commerce and vice president of Pan American Airlines. She had one son and later lived in Sedona, Arizona, where she died in 1990. See "Lois Moran Young Dead at 81; Musical Star and Movie Actress," *New York Times*, July 15, 1990, 1:22.

4. Fitzgerald, *Correspondence*, p. 217; Quoted in Milford, *Zelda*, p. 168; See Gilbert Harrison, *The Enthusiast: A Life of Thornton Wilder* (1983; New York, 1986), pp. 109–110.

5. Edmund Wilson, "A Weekend at Ellerslie" (1952), *The Shores of Light* (1952; New York, 1961), pp. 373, 378–380, 382–383.

6. Quoted in Milford, *Zelda*, p. 168; Fitzgerald, *Letters*, pp. 511–512; Quoted in Turnbull, *Scott Fitzgerald*, p. 186; D. H. Lawrence, *The Lost Girl* (1920; New York, 1968), p. 318.

7. André Chamson, "Remarks of André Chamson," *Fitzgerald-Hemingway Annual*, 5 (1973), 74; Fitzgerald, "A Night at the Fair," *Afternoon of an Author*, pp. 15–16. See James Joyce, *A Portrait of the Artist as a Young Man* (1916; New York, 1964), p. 16; Herbert Gorman, "Glimpses of F. Scott Fitzgerald," *Fitzgerald-Hemingway Annual*, 5 (1973), 116.

8. Zelda Fitzgerald, *Save Me the Waltz*, *Collected Writings*, p. 114; Letter from Scottie Fitzgerald Lanahan to Mizener, July 5,

1950, Princeton; Zelda Fitzgerald, *Save Me the Waltz*, pp. 79, 118. See Gennady Smakov, "Lubov Egorova," *The Great Russian Dancers* (New York, 1984), pp. 19–25, which reproduces several photographs of Egorova.

9. Fitzgerald, "Two Wrongs," *Taps at Reveille*, p. 205; Quoted in Mellow, *Invented Lives*, p. 338; Sheilah Graham, *The Rest of the Story* (New York, 1964), p. 234. Zelda's *Ballerinas* is reproduced in Mellow's biography.

10. Quoted in Dennis Brian, *The True Gen: An Intimate Portrait of Ernest Hemingway by Those Who Knew Him* (New York, 1988), p. 79; Quoted in A. E. Hotchner, *Papa Hemingway* (New York, 1966), p. 121; Hemingway, *Selected Letters*, p. 291.

11. Callaghan, *That Summer in Paris*, pp. 189, 161, 157, 126.

12. *Ibid.*, pp. 214–215; Hemingway, *Selected Letters*, p. 302; I. M. P. [Isabel Paterson], "Turns with a Bookworm," *New York Herald Tribune*, November 24, 1929, sec. XII, p. 27; Callaghan, *That Summer in Paris*, pp. 243, 247. This fight had assumed epic proportions in Hemingway's mind by 1951, when he told Mizener: "Scott let the first round go *thirteen* minutes" (*Selected Letters*, p. 716). In 1964, after even greater distortions, Archibald MacLeish had to refute a claim that Fitzgerald had injured Hemingway's head with a jagged piece of skylight! See MacLeish, "The Bruiser and the Poet," *Times Literary Supplement*, September 3, 1964, p. 803.

13. Fitzgerald, *Ledger*, p. 183; Quoted in Mellow, *Invented Lives*, p. 353; Quoted in Mizener, *Far Side of Paradise*, pp. 229, 220.

14. Fitzgerald, *Correspondence*, pp. 291, 248–249; Saul Bellow, *Herzog* (New York, 1964), p. 5.

15. Hemingway, *The Sun Also Rises*, p. 235; Fitzgerald, "One Trip Abroad," *Afternoon of an Author*, pp. 144, 161, 162, 164.

16. Milford, *Zelda*, pp. 318–319; Interview with Scottie's friend Marie Jemison, Birmingham, Alabama, January 12, 1992; Fitzgerald, "Outside the Cabinet-Maker's," *Afternoon of an Author*, pp. 138, 141.

17. Zelda Fitzgerald, "Show Mr. and Mrs. F. to Number———," *Crack-Up*, pp. 51–52; Interview with Ellen Barry; Henry Dan Piper's interview with John Biggs, Wilmington, June 22, 1945, courtesy of Professor Piper; Quoted in Milford, *Zelda*, p. 130.

18. Quoted in Turnbull, *Scott Fitzgerald*, p. 173; Fitzgerald, *Correspondence*, p. 241.

Chapter Nine: Madness

1. Fitzgerald, "Echoes of the Jazz Age," *Crack-Up*, p. 21; *Arthur Miller and Company*, ed. Christopher Bigsby (London, 1990), p. 201; Fitzgerald, *Notebooks*, p. 204. For a chronology of Zelda's illness, see Appendix II.

2. Quoted in Turnbull, *Scott Fitzgerald*, p. 199; Quoted in Bruccoli, *Some Sort of Epic Grandeur*, p. 293; Fitzgerald, *Tender is the Night*, p. 183.

3. Quoted in Turnbull, *Scott Fitzgerald*, pp. 199–200; Fitzgerald, *Tender is the Night*, p. 181; Fitzgerald, *Correspondence*, p. 253.

4. The information about Dr. Oscar Forel, who has hitherto been a shadowy figure, is based on a long letter of June 4, 1992, from his son, Dr. Armand Forel, to Jeffrey Meyers, and on Armand Forel's fascinating autobiography, *Médecin et homme politique: Entretiens avec Jean-Bernard Desfayes* (Lausanne: Éditions de L'Aire, 1991), which he kindly sent me. See also "Oscar Louis Forel," *Macmillan Biographical Encyclopedia of Photographic Artists and Innovators*, ed. Turner Browne and Elaine Partnow (New York, 1983), p. 202.

5. Quoted in Milford, *Zelda*, p. 222; Quoted in Thomas Campbell, *Dr. Campbell's Diary of a Visit to England in 1775*, ed. James Clifford (Cambridge, England, 1947), p. 58.

6. Quoted in Milford, *Zelda*, pp. 205–207; Fitzgerald, *Tender is the Night*, p. 183; Quoted in Milford, *Zelda*, pp. 226, 213, 209, 217.

7. Fitzgerald, *Correspondence*, pp. 247–248; Quoted in Elizabeth Spindler, *John Peale Bishop: A Biography* (Morgantown, West Virginia, 1980), p. 223; Fitzgerald, *Letters*, pp. 46, 117, 95.

8. Fitzgerald, *Correspondence*, p. 279; Dos Passos, *Best Times*, pp. 209–210; Quoted in Milford, *Zelda*, p. 228; Fitzgerald, *Notebooks*, p. 131; Quoted in Turnbull, *Scott Fitzgerald*, pp. 201–202.

9. Fitzgerald, "One Trip Abroad," *Afternoon of an Author*, p. 161. Fitzgerald's statement was also prophetic, for a great many foreign writers, seeking both refuge and first-rate doctors, have ended their lives in Switzerland: Rilke, Stefan George, Joyce, Musil, Mann, Hesse, Remarque, Nabokov, Silone, Irwin Shaw, Borges, Simenon and Graham Greene.

10. Fitzgerald, *Letters*, p. 364; Fitzgerald, "One Trip Abroad,"

NOTES TO PAGES 203-209   375

Afternoon of an Author, p. 162; Thomas Wolfe, *Letters,* ed. Elizabeth Nowell (New York, 1956), p. 263; Sinclair Lewis, quoted in Hamilton Basso, "Thomas Wolfe," in *After the Genteel Tradition,* ed. Malcolm Cowley (New York, 1937), p. 202; Hemingway, *Selected Letters,* p. 726.

11. *Dear Scott/Dear Max,* p. 168; Fitzgerald, *Letters,* p. 572; Thomas Wolfe, *You Can't Go Home Again* (New York, 1941), p. 715.

12. Compton Mackenzie, *First Athenian Memories* (London, 1931), p. 320; Letter from Anthony Blond to Jeffrey Meyers, September 7, 1992; For a portrait of Lord Alington, see John Rothenstein, *Augustus John* (Oxford, 1945), plate 53; *As Ever, Scott Fitz,* p. 174.

13. The intriguing Bijou has received very little attention from Fitzgerald's biographers. Mizener, Turnbull, Milford and Mellow do not even mention her. Bruccoli devotes one sentence, LeVot and Donaldson one paragraph each to her. My account of Bijou's life is based primarily on her taped interview, *Bijou O'Conor Remembers Scott Fitzgerald* (London: Audio Arts, 1975) and on interviews in England during August 1992 with her cousins The Earl of Minto and Sir Brinsley Ford; her son, Michael O'Conor; her former daughter-in-law, Gillian Plazzota; and her great-nephew, Sir William Young.

Bijou, a great gossip, told Fitzgerald many interesting stories about her cosmopolitan background. He refers to two of them, as well as to her imperious character, in his *Notebooks,* pp. 219, 104, 18: "Sir Francis Elliot, King George, the barley water and champagne"; "Bijou as a girl in Athens meeting German legacy [?Legation] people in secret. Representing her mother"; "Bijou, regarding her cigarette fingers: 'Oh, Trevah! Get me the pumice stone.'" For more on Bijou, see Appendix III.

14. Fitzgerald, "The Hotel Child," *Bits of Paradise,* ed. Matthew Bruccoli (1974; New York, 1976), pp. 273–274, 289.

15. *Arthur Miller and Company,* p. 15; Fitzgerald, *Tender is the Night,* pp. 203–204; Fitzgerald, "On Your Own," *The Price Was High,* p. 325; Fitzgerald, *Correspondence,* p. 262. Matthew Bruccoli, "Epilogue: A Woman, a Gift and a Still Unanswered Question," *Esquire,* 91 (January 30, 1979), 67, reproduces a photograph of Bert Barr.

16. Fitzgerald, *Correspondence,* p. 254; Letter from Scottie Fitzgerald Lanahan to Mizener, March 10, 1950, Princeton; Fitzgerald, *Correspondence,* p. 488; Helen Blackshear, "Mama Sayre, Scott Fitzgerald's Mother-in-Law," *Georgia Review,* 19 (Winter 1965), 467.

17. Fitzgerald, *Correspondence*, p. 236; Letter from Fitzgerald to Rosalind Smith, n.d. (c. June 1930), Princeton.

18. Fitzgerald, *Correspondence*, p. 255; Letter from Scottie Fitzgerald Lanahan to Mizener, July 5, 1950, Princeton; Quoted in Milford, *Zelda*, p. 269.

19. "Babylon Revisited," *The Stories of F. Scott Fitzgerald*, ed. Malcolm Cowley (New York, 1951), pp. 386, 391, 396, 399, 402.

20. Zelda Fitzgerald, *Save Me the Waltz, Collected Writings*, p. 181; Interview with Budd Schulberg; Interview with Ring Lardner, Jr.; Fitzgerald, *Poems*, p. 141; Dwight Taylor, *Joy Ride* (New York, 1959), pp. 242, 244–246.

21. Fitzgerald, *Correspondence*, p. 282; Anita Loos, *Cast of Thousands* (New York, 1977), p. 113; Samuel Marx, *A Gaudy Spree: Literary Life in Hollywood in the 1930s* (New York, 1987), p. 66; Fitzgerald, *Letters*, p. 31.

22. Fitzgerald, "Crazy Sunday," *Stories of Scott Fitzgerald*, pp. 407, 408–409, 415, 416.

23. Zelda Fitzgerald, *Save Me the Waltz*, pp. 9, 181; Fitzgerald, *Correspondence*, p. 308; Zelda Fitzgerald, *Save Me the Waltz*, p. 180; Quoted in Milford, *Zelda*, p. 255.

24. Sir David Henderson, Introduction to *The Collected Papers of Adolf Meyer* (Baltimore, 1950–52), 2:ix–x; Fitzgerald, *Correspondence*, pp. 380, 382, 285; Quoted in Bruccoli, *Some Sort of Epic Grandeur*, p. 351. For more on Rennie, see his obituary in the *New York Times*, May 22, 1956, p. 33.

25. *Dear Scott/Dear Max*, pp. 166–167; Zelda Fitzgerald, *Save Me the Waltz*, p. 180; Fitzgerald, *Correspondence*, p. 286.

26. Hemingway, *The Sun Also Rises*, p. 22; Zelda Fitzgerald, *Save Me the Waltz*, p. 127; *As Ever, Scott Fitz*, p. 249.

Chapter Ten: La Paix and *Tender is the Night*

1. Quoted in Turnbull, *Scott Fitzgerald*, p. 214; Interview with Frances Turnbull Kidder, April 4, 1992; Turnbull, *Scott Fitzgerald*, p. 229.

Andrew, dutifully following Fitzgerald's advice, attended Princeton.

He served in World War II, earned a doctorate at Harvard and taught for a while at MIT. He also edited Fitzgerald's letters and published a life of Thomas Wolfe. Though he adored his mother and two daughters, Andrew suffered severe depression for many years, could not cope with the pain of living and killed himself in 1970.

2. Fitzgerald, *Letters*, p. 365 and deleted phrase quoted in Bruccoli, *Some Sort of Epic Grandeur*, p. 345; Quoted in Matthew Bruccoli, *F. Scott Fitzgerald: A Descriptive Bibliography*, Revised Edition (Pittsburgh, 1987), p. 93; Fitzgerald, *Correspondence*, p. 324.

3. Fitzgerald, *Correspondence*, p. 338; Scottie Fitzgerald Smith, Foreword to *Bits of Paradise*, p. xiii; Interview with Margaret "Peaches" Finney McPherson, May 14, 1992.

4. Fitzgerald, *Tender is the Night*, p. 257; Sheilah Graham, *The Real Scott Fitzgerald*, pp. 94, 72.

5. Turnbull, *Scott Fitzgerald*, p. 237; Quoted in Mizener, *Far Side of Paradise*, p. 258; Zelda Fitzgerald, "Auction—Model 1934," *Crack-Up*, p. 62; Turnbull, *Scott Fitzgerald*, p. 244 (Zelda's odd title was taken from Ernest Boyd's essay, "Aesthete, Model 1924," which appeared in the first issue of Mencken's *American Mercury*); Scottie Fitzgerald Smith, [Foreword] to *Zelda*, exhibition catalogue (Montgomery: Museum of Fine Arts, 1974), n. p.

6. Fitzgerald, *Correspondence*, p. 336; Quoted in Milford, *Zelda*, p. 346; Quoted in Turnbull, *Scott Fitzgerald*, p. 266; Fitzgerald, *Letters*, p. 588.

7. Fitzgerald, *In His Own Time*, p. 283; Fitzgerald, *Correspondence*, p. 474; Fitzgerald, *Letters*, p. 406.

8. Quoted in Turnbull, *Scott Fitzgerald*, p. 200; Letter from Dr. Benjamin Baker to Jeffrey Meyers, October 10, 1992; H. L. Mencken, *Diary*, ed. Charles Fecher (New York, 1989), p. 63.

9. Quoted in Milford, *Zelda*, p. 347; "Work of a Wife," *Time*, 23 (April 9, 1934), 44. Though Zelda's portraits of Scott were lost, her pencil drawing of him, in a letter of October 1934, appears in Bruccoli, *Some Sort of Epic Grandeur*, p. 383. A number of her paintings and drawings are reproduced in color in *The Romantic Egoists*, following page 190.

10. Fitzgerald, *Correspondence*, p. 318; Marion Meade, *Dorothy Parker: What Fresh Hell is This?* (New York, 1988), p. 235.

11. Yeats, "The Choice," *Collected Poems*, p. 242; Quoted in

Mizener, *Far Side of Paradise*, pp. 345–346. The phrase "spoiled priest" appears in Joyce, *Ulysses*, p. 427. Fitzgerald, *Tender is the Night*, p. 304.

12. Fitzgerald, *Tender is the Night*, pp. 301, 87, 64, 88.

13. *Ibid.*, pp. 217, 219; Fitzgerald, *Notebooks*, p. 172; Fitzgerald, *Tender is the Night*, p. 112.

14. Fitzgerald, *Tender is the Night*, pp. 192, 201, 301, 82, 271.

15. Fitzgerald, *Correspondence*, pp. 339, 358; Gilbert Seldes, "True to Type—Scott Fitzgerald Writes Superb Tragic Novel," New York *Evening Journal*, April 12, 1934, p. 23; John Chamberlain, "Books of The Times," *New York Times*, April 13, 1934, p. 17.

16. Mary Colum, "The Psychopathic Novel," *Forum and Century*, 91 (April 1934), 219–223; D. W. Harding, "Mechanisms of Misery," *Scrutiny*, 3 (December 1934), 318; *Journal of Nervous and Mental Disease*, 82 (July 1935), 115.

17. Fitzgerald, *Letters*, p. 327; Hemingway, *Selected Letters*, p. 407; Fitzgerald, *Letters*, p. 443; Fitzgerald, *Correspondence*, p. 425; Hemingway, *Selected Letters*, p. 483.

Chapter Eleven: Asheville and "The Crack-Up"

1. *As Ever, Scott Fitz*, p. 222; Fitzgerald, *Letters*, p. 550; Henry Dan Piper, Interview with Nora Flynn, Tryon, North Carolina, February 10, 1947, courtesy of Professor Piper; Henry Dan Piper, Interview with Margaret Banning, Tryon, North Carolina, April 7, 1947.

2. Thelma Nason, "Afternoon (and Evening) of an Author," *Johns Hopkins Magazine*, 21 (February 1970), 10; *As Ever, Scott Fitz*, p. 220; Christopher Sykes, *Nancy: The Life of Lady Astor* (New York, 1972), p. 488; Fitzgerald, *Notebooks*, pp. 77–78.

3. Arthur Mizener, notes on his conversation with Edmund Wilson, Princeton; Henry Dan Piper, Interview with Zelda Fitzgerald, Montgomery, Alabama, March 13 and 14, 1947; Henry Dan Piper, Interview with Nora Flynn; Fitzgerald, *Letters*, p. 565.

4. Buttitta, *The Lost Summer*, Preface and p. 17; Interview with Tony Buttitta, New York, March 15, 1992.

5. Quoted in Donaldson, *Fool for Love*, p. 131; Laura Guthrie Hearne, "Summer with Scott Fitzgerald," pp. 161–165, 232.

6. Letter from Beatrice Dance to Laura Guthrie, August 7, 1935, Princeton; Letter from Laura Guthrie to Beatrice Dance, August 17, 1935, Princeton; Letter from Beatrice Dance to Laura Guthrie, October 25, 1935, Princeton.

7. Fitzgerald, *Correspondence*, pp. 419, 421, 427; Fitzgerald, *Letters*, pp. 549, 550; Letter from Fitzgerald to Beatrice Dance, November 6, 1940, Princeton.

8. Fitzgerald, *Notebooks*, pp. 78–79; Fitzgerald, *Great Gatsby*, pp. 180–181.

9. *As Ever, Scott Fitz*, p. 224; Fitzgerald, *Notebooks*, p. 260; *As Ever, Scott Fitz*, pp. 228–229; Henry Dan Piper, Interview with Nora Flynn; *As Ever, Scott Fitz*, p. 239.

10. Fitzgerald, *Letters*, p. 508; Edwin Peeples, "Twilight of a God: A Brief, Beery Encounter with F. Scott Fitzgerald," *Mademoiselle*, 78 (November 1973), 171; Graham, *The Real Scott Fitzgerald*, p. 106.

11. Thomas Mann, *Letters to Caroline Newton* (Princeton, 1971), p. 67; Fitzgerald, *Notebooks*, p. 311; Fitzgerald, "Sleeping and Waking," *Crack-Up*, p. 65.

12. George Orwell, "Benefit of Clergy: Some Notes on Salvador Dali" (1941), *Decline of the English Murder* (London, 1953), p. 20; Fitzgerald, *Correspondence*, p. 429; Fitzgerald, *Crack-Up*, p. 69; *Letters of John Keats*, ed. Robert Gittings (Oxford, 1970), p. 43.

13. Fitzgerald, *Crack-Up*, pp. 72, 80, 75; Wilson, *Letters on Literature and Politics*, p. 44; Fitzgerald, *Crack-Up*, pp. 79, 71; Fitzgerald, *Letters*, p. 79.

14. Fitzgerald, *Crack-Up*, p. 327; Frances Fitzgerald Lanahan, Introduction to *Six Tales of the Jazz Age*, p. 7; Mark Schorer, *The World We Imagine* (New York, 1968), p. 364.

15. Fitzgerald, *Crack-Up*, p. 75; Quoted in James West, "Fitzgerald and *Esquire*," *The Short Stories of F. Scott Fitzgerald*, ed. Jackson Bryer (Madison, Wisconsin, 1982), pp. 154–155; Robert Lowell, "Night Sweat," *For the Union Dead* (New York, 1964), p. 68.

16. Advertisement for Highland Hospital, Fitzgerald papers, Princeton; Adolf Meyer, Preface to Robert Carroll's *What Price Alcohol?* (New York, 1941), p. ix; Sherry Honea, "Reminiscing," *Highland Highlights* (Spring 1980), pp. 15, 16. See also Carroll's obituary in the *New York Times*, June 27, 1949, p. 27.

17. Quoted in Bruccoli, *Some Sort of Epic Grandeur,* p. 483; Fitzgerald, *Correspondence,* p. 431; Quoted in Milford, *Zelda,* p. 373; Quoted in Koula Hartnett, *Zelda Fitzgerald and the Failure of the American Dream for Women* (New York, 1990), p. 183.

18. Fitzgerald, *Letters,* p. 446; Fitzgerald, *Correspondence,* p. 471.

19. *Dear Scott/Dear Max,* p. 219; Interview with Tony Buttitta; Quoted in Mizener, *Far Side of Paradise,* p. 312.

20. Fitzgerald, *Notebooks,* pp. 309, 318; Fitzgerald, *Letters,* p. 562; Fitzgerald, *Short Stories,* p. 218; Fitzgerald, *Letters,* p. 561.

21. Hearne, "Summer with Scott Fitzgerald," p. 260; Fitzgerald, *Notebooks,* p. 89; Tomkins, *Living Well is the Best Revenge,* p. 130; Hemingway, *Selected Letters,* p. 407.

22. Hearne, "Summer with Scott Fitzgerald," p. 260; Fitzgerald, *Letters,* p. 331; Fitzgerald, *In His Own Time,* p. 297; Hemingway, *A Farewell to Arms,* p. 249; Hemingway, *Selected Letters,* pp. 437–438, 408.

23. Berg, *Max Perkins,* p. 305; Hemingway, "The Snows of Kilimanjaro," *Short Stories,* p. 72 (this sentence appeared in the third paragraph of "The Rich Boy"); Item 204.8, Hemingway Collection, John F. Kennedy Library, Boston, Mass.; Fitzgerald, *Letters,* pp. 331, 296.

24. Fitzgerald, *Letters,* p. 369; Fitzgerald, *Tender is the Night,* pp. 46, 51; Hemingway, "The Short Happy Life of Francis Macomber," *Short Stories,* pp. 8, 32; Fitzgerald, *Afternoon of an Author,* p. 179.

25. Fitzgerald, *Correspondence,* p. 451; Fitzgerald, *Letters,* p. 561; Interview with Annabel's daughter Courtney Sprague Vaughan, Monte Sereno, California, June 25, 1992; Patricia Sprague Reneau and Courtney Sprague Vaughan, *Remembered and Honored: Clifton A. F. "Ziggy" Sprague, U.S.N., 1896–1955* (Santa Cruz: privately printed, 1992), p. 69n.

26. Letter from Mok's friend Henry Senber to Jeffrey Meyers, July 16, 1992; Letter from Dr. Paul Mok to Jeffrey Meyers, May 23, 1992; Interview with Tony Buttitta. See also Mok's obituary in the *New York Times,* February 3, 1961, p. 25.

27. Fitzgerald, Interview with Michel Mok, *In His Own Time,* pp. 294–295, 299.

28. Marjorie Kinnan Rawlings, *Selected Letters,* ed. Gordon Bigelow and Lauri Monti (Gainesville, Florida, 1983), pp. 309, 125–126; *As Ever, Scott Fitz,* p. 282.

29. Letter from Fitzgerald to Cecilia Taylor, June 11, 1935, Princeton; letter from Scottie Fitzgerald Lanahan to Arthur Mizener, March 10, 1950, Princeton; Letter from Scottie Lanahan to Mizener, March 18, 1948, Princeton.

30. Fitzgerald, *Letters,* p. 28; Quoted in Mizener, *Far Side of Paradise,* p. 74; Scottie Fitzgerald Lanahan, Introduction to Fitzgerald's *Letters to His Daughter,* pp. xii–xiii; Interview with Margaret McPherson.

31. Interview with Fanny Myers Brennan; Hemingway, *Selected Letters,* p. 412; *Letters from the Lost Generation: Gerald and Sara Murphy and Friends,* ed. Linda Miller (New Brunswick, New Jersey, 1991), p. 151; Fitzgerald, *Letters,* pp. 446–447.

Chapter Twelve: The Garden of Allah and Sheilah Graham

1. Fitzgerald, *The Vegetable,* p. 117; *As Ever, Scott Fitz,* p. 216; Fred Zinnemann, *A Life in the Movies* (New York, 1992), p. 46.

2. F. Scott Fitzgerald, *The Last Tycoon,* [ed. Edmund Wilson] (1941; New York, 1986), p. 163; Fitzgerald, *Letters,* p. 31; *As Ever, Scott Fitz,* p. 330; Fitzgerald, *Letters,* p. 624.

3. *Dear Scott/Dear Max,* pp. 238, 241; Fitzgerald, *Letters,* p. 570; Anthony Powell, "Hollywood Canteen: A Memoir of Scott Fitzgerald in 1937," *Fitzgerald-Hemingway Annual,* 3 (1971), 75; Letter from Anthony Powell to Jeffrey Meyers, November 12, 1991. For Powell's favorable critical judgments, see "Fitzgerald," *Miscellaneous Verdicts* (London, 1990), pp. 211–223. See also pp. 235–237.

4. Letter from Charles Warren to Fitzgerald, October 12, 1934, Princeton; Powell, "Hollywood Canteen," p. 75; Interview with Ring Lardner, Jr.; Ring Lardner, Jr., in the BBC documentary on Fitzgerald, script and video courtesy of Ian Hamilton and Jill Evans.

5. Henry Dan Piper, Interview with John O'Hara, Princeton, February 6, 1950, courtesy of Professor Piper; Anita Loos, *Kiss Hollywood Good-by* (1974; New York, 1975), p. 124; *Dear Scott/Dear Max,* p. 177; Fitzgerald, *Correspondence,* p. 477.

6. Zinnemann, *A Life in the Movies,* p. 44; Powell, *Miscellaneous*

Verdicts, p. 213; Jay Martin, *Nathanael West: The Art of His Life* (New York, 1970), p. 205; Raymond Chandler, *Selected Letters*, ed. Frank MacShane (London, 1981), p. 237.

7. Maurice Zolotow, *Billy Wilder* (New York, 1977), p. 72. Nunnally Johnson, *Letters*, ed. Doris Johnson and Ellen Leventhal (New York, 1981), pp. 80, 249.

8. Interview with Joseph Mankiewicz, Bedford, New York, March 15, 1992; Quoted in Aaron Latham, *Crazy Sundays* (1971; New York, 1972), pp. 120–121; Fitzgerald, *The Beautiful and Damned*, p. 265. Paramore died in a freak accident in 1956: "He was sitting in a car which had been raised in a garage on one of those elevators which they use when making repairs. The contrivance fell and killed him" (Edmund Wilson, *The Twenties*, ed. Leon Edel, New York, 1975, p. 31).

9. F. Scott Fitzgerald, *Three Comrades*, ed. Matthew Bruccoli (New York, 1978), p. 51; Fitzgerald, *Letters*, pp. 583–584; Fitzgerald, *The Great Gatsby*, p. 118; Fitzgerald, *Three Comrades*, p. 249. See also Gore Vidal, "Scott's Case" (1980), *The Second American Revolution* (New York, 1982), pp. 3–23.

10. Fitzgerald, *Notebooks*, p. 163; *Dear Scott/Dear Max*, p. 255; Jacques Bontemps and Richard Overstreet, "Measure for Measure: Interview with Joseph Mankiewicz," *Cahiers du Cinema in English*, 18 (February 1967), 31; Meyers, Interview with Joseph Mankiewicz. Mr. Mankiewicz wittily inscribed my copy of *Three Comrades:* "For Jeffrey Meyers—from the 'despoiler' of F. Scott Fitzgerald's Screenplay, Joseph Mankiewicz, Bedford, 1992."

11. Interview with Budd Schulberg; Fitzgerald, *Correspondence*, pp. 489, 516.

12. Fitzgerald, *In His Own Time*, p. 129; Fitzgerald, *The Last Tycoon*, p. 30; Salka Viertel, *The Kindness of Strangers* (New York, 1969), p. 223.

13. Interview with Margaret McPherson; Letters from Scottie Fitzgerald Lanahan to Mizener, January 21, 1964 and March 22, 1948, Princeton; Quoted in Mizener, *Far Side of Paradise*, p. 314; Fitzgerald, *Correspondence*, p. 495.

14. See Jeffrey Meyers, "Scott Fitzgerald and the English," *London Magazine*, 32 (October–November 1992), 31–44, and Jeffrey Meyers, "Scott Fitzgerald and the Jews," *Forward* (New York), Febru-

ary 12, 1993, pp. 9–10; reprinted in *Midstream,* 39 (January 1993), 31–35.

15. Fitzgerald, "Crazy Sunday," *Stories,* ed. Cowley, p. 410. See Sheilah Graham: *Beloved Infidel* (1958), *The Rest of the Story* (1964), *College of One* (1967), *The Garden of Allah* (1970), *A State of Heat* (1972), *The Real Scott Fitzgerald* (1976) and *Hollywood Revisited* (1984). Her last, all-too-familiar word on Fitzgerald was "The Room Where Scott Died," *New York Times Magazine,* July 26, 1987, pp. 20–21.

16. Lord Chamberlain's Office, Buckingham Palace, to Jeffrey Meyers, December 18, 1992; Maureen, Marchioness of Donegall, to Jeffrey Meyers, December 14, 1992.

17. Interview with Ring Lardner, Jr.; Sheilah Graham, in the BBC documentary on Fitzgerald; *Dear Scott/Dear Max,* p. 265.

18. Quoted in Milford, *Zelda,* p. 413; Interviews with Frances Kroll Ring, Budd Schulberg and Joseph Mankiewicz.

19. Sheilah Graham and Gerold Frank, *Beloved Infidel* (1958; New York, 1959), pp. 132, 152, 160, 162–163.

20. Graham, *A State of Heat,* p. 143; Graham, *The Real Scott Fitzgerald,* p. 120; Fitzgerald, "Last Kiss," *Short Stories,* p. 761.

21. Sheilah Graham, *College of One* (New York, 1967), p. 57; Quoted in Latham, *Crazy Sundays,* p. 185; Henry Dan Piper, Interview with Arnold Gingrich, Chicago, March 29, 1944, courtesy of Professor Piper, and Latham, *Crazy Sundays,* p. 130.

22. Graham, *State of Heat,* p. 144; Graham, *Beloved Infidel,* p. 227; Quoted in Latham, *Crazy Sundays,* p. 131; Graham, *The Real Scott Fitzgerald,* pp. 104, 19.

23. Letter from Frances Kroll to Sheilah Graham, December 10, 1939, Princeton; Fitzgerald, *Correspondence,* p. 564; *This Side of Paradise,* inscribed by Fitzgerald to Sheilah Graham, Princeton.

24. Powell, "Hollywood Canteen," p. 77; Judith Thurman, *Isak Dinesen* (New York, 1982), pp. 156–157; Wilson, *Letters on Literature and Politics,* pp. 313–314.

25. Fitzgerald, *Letters,* p. 368; Budd Schulberg, "Old Scott: The Myth, the Masque, the Man," *Four Seasons of Success* (Garden City, New York, 1972), p. 126; Fitzgerald, *Letters,* p. 249.

26. Letter from Frances Kroll Ring to Mizener, June 14, 1948, Princeton; Letter from Fitzgerald to Edgar Allan Poe, Jr., December 26, 1939, Princeton; *As Ever, Scott Fitz,* p. 315.

Chapter Thirteen: Hollywood Hack and
The Last Tycoon

1. David Thomson, *Showman: The Life of David O. Selznick* (New York, 1992), p. 288; Schulberg, *Four Seasons of Success*, p. 102; Interview with Budd Schulberg.

2. Graham, *The Rest of the Story*, p. 211; Quoted in Mizener, *Far Side of Paradise*, p. 315; Budd Schulberg, "In Hollywood," *New Republic*, 104 (March 3, 1941), 311–312.

3. Mizener's notes on his conversation with Schulberg, Princeton; Meyers, Interview with Schulberg.

Wanger had a notoriously fierce temper. In 1951 he served three months in jail for shooting the agent of his actress-wife Joan Bennett.

4. Quoted in Turnbull, *Scott Fitzgerald*, p. 324; Letter from Scottie Fitzgerald Lanahan to Mizener, October 22, 1950, Princeton.

5. *As Ever, Scott Fitz*, p. 403; David Niven, *Bring on the Empty Horses* (New York, 1975), pp. 100–101; Quoted in Latham, *Crazy Sundays*, p. 253; *Dear Scott/Dear Max*, p. 261.

6. Fitzgerald, *In His Own Time*, p. 155; Fitzgerald, *Correspondence*, p. 385; Fitzgerald, *In His Own Time*, p. 160.

7. Fitzgerald, *Letters*, p. 126; *As Ever, Scott Fitz*, p. 415; Frances Scott Fitzgerald, "A Short Retort," *Mademoiselle*, July 1939, p. 41.

8. Letter from Scottie Fitzgerald to Mizener, February 2, 1948, Princeton; Quoted in Marie Jemison's unpublished memoir of Scottie, "Everybody Wants My Parents, Nobody Wants Me," pp. 34, 48–49, courtesy of Marie Jemison; Frances Kroll Ring, *Against the Current: As I Remember Scott Fitzgerald* (Berkeley, 1985), p. 81.

9. Fitzgerald, *Correspondence*, p. 523; Quoted in Milford, *Zelda*, p. 401; Fitzgerald, *Letters*, p. 128; Fitzgerald, *Correspondence*, p. 554.

10. Letter from Scottie Fitzgerald Lanahan to Mizener, March 10, 1950, Princeton; Scott and Zelda Fitzgerald, *Romantic Egoists*, p. 225.

11. *As Ever, Scott Fitz*, pp. 346, 394, 400.

12. Fitzgerald, *Letters*, p. 607; *As Ever, Scott Fitz*, p. 408; *Dear Scott/Dear Max*, pp. 258, 261.

13. Fitzgerald, *Letters*, p. 332; Fitzgerald, *Notebooks*, p. 335;

Ernest Hemingway, *For Whom the Bell Tolls* (New York, 1940), p. 160; Fitzgerald, *The Last Tycoon,* p. 81; Graham, *College of One,* p. 159; Fitzgerald, *Letters,* pp. 146–147. For an evaluation of Hemingway's achievement, see Jeffrey Meyers, *"For Whom the Bell Tolls* as Contemporary History," *The Spanish Civil War in History,* ed. Janet Pérez and Wendell Aycock (Lubbock, Texas, 1990), pp. 85–107.

14. Hemingway, *Selected Letters,* p. 657; Quoted in Jacqueline Tavernier-Courbin, *Ernest Hemingway's "A Moveable Feast": The Making of a Myth* (Boston, 1991), p. 12; Gregory Hemingway, *Papa* (Boston, 1976), p. 103.

In 1941, when Hemingway was competing with the recently dead Fitzgerald, he judged *The Last Tycoon* more severely and disliked Kathleen as much as Fitzgerald had disliked Maria. As Hemingway told Perkins: "Most of it has a deadness that is unbelievable for Scott. . . . The women were pretty preposterous. Scott had gotten so far away from any knowledge of people that they are very strange. He still had the technique and the romance of doing anything, but all the dust was off the butterfly's wing" (*Selected Letters,* p. 527).

15. Fitzgerald, *Correspondence,* p. 557; Fitzgerald, *Letters,* pp. 187, 619; Quoted in Mizener, *Far Side of Paradise,* p. 324.

16. Fitzgerald, *The Last Tycoon,* p. 125; Fitzgerald, *Correspondence,* pp. 451–452. For Thalberg's life, see Bob Thomas, *Thalberg: Life and Legend* (Garden City, New York, 1970) and Samuel Marx, *Mayer and Thalberg: The Make-Believe Saints* (New York, 1975).

17. Fitzgerald, *Correspondence,* p. 549; Fitzgerald, *The Last Tycoon,* pp. 118, 91, 42.

His friendships with Jews, who were invariably kind to Fitzgerald, altered his preconceived hostility and enabled him to see them as individuals. George Jean Nathan published his first stories in the *Smart Set,* Carmel Myers introduced him to the Hollywood elite, Gilbert Seldes wrote the most perceptive review of *The Great Gatsby,* Gertrude Stein generously praised his work, Dorothy Parker was another consistent supporter, Bert Barr (Bertha Weinberg Goldstein) befriended him on the voyage home to his father's funeral, S. J. Perelman was a witty and stimulating friend in Hollywood, Nathanael West was also an admiring colleague, Budd Schulberg tried to take care of him after his binge in Hanover and Frances Kroll was his devoted secretary.

18. *As Ever, Scott Fitz,* p. 351; Fitzgerald, *Correspondence,* p. 561; Fitzgerald, *Letters,* p. 112.

19. J. F. Powers, "Dealer in Diamonds and Rhinestones," *Commonweal,* 42 (August 10, 1945), 408.

20. Fitzgerald, *Correspondence,* p. 594; *The Time is Ripe: The 1940 Journal of Clifford Odets,* Introduction by William Gibson (New York, 1988), p. 293; Fitzgerald, *Correspondence,* p. 614.

21. Fitzgerald, *Letters,* p. 144. Sheilah characteristically gives two quite different versions of Scott's death. In *Beloved Infidel* (1958), p. 251, which I have followed, she said he was still breathing after he fell down. In *The Real Scott Fitzgerald,* p. 15, she said he died instantly. Both Edmund Wilson (*Letters,* p. 328) and Mizener (*Far Side of Paradise,* p. 335) follow the later, less reliable version.

22. Frank Scully, "F. Scott Fitzgerald," *Rogue's Gallery* (Hollywood, 1943), pp. 268–269. Fitzgerald may have been echoing the teenage Tennyson, who in 1824 "had run weeping into the woods at Somersby and despairingly carved 'Byron is dead' into the sandstone" (Robert Bernard Martin, *Tennyson: The Unquiet Heart,* Oxford, 1980, p. 231).

23. Interview with Fanny Myers Brennan; *Letters from the Lost Generation,* p. 259; Lee Reese, *The Horse on Rodney Square* (Wilmington, Delaware, 1977), p. 177; Letter from John Biggs III to Jeffrey Meyers, November 27, 1991.

24. *As Ever, Scott Fitz,* p. 424; *Letters from the Lost Generation,* p. 261.

25. Fitzgerald, *In His Own Time,* p. 472; Wilson, *Letters on Literature and Politics,* pp. 327, 337; Wilson, Foreword to Fitzgerald's *The Last Tycoon,* n.p.; Edmund Wilson, Foreword to Fitzgerald's *The Last Tycoon, The Great Gatsby and Selected Stories* (New York, 1945), p. xi; Wilson, *Letters on Literature and Politics,* p. 343.

26. Wilson, *Letters on Literature and Politics,* p. 337; Wilson, "Dedication" to *The Crack-Up,* pp. 8–9; Wilson, *Letters on Literature and Politics,* p. 335. See Jeffrey Meyers, "Scott Fitzgerald and Edmund Wilson: A Troubled Friendship," *American Scholar,* 61 (Summer 1992), 375–388.

27. Stephen Vincent Benét, "Fitzgerald's Unfinished Symphony," *Saturday Review of Literature,* 24 (December 6, 1941), 10; Wilson, *Letters on Literature and Politics,* p. 475; John Updike, *Hugging the Shore* (New York, 1983), p. 380.

28. See Wilson's *The Crime in the Whistler Room* (1924), Lardner's *What Of It?* (1925), Hemingway's *The Torrents of Spring* (1926), Van Vechten's *Parties* (1930), Zelda's *Save Me the Waltz* (1932), Wolfe's *You Can't Go Home Again* (1941), Schulberg's *The Disenchanted* (1950), George Zuckerman's *The Last Flapper* (1969), James Aldridge's *One Last Glimpse* (1977), Ron Carlson's *Betrayed by Scott Fitzgerald* (1977), Kaye McDonough's *Zelda* (1978), Tennessee Williams' *Clothes for a Summer Hotel* (1980), Donald Davie's poem "The Garden Party" and Theodore Roethke's "Song for the Squeeze-Box."

29. Quoted in Turnbull, *Scott Fitzgerald*, p. 327; Hartnett, *Zelda Fitzgerald*, p. 185; "Fire in Carolina Mental Hospital Kills 9 Women," *New York Herald Tribune*, March 12, 1948.

The catastrophic fire almost ruined Highland. The medical director resigned and was replaced by Dr. Carroll's adopted daughter Charmian, a nurse who had become a psychiatrist and who served as director until 1963.

30. Brendan Gill, *A New York Life* (New York, 1990), p. 315; Interview with Meryle Secrest, November 22, 1992; Interview with Eleanor Lanahan, Hempstead, New York, September 26, 1992.

31. Chandler, *Selected Letters*, p. 239; Toklas, *Staying on Alone*, p. 171.

Bibliography

I. Works on Fitzgerald

Bruccoli, Matthew. *Some Sort of Epic Grandeur: A Life of Scott Fitzgerald.* New York, 1981.

Buttitta, Tony. *The Lost Summer: A Personal Memoir of F. Scott Fitzgerald.* 1974; New York, 1987.

Donaldson, Scott. *Fool for Love: A Biography of F. Scott Fitzgerald.* 1983; New York, 1989.

Donnelly, Honoria Murphy with Richard Billings. *Sara & Gerald: Villa America and After.* New York, 1982.

Graham, Sheilah and Gerold Frank. *Beloved Infidel.* 1958; New York, 1959.

Hemingway, Ernest. *A Moveable Feast.* New York, 1964.

———. *Selected Letters, 1917–1961.* Ed. Carlos Baker. New York, 1981.

LeVot, André. *F. Scott Fitzgerald: A Biography.* Trans. William Byron. 1979; London, 1984.

Mayfield, Sara. *Exiles from Paradise: Scott and Zelda Fitzgerald.* 1971; New York, 1974.

Mellow, James. *Invented Lives: F. Scott and Zelda Fitzgerald.* Boston, 1984.

Meyers, Jeffrey. *Married to Genius.* London, 1977.

———. "Poe and Fitzgerald," *London Magazine,* 31 (August–September 1991), 67–73.

———. "Scott Fitzgerald and Edmund Wilson: A Troubled Friendship," *American Scholar,* 61 (Summer 1992), 375–388.

———. "Scott Fitzgerald and the English," *London Magazine,* 32 (October–November 1992), 31–44.

———. "Scott Fitzgerald and the Jews," *Forward,* February 12, 1993, pp. 9–10; reprinted in *Midstream,* 39 (January 1993), 31–35.

———, ed. *The Great Gatsby.* London: Dent-Everyman, 1993.

———, ed. *Tender is the Night.* London: Dent-Everyman, 1993.

Milford, Nancy. *Zelda.* 1970; New York, 1971.

Mizener, Arthur. *The Far Side of Paradise: A Biography of F. Scott Fitzgerald* (1951). Revised edition. Boston, 1965.

Piper, Henry Dan. *F. Scott Fitzgerald: A Critical Portrait.* New York, 1965.

Ring, Frances Kroll. *Against the Current: As I Remember F. Scott Fitzgerald.* Berkeley, 1985.

Turnbull, Andrew. *Scott Fitzgerald.* 1962; London, 1970.

Wilson, Edmund. *Letters on Literature and Politics, 1912–1972.* Ed. Elena Wilson. New York, 1977.

II. Edmund Wilson on Fitzgerald

"The Literary Spotlight: F. Scott Fitzgerald," *Bookman* (New York), 55 (March 1922), 21–22; reprinted in *The Shores of Light.* New York, 1952. Pp. 27–35.

"Two Young Men and an Old One," *Vanity Fair,* 19 (November 1922), 24.

"A Selection of Bric-à-Brac," *Vanity Fair,* 20 (June 1923), 18.

"Imaginary Conversations, II. Mr. Van Wyck Brooks and Mr. Scott Fitzgerald," *New Republic,* 38 (April 30, 1924), 249–254; reprinted in *Discordant Encounters.* New York, 1926. Pp. 37–60, and as "The Delegate from Great Neck." *The Shores of Light.* New York, 1952. Pp. 141–155.

"Mürger and Wilde on Screen," *New Republic,* 46 (March 24, 1926), 144–145 (positive review of the stage version of *The Great Gatsby*).

"The All-Star Literary Vaudeville" (1926). *The Shores of Light.* New York, 1952. Pp. 232–233.

Foreword to *The Last Tycoon.* [Ed. Edmund Wilson.] New York, 1941. Pp. ix–xi.

The Boys in the Back Room. San Francisco, 1941. Pp. 71–72; reprinted in *Classics and Commercials.* New York, 1950. Pp. 51–52, 56.

"On Editing Scott Fitzgerald's Papers" [poem], *New Yorker,* 18 (May 16, 1942), 17; reprinted as "Dedication" to *The Crack-Up.* New York, 1945. Pp. 7–9, and in *Night Thoughts.* 1953; New York, 1961. Pp. 119–122.

"Thoughts on Being Bibliographed," *Princeton University Library Chronicle,* 5 (February 1944), 51–54; reprinted in *Classics and Commercials.* New York, 1950. Pp. 105–120.

Introduction to John Peale Bishop's *Collected Essays.* New York, 1948. Pp. vii–xiii; reprinted in *The Bit Between My Teeth.* New York, 1965. Pp. 6–15.

"A Weekend at Ellerslie." *The Shores of Light.* New York, 1952. Pp. 373–383.

"Christian Gauss as a Teacher of Literature." *The Shores of Light.* New York, 1952. Pp. 3–26.

"Sheilah Graham and Scott Fitzgerald," *New Yorker,* 34 (January 24, 1959), 115–124; reprinted in *The Bit Between My Teeth.* New York, 1965. Pp. 16–27.

"That Summer in Paris," *New Yorker,* 39 (February 23, 1963), 139–142, 145–148; reprinted in *The Bit Between My Teeth.* New York, 1965. Pp. 515–525.

A Prelude. New York, 1967. Pp. 47, 68–69, 93, 106, 116–117, 148, 180.

The Twenties. Ed. Leon Edel. New York, 1975.

Letters on Literature and Politics, 1912–1972. Ed. Elena Wilson. New York, 1977.

The Nabokov-Wilson Letters, 1940–1971. Ed. Simon Karlinsky. New York, 1979. Pp. 17, 114–115, 157n, 200n.

The Thirties. Ed. Leon Edel. New York, 1980.

The Forties. Ed. Leon Edel. New York, 1983.

The Fifties. Ed. Leon Edel. New York, 1986.

III. Scottie Fitzgerald on Her Father

Fitzgerald, Frances Scott. "A Short Retort," *Mademoiselle*, July 1939, p. 41.

———. "Princeton and F. Scott Fitzgerald," *Nassau Literary Magazine*, 100 (1942), 45; reprinted as: "Princeton & My Father," *Princeton Alumni Weekly*, 56 (March 9, 1956), 8–9.

Lanahan, Frances Scott. "Fitzgerald as He Really Was," Washington *Post* & *Times-Herald*, April 27, 1958, p. E7.

Lanahan, Frances Fitzgerald. Introduction to Scott Fitzgerald's *Six Tales of the Jazz Age*. New York, 1960. Pp. 5–11.

———. "My Father's Letters: Advice Without Consent," *Esquire*, 64 (October 1965), 95–97; reprinted as: Introduction to Scott Fitzgerald's *Letters to His Daughter*. New York, 1965. Pp. ix–xvi.

———. "Scott, Ernest, Arnold and Whoever," *Esquire*, 67 (March 1967), 159 (letter).

Lanahan, Frances Scott Fitzgerald. *When I Was 16*. Ed. Mary Brannum. New York, 1967. Pp. 200–216; reprinted as: "When I Was Sixteen," *Good Housekeeping*, 167 (October 1968), 100–101.

Smith, Scottie Fitzgerald. Foreword to *As Ever, Scott Fitz*. Philadelphia, 1972. Pp. xi–xvi.

Smith, Frances Fitzgerald. "Où sont Les Soleils d'Antan? Françoise 'Fijeralde'?" *F. Scott Fitzgerald and Ernest M. Hemingway in Paris*. Ed. Matthew Bruccoli and C. E. Frazer Clark. Bloomfield Hills, Michigan, 1972. N.p.

Smith, Scottie Fitzgerald. "Christmas as Big as the Ritz," *Washington Post*, December 23, 1973, *Potomac* Magazine, pp. 7–8.

———. Introduction to Scott and Zelda Fitzgerald's *The Romantic Egoists*. New York, 1974. Pp. ix–x.

Smith, Frances Scott Fitzgerald. "Mia is the Daisy Father Had in Mind," *People*, 1 (March 4, 1974), 34.

Smith, Scottie Fitzgerald. Foreword to Scott and Zelda Fitzgerald's *Bits of Paradise*. 1974; New York, 1976. Pp. xi–xvii.

Smith, Frances Scott Fitzgerald, "Notes About My Now-Famous Father," *Family Circle*, 84 (May 1974), 118, 120.

Smith, Scottie Fitzgerald. [Foreword] to *Zelda*, exhibition catalogue. Montgomery: Museum of Fine Arts, 1974. N.p; reprinted as [Foreword] to *The Collected Writings of Zelda Fitzgerald.* New York, 1991. Pp. ix–x.

————. "The Colonial Ancestors of Francis Scott Key Fitzgerald." In Matthew Bruccoli's *Some Sort of Epic Grandeur.* New York, 1981. Pp. 496–509.

See also *In Memoriam: Frances Scott Fitzgerald Smith, 1921–1986.* Privately printed, n.p., n.d.

INDEX

Compiled by Valerie Meyers